IDEAS IN PROCESS

Ideas in Process

AN ANTHOLOGY OF READINGS IN COMMUNICATION

Edited by

C. MERTON BABCOCK

KENNIKAT PRESS
Port Washington, N. Y./London

IDEAS IN PROCESS

Copyright, 1958, by C. Merton Babcock
Reissued in 1971 by Kennikat Press by arrangement
with Harper & Row Publishers, Inc.
Library of Congress Catalog Card No: 72-113343
ISBN 0-8046-1397-4

Manufactured by Taylor Publishing Company   Dallas, Texas

ESSAY AND GENERAL LITERATURE INDEX REPRINT SERIES

CONTENTS

Contents

Arranged by Types and Patterns of Discourse

CRITICISM AND SATIRE

OBSERVATION AND EXPERIENCE

ANALOGY

CLASSIFICATION AND ANALYSIS

PREFACE

THIS IS A BOOK about language and the communication of meaning. It is designed to help college freshmen acquire mastery of four practical language skills: reading, writing, speaking, and listening. Since mastery of each of these skills is thought to depend upon one's ability to think, the central focus of this collection of essays is on clear, straight, and independent thinking. This focus is more than justified by the criticism, perennially leveled against educators, that most students who complete their formal education cannot think creatively, cannot judge critically, and cannot manipulate language in an intellectually mature manner. Bernard Iddings Bell has said: "Most Americans cannot read anything more difficult than a picture-paper or a pulp magazine; they cannot write a letter and make their meaning plain; they rarely speak except in clichés; they are unable to follow argument put in the simplest words; to understand what a speaker is driving at."

The kind of thinking required for mastery of these basic skills is the kind that engages the student in active, creative effort with facts, words, and ideas; not the kind that promotes passive acceptance of prepackaged platitudes based on unsupported myths or unfounded and unchallenged beliefs. What is needed in a language arts course, according to Stephen Leacock, is "not more quantity in the current of words, but a higher voltage of mental interest"—something that will kindle a flame in the mind.

It is probably impossible to teach anyone *how* to think. Each mind has its own method and each method is mysterious and unpredictable. It does seem probable, however, that some conditions are more favorable for creative activity than others, and that certain attitudes of mind, certain linguistic abilities, and certain intellectual capacities will aid one in gaining insights. These include a wide background of personal experience, realistic purposes for using language, a thorough understanding of the nature and functions of words, a scientific detachment toward facts, and the ability to see the interlocking parts of extended discourse in total perspective. This book is planned and organized so as to offer students the kinds of experiences that will foster rational, independent thinking and that will promote mature linguistic behavior.

Important criteria used in the selection of the essays include: clarity of expression, importance and significance of ideas presented, and usefulness of the subject matter in the formation of sound critical judgments and unbiased points of view. Some of the selections are informative, some provocative, some controversial, some critical, and some entertaining. All are purposeful and furnish excellent models of efficient and effective communication. The techniques employed by the various authors demonstrate a wide variety of methods by which ideas may be brought into focus, examined, explained, supported, and adapted to specific readers and listeners. In most instances, the style and idiom of the selections is of our time. Two or three exceptions from nineteenth-century literature are included for their unusual merit in exemplifying specific types of discourse, or for their value in showing the linguistic changes that have occurred in the years since they were written.

One of the virtues of the anthology is that it supplies a subject content for the communication skills course. It brings together basic tenets of general semantics, field theory, operational psychology, linguistic science, and pragmatic philosophy, which when combined offer a set of workable principles for the science and art of communication. The essays are intentionally arranged in a sequence that roughly corresponds with the several steps in the process of communicating ideas: deriving meaning from experience, recording meaning in verbal symbols, creating ideas as solutions to recognized problems, supporting ideas with facts and evidence, recognizing realistic purposes for communication, and understanding the mediums by which ideas are usually disseminated.

A supplementary Table of Contents, arranged by types and patterns of discourse, supplies an index of methods of development and kinds of argument employed by the several authors. Such arrangement furnishes a handy selector for finding essays pertinent to principles under discussion at a given time. It also supplies an index of models for student writing and speaking.

The questions and exercises which accompany the essays are designed to give students practical experience in reporting, discussion, definition of words, persuasion, content analysis, critical evaluation, and problem solving. A great deal of cross-referencing is purposefully incorporated into the exercises in order to insure a balanced perspective of the problems discussed.

The book is open-ended. It is based on the theory that communication is a continuing experience, never crystallized, forever in process. The materials and methods of social communication furnish subject matter for a lifetime course of study. The readings presented here should open the door to the unlimited potential of language in personal, social, civic, and vocational life.

January, 1958

C. M. B.

1. THE SKILLS
OF COMMUNICATION

Communication is a coöperative enterprise requiring the joint action of at least two people who want to share their thoughts. In this respect, it is like a game of tennis. When a tennis ball is passed back and forth across the net which divides the court, both players—the server and the receiver —are actively involved in the play. Just so in communication. When an idea is transmitted from one person to another, both parties in the act have work to do. The receiver as well as the transmitter must conceive the idea if the transfer is to be successfully made.

Communication skill involves the whole of speech, as Peter F. Drucker explains in the opening essay of this volume. To attain maximum proficiency with language, "one must not only know the whole of the 'message,' one must also be able to relate it to the pattern of behavior, personality, situation, and even culture with which it is surrounded." Mr. Drucker's illumination of the "new philosophy" makes a good starting place for a study of the nature of language and its critical importance in human affairs.

The four skills of communication—reading, writing, speaking, and listening—are modes of a mental activity called thinking. All of these skills require active, creative effort. Listening as well as speaking is an intellectual activity by which ideas are structured with the aid of spoken words; and reading as well as writing is an activity by which ideas are structured with the aid of written words. The most important qualification a person

1

can have, then, for successful communication of ideas is the ability to think —logically, rationally, and creatively.

While this ability cannot be acquired solely by reading, the essays in this section of the anthology were selected because they support the theory that meaning is self-conceived, rather than acquired from others, and that knowledge is something to do, rather than something to absorb. Perry and Whitlock, in the essay "The Right to Think—Through Reading," go so far as to suggest that students should introduce a certain impatience, or critical doubt, into the business of reading, a process which they believe should include the capacities to judge, to select, and to discard. The same emphasis may be found in the essays on listening and on writing. Stuart Chase, in "Are You Listening?" speaks of mental barriers which interfere with one's ability to comprehend the spoken word, and Stephen Leacock, in "Anybody Can Learn to Write," shows that a writer must rely upon his own experiences in order to succeed. The necessity for self-training is further established by Stephen Price in "Put Your Best Voice Forward," an essay which anticipates Section II of the anthology.

Many popular fallacies about language are turned inside out by the authors of these selections, not the least of which is the erroneous notion that *how* a thing is said is more important than *what* is said. Donald Lloyd, in "Our National Mania for Correctness," faces this question squarely and argues for a realistic, sensible, and functional approach to matters of usage and grammar.

◆ ◆ ◆

The New Philosophy Comes to Life

PETER F. DRUCKER

IN THE early fall of 1956 two brothers—intelligent, well-educated graduate students in their twenties—went to see "Inherit the Wind," the play based on the notorious Scopes "Monkey"

Reprinted from *Harper's Magazine*, August, 1957, by permission of Peter F. Drucker. Copyright 1957 by Harper & Brothers.

Trial of 1925, in which a schoolteacher in rural Tennessee was convicted for teaching evolution, and in which the great nineteenth-century "conflict between science and religion" reached a climax of absurdity. When they came home they said they were much impressed by the acting but rather baffled by the plot. What, they wanted to know, was all the excitement about? Their father, at their age, had been so deeply stirred by the trial that he gave up the ministry and became a lawyer; but when he tried to explain its meaning and excitement to his sons, they replied, "You are making this up. It makes no sense at all."

The point of this story is that one of the sons is a graduate geneticist, the other a theological student in a Presbyterian and strictly Calvinist seminary. Yet the "conflict between science and religion" could not even be explained to either of them.

It is indeed frightening how fast the obvious of yesteryear is turning incomprehensible. An intelligent and well-educated man of the first "modern" generation—that of Newton, Hobbes, and Locke—might still have been able to understand and to make himself understood up to World War II. But it is unlikely that he could still communicate with the world of today, only fifteen years later. We ourselves, after all, saw in the last election campaign how rapidly the issues, slogans, and alignments of as recent a period as the 'thirties have become irrelevant, if not incomprehensible.

But what matters most for us—the first "post-modern" generation—is the change in fundamentals. We still profess and teach the world view of the past three hundred years. But we no longer see it. We have as yet no name for our new way of looking at things—no tools, no method. But a world view comes first; it is the foundation for philosophical terms and technical vocabulary. And that new foundation is something we have acquired, all of a sudden, within the past fifteen or twenty years.

SUM OF THE PARTS

The world view of the past three hundred years can perhaps be summed up in a word as "Cartesian." Few professional philosophers during these years have followed René Descartes, the early seventeenth-century Frenchman, in answering the major problems of systematic philosophy. Yet the modern age has taken its important cues from him. More than Galileo or Calvin, Hobbes, Locke, or Rousseau, far more even than Newton, Descartes influenced the minds of three centuries— what problems would appear important or even relevant, what would be the scope of men's vision, their assumptions about themselves and their universe, and above all, their concept of what was rational and plausible.

His was a twofold contribution. First he gave to the modern world its basic axiom about the intelligibility of the universe. The best known formulation is that in which the Académie Française, a generation after Descartes' death, defined "science" as "the certain and evident knowledge of things by their causes." Expressed less elegantly and less subtly, this says that "the whole is the sum of its parts"—the oversimplification that might be made by an ordinary man who is neither scientist nor philosopher.

Second, Descartes provided the method to make his axiom effective in organizing knowledge. Whatever the mathematical significance of his "Analytical Geometry," it established the new concept of a world unified in simple quantitative relations that could deal efficiently with motion and change, the flow of time, and even the invisible. The perfecting of this mathematics, and its widespread adoption as a universal symbolic language, made it possible for Lord Kelvin two hundred years later to re-assert the principles of Cartesianism by saying, "I know what I can measure."

The statement that the whole is equal to the sum of its parts also implies that the whole is determined by its parts, that the behavior of the whole is caused by the motion of the parts, and that there is no such thing as wholeness apart from the different sums, structures, and relationships of the parts. These statements are likely to sound obvious today since they have been taken for granted for so long, even though they were radical innovations when first propounded. But though most of us still respond to the familiarity of these assertions, there are no longer many scientists who would accept the definition of the Académie Française—at least not for what they call "science" in their own field. Virtually every one of our disciplines now relies on conceptions which are incompatible with the Cartesian axiom, and with the world view we once derived from it.

PATTERN AND CONFIGURATION

Biology shows this dramatically. Its tremendous development in the past fifty years has resulted directly from our applying the strict "Cartesian" methods to the study of the living organism. But the more "scientific" the biologist has become, the more he has tended to talk in terms such as "immunity" and "metabolism," "ecology" and "syndrome," "homeostasis" and "pattern"—each of them essentially an aesthetic term describing not so much a property of matter or quantity as of a harmonious order.

The psychologist talks about *"Gestalt,"* "ego," "personality," or "behavior"—terms that could hardly be found in serious works before 1910. The social sciences talk about "culture," about "integration," or about the "informal group." The aesthetician talks about "form." These are all concepts of pattern or configuration. Whether one searches for the "drives" in a personality, the complex of chemical, electrical, and mechanical actions in a metabolism, the specific rites and customs in a culture, or the particular colors and shapes in a non-objective painting—all can be understood, explained, or even identified only from their place in a pattern.

Similarly, we have a pattern at the center of our economic life, the business enterprise. "Automation" is merely an ugly word to describe as an entity a new view of the process of production. "Management" is a similar term. In government we talk about "administration" or "political process"; the economist talks about "national income," "productivity," or "economic growth" much as the theologian talks about "existence." Even the physical sciences and engineering, the most Cartesian of all our disciplines, talk about "systems" or—the most non-Cartesian term of all—about "quanta" in which, with one measurement, are expressed mass and energy, time and distance, all absorbed into a single entity.

The most striking change is perhaps to be found in our approach to the study of speech and language. Despite the anguished pleas of teachers and parents, we talk less and less about "grammar"—the study of *parts* of speech—and more and more about "communication." It is the *whole* of speech, including not only the words left unsaid but the atmosphere in which words are said and heard, that "communicates." One must not only know the whole of the "message," one must also be able to relate it to the pattern of behavior, personality, situation, and even culture with which it is surrounded.

All these terms are brand-new. Not one of them had any scientific standing fifty years ago in the vocabulary of scholars and scientists. And all of them are *qualitative*. Quantity does not characterize them; a "culture" is not defined by the number of people who belong to it, nor is a "business enterprise" defined by its size. Quantitative change matters in these configurations only when it becomes qualitative—when, in the words of the old Greek riddle, the grains of sand have become a sand-pile. This is not a continuous but a discontinuous event, a sudden jump over a qualitative threshold at which sounds turn into recognizable melody, words and motions into behavior, procedures into a management philosophy, or the atom of one element into that of another. And, finally, none of these configurations as such is measurable or capable of being expressed—except in the most distorted manner—through the traditional symbols of quantitative relationship.

None of these new concepts, let me emphasize, conforms to the axiom that the whole is the result of its parts. On the contrary, all conform to a new, and by no means as yet axiomatic, assertion that the parts exist in contemplation of, if not for the sake of, the whole.

THE PURPOSEFUL UNIVERSE

Moreover, none of these new concepts has any causality to it. Einstein was thoroughly "modern" in saying that he could not accept the view that the Lord plays dice with the universe. But what Einstein was criticizing was the inability of the physicists— including himself—to visualize any other kind of order except causality; that is, our inability to free ourselves from our Cartesian blinders. Underlying the new ideas, including those of modern physics, is a unifying order, but it is not causality; it is purpose.

Each of these new concepts I have mentioned expresses a purposeful unit. One might even say, as a general "modern" principle, that the elements (for we no longer really talk of "parts") will be found to arrange themselves so as to serve the purpose of the whole. This, for instance, is the assumption that underlies the biologist's attempt to study and to understand organs and cells. It is this "arrangement in contemplation of the purpose of the whole" that we mean today when we speak of "order."

This universe of ours is again a universe ruled by purpose, as was the one that the Cartesian world view displaced three hundred years ago. But our idea of "purpose" is a very different one from that of the Middle Ages or Renaissance. Theirs lay outside of the material, social, and psychological universe, if not entirely outside of anything Man himself could be, could do, or could see. Our "purpose," by sharp contrast, is in the configurations themselves; it is not metaphysical but physical; it is not the purpose *of* the universe, but the purpose *in* the universe.

I read the other day a piece by a leading physicist in which he talked about the "characteristics of sub-atomic particles." A slip of the pen, to be sure; but a revealing one. Only a generation ago it would not have been possible for a physicist, no matter how slipshod, to write of anything but the "properties" of matter. For atomic particles to have "characteristics," the atom—if not matter and energy themselves—must have a "character"; and that means that matter must have a purposeful order within itself.

The new world view, in addition, involves the idea of *process*. Each of the new concepts involves growth, development, dynamism—and these are irreversible, whereas events in the Cartesian universe were as reversible as the symbols on either side of an equation. Never, except in fairy tales, does the grown man become a boy again, nor does lead change back to uranium, nor does a business enterprise return to family partnership. All these changes are irreversible because the process changes its own character; it is, in other words, self-generated change.

Only seventy-five years ago the last remnant of pre-Cartesian thinking, the idea of "spontaneous generation" of living beings, was finally laid to rest by Louis Pasteur. Now it comes back to us in the researches of biologists who look for clues to the origin of life in the laboratory "creation" of amino-acids. Now respectable mathematical physicists seriously talk about something even more grossly shocking to the Cartesian view: a theory of constant and spontaneous self-generation of matter in the form of new stars and new galaxies. And a leading biochemist, Sir Macfarlane Burnet, the Australian pioneer of virus research, recently defined a virus, as "not an individual organism in the ordinary sense of the term but something that could almost be called a stream of biological pattern."

In this new emphasis on "process" may well lie the greatest of all the departures of the new world view. For the Cartesian world was not only a mechanical one, in which all events were finitely determined; it was essentially a static one. Inertia, in the strict meaning of classical mechanics, was the assumed norm. It had been an accepted doctrine since Aristotle that the Unchangeable and Unchanging alone was real and alone was perfect. On this one point Descartes, otherwise so daring an innovator, was the strictest of traditionalists.

In fact it was the great achievement of the Cartesian view to make this traditional axiom usable. Motion so obviously exists;

yet on the basis of inertia it cannot be explained and measured —as was first pointed out two thousand years ago in the famous "paradoxes" of Zeno, such as that of Achilles and the tortoise. Only "calculus"—together with Descartes' Analytical Geometry —could find a way out of the impasse between the idea of inertia and the experience of motion..This it did by a most ingenious trick: by explaining and measuring motion as though it consisted of an infinite number of infinitely small but perfectly static "stills."

It is far from true that this "solved" Zeno's paradox, as the textbooks assert. But it could do what no one before had been able to do—assert the axiom of inertia and yet handle motion with growing assurance—and it could point to its success in actually analyzing, predicting, and controlling physical motion. Today, however, we are becoming all-too-painfully aware that the "solution" is inapplicable to true motion—that is, to growth and development, whether biological or economic, which cannot be explained away as a kind of optical illusion. We assume— and are increasingly aware that we assume—that growth, change, and development are the normal and the real, and that their absence is the abnormal—the imperfect, the decaying, and the dead.

TOWARD A NEW PHILOSOPHY

Within the past twenty or thirty years these new concepts have become the reality of our work and world. They are "obvious" to us. Yet, though we take them increasingly for granted, we do not fully understand them. Though we talk glibly of "configuration," "purpose," and "process," we do not yet know what these terms express. We have abandoned the Cartesian world view; but we have not developed, so far, a new tool box of methods or a new axiom of meaning and inquiry. We have certainly not yet produced a new Descartes. As a result we are in an intellectual and artistic crisis.

True, there is a rapidly growing literature of the "new"

philosophy. Though anticipations of it can be found in numerous thinkers—for example, in Whitehead, Bergson, Goethe, Leonardo, or Aristotle—the earliest to expound the new vision in our time was probably that astounding South African, Jan Christiaan Smuts, with his philosophy of "holism" twenty-five or thirty years ago. There are pronounced reflections of it in the work of two physicists, Lancelot Law Whyte, with *The Next Development in Man*, and Erwin Schroedinger, with his *What Is Life?*, and one of its latest and most persuasive expressions is provided by the distinguished economist, Kenneth Boulding, in a small book called *The Image*. It is hardly an accident, moreover, that one of the contemporary philosophers who sells best in paper-back editions is the late Ernst Cassirer; his books—though anything but "popularly" written; in fact, a veritable thicket of Teutonic abstractions—deal with patterns, configurations, and symbols of order as essential elements in Man's experience.

But the people working in a specific discipline are still in difficult straits. They see the new ideas everywhere around them; indeed, they often see little else. But whenever they want to do rigorous work, all they have to work with are methods based on the old world view, methods which are quite inappropriate to the new.

In the social sciences this shows itself in the glaring discrepancy between our talk of "culture," "personality," or "behavior" and our inability to produce much more than vast collections of empirical data about particular—and therefore largely meaningless—manifestions. In a discipline that is much closer to my own daily interest, the study of management, the situation is equally frustrating. The discipline only exists because we have a new conception of the business enterprise. All of us know and stress continually that the really important things are process-characteristics, such as the "climate" of an organization, the development of people in it, or the planning of its features and purposes. But whenever we try to be "scientific," we are thrown back on mechanistic and static methods, such as work measurement of individual operations or, at best, organization rules and definitions. Or take the physicists: the more they discover about the various sub-atomic particles of matter, the more confused, complicated, and inconsistent become their general theories of the nature of matter, energy, and time.

As a result, the very disciplines that are advancing the fastest, in which therefore there is the most to learn, are rapidly becoming unteachable. There is no doubt that medicine, for instance, has made giant strides in this generation. But virtually every experienced teacher of medicine I know wonders whether the young medical-school graduate of today—the very one who gets "the best medical education the world has to offer"—is as well taught and as well prepared as his much more ignorant predecessor of thirty years ago. The reason is simple. Medical schools are still organized around the idea of disciplines as static bundles of knowledge. But, where a hundred years ago there were at best six or seven such "bundles," there are perhaps fifty today. Each has become in its own right a full-blown "science" which takes a lifetime to master—even to acquire a "smattering of ignorance" in any one of them takes more than the five years of medical training.

In addition we suffer the affliction, perhaps inevitable in a time of philosophical transition, of a maddening confusion of tongues among the various disciplines, and the consequent cheapening and erosion of language and style. Each discipline has its own language, its own terms, its own increasingly esoteric symbols. And whenever we try to re-establish unity all we can do is fall back on the outworn language of the Cartesian world which originally brought disunity upon us.

All of this, it should be firmly said, is not merely the "natural" result of advancing knowledge, as some academicians assert. The "natural" result should be, as it has always been, greater simplicity—greater ease of learning and teaching. If our knowledge becomes constantly more specialized, more complicated, rather than more general, then something essential is lacking—namely, a philosophical synthesis appropriate to the world we actually inhabit.

A BIG ORDER

Yet we now can—as we could not a decade or two ago—foresee what shape the new integration will take, when and if it comes. We can see, first of all, what it will not be. The way out is not to repudiate the Cartesian world view but to overcome and encompass it. Modern physics may have given us cause to rediscover Aristotle on a new level of understanding, but it has not made us more appreciative of astrology. Modern biology and operations research have made us more conscious of the need to measure quality, value, and judgment; they have not made us repudiate strict proof, or abandon the quest for objective measurement.

Another negative prediction: in the coming synthesis, the Cartesian dualism between the universe of matter and the universe of mind will not be retained. This was certainly the most potent, as it was the most central, element in Descartes' own system; and for three hundred years it has paralyzed philosophy —if not all our thinking—by widening the split between "idealist" and "materialist," so that each has built ever-higher fences around his own little plot of reality. If there ever was a useful distinction here, it ceased to be meaningful the day the first experimenter discovered that by the very act of observing phenomena he affected them. Today our task is to understand patterns of biological, social, or physical order in which mind and matter become meaningful precisely because they are reflections of a greater unity.

We can also say something affirmative. We need a discipline rather than a vision, a strict discipline of qualitative and irrevocable changes such as development, growth, or decay, and methods for anticipating such changes. We need a discipline, in other words, that explains events and phenomena in terms of their direction and future state rather than in terms of cause—a "calculus of potential," you might say, rather than one of "probability." We need a philosophy of purpose; a logic of quality, and ways of measuring qualitative change; and a methodology of potential and opportunity, of "turning points" and "critical factors," of risk and uncertainty, of constants and variations, "jump" and continuity. We need a dialectic of polarity, one in which unity and diversity are defined as simultaneous and necessary poles of the same essence.

This may sound like a big order, and one we are as yet far from able to fill. Yet we may have the new synthesis more nearly within our grasp than we think. In philosophy and science—perhaps even more in art—a "problem" begins to be solved the moment it can be defined, the moment the right questions are being asked, the moment the specifications are known which the answers must satisfy, the moment we know what we are looking for.

And that, in one after another of the areas of modern knowledge, we already know.

Questions and Exercises

1. What does Mr. Drucker say of the modern approach to the study of speech and language? How does he describe a communication course? How does such a course differ from traditional freshmen English courses?

2. Drucker says we talk less and less about grammar and more and more about communication. How can you justify this change of orientation in language study? Read "The King's English in a Democratic World," Chapter 16 in Charlton Laird's *The Miracle of Language*. What new directions in the teaching of introductory language courses do you know of that support Drucker's statement?

3. Write a short paper of 200 to 250 words in which you contrast the Cartesian philosophy with what Mr. Drucker calls the "new philosophy."

4. Explain why we are so tardy in accepting the principles of "holism." Cite several instances of our failure to embrace this doctrine.
5. Define each of the following terms as they relate to the "new philosophy" discussed by Drucker: *psychosomatic medicine, Gestalt psychology, integration, synthesis, process, order.*
6. What group of educators, in your opinion, would most likely take exception to Lord Kelvin's principle: "I know what I can measure"?
7. Explain how the new philosophy defends a belief in divine power more so than does the Cartesian philosophy. What was Einstein's idea of God?
8. Explain what Drucker means by purpose "not *of* the universe, but *in* the universe."
9. Explain what is meant by "a dialectic of polarity." How can unity and diversity be necessary parts of a single entity? Explain this with reference to the words *universe* and *university.*
10. Read Kouwenhoven's article in this volume entitled "What's American about America?" and discuss the similarity of Kouwenhoven's and Drucker's points of view.
11. On what philosophy was Robert Louis Stevenson's *Dr. Jekyll and Mr. Hyde* based? Explain.
12. Drucker mentions a familiar dichotomy: materialism and idealism. What other dualities can you think of that might be reconciled?
13. What is the difference between objective and subjective measurement? Which type of measurement is employed by scientists? What courses in college make maximum use of subjective methods of measurement?
14. What is the difference between fact, value, and judgment? Between quantitative and qualitative aspects of a phenomenon?

◆ ◆ ◆

The Right to Think—Through Reading

WILLIAM G. PERRY, JR., and CHARLES P. WHITLOCK

I

"AND," READ Sammy, carefully forming each word after the manner teachers seemed to approve, ". . . and the big wolf was dis-dis-g-runt-ld."

"The big *gray* wolf, Sammy."

"The big *gray* wolf. What does—"

"Very good, Sammy, you only made one mistake on the whole page this time. And now, Margaret—"

"But what does—"

"No questions now, Sammy, we have to go on. I want everybody to read one page today. Now, Margaret—"

Perhaps your school days were old-fashioned enough for you to recognize this scene. Of course no modern teacher would let this happen—except on her "bad days." In any case we shall return to Sammy, hoping he will be somehow familiar.

What we want to talk about is the business of reading faster. We shall not be talking about "remedial" reading, the treatment of severe reading disabilities, but about what the specialists now call "developmental" reading—the training of normally slow-to-moderate readers, such as you may feel yourself to be, in more advanced reading skill.

Nearly everyone is impatient with his reading rate. Our own impatience has given us a special interest in the field, and it is one of our diversions to teach a short course in the art of rapid

Originally published under the title "The Right to Read Rapidly" by William G. Perry, Jr., and Charles P. Whitlock in *The Atlantic Monthly*, November, 1952. Copyright 1952 by William G. Perry, Jr., and Charles P. Whitlock. Reprinted by permission of the authors and The Atlantic Monthly Press.

reading to college students, with the dubious reward of seeing many of them outperform us on standard reading tests.

The demand for this kind of training is astonishing, not only in college, where even professors apply, but at the executive level in government bureaus, in industry, and in the armed services. You have probably read about these courses in "speed reading" and about the ingenious mechanical devices employed—the Rapid-o-Readers, the Flash-o-Scopes (we hope there are no such names), and our own Harvard Reading Films. Perhaps you hope some day to take such a course.

Some of these courses are modest, considered, and helpful. Others are neither modest nor considered; that even these seem often to be helpful should suggest much of interest about reading skills.

Let us examine one of the less considered. "The Ortho-Visual and Speed-Reading Institute" offers to train you out of your pedestrian ways (with due regard for comprehension) and the program is plausible in its simplicity. Everyone knows nowadays that a reader's eye does not sweep across a line but jerks across in little stops, and that the seeing is done in the stops, which take time. The Institute's machines, however, will train you to see more words at a glance, will broaden your "span" so that you may make fewer stops (as good readers do) and so increase your speed. The machines will also train you out of that awful habit of "regressing," of looking back constantly at things you missed.

All this is sound in its way, and based on respectable studies of what good and poor readers actually do with their eyes. Furthermore, if you take the course you will be pleased at your improvement in seeing more letters and numbers at each flash of the machine, and you will probably improve your reading.

But if we should test you before you take this course, you would find that when looking at ordinary *meaningful phrases,* you can already see three or four words at a time in a flash of one fiftieth of a second. This means that, with time allowed for movement from stop to stop, your eyes are already equipped to read at between 3000 and 10,000 words per minute. Even if we cut these figures in half, as an easy concession to plausibility, we can still ask you to explain why you are not reading this article at over 1000 words per minute. It is not your eyes that are holding you back. The chances are that you are not reading above 350 words per minute. Perhaps we should change the subject. Up until now we have been talking about reading as if it went on between the eye and the paper, and everyone could be enthusiastic about improving it. Now our attention is reaching back of the eyeball, and you are embarrassed, and we are embarrassed.

At this point there is no use pretending to be technical. When we get back to the eyeball in reading, the scientists present us with many intriguing problems and no answers. "Seeing," "perceiving," "comprehending," "learning," are words which apply to some continuous neural process at which we can only wonder. No one knows how meaning is constructed; no one even knows why some fast readers report that they can gather meaning directly from "seeing" the words while most of the rest of us feel that we have to "say" or "hear" the words to comprehend them. Nor do the scientists know anything about the neural determinants of mental speed. Perhaps the modern layman has been too ready to credit the scientific reading expert with knowing what he was talking about.

The nature of "comprehension" is of course the heart of the problem. The instructor in a speed-reading course recently reported, in a solemn statistical paper, the extraordinary gains among his pupils. One prize student, call him Mr. Brown, was reported to have improved from 150 words per minute to 1500 words per minute in three weeks, with 80 per cent comprehension. We searched for the material Mr. Brown had read on his tests. This was omitted from the brochure—perhaps for lack of space. The report did, however, include the questions on which Mr. Brown's comprehension score had been based, together with a key to the correct answers. We found that we too could score 80 per cent on these questions, without having read the test material at all. We have learned how most multiple-choice questions are made; so, apparently, has Mr. Brown.

We feel that Mr. Brown learned something much more important than this, and we shall return to it. We wish first to face some vital issues raised by this apparently disreputable incident.

Evidently "comprehension" in this case was what the test-maker thought it was when he made up the questions. The point we wish to make is that this is *always* so. It is so whether someone else is testing you or whether you are judging for yourself "what you got out of" reading something. What "comprehension" is, then, depends on the assumptions you make about the value of reading something at all. How shall we test your comprehension of the Gettysburg Address? Shall we ask you for the meaning of the word "dedicated"? Shall we ask you to state the "main idea" in "your own" words? Or shall we measure your pulse rate?

You will object that there must surely be respectable tests of just plain *reading*. Possibly, and yet in the best of them, "comprehension" is defined by the questions the tester chooses to ask. A useful reading test is supposed to distinguish "good" readers from "poor" readers, but we wager that we could construct an alternate set of questions, demonstrably accurate, which the "good" readers on the original test would answer incorrectly and the "poor" readers correctly. For example, Sammy in our opening paragraphs received a lesson in reading such that if he were asked to fill in the blank in the sentence "The wolf was——" he would answer "gray," whereas a "good" reader might answer "disgruntled."

We are not saying that there are no standards. Though it is possible that Sammy's book might be read for the purpose of finding out the color of the wolf, most educated people would probably agree that for ordinary reading purposes it would be more important to know that the wolf was disgruntled. And despite a wide disagreement about what constitutes "comprehension" of a book like *Moby Dick*, educated men can probably agree about the meaning of most expository prose. This leads inevitably to the question: "Are test-makers educated?" That many of them are is no reason for relaxing a skeptical vigilance, for the educated

man is now being defined by the tests, and soon education will
appear in the tester's own image, just as "intelligence" does now.

We are saying that your reading habits tend to form around
the image of what you expect to do with what you read—or that
more likely they formed long ago around the image of what you
felt you *were expected* to do. Unfortunately, once a habit is
formed, let us say at Sammy's age, it tends to persist as a kind
of assumption about one's relation to the printed page, instead
of giving way to new methods for new purposes.

Now, if "comprehension" of, say, the Bible is defined differently, according to one's purposes, in a Sunday School, in a history course, in a literary discussion, in a religious crisis, or in an
idle evening, what shall be said of reading "rate"? Obviously,
the best of readers would vary his rate in these different contexts
—possibly quite radically. In fact, this would be one of his distinguishing qualities as a good reader. In other words, "rate" cannot be reliably described, much less evaluated, in words-per-min-
ute. The only real question is, "How rapidly are you getting what
you want?" It is pretty hard to phrase an answer to this one,
even when you know what you want.

We suspect that when many people complain about their rate,
they mean that they usually spend more time with a book than
the results are worth to them, or that they suspect that they
are quite capable of getting the same results in half the time. Of
course full capacity itself varies from person to person, and those
of us whose best reading is less rapid than some others' best
have reason for envy. But even the "lightning" reader cannot
read all he "ought" to read, and even he must select and worry.

If both rate and comprehension are so relative to person, purpose, and materials, then a poet reading a poem, a chemist reading a professional paper, and a housewife reading a detective
story are all quite properly engaged in radically different pursuits.
In fact, you may have begun to wonder what is meant by the
word "reading." Here you are in excellent company. Listen to
Dr. Arthur E. Traxler, of the Educational Records Bureau, an
expert among experts: "Specialists in the reading field think of

'reading' as anything from a set of more or less mechanical habits
to something akin to the 'thinking' process itself. No one has yet
been able to identify the components of reading comprehension.
. . . Without a knowledge of these factors our tests of reading
skill are mere shots in the dark." Now if the tests are shots in
the dark, what about the "improvement" which is popularly
demonstrated by them?

II

If we have succeeded in sharing with you our confusion on
these technical problems, perhaps you will be willing to return
with us to Sammy. There is something of Sammy in most of us.
We picture him as a small child, bright and inquisitive. His
parents had striven successfully to imbue him with the feeling
that he was a "good" boy, and he had somehow deduced in the
process that this was the only safe kind of boy to be. This notion,
however, very quickly ran into conflict with his curiosity. His
"whys" and "whats" irritated his elders, who sometimes even
startled him by saying sharply, "Now stop it, Sammy, and don't
ask questions about things like that." It was very clear that a
good boy did not "find out," that he should wait until he was
told.

When he went to school his teacher clinched this conviction
by saying, "Now Sammy, if you'll just wait quietly I'll explain
everything." When he learned to read he found that books were
written by parent-teachers who told one things. And we have
seen him learning the golden rule of "good boy" reading: "Never
skip any words and don't ask questions."

Sammy was intelligent. As he went on in school he perceived
another principle. He saw, without ever having to put it into
words, that more moral value was put on whether reading was
"done" than upon its outcome. He saw that diligent readers were
never scolded even when they didn't know the answers, whereas
Aleck, who always seemed to know the answers without having
"done the reading," was constantly scolded for not making the

best use of his talents. Reading was clearly not a means to an end but a problem of conscience.

Now, since "good" reading required an obedient respect for the dictates of teachers and print, there was no place for his assertive and analytical impulses to go except into sports and gasoline engines. He was therefore much troubled by difficulties of concentration when reading anything but comics. He bewildered himself by periods of academic "laziness." Indeed, he had to drive himself to get through increasingly long assignments, and near his last year of school was discovered to be a "slow reader" with "short eye span." This was less of a surprise than a relief to him, because it explained so much.

We shall not pause to describe Sammy's eye movements. They are, of course, restricted by his assumptions about reading. He therefore cannot directly change them. When he tries to speed up, he becomes terrified of "missing something." Sammy feels that if he looks carefully at every word and misses the whole meaning he is somehow not to blame, but if he should miss some small thing by brazenly skipping it, the burden of responsibility would be overwhelming. He sometimes tries to read fast, and confirms his worst fears; since he is thinking of reading fast, not of getting meaning fast, he does in fact miss the meaning entirely.

When he then returns to looking at every word, to "absorbing" and "being told" rather than finding out, the slow drudgery challenges less than one half of his very good mind, and there is nothing for the other half to do but to go woolgathering. Of course it soon picks up a charming piece of wool and entices the first half into joining the fun. The sudden realization that he has "read" two whole pages without any comprehension at all is an experience common to the Sammy in each one of us.

There are other kinds of slowish readers besides Sammy; at another extreme the arguer, who battles every word and statement. He labors in the fear that through merely understanding the author's views he may involve himself unaware in some modification of his own. Perhaps he is fighting some long lost battle of early school years when one is not only required to learn something but is under constraint to believe it. Beyond these tendencies there are also more dramatic "disabilities" and "blocks," but this article is not about them. In our experience it is Sammy who is ubiquitous, with his assumption that Knowledge is to be passively absorbed, not found out and mastered. For him to judge, to select, and to discard (in short, to think) is to contend impiously with the gods of the printed Word—to "cut and slash" in a way which makes him feel exceedingly uncomfortable. As one student put it, "I wish I could read fast without feeling nasty—er—I mean nervous."

But even the "great" books are not gods; they are tools. Often they are dull tools. Certainly they can never be any sharper than the wits with which we use them. Authors are often dry and discursive; they cannot see our nod of recognition, or catch the signs that would tell them we have guessed the direction of their argument. Instead they must go boorishly on with their monologue, justifying a point we are willing to concede, as no civilized man would do in conversation. If we could remember this, perhaps the Sammy in us would take heart.

Yet to read well we need not bolster our nerve. In bold reading a legitimate contempt is more discriminating than a false courage. What we need is not patience, either, but impatience—the impatience that forces us to consider what we are reading for and to read *for it*. Only in impatience with wasted time will we invest the initial effort to establish the center of energy in our own heads rather than leave it somewhere in the book with the hope that the author will somehow be "stimulating." Interest in most informational reading is born from our own commitment to our purpose, and it is a rare author whose art we can rely on to tease us from page to page. Concentration is not achieved by nobly renouncing a tendency to think of other things, by "keeping thoughts out"; it is a by-product of having a goal that challenges the whole mind. If our goal be knowledge, it is good to remember that knowledge is ours only when we can think it for ourselves, not when we have merely "understood" while someone else thought it. Knowledge is not something we absorb; it is something we do.

III

The job, then, is to help Sammy change his mind so that he may change his ways. This is usually quite feasible. One can do it for oneself, once one gets the idea, or one can get some concentrated practice in a good reading course.

The advantage of a good course is not that it does the job for you, which it cannot, but only that it presents useful materials and those constant checks which assist in the growth of confidence. Such a course focuses not on the reading of good literature, which is a separate problem, but on general informational reading. It provides exercises in analysis and opportunities for radical self-assertion—binges of skimming, gambles in guessing whole paragraphs from their opening words, and scandalous revelations of the long-winded hypocrisy of most conventional prose. Probably the course will offer enough really difficult passages to reassure you that you are not being led down a primrose path.

Our students often rise in wrath midway through our course and accuse us. One cried, "I see what you're doing! You're trying to get us to think while we read. But suppose we think something the author doesn't think, or something the teacher doesn't think. What will happen to us then?" Unfortunately there is much reason in this extraordinary wail. A college professor, like any human being, has his bias, and a wise student respects it. Even in the most liberal colleges a few still reject the slightest deviation from the wording of the book. The student's error lay not so much in his cynicism, which was not our business at the moment, but in his assumption that mastering an author's reasoning demanded a total suspension of his own. What he had to learn was that only by direct comparison with his own reasoning, prejudices, or guesswork could he perceive what the author was saying at all.

We almost forgot: the course may also include practice with

machines. We seem to be in a poor way, after all this talk, to justify the use of machines. They would seem only to confirm Sammy in his delusion that reading goes on "out there," and that he is simply to follow along, or that if he could only get the right eye-movements. . . . But this distortion need follow only if the teacher is himself deluded, or is so insecure that he sets the machine in the center of his course. In its proper place a really good reading gadget can be very useful, especially those which stretch the pace of the reader on regular consecutive reading and then let him discover by a rigorous check that he can do better than he had thought. Such games as this can be great fun and a useful antidote to the tradition that good reading, like all good things, can be learned only in pain.

The best of these devices may also provide some training in the more mechanical processes of reading. Once Sammy is liberated at heart, they may help him work up undeveloped skills in visual selection and in the coördination of eye and brain. We have said only that to start with such training is as useless as to suggest to someone who labors under the necessity of touching every picket in a picket fence that he let one touch stand for three.

We have talked so much about selection and skipping that we must face up to the charge of recommending superficiality. We are really against it. But we do not believe it can be avoided by Sammy's efforts at thoroughness. Instead we believe the gains reported for "Mr. Brown" are the first essential step out of the quagmire of Sammy's own superficiality. We like to think of Mr. Brown with his tongue in his cheek and a conviction of having got his money's worth. We tell our students about him at the outset of our course, and as they laugh we ask them to stop and consider. May he not have discovered the foundation of all reading skill: the confidence to dismiss the trivial? The questions used in the tests of his reading suggest that the material itself was not worth reading, just as the questions were not worth answering. Let us concede that Mr. Brown was getting nothing whatever out of such reading whether he read slowly or fast. His gains were therefore great. He learned how to get nothing out of such reading in one-tenth the time it previously took him to get nothing out of it.

The capacity to get nothing out of useless material without exhausting one's time and attentive energy in the process is a prerequisite, in these days, to the attentive and energetic comprehension of passages which really matter. It takes a bit of practice for Sammy to develop this capacity, which includes the capacity to determine which passage is which. Selection is fundamental to thoroughness, and selection requires some fast and independent thinking.

For students who have attained this capacity we hope some day to develop an advanced course in rapid reading (measured in important ideas per hour) in which we tackle only a single paragraph per day. At present we refer such students to Professor I. A. Richards' book *How to Read a Page*. Of course the understanding of great literature is still another problem, and for this we refer our students to life, to books, and to their courses in literary criticism.

We have not meant to imply that all reading must be energetic. Surely there is a value in lolling, in immersing, and in reverie. Much of what we learn from a good book happens we know not how. Yet when we select our companions for lolling, there is still reason for standards and room for indignation.

This brings us to end with a heartening anecdote. We find it heartening, and feel it sums up what we have tried to say. Perhaps it shows that schools are better than they were, or perhaps simply that whatever problems its young heroine may meet in later life they will not be those of reading comprehension. If it says more, it must speak for itself.

We were once called upon to advise a parent-teacher association of an up-and-coming school on the matter of training good readers for college. We emphasized the skills of judgment and selection, and argued that one must give students not just preselected good books but also bad books so that they may have something to discard. We knew this was quixotic advice, practicable only in the last year of school if at all, for it is hard enough to keep children supplied with one book on a subject, to say nothing of six. But the school was way ahead of us, as so many schools are way ahead of experts. We received shortly a letter from the principal. It ran like this:—

Dear Sirs:

We were glad to have you make the points you made before the association. We have been trying to persuade our parent group of these matters for years and it is very helpful to receive support from outside.

We think you may value an account of an incident which occurred since your visit. The fourth-graders happened to be studying the ancient Hebrew civilization, using the Old Testament as source material. In keeping with the principles you so ably described, the teacher also supplied other books, among them some of those watered-down children's rewrites of the Bible stories. One nine-year-old girl, who seems to have read her Old Testament stories understandingly, perused one of these books and promptly requested to be given back the Bible. The teacher inquired into the pupil's reasons.

"Well," said the girl indignantly, "this book is no good. It says here that Delilah was Samson's wife, and Delilah was not Samson's wife, she was just his very good friend."

Questions and Exercises

1. Considering what the authors say about speed and comprehension in reading, which do they consider more important of the two? Explain fully.
2. What use do the authors feel should be made of machines or mechanical aids and devices in reading training?
3. The authors say, "The chances are you are not reading above 350 words per minute." Have your instructor test your rate of reading, using this or any other of the essays included in this volume. Compare your rate with that of your classmates. Are

you below the mean or average of the class? Is the class mean below 350 words per minute?

4. One writer on the subject of reading skills says that most people find that reading which is in tune with the writer's plan of writing is more productive than the usual "page" reading. It is a serious fallacy, he says, that leads us to think of pages of reading rather than of a sequence of ideas with logical thought relationships. How does this theory agree with the position of the authors of the essay you are studying?

5. The authors mention "seeing," "perceiving," "comprehending," and "learning" as parts of a total neural process which may be called "reading." How does this analysis of the process account for differences in comprehension among students?

6. What do the authors think is the principal weakness of comprehension tests? Can you suggest ways of combating this weakness?

7. Martin Panzer, in "Who Does Your Thinking?" *Coronet,* November, 1954, suggests a simple test to determine your capacity to think. Try this test on yourself:

"Ask yourself, first: did I arrive at this belief as a result of analysis and understanding, or as a result of a lazy reaction to what someone else said or did? Then ask yourself: if anyone asks me why I think or do this, will I be able to give a reasonably intelligent reply or will I have to bluff and flounder? Finally, ask yourself: do I speak or act as I do in a particular instance because I am convinced I am right or because I am guilty of prejudices which have been instilled into me by others?"

8. What do the authors of this essay consider to be the important mental operations in thinking? Compare this analysis with the ideas proposed by John Dewey in *How We Think* (chapter 1) or by James Harvey Robinson in "Four Kinds of Thinking" from *The Mind in the Making.*

9. Explain the authors' contention that "knowledge is not something we absorb, but something we do."

10. According to the authors, reading for a purpose is more productive than merely reading. In addition to acquiring knowledge, what other purposes might one have for reading? List as many as you can.

11. How do you understand the statement that what we need in reading is "not patience, but impatience"? Illustrate your explanation.

12. Point out a paragraph in the essay where the authors suggest that reading is a two-way operation—a coöperative effort on the part of both writer and reader.
13. By referring to your dictionary, determine the authors' meaning of the following words: *ubiquitous, discursive, reverie, pedestrian, quixotic.*
14. What are some of the assumptions, according to the authors, that average readers bring to an assignment in reading? Can you mention some which the authors failed to list?
15. How does the thought of this essay on reading compare with Stuart Chase's discussion of listening in "Are You Listening?" Point out several similarities.
16. How do any of the following essays which appear in this anthology support Perry's and Whitlock's argument that one must learn to think while reading?
    James Thurber, "Oliver and the Other Ostriches"
    Loren C. Eiseley, "The Bird and the Machine"
    H. I. Phillips, "Little Red Riding Hood"
    William Saroyan, "The Circus"
17. What possible connection do you see between the argument of this essay and Lloyd's thesis in "Our National Mania for Correctness"? Explain fully.

◆ ◆ ◆

Anybody Can Learn to Write

STEPHEN LEACOCK

THE BYGONE humorist Bill Nye once inserted in his column of Answers to Correspondents an enthusiastic item which read, "You write a splendid hand, you ought to write for the papers."

Reprinted by permission of Dodd, Mead & Company from *How to Write* by Stephen Leacock. Copyright © 1943 by Dodd, Mead & Company, Inc.

The wilful confusion of mind as to what writing means is very funny. But the confusion is no hazier than that of many young people who "want to write." Bill Nye would have told them that the best writing is done straight from the elbow. It is the purpose of this book to show that it originates in the brain. Writing is thinking.

This confusion between writing as a form of activity and as a form of thought came down to us from the long years during which the mechanical art of writing seemed of itself scholarship. In our immediate day, very brief in comparison, the art of writing has become practically universal among the nations called civilized. If that were all that were needed, everyone might be an author. Indeed, it is hard for us now to realize how very few people in past ages knew how to write. Charlemagne (742–814), who founded schools of learning in his great Empire, couldn't read or write. He tried to learn but he never succeeded. He used to carry round with him—so wrote a monk who was his friend and biographer—tablets and pencils in the hope that he might find time and opportunity to learn. But it was beyond him. It seems strange to imagine his great frame (he was nearly eight feet high) bent over his copy book as he breathed hard in his stubborn effort. It was his own inability to read that led him to found schools for others. There is something pathetic in this ambition of the greatest towards a thing now possessed by the humblest. It has the same human quality in it as when with us a millionaire, debarred from education in his own youth, founds a university and whenever he learns of something new that he doesn't know, founds a new chair in it.

This general inability to read and write lasted for centuries after Charlemagne. Henry the First of England was called Beau-Clerc, the "fine scholar," presumably merely because he could read and write in Latin: he had no further title to scholarship except that he started the first menagerie: but a little went a long way in those days. The barons of the Magna Carta signed with their seals, not their signatures. They couldn't read it. Even in the England of Queen Victoria's early reign over sixty per cent of the young women of the working class who got married signed the marriage register with their mark. For years after that in the country parts of England a "scholar" meant a person who could read and write as opposed to the generality who couldn't.

It is worth while to make this reference to the ability to write, to the mechanical art of writing and its relative rarity in bygone times, and indeed till yesterday. For to this fact is partly due the rather distorted view frequently taken as to what writing means. It is still thought of as if it meant stringing words together, whereas in reality the main part of it is "thinking." People don't realize this. A student says, "I want to write"; he never says "I want to think." Indeed, nobody deliberately wants to think except the heroine in a problem play, who frequently gasps out "I must think," a view fully endorsed by the spectators. "Let me think!" she says; indeed she probably has to go away, to the Riviera, "to think." When she comes back we learn that she is now looking for some way to "stop thinking"—to prevent her from going mad. . . .

All these references are made in order to stress the simple fact that writing is essentially thinking, or at least involves thinking as its first requisite. All people can think, or at least they think they think. But few people can say what they think, that is, say it with sufficient power of language to convey it to the full. Even when they have conveyed it, it may turn out to be not worth conveying. But there are some people whose thoughts are so interesting that other people are glad to hear them, or to read them. Yet even these people must learn the use of language adequate to convey their thoughts; people may sputter and gurgle in a highly interesting way but without the full equipment of acquired language their sputters won't carry far. This, then, is what is meant by writing—to have thoughts which are of interest to other people and to put them into language which reveals the thoughts. These thoughts may come in part from native originality, in part from deliberate search and reflection. In all that concerns writing, spontaneous originality, what we call native gift, is mingled with the result of conscious effort. The threads are interwoven in the cloth, till they blend and often seem indistinguishable.

It is the affectation of many authors to lay stress on the spontaneity of their thought. "This came to me," says such a one, striking a pose, "came to me one day in the heart of the woods." Poets have always loved to compare themselves to birds, singing untaught and unrewarded. Orators persuade themselves that they speak best on the spur of the moment. The truth is otherwise. The bird spends its life in practice; the orator has agonized at home. . . .

Now every child that is born into the world comes to it with a basis of mentality, an interpretation of life that was fashioned so slowly and so long ago that our ten thousand years of work has nothing to do with it. The child's economic world is a wonderful place, in which everybody is doing things because he wants to do them. The child understands that the furnaceman stokes up the furnace for the glorious fun of making the red glow when the poker hits the coals. So the child decides to be a furnaceman when he grows up. The child sees the policeman on the corner —helmet, baton and buttons, and all authority—directing the traffic, and decides to be a traffic policeman when he grows up. Indeed, he can't wait. In a toy helmet with a toy baton he directs traffic in the nursery, blowing his whistle, and thinking—"Here's the life." Or the child wants to run a streetcar, or to be an elevator man. All his little invented games of play are adaptations and anticipations of "work." But he doesn't know it: the future is veiled.

Gradually the veil is drawn aside. The child begins to understand that the furnaceman is not stoking the fire for fun, that the garbage man doesn't love garbage, and that the streetcar conductor doesn't keep the money, as he does in the nursery. The poet Wordsworth has told how "the shades of the prison house begin to close about the growing boy." He is referring to the boy's soul, gradually bruised into forgetfulness of its own immortal origin. But he might have told it also, with perhaps greater immediate pathos, in the economic sense—the fading of the bright vista of the nursery economic world, and the conversion of its glorious company into people working for money to buy food and clothes.

This conversion, though the child cannot know it, is never in reality quite complete. The human mind has a marvellous quality of adaptation. Many people, blessed with good health and conscience, grow to "like their job," begin to do it as if they did it for its own sake. The janitor of the apartment building becomes in his fancy its proprietor. The traffic policeman, in his best hours at any rate, sees himself a commanding general. So shall you find a railway timekeeper who ranks himself with the sun, or a gardener setting out tulips and absorbed to the point of being a tulip himself; a master tailor dreaming, chalk in hand, over the lines of a pair of trousers; and then in one bold sweep carrying his dream into reality. . . .

So then, one wants to "write," and that means to have, or get, ideas that are so interesting that if fully converted into words people want to read them—and will even (though we must pretend to forget that) pay money to read them. So the first inquiry is, How do you set about it to get ideas? Hence arises the question whether we get ideas by looking for them or by not looking for them; that is, by happening to be looking in another direction when they come along. In other words, is what is wanted in writing patient effort and conscientious industry? Or native genius and happy chance? This doesn't seem much of a question at first sight. But in reality it underlies all the discussion of how to write. John Stuart Mill once laid down a proposition so simple that it would require an idiot to deny it, namely that if you cultivate a piece of land more and more and better and better there comes a time when it isn't worth while to cultivate it better still. Having laid down this obvious truth, Mill declared it the most important proposition in Political Economy.

So with the question of whether to write by work or by inspiration. How can you be a writer by trying to be? You either are or you are not. "Poets," said the Romans, "are born, not made." So might you be inclined to believe till there comes the afterthought about the "mute inglorious Miltons" buried in the country churchyard, or the wish that you had seized and expressed the thoughts that have sometimes come to you, as you might have done if you had cultivated the power of expression. . . .

But it is also true that writers, in the mass, would never get far without a great deal of deliberate effort, of conscious pursuit of an idea, of constant practise in suiting words to thought. My own experience has been confined to two fields, both of them aside from the main body of imaginative writing. I can therefore speak from personal experience only of a limited scope. It has been my lot to write a great deal of historical and political stuff, in which imagination only figures as the paint upon the gingerbread—the art of using language to interest and embellish thought. It would insult a historian to ask if he got his facts out of his own head. . . .

We have decided then that writing has got to be done deliberately. We can't wait for it to come. On these terms, I claim that anybody can learn to write, just as anybody can learn to swim. Nor can anybody swim without learning how. A person can thus learn to swim up to the limits imposed by his aptitude and physique. The final result may not be worth looking at, but he can swim. So with writing. Nobody can learn to write without having learned how, either consciously or unconsciously. But it fortunately happens that what we call our education supplies to all of us the first basis for writing, the ability to read and to spell. Indeed our ordinary education, even in any elementary school, gives us a certain training in putting words together. Under the name of "composition" we go through a harrowing set of little exercises in correcting errors in the use of English; we put poetry back into prose, and go so far as to reach up to writing a composition on An Autumn Walk, or The Fidelity of the Dog. This is not "writing" in the sense adopted in this book but it is as essential a preliminary to it as learning to drive a nail into a board is to carpentry. People of exceptional native ability and no schooling sometimes write, and sometimes have reached great eminence without such training. But that is because the bent of their minds was so strong in that direction that unconsciously they weighed and measured words and phrases, fascinated with the power of expression, as an artistic genius, a young Giotto, with the pictured line.

Indeed, an ordinary environment of today gives us an even further start, and nowadays our sight and hearing, through moving pictures, introduces us to a vast world of history, of actual events, and imaginary stories. These and the little circumstances of our own life give us plenty of material for thought. If we put our thoughts into words and write them down, that is writing. There's no more to it. It's just as simple as that.

In other words, anybody can write who has something to say and knows how to say it. Contrariwise, nobody can write who has nothing to say, or nothing that he can put into words.

Now it so happens that most of us have a good deal to say, but when we try to turn it into writing it gets muddled up by all kinds of preconceived ideas of how writing should be done, or is done by other people. So much so that when we write anything down it sounds false from start to finish. Each one of us is the custodian of one first class story, the story of his own life. Every human life is a story—is interesting if it can be conveyed. The poet Gray wrote down the "short and simple annals of the poor," sleeping under the elm trees of a country churchyard with such pathos and interest that they have lasted nearly two hundred years. But the poor couldn't have done it for themselves. Neither can we. We can't surround the story of our life with the majestic diction and the music of Gray's Elegy. But it is interesting, just the same, if we can tell it. Have you never noticed how at times people begin to tell you of their early life and early difficulties, and tell it utterly without affectation or effort, and how interesting it is in such form? Like this:

Our farm was fifteen miles from a high school and it was too far to walk, and I didn't see how I could manage to go, and I couldn't have, but Uncle Al (he was the one who had gone out West) heard about it and he sent me fifty dollars and I started.

I boarded Monday to Friday and walked home Fridays after school . . . and so forth.

That's the way the man talks in an unguarded moment. But set him down to write out his life and see what happens. Either he sits and chews his pen and can't start, or he writes—with the result a hopeless artificiality. The same facts are there but dressed with a false adornment like ribbons on a beggar's coat. Something like this: Our farm was situated some ten miles from the nearest emporium of learning, to wit, a high school, a distance beyond the range of Shanks' mare, the only vehicle within reach of my, or my family's, pecuniary resources . . . etc., etc.

This failure happens because the man in question has been, unknowingly, taught how not to write. The necessarily somewhat artificial training of the schoolroom has led him unconsciously to think of writing as something elevated above the ordinary speaking—like company manners. This knocks out at once the peculiar quality of "sincerity" which is the very soul of literature. "Sincerity" is the nearest word for what is meant; it implies not exactly honesty but a direct relation, a sort of inevitable relation as between the words used and the things narrated. This is the peculiar quality of many of the great writers who wrote without trying to write. . . .

We have just said that the ordinary education of the great mass of people, who go to school but don't go to college, supplies them with at least a sort of elementary beginning in "composition," in the expression of thought in words. What they get is at least something; indeed it is much. But it is mainly negative. It says what not to do. It tells them what errors to avoid. But you can't avoid anything if you are writing nothing. You must write first and "avoid" afterwards. A writer is in no danger of splitting an infinitive if he has no infinitive to split.

It might, therefore, be thought that in order to become a writer it is necessary to go on from school to college, and learn the "real stuff." Fortunately for the world at large this is not true. To go to college may be helpful but it is certainly not necessary. Writing is a thing which, sooner or later, one must do for oneself, of one's own initiative and energy. Those who are debarred from the privilege of attending college may take courage. The college kills writers as well as makes them. It is true that a gifted professor can do a lot; he can show the way, can explain what are the things in literature that the world has found great and why, in his opinion, they are so. Better still, he can communicate his own enthusiasm, and even exalt his pupils on the wings of his own credit. More than that, the college gives companionship in study; it is hard to work alone, harder still to enjoy. Appreciation grows the more it is divided.

But as against all that, college training carries the danger of standardized judgments, of affected admiration, of the pedantry of learning. Students read with one eye, or both, on the examination, classify and memorize and annotate till they have exchanged the warm pulsation of life for the post-mortem of an inquest.

But the main point is that writing, whether done in and by college or without college, has got to be done for and by oneself. If you want to write, start and write down your thoughts. If you haven't any thoughts, don't write them down. But if you have, write them down; thoughts about anything, no matter what, in your own way, with no idea of selling them or being an author. Just put down your thoughts. If later on it turns out that your thoughts are interesting and if you get enough practise to be able to set down what they really are in language that conveys them properly—the selling business comes itself. There are many things in life, as we have said, that come to us as it were "at back rounds." Look for happiness and you find dust. Look for "authorship" and you won't find it; look for self-expression in words, for its own sake, and an editor's check will rustle down from Heaven on your table. Of course you really hoped for it; but you won't get it unless and until self-expression for its own sake breaks through.

What do you write about? You write about anything. Your great difficulty will be, as soon as you apprehend this method, that you can think things but can't say them. Most people live and die in that state; their conversation is stuffed with smothered thoughts that can't get over.

Take an example: Two people are walking out with the crowd from the roar and racket of a football game, just over. One says, "I don't know that I quite believe in all that rooting stuff, eh?" And the other answers, reflectively, "Oh, I don't know; I'm not so sure." That's as far as they can get. What the first man means is that organized hysteria is a poor substitute for spontaneous enthusiasm; and what the other means is that after all even genuine enthusiasm unless organized, unless given the aid of regularity and system—even spontaneous enthusiasm degenerates into confusion; our life, itself artificial, compels a certain "organization." They can't say this, but either of these two spectators would read with pleasure a well-written magazine article under such a title as Should Rooting be Rooted Out? The articles we think really good are those that express the things that we think but can't say. . . .

We are still talking then of how to begin. I would like to offer as a practical suggestion the keeping of a sort of "commonplace book" in which one writes all kinds of random attempts at expression. If you have just read a book write a few words down about it. If a moving picture has deeply moved you, write down the fact and try to explain why. Cultivate admiration of other people's words and phrases that seem to express much, and write them down. Soon you will write your own. In a certain sense all literature begins with imitation. Divergence comes later. . . .

Questions and Exercises

1. How does Mr. Leacock define what he calls *writing?* Copy his precise words.
2. How does the author explain the distorted view many people cherish about what writing actually consists of?

3. Consider the following paragraph from "Writing as Process," by Barriss Mills, and determine to what extent he agrees or disagrees with Leacock's ideas:

    "Unless a communication is purposeful, it is nothing, a meaningless exercise or ritual. And purpose here is twofold —the purpose of the writer and the purpose of the reader. We tend to forget that co-operation from a reader is necessary for the completion of any written communication and that such co-operation must be purposeful. Unless a reader has a purpose for reading what we have written our writing cannot successfully communicate. . . . A sincere attempt to communicate, then, involves not only something to say but also having an audience who want to hear what you have to say."

4. What is Leacock's attitude toward the relationship between native intelligence and the ability to write? Would you expect a student with a high I.Q. to get better grades in composition than one with an average or low I.Q.? Why?

5. To what extent does Leacock believe that writing is largely a matter of inspiration, or proper mood, or state of mind?

6. Before he died, Stephen Leacock was an English teacher at McGill University in Canada. What peculiarities of spelling do you detect in the essay that reflect British rather than American usage? Read in this connection Mario Pei's "The Geography of English."

7. Where does Leacock suggest that one get ideas for writing? How would he feel about the list of subjects usually suggested for exercises in composition in handbooks of English?

8. Can you supply an example, or examples, of the kind of authors Leacock mentions when he says: "People of exceptional native ability and no schooling sometimes write, and sometimes have reached great eminence without such training"?

9. It is often said that no one can teach another how to think. If thinking is as important in writing as Leacock suggests, what can a student who wants to write effectively do about it?

10. What does the author mean by the statement: "The college kills writers as well as makes them"? Read Marion Walker Alcaro's "Colleges Don't Make Sense," and describe the effect college had on her ability to express ideas fluently and effectively.

11. What does Leacock think is one of the greatest drawbacks to college courses in writing? Can you propose a plan for your own class that will overcome this difficulty?

12. The author has some pertinent things to say about sincerity, about writing one's own thoughts, about finding self-expression in words. Compare these ideas with what Rollo May says about "The Experience of Becoming a Person." Does May suggest anything that might help a beginning writer to express himself adequately?
13. Follow Leacock's suggestion about keeping a writing notebook. Write down daily anything which occurs to you as being important. Let your instructor see the notebook at the end of the term.
14. Consider William Saroyan's "The Circus," and Mark Twain's "Huck and Jim on the Raft," both included in this anthology, and discuss the nature of the writing in each case. Do these two authors satisfy Leacock's requirements for a successful writer? Explain.

◆ ◆ ◆

Our National Mania for Correctness

DONALD J. LLOYD

EVERY NOW and then the editors of the university presses let out a disgruntled bleat about the miserable writing done by scholars, even those who are expert in literary fields; and from time to time there are letters and editorials in our national reviews bewailing some current academic malpractice with the English language. At present, even *PMLA* (the Publications of the Modern Language Association), traditionally the repository of some of the worst writing done by researchers, is trying to

Reprinted from *The American Scholar*, Summer, 1952, by permission of Donald J. Lloyd and *The American Scholar*. Copyright 1952 by United Chapters of Phi Beta Kappa.

herd its authors toward more lucid exposition. And at two recent meetings of the august Mediaeval Academy, one at Boston and one at Dumbarton Oaks, bitter remarks were passed about the failure of specialists in the Middle Ages to present their findings in some form palatable to the general reader, so that he can at least understand what they are writing about.

Even admitting that a really compelling style is the result of years of cultivation, much scholarly writing is certainly worse than it needs to be. But it is not alone in this. Generally speaking, the writing of literate Americans whose primary business is not writing but something else is pretty bad. It is muddy, backward, convoluted and self-strangled; it is only too obviously the product of a task approached unwillingly and accomplished without satisfaction or zeal. Except for the professionals among us, we Americans are hell on the English language. I am not in touch with the general run of British writing by non-professionals, but I suspect that it is nothing to make those islanders smug, either.

Furthermore, almost any college professor, turning the spotlight with some relief from himself and his colleagues to his students, will agree that their writing stinks to high heaven, too. It is a rare student who can write what he has to write with simplicity, lucidity and euphony, those qualities singled out by Somerset Maugham; far more graduating seniors are candidates for a remedial clinic than can pass a writing test with honors. And freshman writing is forever the nightmare of the teachers of composition, as it would be of their colleagues if the latter could not escape to the simple inanities of their objective tests.

Yet it was not always so. I have on my desk a little manuscript from the fourteenth century written by an unknown author, which I am in the process of editing. When I read it to one of my classes, as I occasionally do, with no more modernization than my own Great Lakes pronunciation and the substitution of a word for one which has become obsolete, it is a simple, clear and engaging document. "Where is any man nowadays that asketh how I shall love God and my fellow-Christians?" it begins. "How I shall flee sin and serve God truly as a true Christian man should? What man is there that will learn the true law of God, which he biddeth every Christian man to keep upon pain of damnation in hell without end? . . . Unnethe (scarcely) is there any lewd man or lewd woman that can rightly well say his Pater Noster, his Ave Maria, and his Creed, and sound the words out readily as they should. But when they play Christmas games about the fire, therein will they not fail. Those must be said out without stumbling for dread of smiting. But if a lewd man should be smited now for each failing that he maketh in saying of his Pater Noster, his Ave Maria, and his Creed, I trowe he should be smited at the full." And so on, to the beautiful poetic line, "Then think it not heavy to dwell with thy mother in her wide house, thou that laist in the strait chamber of her womb." The spelling in the original is hectic, and the capitalization and punctuation sporadic, to say the least.

Yet there was a man who knew what he had to say and set out about saying it, with no nonsense and no fumbling. He aimed for his audience and, judging by the dog-ears and sweat-marks on the book, which is about the size of one of our pocket books, he hit it. Why cannot we do as well in our time? Indeed, the eighteenth century was about the last age in which almost any man, if he was literate at all, could set down his thoughts—such as they were—so that they did not have to be excavated by the reader. We have an abundance of letters, diaries, pamphlets, and other papers from that period, and they are well written. It was the age, we may recall, not only of Boswell and Johnson, but of Pepys and Franklin as well, and of a host of other men whose main legacy to us was a simple, direct, workmanlike style, sufficient to the man and to the occasion, which said what it had to say and said it well. With the end of that century we go into the foggy, foggy darkness, and God knows whether we shall ever find our way out of it—as a people, that is, as a nation of thinking men and women with something to say.

Nevertheless, there is no question what makes our writing bad, or what we shall have to do to better it. We shall simply have to isolate and root out a monomania which now possesses us, which impedes all language study and inhibits all mastery of our native tongue—all mastery, that is, on paper; for as speakers of English, we Americans are loving and effective cultivators of our expression. I recall the gas station attendant who was filling my car. The gasoline foamed to the top of the tank, and he shut off the pump. "Whew!" I said, "that nearly went over." "When you see white-caps," he replied, "you better stop." "You better had," I said, lost in admiration. But if you had given him a pencil, he would have chewed the end off before he got one word on paper.

The demon which possesses us is our mania for correctness. It dominates our minds from the first grade to the graduate school; it is the first and often the only thing we think of when we think of our language. Our spelling must be "correct"—even if the words are ill-chosen; our "usage" must be "correct"—even though any possible substitute expression, however crude, would be perfectly clear; our punctuation must be "correct"—even though practices surge and change with the passing of years, and differ from book to book, periodical to periodical. Correct! That's what we've got to be, and the idea that we've got to be correct rests like a soggy blanket on our brains and our hands whenever we try to write.

This mania for correctness is another legacy from the eighteenth century, but it did not get a real grip on us until well into the nineteenth. Its power over us today is appalling. Among my other tasks, I teach advanced courses in English language to students preparing to teach. Most of these are seniors and graduate students, and in the summer especially, there is a sprinkling of older men and women, experienced teachers, who are sweating out a master's degree. They have had courses in "English" throughout their schooling. But of the nature and structure of the English language, the nature of language habits, the relation of speech to writing, and the differences in usage which arise from dialect and from differing occupational and educational demands—of all these, they know nothing at all.

Nor do they come to me expecting to learn about these. They want to know two things: what correct usage is and how you beat it into the kids' heads. That there are other considerations important to an English teacher is news to many of them. What they get from me is a good long look at their language.

To trace this monolithic concentration on usage is to pursue a vicious circle, with the linguists on the outside. The literate public seems to get it from the English teachers, and the teachers get it from the public. The attitudes and pronouncements on language of a Jacques Barzun, a Wilson Follett, a Bernard De Voto or a Norman Lewis ("How Correct Must Correct English Be?") mean more to English teachers than anything said by the most distinguished professional students of language—such as Leonard Bloomfield, Robert Hall or Charles Carpenter Fries. Correct usage is pursued and discussed, furthermore, without much reference to the actual writing of literary men. Now and again I amuse myself by blue-penciling a current magazine such as the *Saturday Review* or *Collier's* against the rules. I have to report that error is rampant, if variation is to be considered error. The boys just don't seem to pay attention to the rules. Moreover, having seen some of their first drafts, I am pretty sure that what conformity they do display is the work of their wives, secretaries, editors, proofreaders and typesetters, rather than their own. It takes a determined effort to beat the old Adam out of a readable manuscript.

Thus it is only the determined, consciously creative professional who can build his work on the actual language of men. In a recent issue of the *Saturday Review*, I stumbled on a quotation from Wolfgang Langewiesche. "Well, it isn't crowned by no castle, that's for sure," he wrote, "and by no cathedral either." My eyes popped, and I read it again. I liked it. It looked right; it sounded right; it had a fine Chaucerian swing to it. But I bet it cost him some blood and a fifth of Scotch to get it into print. In my own limited publication, I find "a historical" changed to "an historical," all my "further's" changed to "farther" and all my "farther's" to "further," "than us" watered down to "than we," and many, many more. How E. M. Forster got by with "the author he thinks," and got it reprinted in a freshman handbook a few pages along from the prohibition of such locutions baffles me. A phony standardization of usage appears in print, the work of editors unconscious of the ultimate meaning of what they do.

The result of all this is that a wet hand of fear rests on the heart of every nonprofessional writer who merely has a lot of important knowledge to communicate. He writes every sentence with a self-conscious horror of doing something wrong. It is always a comfort to him if he can fit himself into some system, such as that of a business or governmental office which provides him with a model. It is thus that gobbledegook comes into being. I once braced a distinguished sociologist, a student of occupational myths and attitudes, about the convoluted, mainly nominal turgidity of his writing. He apparently admitted verbs into sentences the way we admit DP's into the United States, reluctantly and with pain. In speech he was racy, confident and compelling, a brilliant lecturer. "It's the only way I can get my work into the periodicals," he told me blandly. "If it's clear and simple, they don't think it's scholarly." With what relief the pedagogues subside into pedagese!

If we really want to get good writing from people who know things, so that we can come to learn what they know as easily as we learn from their talk, we can do it in a generation or so. In school and out, in print and out, we can leave usage to its natural nurse, the unforced imitation of the practices which are actually current among educated people. We can use our English courses in school and college, not to give drill on questionable choices among common alternatives, demanding that one be taken as right and the others as wrong, but to give practice in reading and writing. We can learn to read and write for the idea, and go for the idea without regard for anything else. Then our young people will come to maturity confidently using their pencils to find out what they think and get it down on paper; then our scholars will come to write simply, clearly and brilliantly what they brilliantly know.

In our speech we have arrived, I think, at a decency of discourse which is conducive to effective expression. We listen, with a grave courteous attention, to massive patterns of speaking different from our own because they come from differences in dialect and social status; we listen without carping and without a mean contempt. Furthermore, we participate; we go with a speaker through halts and starts, over abysses of construction, filling in the lacunae without hesitation; we discount inadvertencies and disregard wrong words, and we arrive in genial good will with the speaker at his meaning. In this atmosphere, our speech has thrived, and the ordinary American is in conversation a confident, competent expressive being. In writing he is something else again.

No one flourishes in an atmosphere of repression. It is possible, of course, for a person with special aptitudes and a special drive to bull his way past the prohibitions and achieve an individual style. But with the negative attitude that attends all our writing, those whose main interest lies elsewhere are inhibited by fear of "error" and the nagging it stirs up from setting pen to paper, until the sight of a blank white page gives them the shakes. It is no wonder that their expression is halting and ineffective. They cannot fulfill the demands of a prissy propriety and trace the form of an idea at the same time. They thus arrive at adulthood victims of the steely eye of Mr. Sherwin Cody, whose bearded face stares at them from the countless ads for his correspondence school, demanding, "Do YOU make these mistakes in English?" The locutions he lists are not mistakes, and Mr. Cody knows they are not; but his readers do not know it, and they do not know that they don't matter anyway.

For usage doesn't matter. What matters is that we get done what we have to do, and get said what we have to say. Sufficient conformity is imposed upon us by the patterns of our language and by the general practices of its users so that we do not have to run the idea of conformity into the ground by carping about trivial erratics in expression. Why in this matter of language alone complete conformity should be considered a virtue—except to typists, printers and typesetters—it is difficult to see (unless, perhaps, we are using it as a covert and pusillanimous means of establishing our own superiority). In our other concerns in life, we prize individuality; why in this one matter we should depart from a principle that otherwise serves us well is a puzzle for fools and wise men to ponder, especially since there is no general agreement on what to confrom to, and one man's correctness is another's error. Not until we come to our senses—teachers, editors, writers and readers together—and stop riding each other's backs, will the casual, brisk, colorful, amused, ironic and entertaining talk of Americans find its way into print. We should all be happy to see it there.

Questions and Exercises

1. Find a clear-cut statement of the author's thesis, or central idea, in this essay.
2. Lloyd refers to our concern for correctness in matters of language as a "mania." Find as many emotionally toned words of this nature as you can which exhibit the author's attitude toward "correctness."
3. What is the difference between a mania and a monomania? Write a definition of each word supported by at least one example. You may find an example of monomania in Melville's *Moby Dick*.
4. What is the essential difference between the way Americans talk and the way they write, according to Lloyd? Do you find this true in your own experience?
5. What specific types of evidence does Lloyd employ in developing his thesis? Point them out in the essay.
6. What was the precise "error" that Wolfgang Langewiesche made in his article in *The Saturday Review*?
7. List all the grammatical and technical "errors" referred to in the essay, and determine what the author of your handbook for composition or communication has to say about each of them. Check also Margaret Nicholson's *Dictionary of American-English Usage*.
8. What does the author mean by his statement: "It takes a determined effort to beat the old Adam out of a readable manuscript"?
9. Look up the survey of nineteen disputed expressions as reported by Norma Lewis in *Harper's Magazine*, March, 1949, and

discuss the method by which he arrived at decisions regarding acceptable usage. Do you think he was justified in his decisions?

10. Read a current issue of *Harper's Magazine, The Atlantic*, or *The New Yorker*, and find as many examples as you can of usages which are considered "incorrect" by writers of handbooks for composition courses.

11. What is meant by the term *gobbledegook?* What is its etymology? Find at least one good example of this kind of writing.

12. How would you defend the notion that language must of necessity change from time to time, so that what is considered "incorrect" in one decade may be perfectly acceptable in another?

13. What is the implication for beginning writers of the statement: "He apparently admitted verbs into his sentences the way we admit DP's into the United States, reluctantly and with pain"?

14. The author of this essay is quite obviously addressing himself to professional teachers rather than to students. How many of the expressions he uses must you look up in the dictionary in order to understand his meaning?

15. One critic of the "police-force concept of usage" says, "Too many teachers still behave as though all students' writing should be done in language appropriate for negotiating with deans." What in your opinion should constitute a guiding principle for matters of disputed usage in written discourse?

Are You Listening?

STUART CHASE

LISTENING IS the other half of talking. If people stop listening it is useless to talk—a point not always appreciated by talkers.

Reprinted from *The Reader's Digest*, November, 1953, by permission of Stuart Chase and The Reader's Digest Association, Inc. Copyright 1953 by Stuart Chase.

Listening isn't the simple thing it seems to be. It involves interpretation of both the literal meaning of the words and the intention of the speaker. If someone says, "Why, Jim, you old horse thief!" the words are technically an insult; but the tone of voice probably indicates affection.

Americans are not very good listeners. In general they talk more than they listen. Competition in our culture puts a premium on self-expression, even if the individual has nothing to express. What he lacks in knowledge he tries to make up for by talking fast or pounding the table. And many of us while ostensibly listening are inwardly preparing a statement to stun the company when we get the floor. Yet it really is not difficult to learn to listen— just unusual.

Listening is regarded as a passive thing, but it can be a very active process—something to challenge our intelligence. A stream of messages is coming in to be decoded: how close can we come to their real meaning? What is the speaker trying to say? . . . How does he know it? . . . What has he left out? . . . What are his motives?

Sometimes only about a quarter of an audience understands clearly what a speaker has said. To sharpen the ears of its members, the New York Adult Education Council has inaugurated "listening clinics." One member reads aloud while the others around the table concentrate on what he is saying. Later they summarize what they have heard and compare notes—often to find that the accounts differ widely. Gradually the listeners improve, and often they find themselves transferring the skill to business and home affairs. As one member said:

"I became aware of a new attitude. I found myself attempting to understand and interpret the remarks of my friends and associates from *their* viewpoint, and not from my own as I had done previously."

Some years ago Major Charles T. Estes of the Federal Conciliation Service was called in to help settle a long-term dispute between a corporation and its unions. The Major proceeded to invent a technique for listening that has since had wide application in the labor field. He asked delegates from both union and management to read aloud the annual contract which was in dispute. Each man read a section in his turn; then all discussed it. If a dispute began to develop, the clause was put aside for later examination.

In two days the delegates really knew what was in the contract, and were competent to go back and tell their fellow managers or fellow workers what it contained. "We had conditioned them to communicate," said the Major. The contract was not rewritten but has continued in force with very few changes for ten years. Good listening had transformed bad labor relations into good ones.

Carl R. Rogers, University of Chicago psychologist, suggests a game to be played at a party. Suppose a general discussion—say on the French elections—becomes acrimonious. At this point Rogers asks the company to try an experiment. Before Jones, who is on the edge of his chair, can reply to the statement just made by Smith, he must summarize what Smith has said in such a way that Smith accepts it. Any attempt to slant or distort is instantly corrected by the original speaker. This means careful listening, during which emotion is likely to cool.

The result is that everyone in the circle, by listening and rephrasing, acquires a working knowledge of the other fellow's point of view, even if he does not agree with it. The players are quite likely to increase their knowledge of the subject—something that rarely happens in the usual slam-bang argument. The experiment takes courage, says Rogers, because in restating the other man's position one runs the risk of changing one's own.

F. J. Roethlisberger of the Harvard Business School, in a recent study of training courses for supervisors, describes a significant contrast in listening. An executive calls foreman Bill to his office to tell him about a change in Bill's department. A casting will be substituted for a hand-forged job, and the executive tells Bill how to do it.

"Oh yeah?" says Bill.

Let us follow two steps which the boss might take at this point.

First, suppose he assumes that "Oh yeah" means Bill does not see how to do the new job, and it is up to the boss to tell Bill. This he proceeds to do clearly and logically. Nevertheless, Bill is obviously freezing up, and presently things begin to happen inside the boss. "Can it be," he asks himself, "that I have lost my power to speak clearly? No, Bill just doesn't understand plain English; he's really pretty dumb." The look which accompanies this unspoken idea makes Bill freeze up even harder. The interview ends on a note of total misunderstanding.

But, says Roethlisberger, suppose the boss sees from the "Oh yeah" that Bill is disturbed, and he tries to find out why. He says: "What's your idea about how the change-over ought to be made, Bill? You've been in the department a long time. Let's have it. I'm listening."

Things now begin to happen inside Bill. The boss is not laying it on the line, he's willing to listen. So ideas come out, slowly at first, then faster. Some are excellent ideas and the boss becomes really interested in Bill's approach—"Smarter man than I thought!" A spiral reaction is set up, as Bill begins to realize that he never appreciated the boss before. The interview ends on a note of close harmony.

In the first case, the boss did not listen to Bill, he *told* Bill; and though the telling was clear enough the goal moved farther away. In the second case, the boss listened until he had located what was worrying Bill; then they went along together.

So far, we have been talking about sympathetic listening in face-to-face situations, to make sure we grasp the speaker's full meaning. But critical listening, too, is needed in a world full of propaganda and high-pressure advertisers. Here are some techniques which help to develop critical listening to a speech or a conversation, a sales talk at your door or the testimony of a witness before a jury:

Look for motives behind the words. Is the speaker talking chiefly in accepted, appealing symbols—Home, Mother, the Founding Fathers, Our Glorious Heritage, and so on—avoiding the need for thought, or is he really trying to think? Speeches are often solidly larded with symbols, and the well-trained ear can identify them a long way off.

Is the speaker dealing in facts or inferences? With practice you can train your ear to find this distinction in political and economic talk, and to follow the shifts from one level to the next. The listener should also consider his own attitude toward the speaker. Is he prejudiced for or against him? Is he being fair, objective, sympathetic?

The sum of careful listening is to work actively to discover how the speaker feels about events, what his needs and drives appear to be, what kind of person he is. The appraisal can only be rough, but it can be a decided help in dealing with him, in giving him a fair answer.

One other thing: I find that careful listening also helps me to keep quiet rather than sound off foolishly. The best listeners listen alertly, expecting to learn something and to help create new ideas.

Are you listening?

Questions and Exercises

1. Mr. Chase says that listening can be something to challenge our intelligence. Can you explain listening as an active, creative activity rather than as a passive one? How does this thought agree with Leacock's attitude toward writing in "Anybody Can Learn to Write"?
2. What specific techniques of development does Chase employ in this essay to establish the importance of listening training?
3. Considering the experiments of Major Charles T. Estes and of Carl R. Rogers, as described in this essay, what appears to be a major objective of listening training?
4. List the barriers to successful listening that are suggested by this essay.
5. How many kinds of listening does the author describe? Can you think of other types of listening not specifically mentioned in the essay?

6. Describe the difference between the way Chase discusses "sympathetic listening" and the way he discusses "critical listening." Which method is more beneficial to you?

7. Try the Rogers experiment, explained in the essay, in your own class, following or during a discussion of a debatable topic.

8. Report to the class, in a three-minute talk, any experience you have had which demonstrates the need for effective listening.

9. Find Chase's definition of careful listening, which is expressed in one clear-cut, succinct statement.

10. Assuming that a speaker has an obligation to his listeners as well as they to him, what suggestions could you make that would insure better listening behavior on the part of your classmates?

11. After reading this essay, write a short paper in which you define carefully the essential difference between "hearing" and "listening."

12. Read the articles by Carl R. Rogers and by F. J. Roethlisberger which appear in S. I. Hayakawa's *Language, Meaning, and Maturity,* and list reasons why most Americans are, as Mr. Chase says, not good listeners.

13. Supply adequate definitions of the following terms, as they concern effective listening: *empathy, feedback, two-way communication, rapport.*

14. Ineffective speaking is one of the surest ways of making successful listening impossible. An effective speaker analyzes his audience before he addresses them. Consider Voorhis' "Advice to Forlorn Freshmen," which was addressed to college freshmen during orientation week at Colgate. How well, in your opinion, had Voorhis considered his audience? Explain.

15. How does Gilbert Highet's essay "The Art of Persuasion" focus on the need for effective listening during political campaigns?

16. Someone has said "Creative minds need creative audiences." How does this statement argue the importance of listening training in the college curriculum?

◆ ◆ ◆

Put Your Best Voice Forward

STEPHEN S. PRICE

IF YOU were suddenly chosen from a group and asked to make an informal luncheon talk, or address a business meeting, or even speak to millions of people over radio and TV, how would your voice sound to your listeners?

Would it come over clearly and pleasantly? Or would it sound slurred or harsh, weak or tiresome, breathy or piercing?

Some years ago, when I worked as a radio-TV director and coach for CBS, I often had to single out plain everyday men and women from a studio audience to participate in our quiz and interview shows. It was a tricky experience, because so many people have poor voices. I would try to weed out the hopeless cases beforehand by chatting with many individuals a few seconds to size up their voices.

In a group of 20, I would be lucky to find one who had a really good, interesting voice. I might find 6 or more in the 20 who would rate as fair to good. But the majority had inadequate speech and voices. They would have made listeners feel uncomfortable and we would have lost our audience.

Have you ever heard exactly how your voice sounds to others? If you have not, I suggest that—right now—you step to a corner of a room and, facing closely into the corner, cup your ears and speak a few words or count. But don't be shocked! That stranger you hear talking is you!

It is this voice which, unknown to you, has been labeling you in people's minds more than any other single fact about you. People form their impressions of you more by ear than by eye.

Your voice labels you every time you meet someone at a party
. . . or greet a new customer . . . or stop to chat with a casual
acquaintance . . . or try to express an opinion at a community
meeting. It labels you when you talk to a person for the first time
on the telephone.

The way most Americans neglect to develop their voices and
speech has always struck me as astonishing, in view of the growing
role our speaking voices now play in our everyday lives. For example, voice has become an increasingly important factor in making
us more effective at the earning of a living.

We all know, of course, that anyone who wants to succeed as an
entertainer or public official or lawyer or minister must give a
great deal of thought to his voice. But voice has become more
and more important for millions of people in their everyday
work of making a livelihood—whether you are a salesman,
teacher, nurse, railroad conductor, waitress, doctor, receptionist,
airplane pilot, supervisor, or secretary. At the Katharine Gibbs
Secretarial School, for instance, each girl is carefully coached to
inject clarity and warmth into her voice.

One of my most interesting assignments was to check the
voices of key employees of Gimbels' department store in New
York. These people handled the store's public contacts, and included clerks in the "return" and credit departments, as well as
switchboard operators. I posed as a complaining customer and
talked with each by phone. A few did poorly in this "stress" test,
by showing impatience and irritation in their voices.

Another large department store, this one in the Midwest,
made a survey of customers to find which of its clerks were particularly popular. It turned out that 9 out of 10 of the men and
women who reached high in popularity had improved their
voices by singing in school glee clubs or church choirs or by taking part in amateur plays. Today, when it hires new clerks, this
store pays particular attention to whether or not they have "well-
modulated voices."

Right now one of the clients I am coaching is a man who trains
salesmen for a major corporation. He found he needed help him-

self because, when talking to his men, he tended to swallow his words, run out of breath, stammer slightly, and grope for words. I am helping him get more confidence and smoothness into his voice—mainly by developing his diaphragm power and breath and speech co-ordination to the point where it is easy for him to speak incisively and smoothly.

Men and women who hope to attain executive positions need to give extra thought to their speaking voices. In many firms today, officials do most of their conversing with associates by talking into an intercom on their desk. An acquaintance of mine who seemed to be in line for the vice-presidency of his firm was passed over. When I asked another officer of the firm what happened, he explained: "Joe missed out because—well, to be frank, he doesn't *sound* like a vice-president. Joe has such a thin, uncertain voice that the boss was afraid he might make important customers he dealt with lose confidence in us." Now, I might add, Joe is working to put more assurance into his voice.

Our voices are important, not only in our work, but in our community and social lives. In towns like Bloomington, Illinois, you will find hundreds of people each week rising to say a few words at their lodges, women's clubs, civic affairs, school and church functions. Many of these speakers are housewives.

When the housewife finds herself having the floor at a meeting or party her voice often becomes unpleasantly high and tremulous. And at home wives represent the entire family— for better or worse—many times a day in talking on the phone with tradesmen, school officials, and persons they barely know, whose help they may need in their committee or club work.

In romance, voices are put to perhaps the greatest test of all. More than one woman has confided to me that she first became intrigued by her husband because of the warmth and assurance of his voice. A teen-age boy today puts his voice to a test every time he phones a popular girl and tries to sell her on the idea of a date. And we all know the beauty who ruins her appeal by a naggy voice.

There is not a person in the world who cannot make his or

her voice more appealing. In fact, if there is a "perfect" voice any-where, I've never heard it. And most people who are handicapped by inadequate voices never bother to find out just what is wrong—and never try to correct the condition.

What are our most common vocal shortcomings? My colleagues in the field have devised dozens of names to describe various un-pleasant speaking characteristics. In counseling thousands of peo-ple during the past 21 years, however, I have found that the list can be reduced to 5 major troublemakers. If you have a voice that presents you poorly, it is probably for one or more of these 5 reasons. I will try to show you how to check for these short-comings in yourself—and how to convert them into pleasing voice qualities that will be an asset to you. First, ask yourself these five questions:

"Is my voice and speech slurred rather than clear?"

Do people frequently misunderstand you . . . or ask you to repeat . . . or lean forward as if straining to make out what you say? Try saying this sentence aloud: "Leaves, frost crisped, break from the trees and fall." Did it made you feel a little tongue-tied? If spoken by you several times and your answer is "Yes," then you are probably careless in your speech manipulation and you speak indistinctly.

Perhaps your words seem blurred because you speak too rapidly, and the syllables tumble over one another. Many people talk much too fast. Investigators for the telephone company tell me that the average American speaks too quickly on the phone for ready comprehension, which is more than 125 words a minute. Every New York operator is required daily to practice speaking more slowly and distinctly.

More probably, however, your problem is lip laziness. On trips across America in 1952 and 1953 I was dismayed to hear the slur-ring and grunting that passes for speech. A garageman in Des Moines asked me, "Wha che wan'?" A Tucson waitress in-quired, "J'orda ye'?"

An area where much lip laziness is heard is the Deep South, where I heard such things as "Ah don' keh fow inny." Yet Southern speech, when correctly spoken, is musical and charming. It is relaxed and open—two desirable characteristics. Southerners drawl their vowels (a, e, i, o, u), which are the musical letters in our alphabet. Vowels, being open sounds, are easy to say. You just open your mouth and let the "ahs" roll out. But we get power and clarity into our speech with consonants (especially d, t, b, p, k, g, f, v, z, and s). These sounds take real work. To pronounce them properly you must use the tongue, lips, and teeth energetically.

Lip laziness, however, is an all-American speech fault. Some months ago a New Jersey father asked me if I could do anything to help his 19-year-old daughter. He said she was in good physical health but was moody and unhappy. The boys she liked and was dating were getting engaged to other girls. The father, a successful businessman and speaker, suspected, correctly, that her listless, mumbling speech was the major personality problem. She was pretty but spoiled and had never bothered to learn to put herself across to people.

As an incentive I suggested the father purchase a parakeet which he would teach to talk. The parakeet offers a fine challenge because it will learn only if you systematically repeat over and over, in clearly enunciated form, your phrases. One phrase the girl tried was "Budgie is a nice boy."

I also encouraged her to spend about 30 minutes each morning in front of a face mirror energetically repeating the alphabet and articulation exercises. And I persuaded her to spend 5 minutes every day whistling. That's a wonderful corrective for lip laziness! Within a month the girl was making noticeable progress. And within 2 months other people began noticing a change in her. I get reports from her parents that she is meeting new boys and girls and has become a different, more outgoing person. (And Budgie is doing fine with his talking, too!)

If you need to sharpen the clarity of your enunciation, you might try a similar approach. Also, I suggest that you practice talking like Gary Cooper, the actor. Every impersonator of Gary does his imitation by talking through clenched teeth. With your teeth closed tight, you must make up for the handicap by working your tongue and lips harder; and you must exert more power in your breath. In short, you "energize" your speech. With teeth clenched, read aloud passages from this magazine; first slowly, then rapidly. Next, still with your teeth clenched, try repeating such challenging phrases as:

"He thrust three thousand thistles through the thick of his thumb."

"She sells seashells by the seashore."

When you think you are getting pretty good at enunciating, try this final test: Make up a paragraph of double-talk, then telephone a friend and ask him or her to try to write down what you say, as you speak slowly and surely into the mouthpiece. If he can accurately hear your sounds and repeat after you such things as "What happlet to the portisan on the milliflow this cantaflas," you can be sure your voice and speech are improving!

"Is my voice harsh rather than agreeable?"

Do you ever have the feeling people are uncomfortable when you talk? If so, your harsh tones may be hurting their eardrums. This rasping quality takes many forms. Your voice may seem shrill, grating, hard, piercing, or brassy. These defects all go back, however, to one cause—tension in your throat and jaw.

Tension destroys mellowness. When your throat is tense you can't achieve the warm, relaxed quality essential to a really pleasing voice. And a warm, relaxed quality is now a prime qualification for nurses and elementary-school teachers, among others.

Visiting foreigners often comment unfavorably on the harsh voices of many American women. The reason women are more susceptible to this fault than men is that tension shows up more in a woman's voice. I have noticed that the women who suffer most from a hardness in the voice are often career women or housewives with too many responsibilities.

In helping prepare such renowned figures as Bernard Baruch, Herbert Hoover, and James A. Farley for their speeches on the air, I learned that the more responsibilities a great man has, the more relaxed he is. One of my women clients was a movie casting director. A brilliant girl, she went about her work at a super-charged pace. She was proud that she could talk as tough as any film technician. Her voice pierced you. Suddenly she realized that, although she was successful career-wise, she was failing as a woman, in her home and social life, so she sought help.

First, I taught her how to relax—and you can do it, too. Tension in your throat is frequently part of general bodily tension. It shows up in your voice. So you start by relaxing your whole body. Twice a day, in mid-morning and mid-afternoon, this wound-up woman would seclude herself for a few minutes. She would stretch out on a couch or a comfortable chair and throw herself into a rigid state, tensing every muscle in the body—even to the tips of her fingers and toes. She would hold the tension position for a slow count of 10, and then repeat the process 2 or 3 times. Then she would lie quietly for several minutes, eyes shut, quietly relaxed, imagining she was riding down in an elevator.

Then, to relax her throat muscles, she would slump forward in her chair in the "dead-asleep exercise." You do this by letting your head drop, your jaw sag, and your arms flop like a rag doll's. Now, very slowly and gently, roll your head in a circle. Alternate from right to left and continue circling about 3 minutes. Then you can continue relaxing your jaw muscles by yawning a few times, opening your mouth wide, and saying such words as "clock," "squaw," "gong," "claw," and "paw." Try Theodore Roosevelt's famous exercise: Repeat "ding-dong."

I also coached this woman to get more gentleness into her voice. For at least a few minutes every day she would concentrate on talking slowly and gently to people—as if talking to a baby or a puppy. Gradually, gentleness started pervading all her talk. She confessed that she felt a lot better, and that people now seem to enjoy having her around. Nothing was chasing her any more.

"Is my voice weak rather than firm and well supported?"

You have probably, in all your life, never thought much about your diaphragm, the band of muscles a few inches above your mid-riff. Yet the diaphragm is the bellows that blows the fire of life into your speech and adds oomph to your personality. The perfect exponent here is Betty Hutton. If your diaphragm is lazy or weak, you probably have a thin, uncertain, often shy voice. Have you ever had the feeling that people don't pay much attention to you when you talk, or do they ask you to repeat what you said? Do you find it hard to persuade them to show confidence in you? Perhaps your "bellows" needs strengthening.

A young research expert with a wispy, unsure voice complained to me, "When I talk in a group, I rarely get a chance to finish a sentence. Someone always butts in." He complained that if he is talking with a girl, other men can always divert her attention.

I put my hand on his diaphragm and asked him to say loudly, "Boomlay, boomlay, boomlay. Boom!" His frail diaphragm muscle barely fluttered. A well-developed diaphragm will be firm and really bounce when you say "boom."

We worked first of all to give him a more vigorous diaphragm. I prescribed boxing lessons and daily "deep-breathing walks" to give him a sense of greater vitality. Also, he would lie on the floor, face up, breathing deeply in and out. I suggested he place a heavy book on his diaphragm and watch it rise and fall. Still lying down, he would shout several times, "Hay . . . he . . . ha . . . hi . . . ho . . . who!" Then he would sit up, and after inhaling through his nose, blow out his breath through a very tiny hole formed by pursed lips. (A clay pipestem works fine for this, too.) Next, he would pick up a newspaper and see how long he could read aloud with each breath. As his diaphragm strengthened and his breath control improved, he was able to read for 15, and later 20, seconds in one breath. (25 is excellent.)

At the same time I tackled his shyness by persuading him deliberately to pay honest compliments, smile, and tell short jokes. His voice grew more self-assured and his personality improved. When people interrupted him, he would recapture the spotlight by repeating his last phrase—and in a stronger voice. Now he commands attention. He phoned recently to say he never believed that the pretty girl he now sees would go out with him.

Weak voices are more common among women than men. This is especially so with beauties who sit around a great deal being admired, and who get very little vigorous conversational exercise. Their breathing is shallow. Many lovely movie starlets remain starlets because of their thin, baby-girl voices.

In the latest Miss America contest at Atlantic City, N.J., the five finalists were subjected to just one test of their charm: They were asked to talk briefly about themselves before a microphone. One girl who was sensational in appearance proved to have a surprisingly thin, schoolgirlish voice. She was quickly eliminated. It was significant that the girl finally chosen as Miss America, Lee Ann Meriwether, was a dramatics student who had worked to make her voice strong and rich. I could tell by her voice that she had a well-developed diaphragm. Her voice was low and soft. She had breath control.

It is control, not mere lung capacity, which gives you an outstanding voice. The long-held notes of Lily Pons are an example. Many people have lots of breath capacity but poor control. We call their voice type "breathy." They waste a lot of breath saying words containing the letters "p" and "b." You can check your own breath control by holding a lighted candle about 4 inches from your mouth. Now, trying not to blow out the candle, say, "Peter Piper picked a peck of pickled peppers." If you blow out the flame you have poor breath control.

Whispering aloud, I might add, is an excellent way to develop your breath control and voice power. Have a friend stand across the room, then whisper very loudly to him some phrase such as "Charge of the Light Brigade!" As soon as he can hear you clearly, have him move into another room . . . then go as far away as your voice can reach him.

When I was directing and coaching actors at the Ogonquit, Maine, Playhouse, I trained the weakest-voiced girls so that they could "stage whisper" understandably messages while standing the length of two city blocks away. And once I won a bet by whispering, loud and slow, "Minnie, I want to eat," across a quarter-mile lake in the quiet of early morning. I must confess this involved a little deception. I knew that the water would help me by bouncing the words along.

"Is my voice flat rather than colorful?"

Many people are considered bores simply because they talk in a monotone. Salesmen torture customers by droning. And neighbors with a tiresome monotone make you squirm at Parent-Teacher meetings.

Many others, particularly men, do most of their talking within a range of two or three tones and always with the same volume and rate of speech. Does your voice ever seem to bore people? Do people seem to get restless and look away or cough? One good way to check whether your voice follows a flat, dull line is to try singing the scale with "la" up and down. If you find it too difficult, you probably need to practice putting more expression and feeling into your voice.

A prim New England woman who wanted to make a talk to her club came to me for counsel because she was worried about how she would sound. Her voice was cold and listless. I asked her if she knew anyone who got a big kick out of life. She thought a moment, and said, "Yes, the Italian handyman who helps with our gardening." She told me how much she envied his exuberance and joy of living.

To help bring warmth to her voice, I suggested she spend a few hours each week working along with the handyman in planting shrubs and tending the large vegetable garden. She got down on her knees and dug the earth with her hands. Also, for practice at home, I instructed her to imitate a jolly Santa Claus by laughing out loud, up and down the musical scale. First, she would laugh "ho" up and down the scale, then "ha," "he," and "hoo." She was to do it slowly at first and then faster and faster. She was a little appalled, but followed instructions. Within 2 months her voice took on more warmth and feeling and she began to look at life with a more zestful attitude.

A more widespread cause of flatness, however, is "talking through the nose." The result is a twangy nasality. It is common to many New Englanders, Midwesterners, Southwesterners, newsboys, circus barkers, pessimists, worriers, and women who think it is ladylike to keep their mouth closed while talking. When the sound can't come out the mouth properly it takes the back door through the nose, because that is the first opening the breath encounters.

An easy way to check your own voice for "nose-talking" is to hold your nose and say "meaning." Notice how strangely muffled it sounds. Feel the vibration. That is because the sounds "m," "n," and "ng" (and only those three basic sounds) are resonated mainly in the nose. Say, "Father Manning." You should feel vibration in your nose only when you say "Manning." If any other letters sound muffled, then you are probably nasal in your general speech.

When a person talks through his nose you get a sharp, flat, twangy unpleasantness. He's not using his best resonators—the mouth, throat, and chest. They add the vibrant richness to your voice. The farther you open your mouth, the richer, fuller, and lower your tones will be. Try saying "olive" by opening your lips only slightly. Now repeat it while really opening your mouth and rolling out the word. Notice the greater richness?

You can note the role your chest plays in adding vibrance to your voice by placing your hand on your upper chest and humming a few bars. Feel the vibrations? As a matter of fact, you can add vibrance to your voice by humming at odd moments every day. Hum your favorite songs. Gently hum the scale several times. Then hum the low, tender melody of a Stephen Foster song. Every time I meet up with Gordon MacRae, he is humming happily. That's how his speaking voice flows easily.

Also, you can add a new lilt to your voice by some good, open-throated singing when you are in the shower or bath. Sing whatever strikes your mood, with a relaxed and open throat. It is the melody, not the loudness, that counts.

"Is my voice high-pitched rather than well-modulated?"

There's a woman in my neighborhood who has a French poodle named Soufflé. Almost every afternoon I can hear her impatiently calling, "Soufflé, Soufflé, come here!" in her high-pitched voice. Often I can see the little dog react by scurrying farther away. However, when the woman's son calls, in a low, easy voice, Soufflé comes a-trotting.

Dogs live by sound, and high-pitched, harsh voices make them nervous. To a lesser degree, such sounds make us humans uneasy, too. The harsh, high pitch suggests nervousness and is distressing; while a low tone is soothing.

Yet most people talk at a pitch higher than necessary or natural to them. Women are especially prone to a shrill pitch when they speak on the telephone or when they speak louder, as in the forced saying of good-by. With men, of course, a high pitch is unpleasant, for the added reason that, without basis, it might suggest lack of virility.

Probably the most famous case of voice improvement since Demosthenes (the Greek who overcame stuttering and became a famed orator by practice-speaking with pebbles in his mouth) is that of Mrs. Eleanor Roosevelt. When she first began making public appearances as First Lady her voice was notoriously high pitched. She realized this was a handicap and tried hard to correct it. In recent years, when I worked at CBS I helped her several times prepare for her broadcasts, and find she now has a well-modulated voice. It is nicely paced, relaxed, and her occasional high notes are not conspicuous.

She did not actually "lower" her voice. This is impossible. What she did was increase the use of her lower register. You do this by concentrating on the chest. You practice sounds that can be resonated in the chest, such as, "Alone, alone, all, all alone. Alone on a wide, wide sea."

One easy way to discover where your voice is coming from is by saying, "Hello, how are you?" The first time you say it, put your hand on your forehead and pitch your voice up toward your hand. Now put your hand on your chest and low-pitch your words to the chest. Notice the greater depth and richness? You also can develop the warm lower tones of your voice by breathing more deeply as you talk and striving to speak softly, even when under stress. And at least once a day utter some full tone song, such as, *Row, Row, Row Your Boat,* or your school yell (softly) like: "Sis—Boom-m-m! A-a-ah!" in the deepest tone you can muster.

Beyond all these suggestions I have offered for making your voice and speech clear, relaxed, full-bodied, vibrant, and well modulated, there are some general suggestions that will improve the quality of any voice. For example:

—Join with family and friends in group singing.

—Restore in your family the wonderful old custom of reading aloud various classics such as the Bible. Inspirational passages are best. As you concentrate on these phrases they will challenge and improve your powers of articulation, and your speech rhythm.

—Join the nearest amateur theatrical group, because acting is excellent for voice, speech, and personality development.

If you are seriously interested in understanding and improving your voice you certainly should have a recording of it made. It should be of good quality and certainly should not be made on one of those 25-cent automatic machines. The speech department of the nearest college will probably be glad to do it for a small fee. Many people nowadays are buying or renting wire or tape recorders for "family fun" projects or parties. You can benefit from and have fun with such recordings if you listen carefully to your voice and ask acquaintances you respect for criticism. In listening, you can spot your slurring, your hemming and hawing, your gasps for breath, your nose-talking, and any other irritating speech faults you may have.

As you work to improve your voice and speech, I suggest that you not try it out on others—at least, not at first—lest you become self-conscious. Do your practicing in private. Not even the family should be present unless you invite them! After a month or so of regular practice, your new way of speaking will begin to show signs of automatically becoming a part of you.

As your speech improves, and you greet people more openly and cheerfully, your whole life will show signs of improvement. Your new clear, confident voice will set up a chain reaction both within yourself and within people who hear you. Psychologists have a theory to account for this. When you take on the outward posture of an emotional state—as when you start talking clearly, confidently, and cheerfully—you actually bring about a corresponding feeling within you.

When you sound better, you can't help feeling better. You will then begin to take on the glow that comes from increased respect for yourself. And before you know it, people will start looking at you in a new way, as though they had never noticed you before. As you profit by this experience, the whole world starts looking like a nice place in which to live.

Questions and Exercises

1. On what basis does the author argue that speaking is more important than writing? Here is a point that should be seriously considered by curriculum makers. Why?
2. How does Price show that he is interested in the successful communication of meaning between people?
3. Explain the organization of this essay in detail. Make a sentence outline of its principal points.
4. Judging from the five vocal shortcomings discussed by the author, what would you say is the criterion of effectiveness in oral discourse defended in the essay? What other criteria might be used?
5. Consider the persuasive qualities of the essay. How does the author set about to convince you that you can improve your present voice? Which kind of persuasion discussed by Gilbert Highet in "The Art of Persuasion" does Price employ?
6. The author has little if anything to say of stagefright in his discussion of effective speaking. Which of his suggestions for voice improvement might be expected to combat stagefright?
7. Make a list of items you consider important in delivering a talk or speech. How important among these is vocal control?
8. Price, in this essay, makes mention of students coming to him for counsel and advice. To what extent does he suggest that a speech clinician must be consulted for improving your voice? Explain.
9. In the next round of speeches in your class, diagnose your classmates' vocal deficiencies by using the five categories discussed in this essay.
10. If a person's voice is a reflection of his personality, as the author seems to suggest, what psychological steps might be taken to improve the quality of one's voice? Discuss the cause-effect relationship of voice quality and emotional stability. What are the persuasive potentials of a pleasing voice?

11. Make a tape recording of your own voice, before and after following the suggestions for voice improvement offered by Price. Do you notice any marked improvement in your effectiveness?

12. Bernard Shaw's *Pygmalion* is based on a hypothetical experiment in voice correction. Read this play and point out the weaknesses of imitation as a method of learning to speak "properly."

13. Scholars often distinguish between what they call "expressing" an idea and "communicating" an idea. Which of these functions does the author emphasize? Defend your answer with specific quotations from the essay.

14. How would the author of this essay explain the fact that there are hundreds of "beautiful" girls in Hollywood who have been unsuccessful in getting into motion pictures. What statement in the essay best explains his position on this subject?

15. In "The Experience of Becoming a Person," Rollo May talks of "the ability to see ourselves as others see us." Compare the approach to this problem made by May with that made by Price. In what respects do the two authors agree? How do they disagree?

16. Read Stephen Leacock's essay "Anybody Can Learn to Write." Compare Leacock's attitude toward the problem of effective writing with Price's attitude toward the problem of effective speaking. How do these two attitudes differ?

17. Your instructor will offer you frequent opportunities to read aloud in class. Practice the suggestions offered by Price in this essay. Solicit criticism from your instructor and your classmates.

18. One critic of American radio broadcasters has this to say of the ineffectiveness of expression usually displayed by announcers and other radio speakers:

    "Listening to the radio, we are all too often pained and bored by fumbling broadcasters who read separate words rather than paragraphs, sentences, or even unified phrases. They not only miss the forest for the trees; they miss the trees for the branches or even individual leaves. Inevitably they distort emphasis by giving forceful utterance to the wrong items, not seeing them in their proper place as details of a unified whole."

    Which of the exercises outlined in this essay by Price are designed to correct the deficiencies detailed here?

II. EXPERIENCE AND MATURITY

Anyone who hopes to acquire skill in the use of language, whether in reading, writing, speaking, or listening, must first of all understand himself. The psychological dimension of words is just as important in the definition of meaning as any other dimension of language, and the more we know about why words have particular connotations or private meanings for us, the more likely are we to have successful experiences in the transmission and reception of ideas. Since, in a very large degree, every man is his own Webster, the simple maxim of the Greeks, "Know thyself," is excellent advice for those who would learn how to use language most effectively in oral and written discourse. Each person has in his possession something that can be fulfilled in him and him alone.

The very essence of communication skill lies in the persistent and progressive remaking of self. Personal resentments, cherished grudges, selfish conceit, uncompromising prejudices block one's achievement in all matters pertaining to language. Personality is a complicated organization of physical, social, intellectual, and linguistic traits, attitudes, and habits. It is something you are continually building as you engage in the daily activities of living—especially the activities which involve language. Words are so intimately related to acquired beliefs, superstitions, prejudices, and dispositions as to constitute a most valuable index to personality and character.

A systematic study of arbitrary codes of grammar and syntax cannot be expected to alleviate feelings of insecurity and frustration which stifle spontaneity and otherwise seriously interfere with successful communication of ideas. Coddling and spoon-feeding, also, have a tendency to stunt one's linguistic growth, and if continued may cripple one's intellectual powers. Maturity is not the attainment of a specified level of achievement, but is a process of continual development toward the highest human potential.

In this section of the anthology, the focus is on understanding one's self. Rollo May, in "The Experience of Becoming a Person," gets at the heart of the matter by pointing up the psychological causes of emotional insecurity that lie buried beneath consciousness. Mrs. Rawlings, in "An Ancient Enmity," shows how she personally came to grips with a paralyzing fear and triumphed over it by learning how to face facts and deal with them in an unemotional, objective manner. William Saroyan, in his story "The Circus," dramatizes the difference between a mature and immature attitude toward a specific educational problem. The other essays in the section deal directly with adjustment to college. "How to Stay in College" shows how essential communication skill is to academic success, and thereby justifies this book and the course of study for which it is prepared.

◆ ◆ ◆

The Experience of Becoming a Person

ROLLO MAY

To UNDERTAKE this "venture of becoming aware of ourselves," and to discover the sources of inner strength and security which are the rewards of such a venture, let us start at the beginning

Reprinted from *Man's Search for Himself* by Rollo May. By permission of W. W. Norton & Company, Inc. Copyright 1953 by W. W. Norton & Company, Inc.

by asking, What is this person, this sense of selfhood we seek?

A few years ago a psychologist procured a baby chimpanzee the same age as his infant son. In order to do an experiment, such as is the wont of these men, he raised the baby chimp and baby human being in his household together. For the first few months they developed at very much the same speed, playing together and showing very little difference. But after a dozen months or so, a change began to occur in the development of the little human baby, and from then on there was a great difference between him and the chimp.

This is what we would expect. For there is very little difference between the human being and any mammal baby from the time of the original unity of the foetus in the womb of its mother, through the beginning of the beating of its own heart, then its ejection as an infant from the womb at birth, the commencing of its own breathing and the first protected months of life. But around the age of two, more or less, there appears in the human being the most radical and important emergence so far in evolution, namely his consciousness of himself. He begins to be aware of himself as an "I." As the foetus in the womb, the infant has been part of the "original we" with its mother, and it continues as part of the psychological "we" in early infancy. But now the little child—for the first time—becomes aware of his freedom. He senses his freedom, as Gregory Bateson puts it, within the context of the relationship with his father and mother. He experiences himself as an identity who is separated from his parents and can stand against them if need be. This remarkable emergence is the birth of the human animal into a person.

CONSCIOUSNESS OF SELF—THE UNIQUE MARK OF MAN

This consciousness of self, this capacity to see one's self as though from the outside, is the distinctive characteristic of man. A friend of mine has a dog who waits at his studio door all morning and, when anybody comes to the door, he jumps up and barks, wanting to play. My friend holds that the dog is saying in his barking: "Here is a dog who has been waiting all morning for someone to come to play with him. Are you the one? This is a nice sentiment, and all of us who like dogs enjoy projecting such cozy thoughts into their heads. But actually this is exactly what the dog cannot say. He can show that he wants to play and entice you into throwing his ball for him, but he cannot stand outside himself and see himself as a dog doing these things. He is not blessed with the consciousness of self.

Inasmuch as this means the dog is also free from neurotic anxiety and guilt feelings, which are the doubtful blessings of the human being, some people would prefer to say the dog is not *cursed* with the consciousness of self. Walt Whitman, echoing this thought, envies the animals:

> I think I could turn and live with animals. . . .
> They do not sweat and whine about their condition,
> They do not lie awake in the dark and weep for
>   their sins. . . .

But actually man's consciousness of himself is the source of his highest qualities. It underlies his ability to distinguish between "I" and the world. It gives him the capacity to keep time, which is simply the ability to stand outside the present and to imagine oneself back in yesterday or ahead in the day after tomorrow. Thus human beings can learn from the past and plan for the future. And thus man is the historical mammal in that he can stand outside and look at his history; and thereby he can influence his own development as a person, and to a minor extent he can influence the march of history in his nation and society as a whole. The capacity for consciousness of self also underlies man's ability to use symbols, which is a way of disengaging something from what it is, such as the two sounds which make up the word "table," and agreeing that these sounds will stand for a whole class of things. Thus man can think in abstractions like "beauty," "reason," and "goodness."

This capacity for consciousness of ourselves gives us the ability to see ourselves as others see us and to have empathy with others. It underlies our remarkable capacity to transport ourselves into someone else's parlor where we will be in reality next week, and then in imagination to think and plan how we will act. And it enables us to imagine ourselves in some one else's place, and to ask how we would feel and what we would do if we were this other person. No matter how poorly we use or fail to use or even abuse these capacities, they are the rudiments of our ability to begin to love our neighbor, to have ethical sensitivity, to see truth, to create beauty, to devote ourselves to ideals, and to die for them if need be.

To fulfill these potentialities is to be a person. This is what is meant when it is stated in the Hebrew-Christian religious tradition that man is created in the image of God.

But these gifts come only at a high price, the price of anxiety and inward crises. The birth of the self is no simple and easy matter. For the child now faces the frightful prospect of being out on his own, alone, and without the full protection of the decisions of his parents. It is no wonder that when he begins to feel himself an identity in his own right, he may feel terribly powerless in comparison with the great and strong adults around him. In the midst of a struggle over her dependency on her mother one person had this eloquent dream: "I was in a little boat tied to a big boat. We were going through the ocean and big waves came up, piling over the sides of my boat. I wondered whether it was still tied to the big boat."

The healthy child, who is loved and supported but not coddled by his parents, will proceed in his development despite this anxiety and the crises that face him. And there may be no particular external signs of trauma or special rebelliousness. But when his parents consciously or unconsciously exploit him for their own ends or pleasure, or hate or reject him, so that he cannot be sure of minimal support when he tries out his new independence, the child will cling to the parents and will use his capacity for independence only in the forms of negativity and stubbornness. If, when he first begins tentatively to say "No," his parents beat him down rather than love and encourage him, he thereafter will say "No" not as a form of true independent strength but as a mere rebellion.

Or if, as in the majority of cases in the present day, the parents themselves are anxious and bewildered in the tumultuous seas of the changing times, unsure of themselves and beset by self-doubts, their anxiety will carry over and lead the child to feel that he lives in a world in which it is dangerous to venture into becoming one's self.

This brief sketch is schematic, to be sure, and it is meant to give us as adults a kind of retrospective picture in the light of which we can better understand how one fails to achieve selfhood. Most of the data for these conflicts of childhood come from adults who are struggling, in dreams, memories or in present-day relations, to overcome what in their past lives originally blocked them in becoming fully born as persons. Almost every adult is, in greater or lesser degree, still struggling on the long journey to achieve selfhood on the basis of the patterns which were set in his early experiences in the family.

Nor do we for a moment overlook the fact that selfhood is always born in social context. Genetically, Auden is quite right:

> . . . for the ego is a dream
> Till a neighbor's need by
> name create it.[1]

Or, as we put it above, the self is always born and grows in interpersonal relationships. But no "ego" moves on into responsible selfhood if it remains chiefly the reflection of the social context around it. In our particular world in which conformity is the great destroyer of selfhood—in our society in which fitting the "pattern" tends to be accepted as the norm, and being "well-liked" is the alleged ticket to salvation—what needs to be emphasized is not only the admitted fact that we are to some extent created by each other but also our capacity to experience, and create, ourselves.

On the very day I was writing these words, a young intern

[1] *The Age of Anxiety*, New York, Random House, p. 8.

reported in his psychoanalytic session a dream which is essentially parallel to the dreams of almost everyone who is in a crisis in his growth. This young man had originally come for psychoanalytic help as a medical student because of attacks of anxiety so severe and prolonged that he was on the verge of dropping out of medical school. His problems were chiefly due to his close tie to his mother, a very unstable but strong and dominating woman. Having by now completed his medical studies, he was a successful intern and had applied for the most responsible residency in the hospital for the next year. The day preceding the night on which he had this dream, he had received a letter from the hospital directors awarding him the residency and paying him compliments on his excellent work as an intern. But instead of being pleased, he had been suddenly seized with an attack of anxiety. The dream follows in his own words:

I was bicycling to my childhood home where my father and mother were. The place seemed beautiful. When I went in, I felt free and powerful, as I am in my real life as a doctor now, not as I was as a boy. But my mother and father would not recognize me. I was afraid to express my independence for fear I would be kicked out. I felt as lonely and separate as though I were at the North Pole and there were no people around but only snow and ice for thousands of miles. I walked through the house, and in the different rooms were signs tacked up, "Wipe your feet," and "Clean your hands."

The anxiety after his being offered the desired position indicates that something in it, or in the responsibility it entailed, very much frightened him. And the dream tells us why. If he is a responsible, independent person in his own right—in contrast to the boy tied to his mother's apron strings—he will be ejected from his family, and will be isolated and alone. The fascinating vignettes in the form of the "wipe-your-feet" signs add a footnote which says the house is like a military camp and not a loving home at all.

The real question facing this young man, of course, was why he dreamed of going home at all—what need was there within

himself to go back to mother and father and the house he
pictured as externally beautiful in the dream, when he is confronted with responsibility? This is a question we shall deal with
later. Here let us only emphasize how becoming a person, an
identity in one's own right, is the original development which
begins in infancy and carries over into adulthood no matter
how old one may be; and the crises it involves may cause
tremendous anxiety. No wonder many persons repress the conflict and try all their lives to run from the anxiety!

What does it mean to experience one's self as a self? The experience of our own identity is the basic conviction that we all
start with as psychological beings. It can never be proven in a
logical sense, for consciousness of one's self is the presupposition
of any discussion about it. There will always be an element of
mystery in one's awareness of one's own being—mystery here
meaning a problem the data of which encroach on the problem.
For such awareness is a presupposition of inquiry into one's
self. That is to say, even to meditate on one's own identity as a
self means that one is already engaging in self-consciousness.

Some psychologists and philosophers are distrustful of the
concept of self. They argue against it because they do not like
separating man from the continuum with animals, and they
believe the concept of self gets in the way of scientific experi-
mentation. But rejecting the concept of "self" as "unscientific"
because it cannot be reduced to mathematical equations is roughly
the same as the argument two and three decades ago that Freud's
theories and the concept of "unconscious" motivation were "unscientific." It is a defensive and dogmatic science—and therefore
not true science—which uses a particular scientific method as a
Procrustean bed and rejects all forms of human experience which
don't fit. To be sure, the continuum between man and animals
should be seen clearly and realistically; but one need not jump
to the unwarranted conclusion that therefore there is no distinction between man and animals.

We do not need to prove the self as an "object." It is only
necessary that we show how people have the capacity for self-

relatedness. The self is the organizing function within the individual and the function by means of which one human being can relate to another. It is prior to, not an object of, our science; it is presupposed in the fact that one can be a scientist. Human experience always goes beyond our particular methods of understanding it at any given moment, and the best way to understand one's identity as a self is to look into one's own experience. Let us, for example, imagine the inner experience of some psychologist or philosopher writing a paper to deny the concept of consciousness of self. During the weeks he was considering writing this paper, he no doubt many times pictured himself sitting at his desk at some future day writing away. And from time to time, let us say, both before he actually began to write and later as he sat at his desk at work on the paper, he considered in fantasy what his colleagues would say about the paper, whether Professor So-and-So would praise it, whether still others might think it stupid, and so on. In every thought he is seeing himself as an identity as definitely as he would see a colleague walking across the street. His every thought in the process of arguing against the consciousness of self proves this very consciousness in himself.

The consciousness of one's identity as a self certainly is not an intellectual idea. The French philosopher Descartes, at the beginning of the modern period three centuries ago, crawled into his stove, according to legend, to meditate in solitude all one day trying to find the basic principle for human existence. He came out of his stove in the evening with the famous conclusion "I think, therefore I am." That is to say, I exist as a self because I am a thinking creature. But this is not enough. You and I never think of ourselves as an idea. We rather picture ourselves as doing something, like the psychologist writing his paper, and we then experience in imagination the feelings that we will have when we are in actuality doing that thing. That is to say, we experience ourselves as a thinking-intuiting-feeling and acting unity. The self is thus not merely the sum of the various "roles" one plays—it is the capacity by which one *knows* he plays these roles; it is the center from which one sees and is aware of these so-called different "sides" of himself.

After these perhaps high-sounding phrases, let us remind ourselves that after all the experience of one's own identity, or becoming a person, is the simplest experience in life even though at the same time the most profound. As everyone knows, a little child will react indignantly and strongly if you, in teasing, call him by the wrong name. It is as though you take away his identity—a most precious thing to him. In the Old Testament the phrase "I will blot out their names"—to erase their identity and it will be as though they never had existed—is a more powerful threat even than physical death.

Two little girl twins gave a vivid illustration of how important it is for a child to be a person in her own right. The little girls were good friends, a fact made especially possible because they complemented each other, one being extrovert and always in the center of the crowd if people came to visit in the house, the other being perfectly happy by herself to draw with her crayons and make up little poems. The parents, as parents generally do with twins, had dressed them alike when they went out walking. When they were about three and a half, the little extrovert girl began to want always to wear a different kind of dress from her sister. If she dressed after her sister, she would even, if necessary, wear an older and less pretty dress so that it would not be the same as the twin was wearing. Or if the sister dressed after her before they went out, she would beg her, sometimes weeping, not to put on the matching dress. For days this puzzled the parents, since the child was not anxious in other ways. Finally the parents, on a hunch, asked the little girl, "When you two go out walking do you like to have people on the street say, 'Look at these nice twins'?" Immediately the little girl exclaimed, "No, I want them to say, 'Look at these two different people!'"

This spontaneous exclamation, obviously revealing something very important to the little girl, cannot be explained by saying that the child wanted attention; for she would have gotten more attention if she had dressed as a twin. It shows, rather, her demand to be a person in her own right, to have personal identity—a need which was more important to her even than attention or prestige.

The little girl rightly stated the goal for every human being—to become a person. Every organism has one and only one central need in life, to fulfill its own potentialities. The acorn becomes an oak, the puppy becomes a dog and makes the fond and loyal relations with its human masters which befit the dog; and this is all that is required of the oak tree and the dog. But the human being's task in fulfilling his nature is much more difficult, for he must do it in self-consciousness. That is, his development is never automatic but must be to some extent chosen and affirmed by himself. "Among the works of man," John Stuart Mill has written, "which human life is rightly employed in perfecting and in beautifying, the first importance surely is man himself. . . . Human nature is not a machine to be built after a model and set to do exactly the work prescribed for it, but a tree, which requires to grow and develop itself on all sides, according to the tendency of the inward forces which make it a living thing." In this charmingly expressed thought, John Stuart Mill has unfortunately omitted the most important "tendency of the inward forces" which make man a living thing, namely that man does not grow automatically like a tree, but fulfills his potentialities only as he in his own consciousness plans and chooses.

Fortunately the long protracted period of infancy and childhood in human life—in contrast to the condition of the acorn, which is on its own as soon as it falls to the soil, or of the puppy which must fend for itself after a few weeks—prepares the child for this difficult task. He is able to acquire some knowledge and inner strength so that as he must begin to choose and decide, he has some capability for it.

Man, furthermore, must make his choices as an individual, for individuality is one side of one's consciousness of one's self. We can see this point clearly when we realize that consciousness of one's self is always a unique act—I can never know exactly how you see yourself and you never can know exactly how I relate to myself. This is the inner sanctum where each man must stand alone. This fact makes for much of the tragedy and inescapable isolation in human life, but it also indicates again that we must find the strength in ourselves to stand in our own inner sanctum as individuals. And this fact means that, since we are not automatically merged with our fellows, we must through our own affirmation learn to love each other.

If any organism fails to fulfill its potentialities, it becomes sick, just as your legs would wither if you never walked. But the power of your legs is not all you would lose. The flowing of your blood, your heart action, your whole organism would be the weaker. And in the same way if man does not fulfill his potentialities as a person, he becomes to that extent constricted and ill. This is the essence of neurosis—the person's unused potentialities, blocked by hostile conditions in the environment (past or present) and by his own internalized conflicts, turn inward and cause morbidity. "Energy is Eternal Delight," said William Blake; "He who desires but acts not, breeds pestilence."

Kafka was a master at the gruesome task of picturing people who do not use their potentialities and therefore lose their sense of being persons. The chief character in *The Trial* and in *The Castle* has no name—he is identified only by an initial, a mute symbol of one's lack of identity in one's own right. In the staggering and frightful parable, *Metamorphosis*, Kafka illustrates what happens when the human being forfeits his powers. The hero of this story is a typical, empty modern young man, who lives a routine, vacuous life as a salesman, returning regularly to his middle-class home, eating the same menu of roast beef every Sunday while his father goes to sleep at the table. The young man's life was so empty, implies Kafka, that he woke up one morning no longer a human being but a cockroach. Because he had not fulfilled his status as a man, he forfeited his human potentialities. A cockroach, like lice and rats and vermin, lives off others' leavings. It is a parasite, and in most people's minds a symbol for what is unclean and repugnant. Could there be any more powerful symbol of what happens when a human being relinquishes his nature as a person?

But to the extent that we do fulfill our potentialities as persons, we experience the profoundest joy to which the human being is heir. When a little child is learning to walk up steps or lift a box, he will try again and again, getting up when he falls down and starting over again. And finally when he does succeed, he laughs with gratification, his expression of joy in the use of his powers. But this is nothing in comparison to the quiet joy when the adolescent can use his newly emerged power for the first time to gain a friend, or the adult's joy when he can love, plan and create. Joy is the affect which comes when we use our powers. Joy, rather than happiness, is the goal of life, for joy is the emotion which accompanies our fulfilling our natures as human beings. It is based on the experience of one's identity as a being of worth and dignity, who is able to affirm his being, if need be, against all other beings and the whole inorganic world. This power in its ideal form is shown in the life of a Socrates, who was so confident in himself and his values that he could take his being condemned to death not as a defeat but as a greater fulfillment than compromising his beliefs. But we do not wish to imply such joy is only for the heroic and the outstanding; it is as present qualitatively in anyone's act, no matter how inconspicuous, which is done as an honest and responsible expression of his own powers. . . .

Questions and Exercises

1. Rollo May says that consciousness of self gives one "the ability to stand outside the present and to imagine oneself in yesterday or ahead in the day after tomorrow." How is the same capacity explained by Susanne Langer in "Language and Creative Thought"?
2. Define *empathy* and *ethical sensitivity*. Use at least two examples to clarify your meaning in each case.

3. Compare May's ideas about correcting delinquent children with those suggested by William Saroyan's story, "The Circus." Are either of these theories an endorsement of "Spare the rod and spoil the child"?

4. How does May's discussion of "psychological blocks" supplement and reinforce what Stuart Chase says about barriers to listening in "Are You Listening?"

5. A Colgate professor has affirmed that "the initiative for the education of students in America rests squarely on the head of the professor," that "he must not only lead his students to the wellspring, but that he must somehow force them by devious means to drink." What is May's attitude toward this state of affairs in American education? Explain.

6. How does May's attitude toward conformity compare with ideas expressed by Mark Twain in "Huck and Jim on the Raft"?

7. What is meant by *extravert* and *intravert*? To what extent are these terms employed by modern psychologists to characterize human behavior? What other labels for personality types are used?

8. How does May's idea that a person "fulfills his potentialities only as he in his own consciousness plans and chooses" oppose a fatalistic orientation to life? What are the implications of this idea for students of communication skill?

9. In criticizing John S. Mill's comparison of a human being to a tree, what fallacy in reasoning has May put his finger on? Can you mention other examples of this fallacy in literature?

10. What is the significance of what May calls the "essence of neurosis" in the successful communication of ideas?

11. How does May show that values and beliefs are an essential part of a well-organized self?

12. How would May answer Mrs. Alcaro's argument in "Colleges Don't Make Sense"?

13. Show how May's ideas in this essay point up the partial-truths contained in stereotypes. See John Steinbeck's "How to Tell Good Guys from Bad Guys."

14. Show how Paul Fisher's contention, that the tramp printer in America was a good thing for the newspaper business, harmonizes with May's concept of self-consciousness. See "A Forgotten Gentry of the Fourth Estate."

15. How does May support his argument in this essay? Considering the language employed, what school of psychology does he belong to?

16. Consider the following statement by William Graham Sumner quoted from *What Social Classes Owe to Each Other* (1883). Write a paper in which you take this statement as your thesis. Support the idea with specific examples from your own experiences.

"Every man and woman in society has one big duty. That is, to take care of his or her own self. This is a social duty. For, fortunately, the matter stands so that the duty of making the best of one's self individually is not a separate thing from the duty of filling one's place in society, but the two are one, and the latter is accomplished when the former is done."

◆ ◆ ◆

An Ancient Enmity

MARJORIE KINNAN RAWLINGS

I CAME to Cross Creek with such a phobia against snakes that a picture of one in the dictionary gave me what Martha calls "the all-overs." I had the common misconception that in Florida they were omnipresent. I thought, "If anything defeats me, sends me back to urban civilization, it will be the snakes." They were not ubiquitous as I had expected, but I saw one often enough to keep my anxiety alive. A black snake actually ran at me, and a chicken snake thrust his face into mine from a pantry shelf. These were harmless, I knew, but none the less revolting. I took my first faltering steps of progress through sheer shame. In a section where the country women possess great physical fearlessness, I felt feeble-minded to find myself screaming at the sight of a king snake that asked nothing more than a chance to destroy the rats that infested the old barn. I forced myself to stand still when I saw a snake in the weeds of the neglected house yard, at least long enough to determine its non-venomous nature. The only poisonous reptiles in Florida, I knew, were the rattlesnake and the cottonmouth moccasin, which I had already seen with horror, and the coral snake, which I did not know.

My determination to use common sense might have been my undoing. One late winter day in my first year I discovered under the palm tree by the gate a small pile of Amaryllis bulbs. The yard was desperate for flowers and greenery and I began separating the bulbs to set out for spring blooming. I dug with my fingers under the pile and brought out in my hand not a snake, surely, but a ten-inch long piece of Chinese lacquer. The slim inert reptile was an exquisite series of shining bands of yellow and black and vermilion, with a tiny black nose. I thought, "Here is a snake, in my hands, and it is as beautiful as a necklace. This is the moment in which to forget all nonsense." I let it slide back and forth through my fingers. Its texture was like satin. I played with it a long time, then killed it reluctantly with a stick, not for fear or hate, but because I decided to cure the skin for an ornament on the handle of a riding crop. I salted the hide and tacked it to a sunny wall. I showed it proudly to my friend Ed Hopkins, who was teaching me the Florida flora and fauna.

He said, "God takes care of fools and children."

The snake was the deadly coral snake. Its venom is of the cobra type, killing within a few minutes by a paralyzing of the nerves. The old terror was back again, and it seemed to me that I should never now be able to pass beyond it. I had no fear of death as death, but the medium was another matter, and one is certainly entitled to one's prejudices in so personal a matter. I found that I had still the blind, unthinking, "instinctive" horror of coming on a poisonous serpent. Nothing could warm the frozen column that replaced my spine at the thought of finding myself face to face with a Florida diamond-back rattler. In a varied life I had discarded one physical fear after another, finding them harmless when confronted. I said, "I am only afraid of the intangibles." Yet even such intangibles as poverty and loneliness might be, simply, accepted, and so disarmed. I discovered that for me rattlesnakes represented the last outpost of physical fear.

I discovered this when Ross Allen, a young Florida herpetologist, invited me to join him on a hunt in the upper Everglades—for rattlesnakes. . . .

Ross and I drove to Arcadia in his coupé on a warm January day.

I said, "How will you bring back the rattlesnakes?"

"In the back of my car."

My courage was not adequate to inquire whether they were thrown in loose and might be expected to appear between our feet. Actually, a large portable box of heavy close-meshed wire made a safe cage. Ross wanted me to write an article about his work and on our way to the unhappy hunting grounds I took notes on a mass of data that he had accumulated in years of herpetological research. The scientific and dispassionate detachment of the material and the man made a desirable approach to rattlesnake territory. As I had discovered with the insects and varmints, it is difficult to be afraid of anything about which enough is known, and Ross' facts were fresh from the laboratory.

The hunting ground was Big Prairie, south of Arcadia and west of the northern tip of Lake Okeechobee. Big Prairie is a desolate cattle country, half marsh, half pasture, with islands of palm trees and cypress and oaks. At that time of year the cattlemen and Indians were burning the country, on the theory that the young fresh wire grass that springs up from the roots after a fire is the best cattle forage. Ross planned to hunt his rattlers in the forefront of the fires. They lived in winter, he said, in gopher holes, coming out in the midday warmth to forage, and would move ahead of the flames and be easily taken. We joined forces with a big Cracker named Will, his snake-hunting companion of the territory, and set out in early morning, after a long rough drive over deep-rutted roads into the open wilds.

I hope never in my life to be so frightened as I was in those first few hours. I kept on Ross' footsteps, I moved when he moved, sometimes jolting into him when I thought he might leave me behind. He does not use the forked stick of conventional snake hunting, but a steel prong, shaped like an L, at the end of a long stout stick. He hunted casually, calling my attention to the varying vegetation, to hawks overhead, to a pair of the rare whooping cranes that flapped over us. In mid-morning he stopped short, dropped his stick, and brought up a five-foot rattlesnake draped limply over the steel L. It seemed to me that I should drop in my tracks.

"They're not active at this season," he said quietly. "A snake takes on the temperature of its surroundings. They can't stand too much heat for that reason, and when the weather is cool, as now, they're sluggish."

The sun was bright overhead, the sky a translucent blue, and it seemed to me that it was warm enough for any snake to do as it willed. The sweat poured down my back. Ross dropped the rattler in a crocus sack and Will carried it. By noon, he had caught four. I felt faint and ill. We stopped by a pond and went swimming. The region was flat, the horizon limitless, and as I came out of the cool blue water I expected to find myself surrounded by a ring of rattlers. There were only Ross and Will, opening the lunch basket. I could not eat. Ross never touches liquor and it seemed to me that I would give my hope of salvation for a dram of whiskey. Will went back and drove his truck closer, for Ross expected the hunting to be better in the afternoon. The hunting was much better. When we went back to the truck to deposit two more rattlers in the wire cage, there was a rattlesnake lying under the truck.

Ross said, "Whenever I leave my car or truck with snakes already in it, other rattlers always appear. I don't know whether this is because they scent or sense the presence of other snakes, or whether in this arid area they come to the car for shade in the heat of the day."

The problem was scientific, but I had no interest.

That night Ross and Will and I camped out in the vast spaces of the Everglades prairies. We got water from an abandoned well and cooked supper under buttonwood bushes by a flowing stream. The camp fire blazed cheerfully under the stars and a new moon lifted in the sky. Will told tall tales of the cattlemen and the Indians and we were at peace.

Ross said, "We couldn't have a better night for catching water snakes."

After the rattlers, water snakes seemed innocuous enough. We worked along the edge of the stream and here Ross did not use his L-shaped steel. He reached under rocks and along the edge of the water and brought out harmless reptiles with his hands. I had said nothing to him of my fears, but he understood them. He brought a small dark snake from under a willow root.

"Wouldn't you like to hold it?" he asked. "People think snakes are cold and clammy, but they aren't. Take it in your hands. You'll see that it is warm."

Again, because I was ashamed, I took the snake in my hands. It was not cold, it was not clammy, and it lay trustingly in my hands, a thing that lived and breathed and had mortality like the rest of us. I felt an upsurgence of spirit.

The next day was magnificent. The air was crystal, the sky was aquamarine, and the far horizon of palms and oaks lay against the sky. I felt a new boldness and followed Ross bravely. He was making the rounds of the gopher holes. The rattlers came out in the mid-morning warmth and were never far away. He could tell by their trails whether one had come out or was still in the hole. Sometimes the two men dug the snake out. At times it was down so long and winding a tunnel that the digging was hopeless. Then they blocked the entrance and went on to other holes. In an hour or so they made the original rounds, unblocking the holes. The rattler in every case came out hurriedly, as though anything were preferable to being shut in. All the time Ross talked to me, telling me the scientific facts he had discovered about the habits of the rattlers.

"They pay no attention to a man standing perfectly still," he said, and proved it by letting Will unblock a hole while he stood at the entrance as the snake came out. It was exciting to watch the snake crawl slowly beside and past the man's legs. When it was at a safe distance he walked within its range of vision, which he had proved to be no higher than a man's knee, and the snake whirled and drew back in an attitude of fighting defense. The rattler strikes only for paralyzing and killing its food, and for defense.

"It is a slow and heavy snake," Ross said. "It lies in wait on a small game trail and strikes the rat or rabbit passing by. It waits a few minutes, then follows along the trail, coming to the small animal, now dead or dying. It noses it from all sides, making sure that it is its own kill, and that it is dead and ready for swallowing."

A rattler will lie quietly without revealing himself if a man passes by and it thinks it is not seen. It slips away without fighting if given the chance. Only Ross' sharp eyes sometimes picked out the gray and yellow diamond pattern, camouflaged among the grasses. In the cool of the morning, chilled by the January air, the snakes showed no fight. They could be looped up limply over the steel L and dropped in a sack or up into the wire cage on the back of Will's truck. As the sun mounted in the sky and warmed the moist Everglades earth, the snakes were warmed too, and Ross warned that it was time to go more cautiously. Yet having learned that it was we who were the aggressors; that immobility meant complete safety; that the snakes, for all their lightning flash in striking, were inaccurate in their aim, with limited vision; having watched again and again the liquid grace of movement, the beauty of pattern, suddenly I understood that I was drinking in freely the magnificent sweep of the horizon, with no fear of what might be at the moment under my feet. I went off hunting by myself, and though I found no snakes, I should have known what to do.

The sun was dropping low in the west. Masses of white cloud hung above the flat marshy plain and seemed to be tangled in the tops of distant palms and cypresses. The sky turned orange, then saffron. I walked leisurely back toward the truck. In the distance I could see Ross and Will making their way in too. The season was more advanced than at the Creek, two hundred miles to the north, and I noticed that spring flowers were blooming among the lumpy hummocks. I leaned over to pick a white violet. There was a rattlesnake under the violet.

If this had happened the week before, if it had happened the day before, I think I should have lain down and died on top of the rattlesnake, with no need of being struck and poisoned. The snake did not coil, but lifted its head and whirred its rattles lightly. I stepped back slowly and put the violet in a buttonhole. I reached forward and laid the steel L across the snake's neck, just back of the blunt head. I called to Ross:

"I've got one."

He strolled toward me.

"Well, pick it up," he said.

I released it and slipped the L under the middle of the thick body.

"Go put it in the box."

He went ahead of me and lifted the top of the wire cage. I made the truck with the rattler, but when I reached up the six feet to drop it in the cage, it slipped off the stick and dropped on Ross' feet. It made no effort to strike.

"Pick it up again," he said. "If you'll pin it down lightly and reach just back of its head with your hand, as you've seen me do, you can drop it in more easily."

I pinned it and leaned over.

"I'm awfully sorry," I said, "but you're pushing me a little too fast."

He grinned. I lifted it on the stick and again as I had it at head height, it slipped off, down Ross' boots and on top of his feet. He stood as still as a stump. I dropped the snake on his feet for the third time. It seemed to me that the most patient of rattlers might in time resent being hauled up and down, and for all the man's quiet certainty that in standing motionless there was no danger, would strike at whatever was nearest, and that would be Ross.

I said, "I'm just not man enough to keep this up any longer," and he laughed and reached down with his smooth quickness and lifted the snake back of the head and dropped it in the cage. It slid in among its mates and settled in a corner. The hunt was over and we drove back over the uneven trail to Will's village and left him and went on to Arcadia and home. Our catch for the two days was thirty-two rattlers.

I said to Ross, "I believe that tomorrow I could have picked up that snake."

Back at the Creek, I felt a new lightness. I had done battle with a great fear, and the victory was mine.

Questions and Exercises

1. The title of this narrative refers to the Biblical account of Eve and the serpent in the Garden of Eden. See Genesis 3:15. How does Mrs. Rawlings' account refute the Biblical prediction?
2. Read A. E. Mander's "Groundless Beliefs," and decide to what extent fear of snakes may be considered groundless.
3. Mrs. Rawlings called her fear of snakes a *phobia*. Considering her account of the experience, what is suggested about ridding oneself of any phobia? How do these suggestions compare with a psychologist's recommendations? Check any recently published book on the psychology of fear.
4. How can you account for the apparently "incredible" fact that the deadly coral snake, discussed in the second paragraph, did not attack the author?
5. What principle regarding the effects of the emotions on the physical functions of the body is demonstrated by the fact that the author could not eat when she imagined herself surrounded by snakes? Cite other examples that demonstrate this same principle.

6. Read S. I. Hayakawa's discussion of "Delusional Worlds," in *Language in Thought and Action*, pp. 192–193, and explain Mrs. Rawlings' fear of snakes with reference to this discussion.
7. Considering what the author says about fear of snakes, what would you say is the basis of prejudice? Why are prejudicies so difficult to get rid of?
8. What specific words and devices in the narrative call attention to the author's emotional experience, her feelings, her assumptions, her judgments?
9. What points of similarity do you find between Mrs. Rawlings' and Loren C. Eiseley's experiences with snakes? See Loren C. Eiseley's "The Bird and the Machine."
10. Write in a single, declarative sentence the main idea or thesis of Mrs. Rawlings' narrative.
11. How does the account of the author's difficulties of getting the captured rattler into the cage help to make the point of the narrative?
12. Write a paper in which you describe the method by which you overcame an unjustifiable fear, such as fear of the dark, fear of strangers, fear of high places, fear of being alone, stagefright, or claustrophobia.
13. What connection do you see between a phobia for snakes and an inflexible set of beliefs, such as possessed by Stafford in William Saroyan's story "The Circus"?
14. Explain how fears and prejudices are easily responsible for one's inability to think straight.
15. How does Mrs. Rawlings' getting the "all-overs" by looking at a picture of a snake demonstrate the pernicious aspects of emotional blocks or verbal fixations? What connection do you find between this experience and Stuart Chase's discussion of blocks to effective listening in "Are You Listening?" Read Margaret Schlauch's *The Gift of Tongues*, pp. 113–117, for illumination on the subject of emotional associations.

◆ ◆ ◆

Advice for Forlorn Freshmen

HAROLD O. VOORHIS

ONE SUNDAY afternoon a few weeks ago, I experienced a distinct contribution to my own education from the vantage point of a ringside seat at a bullfight in the venerable city of Barcelona. Now I am not quite sure whether this was good or bad education, but in any case amidst the tumult of the throng that rocked the colosseum, a glittering array of toreador talent had already dispatched a number of infuriated bulls in an ascending pattern of bravado, when it suddenly appeared that the most ferocious *torro* of them all was about to be admitted to the arena. Came a hush from the *aficionados* as the great, fawn-colored beast, broad of beam and wicked of horn, pawed the earth on entry and rippled the sawdust afar with contemptuous snorts of indignation. The *picadors*, the *banderilleros*, and the *matadore* took to their barricades with unusual alacrity as the vicious animal trotted around the ring casing the joint. Having made the circuit, he took up a central position facing the president's box, gave his massive horns a practice hook or two, then stood stock-still, disdainful of the intimidated fighters, released an unmistakable yawn, sat down on his haunches, head between his forelegs, and refused thenceforth to budge.

Now any resemblance between that bull ring and this circle is purely coincidental. Yet I perceive something of a fringe analogy: For some days now you have been trotting around this campus, casing the joint; getting oriented, I believe they call it in

Adapted from remarks given at freshmen orientation meeting, Colgate University, Hamilton, New York, September 18, 1953. An abridged version of the address appeared in *School and Society*, April 17, 1954. Reprinted by permission of Harold O. Voorhis, vice president and secretary of New York University, and of Stanley Lehrer, managing editor of *School and Society*.

the catalogue. This soiree, I am told, is a part of that process. Now if any of you succumb to boredom and sleep the rest of this session out, I shall remember the Barcelona precedent with sympathetic understanding.

I realize that you have already been surfeited with advice from many quarters to the point of groggy weariness. I know what it means. For fifty years, man and boy, I have been on the receiving end of as good advice, I venture, as was ever dispensed. Of course, the fact that it has done me so little good is demonstrated by my very presence here in an advisory capacity. I ought to know better than add to your punishment. Yet it is something more than petty vengeance that puts me before you. I am here to test a theory. I have observed that good advice is so often conducive to contrary action—or, at all events, seems to be so frequently honored in the breach—that I am tempted to resort to reverse English, to reach deep in the bag of personal experience and offer you some of the choicest bad advice that can be dished out in the few remaining moments at my disposal. Just please don't get confused. This is straight from the heel bad advice, and nothing else but.

Colgate is one big happy family, but like all families it has its faults. Its faults keep it from being too stuffy. Perhaps if you try hard enough you can contribute to some of the faults. First, take the matter of traditions. You will find that this college, like most such institutions, is built on traditions. Some new students make the mistake of getting acquainted with these traditions and getting into the swing of them. Such creatures are nothing but supine conformists. Be original. Don't hesitate to flout the traditions and set up a pattern of your own. Such a course of action, diligently and vigorously pursued, will bring you well-merited distinction; and if your hide is tough enough you may survive the consequences of that distinction.

Most of you have excelled one way or another in secondary school else you wouldn't be here. Don't fail to impress the campus early with the precise nature and extent of those achievements. The director of admissions may know about them but you can't depend upon him to broadcast the intelligence. Wear your block-lettered sweaters nonchalantly. Leave a marked copy of the high-school yearbook where it will be seen. Laudatory clippings from high-school days posted on the dormitory bulletin board never fail to attract attention. Don't hide your light under a beanie. Reticence here is reserved for sophomores.

Some of you, perhaps, are away from home for an extended stretch for the first time. A few of you may have been admonished to write the family now and then. Don't take that suggestion too seriously. Far better never to write until you need money; otherwise your folks may get the idea you are homesick. The manly fellow will never labor the home-town postman until he is flat broke.

Meantime, don't waste effort keeping an expense account. Remember there is more where the last remittance came from. Besides, the world owes you a living—never forget that. Later on in life, when you try to collect, you will learn the facts about this. But you needn't worry about it yet; there is plenty of time. It's a dangerous thing for any man to skimp before he has to; he might wind up with money and nothing else. If your Jaguar needs another horn, go out and buy it. Nothing like two horns on a Jaguar as well as a self-respecting dilemma.

Now, about your courses of study. A few of you, possibly, have come here for the purpose of study. You are probably stuck with your program for the first semester and can't shift. You're probably saddled with a few tough courses. My earnest counsel is this. Just as soon as you get the chance hereafter, pick nothing but snap courses. You may be told there are no snap courses at Colgate. Don't be deceived. Discover them and seize upon them. Remember, the Lord has blessed each of you with only a limited amount of gray matter which you are going to need, I trust, for a long time to come. The less wear and tear on the brains now, the better. You must conserve what precious little you have. You'll need them most after you are released from this blessed haven into the stormy seas of real life.

Having, with all the resourcefulness at your command, discovered and elected the snap courses, don't study the books relating thereto, but study the professors. If you will only master the moods, the whims, and the pet theories of the prof, you will be all set; you need never crack a book. Feed what he puts out right back to him—he will love it. There's Phi Beta Kappa gold in that simple formula.

Books, to the enterprising college man, are nothing but unabated nuisances. Take note that the library on this campus is not its most attractive adornment. It was, of course, designed that way, as a place to be shunned. There are ghosts of well-meaning scholars of all generations rattling around in the bowels of that granite tomb who yearn for your company. Give them wide berth. Seek ye, instead, the fleshpots of this Valley. They are here to serve you prodigally just as they have served your elders.

So arrange your habits as always to arrive at class just late enough to get under the wire and then after class is over make it a practice to linger a while for a personal word with the professor. This will attract most helpful attention to yourself, and thus you won't be lost in the shuffle. Even though a professor may be ever so anxious to shake off the class and get on to more important pursuits, it always pleases him no end to be plucked on the sleeve and pleasantly detained by a truly eager disciple. Such a practice, moreover, will classify you permanently in the estimation of your fellow students.

I've heard it said that one of the most important things for the college freshman to do is to pick the right kind of college friends—friends who will be with him for a 50-year journey— some of whom may write his obituary. This, of course, is all nonsense. Close campus friends may well prove a serious liability. Play it safe. Don't make the mistake of warming up to fellow students. The guy who keeps his own company may find it a little dismal at times but he is less apt to get in trouble. There is nothing more hazardous and mischievous than the reposal of trust and confidence in one's fellow men.

If, due to circumstances beyond your control, you should eventually be impelled to join a fraternity and are given any choice in the matter, pick the gang that makes the most noise, the crowd with the biggest flash. It will be easier to lose yourself in that outfit and be let alone. Fraternities are nothing but conspiracies to destroy the individual. They are tolerated for fictitious values which, strangely enough, manage to fool some people all their lives. Even my own jaundiced eyes still well up with emotion at the strains of "Pass the Loving Cup Around."

Whatever you do, don't be pushed around. If somebody tries to get you to go out for some student activity, athletic or otherwise, resist it with all your might. Such business is the thief of the precious leisure to which you are so rightly entitled as respite from your ardous studies of the professors. Men who go in for such voluntary things are the busybodies who run things around town after college days are over. They are the guys who make mature life so hectic for the rest of us.

I could go on with such vicious hints but I won't; if I say too much in this vein you may not take me seriously. But one final word of perverted advice: I used to think just as our alumni secretary thinks that the admirable college man as well as the truly worth-while alumnus is the man who, among other things, shows genuine pride in his college; and that it is the extent of this collective pride that somehow sets one college above another in public esteem. That, of course, is all the bunk. As a conscientious Colgate man you should be ever on the alert for flies in the oatmeal. If you have any complaint about Colgate be sure to talk it up on the outside. Your criticism may fall on the ears of some wealthy old coot who, impressed by your articulate despondency, will leave his fortune to this institution to redeem its deficiencies.

So much for my humble share in your orientation to Colgate. If what I have said makes nonsense in your interpretation I trust you will be guided accordingly. I am not sure I have made myself altogether clear in this last entreaty, but this I do know—that a long, long line of Colgate men ahead of you, who love this institution, welcome you most heartily to this friendly association, confident in your ability and determination to magnify the glory of this college to the enduring benefit of the common weal. Good luck to you!

Questions and Exercises

1. In order to avoid using clichés and platitudes, the author of this address has resorted to what he calls "reverse English." In what way is this method of communicating an idea justified under the existing circumstances?
2. Make a list of slang and colloquial expressions employed by Voorhis in his address. How can these expressions be justified? What is the attitude of Donald J. Lloyd toward such usages as explained in "Snobs, Slobs, and the English Language"?
3. What is Voorhis' real purpose or aim in this address? By what precise method does he develop his idea: analysis, analogy, reasons, examples, directions?
4. Study the unity of the paragraphs into which the address is divided. What is the controlling idea, or focal point, in each case?
5. Rewrite the portion of the address that is couched in "reverse English" in direct, positive statements that are devoid of irony. Pay particular attention to parallel structure in the sentences you construct.
6. Make a list of the educational doctrines that Voorhis would support. Defend this list by citing specific passages in the address.
7. Specify three separate ways by which Voorhis adapts his discourse to his listeners? How effective are these devices as far as you are personally concerned?
8. How would you defend the idea that Voorhis believes a college man or woman should learn to think for himself? Does he agree or disagree with the principal idea set forth by Perry and Whitlock in "The Right to Think—Through Reading"?
9. Compare Voorhis' ideas about college life with those expressed by Jameson in "How to Stay in College." What points of similarity do you detect?
10. Roger W. Holmes, in "What Every Freshman Should Know," *American Mercury*, November, 1940, discusses the topic of

Voorhis' speech, although from a slightly different point of view. Read this essay, and determine how many of the items discussed by Voorhis are also mentioned by Holmes. Which of the two treatments of the subject do you consider more effective? Why?

11. Colgate is a small liberal arts college. How does the author reveal his attitude toward a liberal education in this address? Explain fully. How would he answer the argument presented by Marion Walker Alcaro in "Colleges Don't Make Sense"?

12. Read the following statement concerning the community aspects of college life, and determine to what extent Voorhis would endorse the inherent belief:

"The modern student lives in a world of unprecedented stresses, strains, and demands. Whatever scholarly capacity he may have will emerge only under certain conditions. . . . It is fairly certain that *some* promising students can be thwarted by excessively one-sided conditions of development. In a college, study takes place under social auspices, however individualized the pattern of study. The college is perforce a community, even if it be a cloister. . . . Intellectual development can be guarded as well as nurtured by circumstances of friendly association, informal guidance, and the minimization of tense competition. Those that think scholarship will out, no matter what, are a little naive."

◆ ◆ ◆

The Circus

WILLIAM SAROYAN

ANYTIME A circus used to come to town, that was all me and my old pal Joey Renna needed to make us run hog-wild, as the

From *My Name Is Aram*. Copyright 1937, 1938, 1939, 1940 by William Saroyan. Reprinted by permission of Harcourt, Brace and Company, Inc.

saying is. All we needed to do was see the signs on the fences and in the empty store windows to start going to the dogs and neglecting our educations. All we needed to know was that a circus was on its way to town for me and Joey to start wanting to know what good a little education ever did anybody anyway. After the circus *reached* town we were just no good at all. We spent all our time down at the trains, watching them unload the animals, walking out Ventura Avenue with the wagons with lions and tigers in them and hangıng around the grounds, trying to win the favor of the animal men, the workers, the acrobats, the clowns.

The circus was everything everything else we knew wasn't. It was adventure, travel, danger, skill, grace, romance, comedy, peanuts, popcorn, chewing-gum, and soda-water. We used to carry water to the elephants and stand around afterwards and try to seem associated with the whole magnificent affair, the putting up of the big tent, the getting everything in order, and the worldly-wise waiting for the people to come and spend their money.

One day Joey came tearing into the classroom of the fifth grade at Emerson School ten minutes late, and without so much as removing his hat or trying to explain his being late, shouted, Hey, Aram, what the hell are you doing here? The circus is in town.

And sure enough I'd forgotten. I jumped up and ran out of the room with poor old Miss Flibety screaming after me, Aram Garoghlanian, you stay in this room. Do you hear me, Aram Garoghlanian?

I heard her all right and I knew what my not staying would mean. It would mean another powerful strapping from old man Dawson. But I couldn't help it. I was just crazy about a circus.

I been looking all over for you, Joey said in the street. What happened?

I forgot, I said. I knew it was coming all right, but I forgot it was today. How far along are they?

I was at the trains at five, Joey said. I been out at the grounds since seven. I had breakfast at the circus table. Boy, it was good.

Honest, Joey? I said. How were they?

They're all swell, Joey said. Couple more years, they told me, and I'll be ready to go away with them.

As what? I said. Lion-tamer, or something like that?

I guess maybe not as a lion-tamer, Joey said. I figure more like a workman till I learn about being a clown or something, I guess. I don't figure I could work with lions right away.

We were out on Ventura Avenue, headed for the circus grounds, out near the County Fairgrounds, just north of the County Hospital.

Boy, what a breakfast, Joey said. Hot-cakes, ham and eggs, sausages, coffee. Boy.

Why didn't you tell me? I said.

I thought you knew, Joey said. I thought you'd be down at the trains same as last year. I would have told you if I knew you'd forgotten. What made you forget?

I don't know, I said. Nothing, I guess.

I was wrong there, but I didn't know it at the time. I hadn't really forgotten. What I'd done was *remembered*. I'd gone to work and remembered the strapping Dawson gave me last year for staying out of school the day the circus was in town. That was the thing that had kind of kept me sleeping after four-thirty in the morning when by rights I should have been up and dressing and on my way to the trains. It was the memory of that strapping old man Dawson had given me, but I didn't know it at the time. We used to take them strappings kind of for granted, me and Joey, on account of we wanted to be fair and square with the Board of Education and if it was against the rules to stay out of school when you weren't sick, and if you were supposed to get strapped for doing it, well, there we were, we'd done it, so let the Board of Education balance things the best way they knew how. They did that with a strapping. They used to threaten to send me and Joey to Reform School but they never did it.

Circus? old man Dawson used to say. I see. *Circus*. Well, bend down, boy.

So, first Joey, then me, would bend down and old man Dawson would get some powerful shoulder exercise while we tried not to howl. We wouldn't howl for five or six licks, but after that we'd howl like Indians coming. They used to be able to hear us all over school and old man Dawson, after our visits got to be kind of regular, urged us politely to try to make a little less noise, inasmuch as it was a school and people were trying to study.

It ain't fair to the others, old man Dawson said. They're trying to learn something for themselves.

We can't help it, Joey said. It hurts.

That I know, old man Dawson said, but it seems to me there's such a thing as modulation. I believe a lad can overdo his howling if he ain't thoughtful of others. Just try to modulate that awful howl a little. I think you can do it.

Then he gave Joey a strapping of twenty and Joey tried his best not to howl so loud. After the strapping his face was very red and old man Dawson was very tired.

How was that? Joey said.

That was better, old man Dawson said. By far the most courteous you've managed yet.

I did my best, Joey said.

I'm grateful to you, old man Dawson said.

He was tired and out of breath. I moved up to the chair in front of him that he furnished during these matters to help us suffer the stinging pain. I got in the right position and he said, Wait a minute, Aram. Give a man a chance to get his breath. I'm not twenty-three years old. I'm sixty-three. Let me rest a minute.

All right, I said, but I sure would like to get this over with.

Don't howl too loud, he said. Folks passing by in the street are liable to think this is a veritable chamber of tortures. Does it really hurt that much?

You can ask Joey, I said.

How about it, Joey? old man Dawson said. Aren't you lads exaggerating just a little? Perhaps to impress someone in your room? Some girl, perhaps?

We don't howl to impress anybody, Mr. Dawson, Joey said. We wouldn't howl if we could help it. Howling makes us feel ashamed, doesn't it, Aram?

It's awfully embarrassing to go back to our seats in our room after howling that way, I said. We'd rather not howl if we could help it.

Well, old man Dawson said, I'll not be unreasonable. I'll only ask you to try to modulate it a little.

I'll do my best, Mr. Dawson, I said. Got your breath back yet?

Give me just a moment longer, Aram, Mr. Dawson said.

When he got his breath back he gave me my twenty and I howled a little louder than Joey and then we went back to class. It was awfully embarrasing. Everybody was looking at us.

Well, Joey said, what did you expect? The rest of you would fall down and die if you got twenty. You wouldn't *howl a little*, you'd die.

That'll be enough out of you, Miss Flibety said.

Well! it's true, Joey said. They're all scared. A circus comes to town and what do they do? They come to school. They don't go out to the circus.

That'll be enough, Miss Flibety said.

Who do they think they are, giving us dirty looks? Joey said.

Miss Flibety lifted her hand, hushing Joey.

Now the circus was back in town, another year had gone by, it was April again, and we were on our way out to the grounds. Only this time it was worse than ever because they'd seen us at school and knew we were going out to the circus.

Do you think they'll send Stafford after us? I said.

Stafford was truant officer.

We can always run, Joey said. If he comes, I'll go one way, you go another. He can't chase *both* of us. At least one of us will get away.

All right, I said. Suppose one of us gets caught?

Well, let's see, Joey said. Should the one who isn't caught give himself up or should he wreck Stafford's Ford?

I vote for wreck, I said.

So do I, Joey said, so wreck it is.

When we got out to the grounds a couple of the little tents were up, and the big one was going up. We stood around and watched. It was great the way they did it. Just a handful of guys who looked like tramps doing work you'd think no less than a hundred men could do. Doing it with style, too.

All of a sudden a man everybody called Red hollered at me and Joey.

Here, you Arabs, he said, give us a hand.

Me and Joey ran over to him.

Yes, sir, I said.

He was a small man with very broad shoulders and very big hands. You didn't feel that he was small, because he seemed so powerful and because he had so much thick red hair on his head. You thought he was practically a giant.

He handed me and Joey a rope. The rope was attached to some canvas that was lying on the ground.

This is going to be easy, Red said. As the boys lift the pole and get it in place you keep pulling the rope, so the canvas will go up with the pole.

Yes, sir, Joey said.

Everybody was busy when we saw Stafford.

We can't run now, I said.

Let him come, Joey said. We told Red we'd give him a hand and we're going to do it.

I'll tell you what, I said. We'll tell him we'll go with him after we get the canvas up; then we'll run.

All right, Joey said.

Stafford was a big fellow in a business suit who had a beef-red face and looked as if he ought to be a lawyer or something. He came over and said, All right, you hooligans, come along with me.

We promised to give Red a hand, Joey said. We'll come just as soon as we get this canvas up.

We were pulling for all we were worth, slipping and falling.

The men were all working hard. Red was hollering orders, and then the whole thing was over and we had done our part.

We didn't even get a chance to find out what Red was going to say to us, or if he was going to invite us to sit at the table for lunch, or what.

Joey busted loose and ran one way and I ran the other and Stafford came after *me*. I heard the circus men laughing and Red hollering, Run, boy, run. He can't catch *you*. He's soft. Give him a good run. He needs the exercise.

I could hear Stafford, too. He was very sore and he was cussing.

I got away, though, and stayed low until I saw him drive off in his Ford. Then I went back to the big tent and found Joey.

We'll get it this time, Joey said.

I guess it'll be Reform School this time, I said.

No, Joey said. I guess it'll be thirty. We're going to do some awful howling if it is. Thirty's a lot of whacks even if he *is* sixty-three years old. He ain't exactly a weakling.

Thirty? I said. Ouch. That's liable to make me cry.

Maybe, Joey said. Me too, maybe. Seems like ten can make you cry, than you hold off till it's eleven, then twelve, and you think you'll start crying on the next one, but you don't. We haven't so far, anyway. Maybe we will when it's thirty.

Oh, well, I said, that's tomorrow.

Red gave us some more work to do around the grounds and let us sit next to him at lunch. It was swell. We talked to some acrobats who were Spanish, and to a family of Italians who worked with horses. We saw both shows, the afternoon one and the evening one, and then we helped with the work, taking the circus to pieces again; then we went down to the trains, and then home. I got home real late. In the morning I was sleepy when I had to get up for school.

They were waiting for us. Miss Flibety didn't even let us sit down for the roll call. She just told us to go to the office. Old man Dawson was waiting for us, too. Stafford was there, too, and very sore.

I figured, Well, here's where we go to Reform School.

Here they are, Mr. Dawson said to Stafford. Take them away, if you like.

It was easy to tell they'd been talking for some time and hadn't been getting along any too well. Old man Dawson seemed irritated and Stafford seemed sore at him.

In *this* school, old man Dawson said, I do any punishing that's got to be done. Nobody else. I can't stop you from taking them to Reform School, though.

Stafford didn't say anything. He just left the office.

Well, lads, old man Dawson said. How was it?

We had lunch with them, Joey said.

Let's see now, old man Dawson said. What offense is this, the sixteenth or the seventeenth?

It ain't that many, Joey said. Must be eleven or twelve.

Well, old man Dawson said, I'm sure of one thing. This is the time I'm supposed to make it thirty.

I think the next one is the one you're supposed to make thirty, Joey said.

No, Mr. Dawson said, we've lost track somewhere, but I'm sure this is the time it goes up to thirty. Who's going to be first?

Me, I said.

All right, Aram, Mr. Dawson said. Take a good hold on the chair, brace yourself, and try to modulate your howl.

Yes, sir, I said. I'll do my best, but thirty's an awful lot.

Well, a funny thing happened. He gave me thirty all right and I howled all right, but it *was* modulated howl. It was the most modulated howl I ever howled; because it was the *easiest* strapping I ever got. I counted them and there were thirty all right, but they didn't hurt, so I didn't cry, as I was afraid I might.

It was the same with Joey. We stood together waiting to be dismissed.

I'm awfully grateful to you boys, old man Dawson said, for modulating your howls so nicely this time. I don't want people to think I'm killing you.

We wanted to thank him for giving us such easy strappings, but we couldn't say it. I think he knew the way we felt, though, because he smiled in a way that gave us an idea he knew.

Then we went back to class.

It was swell because we knew everything would be all right till the County Fair opened in September.

Questions and Exercises

1. Notice the nonparallel structure in this statement from Saroyan's story: "The circus was adventure, travel, danger, skill, grace, romance, comedy, peanuts, popcorn, chewing-gum and soda-water." How does this structure help to describe the circus?
2. Compare the attitudes of Miss Flibety, Mr. Stafford, and Mr. Dawson toward "juvenile delinquency." Engage in group discussion on the problem: "Which of the three attitudes promises to achieve the best long-range results for the recalcitrant boys?"
3. Mrs. Jean Doyle in "What Nobody Knows about Juvenile Delinquency," *Harper's Magazine*, August, 1956, suggests that Americans have relaxed disciplinary measures to such an extent that it is little wonder crime is so rampant among teen-aged youth. Read her article, and then decide whether Stafford or Mr. Dawson was better justified in his position regarding the boys in Saroyan's story.
4. Do you think corporal punishment is justified in the American public school system? Investigate this topic by engaging in library research, and write a paper in which you present the evidence you are able to collect.
5. Using this story as a case history, engage in an organized group discussion with members of your class in which you attempt to suggest ways of improving student-teacher relationships in public schools.
6. What would you say is the unifying theme of Saroyan's story? Does this theme clash with your beliefs about human nature?
7. In the light of what Steinbeck says in "How to tell Good Guys from Bad Guys," who, from your point of view, are the good guys and bad guys in Saroyan's story? Explain.

8. Do you consider Miss Flibety incapable of controlling her class? Why was she unable to keep the boys from running off to the circus?

9. Do you think the boys were hopeless as far as regulated education is concerned? Explain.

10. Consider Joey's behavior in the light of what Rollo May has to say about "The Experience of Becoming a Person." Do you see any merit in his independent and daring attitude toward his overregulated environment?

11. Aram Garoghlanian, the central character in the collection of stories which make up *My Name Is Aram*, has been called a foreign-born Tom Sawyer. Compare the technique used by Saroyan in this story and that used by Mark Twain in "Huck and Jim on a Raft." Which author's characters come most nearly alive for you?

12. The American Council on Education has published a book called *Helping Teachers Understand Children*. Locate this book in your library, and compare the thoughts expressed on the subject with the idea inherent in Saroyan's story.

13. Consider the language used by Saroyan in this story. What would you say of the necessity of using erudite language to express profound ideas?

◆ ◆ ◆

How to Stay in College

ROBERT U. JAMESON

AT LEAST 2,500,000 young Americans are in college this fall. Of these, about 1,000,000 are freshmen. These figures are impressive; they seem to indicate that the ideal of a college-educated

Reprinted from *The Saturday Evening Post*, October 6, 1954. Copyright 1954 by The Curtis Publishing Company. Reprinted by permission of Robert U. Jameson.

democracy is on the way to realization. Yet the unhappy fact is that more than a third of the men and women who enter college fail to graduate. Why?

To find the answer to this question, I have talked to deans and instructors in several colleges and to a large number of young men and women who have just finished their freshman year in colleges all across the United States. Some facts are clear.

Of those who drop out of college, some leave for financial reasons, and this is often tragic because these people in many cases do well in college before they have to leave. Some leave because of poor health. A few are drafted. Many leave for "personal" reasons—marriage, family mix-ups or just the realization that college is not the place for them.

But the principal concern of the colleges is the disappearance of students who should graduate, but who simply fail instead. Therefore the real question is this: Why do students fail in college?

Although they may state it differently, all college deans from coast to coast agree on one point: The major problem of the college freshman is that of adjusting to a new kind of life, in which he is expected to behave like an adult. The Assistant Dean of Freshmen at Yale, Harold B. Whiteman, Jr., calls this "the acquiring of self-discipline." Dr. J. W. Graham, Assistant Dean at Carnegie Tech, calls the same process "learning to think." Diogenes, among others, said simply "Know thyself." In one way or another, what happens in the first year or two of college depends largely upon this one thing: Is the college student ready to grow up, to understand what college is?

What is college? By the end of this article, I believe that the question will be answered fairly. To begin with, here are some general statements about what college is. Robert B. Cox, Dean of Men at Duke University, says that his fervent wish is to be able some day to prove to an entering class that the freshman year is not Grade 13 in high school. Father Edward Dwyer, of Villanova College, says this: "I wish that it were possible for us to demonstrate that college is a place for adults, not an advanced school for children." And a young man who has just finished his first year at Princeton says this: "The most important problems facing a freshman are those of adjustment to a unique society, one totally different from high school."

Can college be defined?

In the first place, college is a place in which a person can learn how to learn. In school, boys and girls are taught something about how to pass courses in order to get a school diploma. Often enough they get the diploma at a certain age even with a record of failure. In college, on the other hand, these boys and girls are asked to learn to think, to meet complex intellectual problems and to handle these problems on their own. Intellectual independence, the first requisite of college, is often a distinct shock to a freshman.

An example of one college's method will perhaps make the point clearer. At The Carnegie Institute of Technology, English composition courses are quite unlike high-school courses. Students may be given several opposing points of view about a single topic and told to reach a logical, unbiased conclusion in a composition about this topic. The unwary freshman is thus faced with the necessity of using logic, of discarding personal prejudices and of writing carefully in order to prove to his instructor that he is capable of thinking through a problem. This "case-study" method is used in more than one freshman course in college.

Another course will present a student with the necessity of doing a large volume of reading and drawing conclusions from the reading. Or an instructor may say something like this: "What happened in England during the first week of July, 1751?" The freshman who asks how to find out such things will probably be rewarded with an icy stare and a map showing where the college library is—no more.

How do freshmen react to situations like these? Unfortunately, many will react badly because the spoon feeding of the high school, the parents eager to help with homework, the teacher who leads classes by the nose are all missing. Now the human brain, perhaps the least-used muscle in the human body, has to start working on its own.

A student who has finished a year at Washington and Lee says this: "I have just begun to realize, at the end of a rough year, what college has to offer. I hope that next year I will do a better job." "In college," says a girl at Michigan, "you get nowhere until you grow up."

But no college dean or adviser can possibly walk up to a floundering freshman and say, "You will do all right as soon as you grow up." Instead, all colleges provide elaborate programs to introduce the college to the freshmen, to warn the young people about what is ahead.

When the 1,000,000 new freshmen arrive for Freshman Week at any of the nearly 2000 colleges in the land, they are put through a complicated and sometimes bewildering mill. They meet their roommates. They meet their advisers. They take placement tests and aptitude tests and reading tests and physical examinations. They meet the president. They are invited to buy the school paper, pennants, beer mugs, rugs, laundry service and everything else under the sun. They attend a football rally and chapel and a dance or two and a picnic and a number of meetings for indoctrination in the methods of study.

They are breezed through a very pleasant week—dizzying, perhaps, but new and different. They don't even have time to get homesick. That comes about two weeks later. Now, during this week, deans and advisers say many things which freshmen may, to their sorrow, ignore:

Start studying at once.
Get to know the library immediately.
Set up a schedule for yourself—revise it later, if necessary—to include both social and academic activities.
Join one or two extracurricular activities, but not every one in sight.
Get enough sleep.
Don't forget chapel.
Don't cut classes.

You're on your own; make the most of your independence. But if you get into trouble, see your adviser right away.

Then classes begin, and the realities of college are suddenly all too evident. The first theme is written; the first history test is taken; the first physics experiment is done. And the first blast comes from a teacher, who, unlike lovable old Mr. Chips at home in the high school, is apparently half devil and half dragon.

An angry English instructor throws a theme on the desk in front of the dean of admissions and says acidly, "Would you be good enough to tell me why this man, who is obviously an idiot, has been admitted to this college?"

A freshman hands in a paper two days late and wonders why he gets an E. Another is stymied by the fact that his edition of King Lear has no footnotes to explain the text. "How am I supposed to be able to understand this stuff?"

A freshman's reaction to failure is a clear indication of whether he is a child or an adult. The adult simply works harder. The child may get surly. He may blame the instructor, not realizing that it is he, not the instructor, who has failed. He may look for excuses to explain his failure—headaches, a loud-mouthed roommate, the radio across the hall.

Because the college is concerned about the student who is in trouble and wants to save him, elaborate counseling programs have been set up in every college. The counselors, or advisers, try first to find out why students fail and then try to correct the trouble.

Among the causes for freshman failure, certainly the most important is lack of adequate training in secondary school. Overworked and underpaid teachers are simply not finding it possible to condition many of their students for the rigors of college work, particularly in the one most important subject of all: English.

According to almost every administrative officer in the colleges, the average freshman is deficient in the basic skills of reading and composition. Poor reading is usually caused by lack of practice. The average student today simply does not read many books; consequently, when he has to face long and complicated reading assignments in college, he may find that he has to study forty or fifty hours a week to keep his head above water. Or he may throw up his hands, say the assignments are impossible and go to the movies. In the latter case he will probably be on probation before long.

Colleges all over the land are finding it necessary to establish reading clinics for the most seriously retarded readers. Yet the number of students who get clinical attention is usually limited because few colleges are rich enough to set up a really adequate reading center. The student who is in trouble here should, however, at least go over the problem with his adviser, who will be able to give sound advice about the art of studying.

A large number of young men and women, college Class of 1958, say that one of their most serious freshman-year mistakes was not seeing their advisers often enough.

If reading by freshmen is poor, composition is generally even worse. It is pathetic to see items like this in college catalogues: "English W-1. Remedial course in composition. M.W.F. 9. Required of students who show insufficient preparation for English A. Students who pass the course with an A or B receive two points credit. Others receive no credit and are required to take English A."

English W-1 and its counterparts in hundreds of colleges waste time doing high-school work while advanced work has to wait. But college students must be able to communicate an idea, whether in literature or physics. College advisers wish that all schools could somehow graduate all students with at least a rudimentary idea of what a good sentence is.

This description of poor preparation in English, which is commented on again and again in the colleges—a Harvard faculty report in 1898 made the complaint—is not intended to condemn the high-school English teachers of America. Nor is it to be understood that every freshman is poorly prepared. The majority of freshmen have been in classes so large that no teacher can be expected to assign a weekly theme, much less correct the theme and confer with every student about the paper. Thus the freshman is too often in trouble because of shortcomings which have nothing to do with his ability. Under the circumstances, the best advice for a high-school student may well be this: beginning two or three years before you go to college, work on English composition and read a lot of books. Otherwise you may have serious trouble in all your college work, even if you are going to study animal husbandry or mining engineering.

The next academic problem of the freshman year—and this applies to all students, whether or not they have specific subject-matter difficulty—is that of how to study and how much to study.

According to most college authorities, high-school graduates, not usually so coddled as private-school students, get at their work early but do not realize how much is demanded of them. Independent-school graduates are likely to coast during the first part of the freshman year, because much of what they are being taught is in some way a repetition of their prep-school work. Then they may fall into the habit of thinking that college is easy.

"Because of my excellent high-school preparation, I did not have to work very hard during the first term," writes a young man who had hard sledding at Cornell last year. "Most of the material was review, and I became overconfident, ending the term with a 74. When I began learning completely new material in the second term, I did not improve my study habits enough to maintain the standards set by the faculty. I learned how to study the hard way, by 'busting out.' If I had the year to do over, I would study regularly and keep up with assignments, even though the material was neither new nor interesting. I do not like summer school."

Every college adviser tells his advisees the same thing. Some listen. A hundred freshmen, at the end of the year, say the same thing: start to study at once. Don't get behind. "Boy, if I dropped a pencil in the lecture room, I missed a semester's work," said a Penn State Marine Corps veteran.

This "busting out," or flunking, by well-prepared, intelligent students is what the Dean of Freshmen at Duke calls the "G-Factor." G stands for Goof, in the current slang use of the word. The bright boy who goofs is a very big headache to his college and a terrible waste of money, brains, effort and teaching. Obviously a number of these G-boys find themselves. What is tragic is that failure is the only way to show such a bright boy or girl that the college means business.

The jolt of failure sometimes produces results other than recovery. One common reaction is to blame the instructor. But no college adviser has much time for such an attitude. "I always tell characters like that," says a dean of a Southern college, "that I don't care what he thinks of the teacher. I tell him the library is right across the street. He can learn a lot there."

Or failure may bring a defeatist attitude, particularly to a student who has always done well in school. Colleges are on the watch for the defeatist, because they want to salvage at least something which the student has to offer, and they want also to keep him on an even keel emotionally. Deans, advisers, the college health service, coaches and others go into action. The student who fails to react to the collective wisdom of a group like this eventually will probably be dropped.

On the other hand is the family, not college-trained, which has laudable but often unrealistic hopes for a son or daughter: my son is going to be a doctor or an engineer; my daughter is going to be a nurse. In many instances these students become discouraged easily, and many of them drop out when they realize that they are not college material.

This particular problem is one found more often in the large state universities than in the smaller colleges, whose admissions requirements are stricter, and in which the student's purposes are more closely investigated before he is admitted.

But academic failure is by no means the only cause of trouble in college. Since college life is a complete and complicated existence, failure often comes to the student who cannot preserve the important balance between his academic and his social life.

Overemphasis on extracurricular activities, too much drinking, too much dating, too much fraternity activity—all of these will lead to trouble.

College, like life, is far too full of temptations. "My hardest job," says a bright young man, "was to take over where my parents left off—to learn to face facts: when you have to work, work; don't go to the movies." Another writes this way: "All people had to do was mention a party and I left the books."

In college, as in the world, the herd instinct is very strong. Offer cigars to a group of teen-agers and see what happens. (No youngster actually likes cigars.) If the first boy refuses, all may refuse. If the first accepts the gift, who will have the courage to refuse?

Eugene S. Wilson, Dean of Freshmen at Amherst College, has a very sound piece of advice: "The big job is to get students to be themselves. Most people don't dare to be a nobody; they must conform, be like everybody else. We try to tell our students that they should not be afraid to be good students—to study instead of holding a 'bull session.'" Or, to quote Emerson: "Whoso would be a man must be a nonconformist."

Activities in college are very attractive, and every student will miss a great deal if he stays completely away from them. From varsity football to the radio station, from intramural field hockey to folk dancing, there is something of interest to everyone on the campus. The problem is one of proportion.

Here are student comments:

"If I had the year to do over, I would say 'no' to all but one carefully chosen extracurricular activity." (Cornell)

"Athletics are good, but don't try to be a three-letter man. Actually, one sport is enough, due to the tremendous drain on one's studying time." (Princeton)

"If you don't have time for intercollegiate sports, get into the intramural program. That is enough exercise for anybody." (Amherst)

"Join some clubs, but don't stress them over classes." (Middlebury)

"Watch out for varsity athletics. Intramurals take less time." (Oklahoma)

Colleges vary considerably in their approach to extracurricular activities, to be sure—from the institution which has abolished intercollegiate sports to the one which provides scholarships for athletes. But all colleges agree that too much nonacademic exertion is certain to upset a student's normal balance.

Every freshman dean advises his charges to join a team or a club if it can be done without letting classwork suffer. Every dean also advises his charges not to join everything in sight. The wonderful independence of the freshman cannot be allowed to turn into license. One college simply advises its students to spend eight hours sleeping, eight hours in study and classes, and eight hours on everything else—as an average.

There are extracurricular activities which seem to help the student's over-all maturing in judgment and balance: the "cultural" clubs—music and dramatics—and, of increasing importance, religious activities. Nearly all campuses report an increasing awareness of the need for personal religion. This need, reflecting perhaps the uncertainty of the times, is filled by prayer groups and religious-discussion groups. Many colleges, like Dartmouth and the University of North Carolina, report increased activity on the part of the Christian Union and the Y.M.C.A., which carry on extensive social-work projects in the college and in the community. At Yale, among other groups, there is even a U.S. Grant Institute, which gives free tutoring to Negro children in New Haven. Ohio State University has every year a popular Religion in Life Week, organized by student church groups and presenting an imposing array of speakers and discussion leaders.

A serious social problem on most campuses is a three-way problem: drinking, dating and driving. These, or at least the first and third, concern some colleges more than others. Most college freshmen can be realistic about drinking. Nearly all of them say: drink moderately, if at all; date on weekends only—otherwise marks suffer. One Wellesley girl thinks that learning to drink is as important as other types of education. But she drinks "rye and ginger (one)" only if her date drinks. And a young man at Middlebury makes this astute remark: "Being a big drinker doesn't make you popular or a big wheel on campus. Far from it. If anything, it hinders your chances of making lasting friends."

College authorities vary in their approach to the question of drinking, especially when college policy in the matter is not rigid. Big-city colleges like Columbia realistically accept the fact that no "prohibition" is possible on a campus surrounded by several dozen New York City taprooms. Many colleges urge the prosecution of bars which serve minors, and a number of such places have been closed—temporarily. Some colleges simply ban liquor from the campus and hope for the best. Still others put into their Campus Code the stipulation that drinking in public is not gentlemanly. And while all colleges will expel students who make public nuisances of themselves, nearly all are philosophical about the problem.

But when, as in the small-town college or the college in a "dry" county, driving and drinking are combined, administrations have a real problem. When students who want a drink have to go to the next county or even the next state, or when they have to go a distance for a date, they go by automobile. When alcohol is added, disaster sometimes occurs.

As to the automobile by itself—it is here to stay, whether colleges allow it or not. And it is a difficult problem for both college authorities and college students.

At Dartmouth, for instance, about half of the upperclassmen have cars. Hanover, New Hampshire, is a long way from girls, and on Friday there is a major exodus and too little weekend studying. Big-city colleges have another kind of problem. At Ohio State, for instance, students "need" cars to get to class. In order to pay for the upkeep of the automobile, large numbers of car owners get part-time jobs which often use up so many hours that little time is left for study. Then academic failure appears just because of a car. Fathers are culprits in this thing too. They often give their college sons cars in order to maintain social status. Here again, maturity is what matters—even in father.

"Don't spend too much time with a car," one freshman says, "because it just costs too much." Sound advice.

Many colleges allow only juniors and seniors to drive cars. Others crack down when a student is in academic trouble. A few allow no cars at all. But in spite of the ban on cars at one college in the Philadelphia area, the dean shakes his head and says, "When our graduates die and go to heaven, the first thing they will say is, 'Where can I get a car?'"

Good advice to freshmen, agreed to by all sources, would surely be this: leave your car at home and for a year or two find out what college has to offer you, other than a parking lot. You are presumably in college for somethings besides automobile mechanics.

Indeed, what are the reasons why people are in college today? This is the big question, and the answers which college freshmen give to the question will indicate pretty clearly that there is an enormous amount of misunderstanding about what college is, what it means to students, what it can do for students. This last major item must be explored in some detail.

Some of the commonly accepted values of a college education are these:

> One can join many clubs.
> One can meet the right people.
> One can continue a distiguished career in athletics.
> One can stay out of the Army.
> One can learn a business.
> One can get a degree.
> One can learn to be a research scholar.
> One can prepare for a profession.
> One can get a background of culture.
> One can learn how to think.

The first five of these are unworthy or invalid objectives for the college student. Yet they exist, and they cause trouble. Overemphasis on social life—the first two in the list—has already been discussed, but the others need some attention.

It is no secret that the high pressure of interscholastic and intercollegiate athletics is itself responsible for confusion in the minds of many muscular young men. They have been coddled in school because they could throw passes accurately. Colleges bid for their services, often pay them well. Hence they expect to slide through colleges as athletes, and, in some colleges, they do just this. The coddling goes on, and the happy students move serenely to the Chicago Bears or the Detroit Tigers. Thus for some individuals there is no problem except that college education is perhaps an inaccurate description of what they have been doing.

But most colleges fortunately have a philosophy different from this. In most colleges, athletes must pass their courses or run the risk of probation and ineligibility. In these colleges much time is spent on the guidance of athletes in an attempt to keep the men on an even keel. At Columbia, for instance, nearly all of the coaches have professorial rank and attend faculty meetings, where athletic policy and academic problems are both discussed. The coaches are educators, and many of them are student counselors. Most colleges attempt to orient the student, athletically, by organizing an extensive intramural-sports program, which ordinarily enlists the support of most of the students in games for fun, not for dollars. The thoughtful freshman will put athletics into reasonable balance with his other activities.

Selective Service still looms large in young men's minds, for obvious reasons. But the draft is not nearly so strong an upsetting factor as it was even two or three years ago. Today, thanks to provisions in the Selective Service Act which temporarily defer most college students who stay out of academic trouble, "draft jitters" is a minor problem on most campuses.

What is more, ROTC programs are proving attractive and profitable to many young men, some of whom "find" themselves only while in the service and make a career of the Army or Navy. In some colleges, ROTC programs are compulsory for the first two years, then elective; in others they are elective all the way. The freshman who has the option of electing or not electing

ROTC may find himself in a quandary. His draft deferment is more certain if he joins. On the other hand, college deans point out that many freshmen are unhappy about joining because the quality of instruction in ROTC courses is often not so good as that in the academic courses which the student wants to take. The serious student may find Military Science and Tactics, to say nothing of drill, a waste of time.

The attitude of the administrations and advisers varies markedly, and the freshman should certainly listen to the advice which is apt for his college. At least one Eastern college advises freshmen not to enroll in ROTC. More than one dean is in favor of universal military training. Many others simply point out what the program has to offer and leave the decision up to the student. Advisers will probably have two main things to say: (1) Students who stay in the upper half of their class, scholastically, have a good chance of keeping their I-S classification until they graduate. And (2) students who go into ROTC and graduate with a commission will probably have a more enjoyable time when they do go into service.

And all college deans to whom I mentioned the matter are agreed on one final point about the draft. Students who worry most about being drafted are almost always those who are doing poor work and want something to blame for their failure. It is easy for the student failing two or three subjects to think that the international situation did it. Such men are often advised to drop out of college, do their stretch in the service and then come back to college. Service has a habit of making the immature grow up.

Many failures in college happen because freshmen think that college is a place in which to learn a trade or business. Having received high-school credit for typing, shorthand, automobile driving, band, and what not, they are chagrined to learn that college is not like that. Dean Whiteman, of Yale, says that students often complain about courses such as economics on the ground that these courses do not tell anyone how to run a business; they just teach theories. In much the same way, every college of engineering has on its hands a number of freshmen who are misfits at the start because they are not working with their hands, but are exposed to English, history and psychology. A college course in electricity is not for the embryo television-repair man, who should go to trade school, not college. Those who have this mistaken idea often drop out of the technical schools, where mortality is high anyway. In liberal-arts colleges, students more often than not can adjust themselves to the idea of a liberal education. But the adjustment is painful and often takes two or three years.

Colleges aim not to produce what Dr. J. W. Graham, of Carnegie Tech, calls the "complete technician," but instead a man whose education makes him able to fit a problem into its historical frame. Or, as a professor of chemistry in a small liberal-arts college puts it, "In three or four years all one can learn is that there are unsolved problems for research."

There are two real reasons for college education, and the two are actually the same stated differently: preparation for one of the professions, and acquisition of an idea of culture. Together, these two things mean the beginning of the development of the adult mind. Woodrow Wilson once said, "The object of a university is intellect."

Part of a circular given to each entering freshman at Columbia in 1953 reads as follows: "A liberal-arts education is one that aids the youth to grow into a mature, well-rounded individual who knows how to think objectively, to make the best use of his talents and to understand his responsibilities in a democratic society."

A liberal-arts education means, of course, a general education in which the humanities (literature, language, fine arts), the social sciences (history, economics, political science) and the natural sciences (chemistry, biology, physics) are about equally balanced.

During the war, emphasis in colleges lay in the turning out of people with the specific skills which a complicated war economy required. But today, all over the United States, the trend is returning to the kind of education described as the liberal arts. Even professional schools are now asking for students who have a broad academic background. For example, the Harvard Medical School does not require its candidates to have majored in science any more: some science, of course, but not just science. About a quarter of the curriculum at Carnegie Tech is made up of humanities courses. Massachusetts Institute of Technology has working arrangements with a number of small liberal-arts colleges under which students take "general-education" courses for two or three years and then transfer to M.I.T. for engineering.

Understanding the aims of the liberal-arts program in the American college is probably the hardest and also the most important job for the freshman today. Some freshmen—indeed, some graduate students—will never understand why general education is valuable. They may finish their course, but they will have wasted a lot of time and money. Some freshmen will drop out of college because, not understanding, they will simply fail their courses for lack of direction. Fortunately many freshmen will get the point and will come out of college with at least the beginning of a conception of what learning is.

If the freshman will take advantage of his adviser's experience, of his teachers' knowledge and of the wealth of his college library, and if he will study on his own, most of his minor adjustment problems will disappear. He will stop thinking of the college degree as a high-class work permit, a ticket of admission to this or that job. He will know that hard, analytical study is required in college. He will realize that liberal education means a good balance between academic, athletic and social life. And he will quite surely, out of his broad background, find a special interest to develop into a college major, even if it turns out to be an "impractical" field like Chinese, Indic philology or archaeology.

And the man or woman who finds out what education means has grown up. Surely the proof of the broad education which Americans can get if they want it is a deep understanding of how good that education can be.

Questions and Exercises

1. How does Jameson propose to answer the question stated in paragraph 1? What specific methods of development does he employ in order to accomplish this?
2. How does Jameson's definition of a college compare with the implied definitions in Mrs. Alcaro's "Colleges Don't Make Sense" and in Robert M. Hutchins' "Why Go To College?" Read in this connection Edgar G. Cummings, "What Is a College?" *School and Society*, March 20, 1954.
3. Write a paper on the subject "Why Students Fail in College" taking one or more of the arguments advanced by Jameson and supporting them by your own personal observations and experiences.
4. Is Jameson an advocate for small or large college composition or communication classes? Explain. Do you think he would support a movement to teach composition by closed-circuit television?
5. Compare the reasons for failure in college advanced by Jameson with those suggested by Davis in "The Fable of the Man Who Read the Papers." Also compare them with those of Voorhis in "Advice to Forlorn Freshmen" or of Hutchins in "Why Go To College?"
6. How does Jameson's attitude toward college football compare with the idea expressed by Hutchins in "Why Go To College?" (in this anthology), or "Gate Receipts and Glory," *The Saturday Evening Post*, December 3, 1938?
7. What is Jameson's answer to the argument advanced by Marion Walker Alcaro in "Colleges Don't Make Sense"?
8. Point out two essential ideas developed in this essay. Which one is most adequately developed and supported? Explain.
9. Read the following statement about "Going to College" by Ex-President Bancroft Beatley of Simmons College, and decide to what extent Jameson agrees with the ideas set forth.
   "A college education is an invaluable experience for many young men and women, but it is a mistake to assume that it is so for all. Going to college has become so much the habit of mind of the American people that we tend to close our eyes to the large number of young people for whom the college experience is harmful rather than helpful. To be success-

ful in college a young man or woman must have high intelligence, social maturity, and a real purpose in life, which the college of his choice can help him achieve."

10. Criticize the following statement which appeared in *The Daily Oklahoman*, October 5, 1955. How does this idea compare with Jameson's convictions?

"In view of the current projections of future enrollments it's possible that the time has come to ask whether higher education isn't trying to run over too many rabbits. Certainly it's time to ask whether employers aren't putting too much emphasis on the value of a college degree in certain lines of endeavor where other qualifications are obviously more important. It's only a slight exaggeration to say that a college degree is necessary to get a job driving a truck."

III. LANGUAGE AND MEANING

A proper study of words and their meanings is of utmost significance and importance in the lives of every human being, for social organization is impossible without a system of communication between and among people. The attainment of every want, desire, purpose, goal, no matter how trivial, depends upon a systematic use of language. Man's supremacy in the world was largely achieved by verbal "magic": the capacity to recapture and record the past and to anticipate and fashion the future. Civilization as we know it today could not have developed without language or some equally satisfactory medium of communication.

Susanne Langer, author of *Philosophy in a New Key*, has given much thought and attention to the importance of language in human affairs. In her essay "Language and Creative Thought," she shows how language originated and how it developed among human beings, how sign language differs from symbolic language, how symbols are used in the creation of ideas, and how language makes community life possible. Of basic importance in the attainment of communication skill is a thorough knowledge of the universe of words in which we live and an understanding of how language permits us to behave with a degree of purposefulness, perseverance, and consistency unknown to other animals.

Nor is this the end of the matter. Not only can men use words to achieve their purposes, but words can also use men. Language can be twisted into vicious thoughts and treacherous ideas. The power of words to distort truth is graphically explained in "The Reconstruction of Hidden Value Judgments," the outline of a method by which we may achieve a greater degree of tolerance and freedom in our society. Dale Warren, in "Aunt Lizzie's Lexicon," also touches on this matter and shows how words may manipulate the minds, and therefore the lives, of uncritical people.

Donald Lloyd, in "Snobs, Slobs, and the English Language," has proposed a common-sense analysis of language which reveals its true nature as a medium of communication. Other essays in this section of the anthology treat in a more detailed manner the qualities and characteristics of language outlined by Lloyd. Words do not carry meanings tied to them like labels on jars of preserves. They alter their colors with every context into which they are introduced. They have different meanings for different people, in different places, at different times, and under different circumstances. The essays by Monroe C. Beardsley, Dale Warren, and Mario Pei have been included here because they focus clearly on these important matters.

◆ ◆ ◆

Language and Creative Thought

SUSANNE K. LANGER

OF ALL born creatures, man is the only one that cannot live by bread alone. He lives as much by symbols as by sense report, in a realm compounded of tangible things and virtual images, of actual events and omnious portents, always between fact and

From *The Lord of Creation* by Susanne K. Langer. Reprinted by Special Permission from the January, 1944, issue of *Fortune Magazine*; © 1944 by Time Inc.

fiction. For he sees not only actualities but meanings. He has, indeed, all the impulses and interests of animal nature; he eats, sleeps, mates, seeks comfort and safety, flees pain, falls sick and dies, just as cats and bears and fishes and butterflies do. But he has something more in his repertoire, too—he has laws and religions, theories and dogmas, because he lives not only through sense but through symbols. That is the special asset of his mind, which makes him the master of earth and all its progeny.

By the agency of symbols—marks, words, mental images, and icons of all sorts—he can hold his ideas for contemplation long after their original causes have passed away. Therefore, he can think of things that are not presented or even suggested by his actual environment. By associating symbols in his mind, he combines things and events that were never together in the real world. This gives him the power we call imagination. Further, he can symbolize only part of an idea and let the rest go out of consciousness; this gives him the faculty that has been his pride throughout the ages—the power of abstraction. The combined effect of these two powers is inestimable. They are the roots of his supreme talent, the gift of reason. . . .

A symbol is not the same thing as a sign; that is a fact that psychologists and philosophers often overlook. All intelligent animals use signs; so do we. To them as well as to us sounds and smells and motions are signs of food, danger, the presence of other beings, or of rain or storm. Furthermore, some animals not only attend to signs but produce them for the benefit of others. Dogs bark at the door to be let in; rabbits thump to call each other; the cooing of doves and the growl of a wolf defending his kill are unequivocal signs of feelings and intentions to be reckoned with by other creatures.

We use signs just as animals do, though with considerably more elaboration. We stop at red lights and go on green; we answer calls and bells, watch the sky for coming storms, read trouble or promise or anger in each other's eyes. That is animal intelligence raised to the human level. Those of us who are dog lovers can probably all tell wonderful stories of how high our dogs have sometimes risen in the scale of clever sign interpretation and sign using.

A sign is anything that announces the existence or the imminence of some event, the presence of a thing or a person, or a change in a state of affairs. There are signs of the weather, signs of danger, signs of future good or evil, signs of what the past has been. In every case a sign is closely bound up with something to be noted or expected in experience. It is always a part of the situation to which it refers, though the reference may be remote in space and time. In so far as we are led to note or expect the signified event we are making correct use of a sign. This is the essence of rational behavior, which animals show in varying degrees. It is entirely realistic, being closely bound up with the actual objective course of history—learned by experience, and cashed in or voided by further experience.

If man had kept to the straight and narrow path of sign using, he would be like the other animals, though perhaps a little brighter. He would not talk, but grunt and gesticulate and point. He would make his wishes known, give warnings, perhaps develop a social system like that of bees and ants, with such a wonderful efficiency of communal enterprise that all men would have plenty to eat, warm apartments—all exactly alike and perfectly convenient—to live in, and everybody could and would sit in the sun or by the fire, as the climate demanded, not talking but just basking, with every want satisfied, most of his life. The young would romp and make love, the old would sleep, the middle-aged would do the routine work almost unconsciously and eat a great deal. But that would be the life of a social, superintelligent, purely sign-using animal.

To us who are human, it does not sound very glorious. We want to go places and do things, own all sorts of gadgets that we do not absolutely need, and when we sit down to take it easy we want to talk. Rights and property, social position, special talents and virtues, and above all our ideas, are what we live for. We have gone off on a tangent that takes us far away from the mere biological cycle that animal generations accomplish;

and that is because we can use not only signs but symbols.

A symbol differs from a sign in that it does not announce the presence of the object, the being, condition, or whatnot, which is its meaning, but merely *brings this thing to mind*. It is not a mere "substitute sign" to which we react as though it were the object itself. The fact is that our reaction to hearing a person's name is quite different from our reaction to the person himself. There are certain rare cases where a symbol stands directly for its meaning: in religious experience, for instance, the Host is not only a symbol but a Presence. But symbols in the ordinary sense are not mystic. They are the same sort of thing that ordinary signs are; only they do not call our attention to something necessarily present or to be physically dealt with—they call up merely a conception of the thing they "mean."

The difference between a sign and a symbol is, in brief, that a sign causes us to think or act *in face of* the thing signified, whereas a symbol causes us to think *about* the thing symbolized. Therein lies the great importance of symbolism for human life, its power to make this life so different from any other animal biography that generations of men have found it incredible to suppose that they were of purely zoological origin. A sign is always embedded in reality, in a present that emerges from the actual past and stretches to the future; but a symbol may be divorced from reality altogether. It may refer to what is *not* the case, to a mere idea, a figment, a dream. It serves, therefore, to liberate thought from the immediate stimuli of a physically present world; and that liberation marks the essential difference between human and nonhuman mentality. Animals think, but they think *of* and *at* things; men think primarily *about* things. Words, pictures, and memory images are symbols that may be combined and varied in a thousand ways. The result is a symbolic structure whose meaning is a complex of all their respective meanings, and this kaleidoscope of *ideas* is the typical product of the human brain that we call the "stream of thought."

The process of transforming all direct experience into imagery or into that supreme mode of symbolic expression, language, has so completely taken possession of the human mind that it is not only a special talent but a dominant, organic need. All our sense impressions leave their traces in our memory not only as signs disposing our practical reactions in the future but also as symbols, images representing our *ideas* of things; and the tendency to manipulate ideas, to combine and abstract, mix and extend them by playing with symbols, is man's outstanding characteristic. It seems to be what his brain most naturally and spontaneously does. Therefore his primitive mental function is not judging reality, but *dreaming his desires.*

Dreaming is apparently a basic function of human brains, for it is free and unexhausting like our metabolism, heartbeat, and breath. It is easier to breathe than to refrain from breathing. The symbolic character of dreams is fairly well established. Symbol mongering, on this ineffectual, uncritical level, seems to be instinctive, the fulfillment of an elementary need rather than the purposeful exercise of a high and difficult talent.

The special power of man's mind rests on the evolution of this special activity, not on any transcendently high development of animal intelligence. We are not immeasurably higher than other animals; we are different. We have a biological need and with it a biological gift that they do not share.

Because man has not only the ability but the constant need of *conceiving* what has happened to him, what surrounds him, what is demanded of him—in short, of symbolizing nature, himself, and his hopes and fears— he has a constant and crying need of *expression.* What he cannot express, he cannot *conceive;* what he cannot conceive is chaos, and fills him with terror.

If we bear in mind this all-important craving for expression we get a new picture of man's behavior; for from this trait spring his powers and his weaknesses. The process of symbolic transformation that all our experiences undergo is nothing more nor less than the process of *conception,* which underlies the human faculties of abstraction and imagination.

When we are faced with a strange or difficult situation, we cannot react directly, as other creatures do, with flight, aggression, or any such simple instinctive pattern. Our whole reaction depends on how we manage to conceive the situation—whether we cast it in a definite dramatic form, whether we see it as a disaster, a challenge, a fulfillment of doom, or a fiat of the Divine Will. In words or dreamlike images, in artistic or religious or even in cynical form, we must *construe* the events of life. There is great virtue in the figure of speech, "I can *make* nothing of it," to express a failure to understand something. Thought and memory are processes of *making* the thought content and the memory image; the pattern of our ideas is given by the symbols through which we express them. And in the course of manipulating those symbols we inevitably distort the original experience, as we abstract certain features of it, embroider and reinforce those features with other ideas, until the conception we project on the screen of memory is quite different from anything in our real history.

Conception is a necessary and elementary process; what we do with our conceptions is another story. That is the entire history of human culture—of intelligence and morality, folly and superstition, ritual, language, and the arts—all the phenomena that set man apart from, and above, the rest of the animal kingdom. As the religious mind has to make all human history a drama of sin and salvation in order to define its own moral attitudes, so a scientist wrestles with the mere presentation of "the facts" before he can reason about them. The process of *envisaging* facts, values, hopes, and fears underlies our whole behavior pattern; and this process is reflected in the evolution of an extraordinary phenomenon found always, and only, in human societies —the phenomenon of language.

Language is the highest and most amazing achievement of the symbolistic human mind. The power it bestows is almost inestimable, for without it anything properly called "thought" is impossible. The birth of language is the dawn of humanity. The line between man and beast—between the highest ape and the lowest savage—is the language line. Whether the primitive Neanderthal man was anthropoid or human depends less on his cranial capacity, his upright posture, or even his use of tools and fire, than on one issue we shall probably never be able to settle —whether or not he spoke.

In all physical traits and practical responses, such as skills and visual judgments, we can find a certain continuity between animal and human mentality. Sign using is an ever evolving, ever improving function throughout the whole animal kingdom, from the lowly worm that shrinks into his hole at the sound of an approaching foot, to the dog obeying his master's command, and even to the learned scientist who watches the movements of an index needle.

This continuity of the sign-using talent has led psychologists to the belief that language is evolved from the vocal expressions, grunts and coos and cries, whereby animals vent their feelings or signal their fellows; that man has elaborated this sort of communion to the point where it makes a perfect exchange of ideas possible.

I do not believe that this doctrine of the origin of language is correct. The essence of language is symbolic, not signific; we use it first and most vitally to formulate and hold ideas in our own minds. Conception, not social control, is its first and foremost benefit.

Watch a young child that is just learning to speak play with a toy; he says the name of the object, e.g.: "Horsey! horsey! horsey!" over and over again, looks at the object, moves it, always saying the name to himself or to the world at large. It is quite a time before he talks to anyone in particular; he talks first of all to himself. This is his way of forming and fixing the *conception* of the object in his mind, and around this conception all his knowledge of it grows. Names are the essence of language; for the *name* is what abstracts the conception of the horse from the horse itself, and lets the mere idea recur at the speaking of the name. This permits the conception gathered from one horse experience to be exemplified again by another instance of a horse, so that the notion embodied in the name is a general notion.

To this end, the baby uses a word long before he asks for the object; when he wants his horsey he is likely to cry and fret, because he is reacting to an actual environment, not forming ideas. He uses the animal language of *signs* for his wants; talking is still a purely symbolic process—its practical value has not really impressed him yet.

Language need not be vocal; it may be purely visual, like written language, or even tactual, like the deaf-mute system of speech; but it *must be denotative.* The sounds, intended or unintended, whereby animals communicate do not constitute a language, because they are signs, not names. They never fall into an organic pattern, a meaningful syntax of even the most rudimentary sort, as all language seems to do with a sort of driving necessity. That is because signs refer to actual situations, in which things have obvious relations to each other that require only to be noted; but symbols refer to ideas, which are not physically there for inspection, so their connections and features have to be represented. This gives all true language a natural tendency toward growth and development, which seems almost like a life of its own. Languages are not invented; they grow with our need for expression.

In contrast, animal "speech" never has a structure. It is merely an emotional response. Apes may greet their ration of yams with a shout of "Nga!" But they do not say "Nga" between meals. If they could *talk about* their yams instead of just saluting them, they would be the most primitive men instead of the most anthropoid of beasts. They would have ideas, and tell each other things true or false, rational or irrational; they would make plans and invent laws and sing their own praises, as men do.

The history of speech is the history of our human descent. Yet the habit of transforming reality into symbols, of contemplating and combining and distorting symbols, goes beyond the confines of language. All *images* are symbols, which make us think about the things they mean.

This is the source of man's great interest in "graven images," and in *mere appearances* like the face of the moon or the human profiles he sees in rocks and trees. There is no limit to the meanings he can read into natural phenomena. As long as this power is undisciplined, the sheer enjoyment of finding meanings in everything, the elaboration of concepts without any regard to truth and usefulness, seems to run riot; superstition and ritual in their pristine strength go through what some anthropologists have called a "vegetative" stage, where the dreamlike symbols, gods and ghouls and rites, multiply like the overgrown masses of life in a jungle. From this welter of symbolic forms emerge the images that finally govern a civilization; the great symbols of religion, society, and selfhood.

What does an image "mean"? Anything it is thought to resemble. It is only because we can abstract quite unobvious forms from the actual appearance of things that we see line drawings in two dimensions as images of colored, three-dimensional objects, find the likeness of a dipper in a constellation of seven stars, or see a face on a pansy. Any circle may represent the sun or moon; an upright monolith may be a man.

Whenever we can fancy a similarity we tend to see something represented. The first thing we do, upon seeing a new shape, is to assimilate it to our own idea of something that it resembles, something that is known and important to us. Our most elementary concepts are of our own actions, and the limbs or organs that perform them; other things are named by comparison with them. The opening of a cave is its mouth, the divisions of a river its arms. Language, and with it all articulate thought, grows by this process of unconscious metaphor. Every new idea urgently demands a word; if we lack a name for it, we call it after the first namable thing seen to bear even a remote analogy to it. Thus all the subtle and variegated vocabulary of a living language grows up from a few roots of very general application; words as various in meaning as "gentle" and "ingenious" and "general" spring from the one root "ge" meaning "to give life."

Yet there are conceptions that language is constitutionally unfit to express. The reason for this limitation of our verbal powers is a subject for logicians and need not concern us here. The point of interest to us is that, just as rational, discursive thought is bound up with language, so the life of feeling, of direct personal and social consciousness, the emotional stability of man and his sense of orientation in the world are bound up with images directly given to his senses: fire and water, noise and silence, high mountains and deep caverns, the brief beauty of flowers, the persistent grin of a skull. There seem to be irresistible parallels to the expressive forms we find in nature and the forms of our inner life; thus the use of light to represent all things good, joyful, comforting, and of darkness to express all sorts of sorrow, despair, or horror, is so primitive as to be well-nigh unconscious.

A flame is a soul; a star is a hope; the silence of winter is death. All such images, which serve the purpose of metaphorical thinking, are *natural symbols*. They have not conventionally assigned meanings, like words, but recommend themselves even to a perfectly untutored mind, a child's or a savage's, because they are definitely articulated *forms*, and to see something expressed in such forms is a universal human talent. We do not have to learn to use natural symbols; it is one of our primitive activities.

The fact that sensuous forms of natural processes have a significance beyond themselves makes the range of our symbolism, and with it the horizon of our consciousness, much wider and deeper than language. This is the source of ritual, mythology, and art. Ritual is a symbolic rendering of certain emotional *attitudes*, which have become articulate and fixed by being constantly expressed. Mythology is man's image of his world, and of himself in the world. Art is the exposition of his own subjective history, the life of feeling, the human spirit in all its adventures. . . .

Questions and Exercises

1. Several theories of the origin of language have been advanced by scholars and linguists: the "bow-wow" theory, the "pooh-pooh" theory, the "ding-dong" theory, etc. Find an explanation

of these various theories and decide to what extent you can agree with the notion supported by Langer in this essay.

2. How does Langer suggest that a proposed universal language, such as *Esperanto*, will probably never be universally adopted?

3. Langer suggests that from symbolic forms emerge images that finally govern a civilization. List a number of symbols that may be said to regulate American life in the twentieth century. How many of Kouwenhoven's list of things characteristic of this country, presented in "What's American about America?" are examples? Read in this connection C. Hartley Grattan's "The Things the World Wants," *Harper's Magazine*, November, 1956.

4. Define *imagination* as it relates to words, symbols, and experiences. The opening paragraph of Loren C. Eiseley's "The Bird and the Machine" may help you.

5. Explain the concept of abstraction by making use of the "abstraction ladder" discussed by S. I. Hayakawa in *Language in Thought and Action*, pp. 168–170.

6. What parallel do you find between Langer's discussion of language and Rollo May's "The Experience of Becoming a Person"?

7. What do you understand to be the essential difference between dreaming and creative thinking? What influence may one have on the other?

8. Explain the difference between the denotation and the connotation of a word. Cite several examples in order to clarify the distinction.

9. Explain on the basis of one's capacity to symbolize how the Rorschach (ink blot) tests can reveal characteristics of personality.

10. Read Ralph Waldo Emerson's discussion of "Language" in his essay "Nature," and compare his idea of "language as fossil poetry" with Langer's point of view about symbols.

11. Select some familiar myth, legend, rite, custom, or superstition, and write a paper in which you explain it in terms of symbolization, as set forth in this essay. In this connection, read Marjorie Kinnan Rawlings' "An Ancient Enmity," included in this volume.

12. Langer's discussion of symbols is largely concerned with showing how they facilitate thinking. In what respects may symbols actually *stop* thought? Consider, for example, Dale Warren's discussion of "men of distinction" in "Aunt Lizzie's Lexicon." Read also Thomas Hornsby Ferril's "Western Half-Acre," *Harper's Magazine*, July, 1946.

13. Read Stuart Chase's "Talk Makes Us Human" in *Roads to Agreement*, p. 196, and compare his idea with Langer's theory of "the language line."

14. Very little is known actually concerning what happens in the mind when a thought is created or an insight gained. What are the probable steps in the process, between recognizing a problem and finding an adequate solution to it? What is the function of the emotions in this process? Of the intellect? Of the senses? You may get some hints from Perry and Whitlock "The Right to Think—Through Reading."

15. Aldous Huxley in "Behavior That Language Makes Possible," quoted in Irving J. Lee's *The Language of Wisdom and Folly*, suggests that words may be responsible for war. Read this essay and explain to the class the argument advanced.

◆ ◆ ◆

Snobs, Slobs and the English Language

DONALD J. LLOYD

THERE IS at large among us today an unholy number of people who make it their business to correct the speech and writing of others. When Winston Churchill says, "It's me" in a radio address, their lips purse and murmur firmly, "It is I," and they sit down and write bitter letters to the New York *Times* about What is Happening to the English Language. Reading "I only had five dollars," they circle *only* and move it to the right of *had*, producing "I had only five dollars" with a sense of virtue

Reprinted from *The American Scholar*, Summer, 1951, by permission of Donald J. Lloyd and *The American Scholar*. Copyright 1951 by United Chapters of Phi Beta Kappa.

that is beyond the measure of man. They are implacable enemies of "different than," of "loan" and "contact" used as verbs, and of dozens of other common expressions. They put triumphant exclamation marks in the margins of library books. They are ready to tangle the thread of any discussion by pouncing on a point of grammar.

If these people were all retired teachers of high-school English, their weight in the community would be negligible; but unfortunately they are not. They are authors, scholars, business men, librarians—indeed, they are to be found wherever educated people read and write English. And they are moved by a genuine concern for the language. They have brought us, it is true, to a state in which almost anybody, no matter what his education or the clarity of his expression, is likely to find himself attacked for some locution which he has used. Yet their intentions are of the best. It is only that their earnest minds are in the grip of two curious misconceptions. One is that there is a "correct" standard English which is uniform and definite and has been reduced to rule. The other is that this "correct" standard can only be maintained by the vigilant attention of everybody concerned with language—indeed, by the whole body of educated men and women.

The enemy these self-appointed linguistic sentries see lurking in every expression which stirs the corrector's instinct in them is something they call illiteracy—which is not a simple state of being unlettered, but something more. This illiteracy is a willful and obstinate disregard for the standards of civilized expression. It stirs anger in them when they think they see it, because it seems to them a voluntary ignorance, compounded out of carelessness and sloth. When they think they find it in men who hold responsible positions in the community, they feel it to be a summation of all the decline of the graces of culture, the last reaches of a great wave of vulgarity which is eroding the educated and literate classes. It seems to them to be a surge of crude populism; they hear in each solecism the faint, far-off cries of the rising mob. It is really a sort of ringing in their ears.

In view of the general agreement among the literate that a "correct" standard English exists, and in view of the vituperation directed at anyone suspected of corrupting it, one would expect some kind of agreement about what is correct. There is little to be found; the easy utterance of one educated man is the bane of another. "For all the fussiness about which and that," remarks Jacques Barzun in the *Nation*, "the combined editorial brass of the country have feebly allowed the word 'disinterested' to be absolutely lost in its original sense. One finds as careful a writer as Aldous Huxley using it to mean uninterested, so that by now a 'disinterested judge' is one that goes to sleep on the bench." And on the subject of what surely is a harmless word, *whom*, Kyle Crichton, associate editor of *Collier's*, is quoted in *Harper's:* "The most loathsome word (to me at least) in the English language is 'whom.' You can always tell a half-educated buffoon by the care he takes in working the word in. When he starts it I know I am faced with a pompous illiterate who is not going to have me long as company."

Probably only a cynic would conclude from the abundance of such comments that those who demand correct English do not know it when they meet it; but some students of language must have been led to wonder, for they have made up lists of disputed locutions and polled the literate on them. So far, the only agreement they have reached has to be expressed in statistical terms.

The latest of these surveys, a questionnaire containing nineteen disputed expressions, was reported by Norman Lewis in *Harper's Magazine* for March, 1949. Lewis sent his list to 750 members of certain groups chosen mainly for their professional interest in the English language: lexicographers, high school and college teachers of English, authors, editors, journalists, radio commentators, and "a random sampling of *Harper's* subscribers."

If we count out two groups on the basis of extremely special knowledge and interest—the college professors of English and the lexicographers—we find all the others accepting about half the expressions. The authors and editors (book and magazine) were highest with about 56 per cent, and the editors of women's magazines lowest with about 45. (The expression which was least favored was *less* in the sense of *fewer*—"I encountered less difficulties than I had expected"—but even that received an affirmative vote of 23 per cent.) The distinguished electors seem individually to have played hop, skip and jump down the column, each finding among the nineteen expressions about ten he could approve of. If any two fell on the same ten, it was merely a coincidence.

A person innocent in the ways of this controversy, but reasonably well-informed about the English language, noticing that the disputants ignore the massive conformity of most writers in most of their language practices, in order to quibble about fringe matters, might assume that they would welcome the cold light of linguistic science. This is a naive assumption. In response to an attempt of mine to correct some of the misapprehensions I found in Mr. Barzun's article—among them his curious notion that "detached" and not "uninterested" was the original meaning of "disinterested"—he replied by letter that I represented a misplaced and breezy scientism, and that what I said struck him as "the raw material of 'populism' and willful resistance to Mind. . . . All dictionaries to the contrary notwithstanding, the word disinterested is now prevailingly used in the meaning I deprecated. . . . The fact that an illiterate mistake may become the correct form . . . is no reason for not combating it in its beginnings. . . ." This rejection both of the professional student of language and of the dictionary, when they disagree with the opinions of the writer, has the effect of making each man his own uninhibited authority on language and usage—an effect which I do not believe was exactly what Mr. Barzun had in mind.

What he did have in mind he stated clearly in one distinguished paragraph:

A living culture in one nation (not to speak of one world) must insist on a standard of usage. And usage, as I need not tell you, has important social implications apart from elegance and expressiveness in literature. The work of communication in law, politics, and diplomacy, in medicine, technology, and moral speculation depends on the maintenance of a medium of exchange whose values must be kept fixed, as far as possible, like those of any other reliable currency. To prevent debasement and fraud requires vigilance, and it implies the right to blame. It is not snobbery that is involved but literacy on its highest plane, and that literacy has to be protected from ignorance and sloth.

It is a pity that these sentiments, so deserving of approval, should receive it from almost all educated people except those who really know something about how language works. One feels like an uncultivated slob when he dissents—one of the low, inelegant, illiterate, unthinking mob. Yet as a statement about the English language, or about standard English, it is not merely partly true and partly false, but by the consensus of most professional students of language, totally false. It is one of those monstrous errors which gain their original currency by being especially plausible at a suitable time, and maintain themselves long after the circumstances which give rise to them have vanished. Mr. Barzun's remarks are an echo from the eighteenth century; they reek with an odor mustier than the lavender of Grandmother's sachet. They have little relevance to the use of the English language in America in our day.

In actual fact, the standard English used by literate Americans is no pale flower being overgrown by the weeds of vulgar usage: it is a strong, flourishing growth. Nor is it a simple, easily describable entity. Indeed, it can scarcely be called an entity at all, except in the loose sense in which we call the whole vast sum of all the dialects of English spoken and written throughout the world a single language. In this sense, standard American English is the sum of the language habits of the millions of educated people in this country. It is rooted in the intellectual life of this great and varied people. Its forms express what its users wish to express; its words mean what its users think they mean; it is correctly written when it is written by those who write it, and correctly spoken by those who speak it. No prim and self-conscious hoarding of the dead fashions of a superior class gives it its power, but its negligent use by minds intent on stubborn and important problems. There is no point in a tiresome carping about usage; the best thing to do is relax and enjoy it.

There are five simple facts about language in general which we must grasp before we can understand a specific language or pass judgment on a particular usage. It is a pity that they are not more widely known in place of the nonsense which now circulates, for they would relieve the native-born speaker of English of his present uncertainty, and give him a proper authority and confidence in his spontaneous employment of his mother tongue. They arise from a common-sense analysis of the nature of language and the conditions of its use.

In the first place, language is basically speech. Speech comes first in the life of the individual and of the race. It begins in infancy and continues throughout our lives; we produce and attend to a spoken wordage much greater than the written. Even the mass of writing which floods in upon us today is only the froth on an ocean of speech. In history, also, speech comes first. English has been written for only about fifteen hundred years; before this, it is of incalculable antiquity. In speech, its grammar was developed; from changes in the sounds of speech, changes in its grammar come. The educated are inclined to feel that the most important aspect of language is the written form of it, and that the spoken language must and should take its standards from this. Actually, the great flow of influence is from speech to writing. Writing does influence speech somewhat, but its influence is like the interest a bank pays on the principal entrusted to it. No principal, no interest.

In the second place, language is personal. It is an experience and a pattern of habits of a very intimate kind. In the home, the family, the school and the neighborhood we learn the speechways of our community, learning to talk as those close to us talk in the give and take of daily life. We are at one with our nation in our easy command of the pitch, tune and phrase of our own home town. Language is personal, also, in that our grasp of it is no greater than our individual experience with it. The English we know is not that vast agglomeration of verbal signs which fills and yet escapes the largest lexicons and grammars, but what we have personally heard and spoken, read and written. The best-read man knows of his native language only a limited number of forms in a limited number of combinations. Outside of these, the wealth which a copious tongue has as its potential is out of his world, and out of everybody's, for no dictionary is so complete or grammar so compendious as to capture it.

The third fact about language is that it changes. It changes in its sounds, its meanings and its syntax. The transmission of sounds, words, and meanings from generation to generation is always in some respects imprecise. Minute differences add up in time to perceptible changes, and changes to noticeable drifts. Difference in changes and in rates of change make local speech sounds, pitches, tones and vocabularies draw subtly and persistently away from one another. And all it takes to produce an identifiable dialect is sufficient segregation over a sufficient length of time.

The fourth great fact about language, then, is that its users are, in one way or another, isolated. Each has with only a few others the sort of familiar relationships which join them in one language community. Yet there are upward of two hundred million native speakers of English in the world. Obviously they cannot all be in close touch with one another. They congeal in nuclei— some stable, some transitory—which by a kind of double-action draw them together and enforce isolation of many more-or-less shifting kinds: the isolation of distance, of education, of economic levels, of occupation, age and sex, of hobbies, and political boundaries. Any one of these will be reflected in language habits; any two or three will bring about, in one community, speech differences as great as those caused by oceans and mountain ranges.

The fifth great fact about language is that it is a historical growth of a specific kind. The nature of English is one of the absolutes of our world, like air, water and gravity. Its patterns are not subject to judgment; they simply are. Yet they have not always been what they are; like the physical world, they have changed with time, but always in terms of what they have been. *Boy loves girl* means something different from *girl loves boy*. It is futile for us to prefer another way of conveying these meanings: that is the English way, and we must live with it. Yet students of the language see in this simple pattern the result of a cataclysmic change, great and slow like the geologic upheavals that have brought old salt beds to the very tops of mountain ranges, and as simple. Each is what it is because of what it has been before.

Language as a social instrument reflects all the tides which sweep society, reacting in a local or surface way easily and quickly as a beach changes its contours to suit the waves—but it offers everywhere a stubborn rock core that only time and massive pressures can move. The whim of a girl can change its vocabulary, but no will of man can touch its essential structure; this is work for the long attrition of generations of human use. Ever lagging a little behind human needs, it offers a multitude of terms for the things men no longer care about, but keeps them improvising to say what has not been said before.

Spoken English is, then, by its own nature and the nature of man, a welter of divergences. The divergences of class and place are sharpest in Britain, where the same dialects have been spoken in the same shires and villages for more than a thousand years. Although these can be heard in America by any traveler, no matter how dull his ear, they are relatively slight, for our language is essentially and repeatedly a colonial speech. Each of the American colonies drew settlers from various parts of Britain; each worked out a common speech based mainly on the dialect of its most influential group of immigrants (which differed from colony to colony); each remained in relative isolation from the others for about a hundred years. Then many colonists began to move to the interior: wave after wave of settlers traveled along rather distinct lines of advance until the continent was covered. Everywhere there was a mingling of dialects, with a composite speech arising, based mainly on the speech of the dominant local group. And so we have a Northern speech fanning out from the

Northeastern states, a Midland speech fanning out from the Mid-Atlantic states, and a Southern speech in the land of cotton-raisers, all crossing and merging as the pioneers moved west. Local differences are greatest along the Atlantic coast.

Wherever our people settled, they worked out local ways of talking about the things of common experience, and found their own verbal symbols of class distinctions. Here and there are areas where foreign-speaking groups clung together and developed special exotically-flavored dialects, but otherwise most speech patterns in America can be traced back to the dialects of Britain. Everywhere there is a common speech used by the multitude which works with its hands, and a slightly different dialect spoken by the professional and leisure classes.

The standard English written by Americans is not, however, the written form of educated speech, which shows great local variation. Its spellings have only a rough equivalence to the sounds we make; its grammatical system, which has nationwide and even worldwide currency, had its origin in the educated speech of the Northeastern states, and before that in the dialect of London, England. The concentration of schools, colleges, publishing houses and print shops in early New England and New York had the same effect in this country as the concentration in England, for centuries, of political power, commercial activity and intellectual life in London: it established a written standard, native only to those who grew up near the Hudson River or east of it. Elsewhere in America this written standard has been a learned class dialect—learned in the schools as the property and distinguishing mark of an educated class. Like many of its spellings, it is itself a relic of the past, an heirloom handed down from the days when the whole nation looked to the schoolmasters of New England for its book-learning.

The present controversy about usage is simply a sign that times have changed. The several vast and populous regions of this country have grown self-sufficient and self-conscious, and have taken the education of their youth into their own hands. Where the young once had to travel to the East for a respectable education, they receive it now in local public systems of rapid growth and great size. From local schools they may go to local universities of fifteen to fifty thousand students, where they can proceed to the highest degrees. Yale University is overcrowded with some six thousand students; in the community colleges alone of California more than 150,000 are enrolled. Most of these young people take their diplomas and go to work among their own people. They form a literate class greater in numbers and in proportion to the total population than the world has ever seen before. Speaking the speech of their region, they mingle naturally and easily with its people. When they write, they write the language they know, and they print it, for the most part, in presses close at hand. Everywhere they speak a standard literate English—but with differences: a regional speech derived from the usages of the early settlers.

Standard written English is, after all, an abstraction—a group of forms rather arbitrarily selected from the multitude offered by the language as a whole—an abstraction which serves the peculiar needs of the intellect. It achieves its wide currency because the interests of its users are the common interests of the educated, which transcend frontiers and negate distances—law, literature, science, industry and commerce. It is the tool of intelligence. Any thinking person must use it, because only this form of the language provides the instruments of delicate intellectual discrimination. And it is not static. As the needs of the intellect change, standard English changes. Change is its life, as anyone can see who picks up a book written only a little time ago, or examines almost any old newspaper.

The common speech of the uneducated, on the other hand, is comparatively static. Though it varies greatly from place to place, it is everywhere conservative; far from corrupting the standard language, it follows slowly after, preserving old forms long ago given up by literate speakers. "Them things" was once standard, and so were "he don't," "giv," and "clumb" and "riz." Its patterns are archaic, its forms homely and local. Only its vocabulary is rich and daring in metaphor (but the best of this is quickly swiped by writers of standard English). Seldom written because its speakers seldom write, it is yet capable of great literary beauties, uncomplicated force, compact suggestion, and moving sentiment. But it will not bear the burden of heavy thinking, and anyhow, heavy thinkers have a better tool to use. It is about as much danger to the standard language as an old house cat.

I have often wondered at the fear of common English and its speakers which the cultural aristocracy display, at their curious definition of illiteracy, and at the intemperance of their terms, which verges on the pathological. A Freudian should have a picnic with them. They use such epithets as illiteracies, crudities, barbarism, ignorance, carelessness and sloth. But who is not negligent in language, as in the mechanics of driving a car? They mutter darkly about "inchoate mob feelings." They confess themselves snobs by denying that their attitudes are snobbish. The stridency of their self-assurance puzzles the mind.

We might better adjust our minds to the divergences of usage in standard written English, for time, space and the normal drift of culture have put them there. We need not raise our eyebrows at a different twist of phrase, but enjoy it as an echo of a way of life somewhat different from our own, but just as good. We could do more than enjoy these things; we could recognize that the fixed forms of the language which do not come to our attention were developed in the past. We have come too late for the show. It is the changing forms that evidence the life in our language and in our society; we could learn much about our people and their ways by simply and objectively observing them.

If there is one thing which is of the essence of language, it is its drive to adapt. In an expanding culture like ours, which is invading whole new realms of thought and experience, the inherited language is not wholly suited to what we have to say. We need more exact and expressive modes of utterance than we have; we are working toward finer tolerances. The fabric of our language is flexible, and it can meet our needs. Indeed, we cannot stop it from doing so. Therefore it would be well and wholesome for us to see, in the locutions of the educated which bring us up sharply as we read, not evidences of a rising tide of illiteracy (which they are not), but marks of a grand shift in modes of expression, a self-reliant regionalism, and a persistent groping toward finer distinctions and a more precise utterance.

Questions and Exercises

1. Usage by well-known and educated writers and speakers has been considered a proper criterion of appropriateness in language choices for a long time. (See, for example, Arthur G. Kennedy's *English Usage.*) How does Lloyd explode the usefulness of such a criterion?
2. Norman Lewis' method of determining correct usage is similar to the method used to poll public opinion. How would you attack the validity of this method?
3. Norman Lewis patterned his study of nineteen disputed expressions after a much more comprehensive study made by S. A. Leonard, and publicized in *Facts About Current English Usage* by Albert H. Marckwardt and Fred Walcott. Compare the percentages obtained in the Lewis study with the percentages for the same items obtained in the Leonard study. What conclusions can you draw?
4. Make a list of so-called "grammatical errors" and "vulgar usages" which you find in *Harper's Magazine, The Saturday Review, The Atlantic,* or *The New Yorker* and any of the professional journals. What does this evidence tell you about the levels of usage theory?
5. A past president of the Speech Association of America, while addressing a group of business executives, employed the expression "snafued." How would Lloyd defend this usage?
6. Louis E. Foley published a paper in *School and Society,* May 5, 1951, entitled "The Modern Crime of Linguicide." Read this paper and compare its central thought with Lloyd's point of view.
7. This essay is part of a debate between Lloyd and Jacques Barzun. Barzun's answer to Lloyd may be found in *The American Scholar,* Summer, 1951, under the title "The Retort Circumstantial." Read Barzun's retort, and compare the attitudes of the two men. Which position seems more tenable to you?

8. According to Lloyd, what precisely is standard American English? How does this compare with A. H. Marckwardt's idea in "What Is Good English?" from *Talks* (published by the Columbia Broadcasting System, Inc., 1937)? How does it compare with Margaret Nicholson's idea in "What Is Good English?" *The Atlantic*, May, 1957, pp. 71–73?

9. What other essays in this section of the anthology support one or more of the five principal facts about language which Lloyd discusses in the essay?

10. According to Lloyd, which changes more rapidly, the English vocabulary or the grammatical structure of English? Mention examples of both varieties of change.

11. Louis Foley has said: "In learning a language, the fundamental thing is to learn the *system*—that is to say the 'grammar'— which is a 'technique' in the true sense of that much-abused term. Then, the rest of one's life, one learns *words*. And that we manage to do easily enough in real situations." How does this point of view regarding language agree with what Lloyd says in the essay?

12. What significance, as far as usage is concerned, do you see in the fact that spoken language preceded written language in the social history of mankind?

13. What nineteenth-century usages do you find in Melville's chapter from *Moby Dick* (included in this anthology) that are no longer current in American English? Why have they been altered or omitted from our language?

14. Write a paper of about 250 words explaining why language must change if it is to be useful as a social tool in the affairs of human beings.

15. Following is a defense of English written by Thomas Nash in 1594. Translate it into modern English, making whatever changes are appropriate in both vocabulary and structure:
    "Our English tongue of all languages most swarmeth with the single money of monosillables, which are the only scandall of it. Bookes written in them and no other seeme like shop-keepers boxes, that contain nothing else, save half-pence, three-farthings tow-pence, therefore, what did me I, but having a huge heape of those worthlesse shreds of small English in my Pia Maters purse to make the royaller shew with them to mens eyes, had them to the compounders immediately and exchanged them foure into one and others into more, according to the Greek, French, Spanish, and Italian."

16. Translate the following passage of pedagese into plain English:
    "Johnnie is adjusting well to his peer group and achieving to expectancy in skill subjects. But I'm afraid his growth in content subjects is blocked by his reluctance to get on with his development tasks."
17. Read Clifton Fadiman's "Is There an Upper-Class Language?" *Holiday*, October, 1956, and determine to what extent swearing is approved by the culturally elite in America.

◆ ◆ ◆

Meaning and Context

MONROE C. BEARDSLEY

ONE OF the fundamental facts about words is that the most useful ones in our language have many meanings. That is partly why they are so useful; they work overtime (but, as we shall see, not for nothing). Think of all the various things we mean by the word "foot" on different occasions: one of the lower extremities of the human body, a measure of verse, the ground about a tree, twelve inches, the floor in front of the stairs. The same is true of nearly every common noun or verb. The editors of *The American College Dictionary*, in their preliminary investigation of words most frequently used, found 55 distinct senses of the word "point" in 1,100 occurrences of the word, and they distinguished 109 different senses of the word "run."

Considering the number of ways of taking a particular word, the task of speaking clearly and being understood would seem pretty hopeless if it were not for another very important fact

From Monroe C. Beardsley, *Thinking Straight*, 2nd Ed. Copyright, 1950, 1956, by Prentice-Hall, Inc., Englewood Cliffs, N.J., pp. 153–159. Reprinted by permission of the publisher.

about language. Though a word may have many senses, these senses can be controlled, up to a point, by the context in which the word is used. When we find the word in a particular verbal setting—that is, take it with the words that come before and after it in a discourse—we can usually decide quite definitely which of the many senses of the word is relevant. If a poet says his verse has three feet, it doesn't occur to you that he could mean it's a yard long or is three-legged (unless perhaps you are a critic planning to puncture the poet with a pun about his "limping verse"). The context rules out these maverick senses quite decisively.

We might be puzzled if we read in a newspaper that "in the suicide's pocket the police found a large envelope full of bills." In this sentence, as it stands, the word "bills" can easily be taken in two very different senses. But if the context were expanded so as to read, "The police were surprised to find in the suicide's pocket a large envelope full of bills of various denominations," we should understand that "bills" meant *paper* money, and we might wonder whether it was indeed suicide or accident. Or if the context were expanded differently, so as to read, "The police were surprised to find in the suicide's pocket a large envelope full of unpaid bills," we should understand that "bills" meant *requests for payment of a debt*, and we might wonder whether that explains the suicide.

This is a rather simple illustration of the way in which the context of a word helps to pick out one of its senses and fix that sense. But of course "context" is used broadly here: it may be the rest of a sentence (the *immediate* context), a page, a whole book, or a newspaper file. A "shady street" is one thing; a "shady neighborhood" is something else. The word "strike" means one action on the front page of a paper and another action on the sports page; the words "liberal" and "patriotic" mean certain attitudes in *The New York Times* and mostly different ones in *The Chicago Tribune*. When some time ago a British physicist announced with pleasure that the hydrogen bomb is "safe," his statement caused gasps of surprise; in the technical talk of atomic scientists, "safe" apparently means that it couldn't set off a chain reaction that might destroy the earth itself. This is not the way the man in the street uses the word.

Many common words like "line," "pipe," "base," "stock," and "head" have acquired many serviceable meanings in different occupational contexts—say, in the shoptalk of plumbers, pitchers, or plastic engineers. Think of what the word "wing" means to a birdwatcher, an airman, a stagehand, a general, or an architect. But just because these meanings are so completely distinct—no one can confuse the wing of an airplane with the wing of a house—it is easy to control them by very light contextual pressure. A word or two makes it clear that it is the airman's wing rather than the architect's that is referred to. But when the differences between the senses of a word are slighter and subtler (they may be even more important, however), the most careful management of the context may be required to get and keep one sense in focus. The exact meaning of a word like "middle class" or "evolution" or "justice" may depend upon the whole book in which it appears.

That is why it is often easy to misrepresent what someone has said by quoting some of his remarks out of their context. The words may not, strictly speaking, be *mis*quoted, but their meaning has been changed. The political candidate's promise to obtain peace or balance the budget is echoed and attacked by his opponent—who is careful to leave out the conditions and qualifications that originally surrounded it. Even if a writer is scrupulous enough to put in dots to indicate that something has been left out, he may not be *quite* scrupulous enough to stick to the original meaning. You have seen advertisements of a new play, with a few words from a review. The phrase ". . . emotional subtlety . . . (Bridgeport *Post*)" may be from a sentence that goes: "It has all the emotional subtlety of a barroom brawl." The phrase ". . . great drama . . . (New Haven *Register*)" may be from a sentence that goes: "No doubt it was considered a great drama when it first appeared in 1927, but. . . ." And this is nothing to what a professional wiretapper can do if he records a telephone conversation and picks out words to rerecord on a new tape.

Representative Wayne L. Hays, a member of the Special House

Committee set up by the 83rd Congress to investigate tax-exempt foundations, frequently argued during the committee's hearings that the "research directors" of the committee were willing to make judgments on passages torn out of contexts that might change their meaning considerably. He finally made a dramatic demonstration of this by producing three paragraphs which the associate research director testified were "closely comparable" with, and parallel to, Communist literature that he had read. They were excerpts from two papal encyclicals.

A loose and sloppy writer lays himself open particularly to accidental misquotation, but any writer would find it very hard to write a paragraph that is proof against a deliberate and skillful excerptlifter. Dean Sturges of the Yale Law School perhaps came as close as anyone can when, in 1949, the Harvard Law School *Record* asked him for an appropriate comment on the Harvard Law School's decision to admit women students for the first time. Dean Sturges is reported to have sent the following telegram:

YALE LAW FACULTY AND STUDENT BODY DEEPLY MOVED. FEEL IT QUITE POSSIBLE HARVARD MAY MAKE CONTRIBUTION TO WOMANHOOD. DOUBT MANY ADVERSE CONSEQUENCES HARVARD FACULTY OR STUDENT BODY. WE HAVE ALWAYS FOLLOWED WITH GENUINE INTEREST LONG STRUGGLE HARVARD LIBERALS IN THIS MATTER. OUR MANY GENERATIONS OF WOMEN GRADUATES ARE OF COURSE A PRIDE AND JOY. BEST WISHES.

Try digging a quotable compliment out of that.

The importance of context in the interpretation of meaning varies from one discourse to another. In a technical article on mathematics or physics, most sentences can stand pretty much on their own feet and be well understood apart from their context. Scientific terms are designed to resist the influence of context so that they can pass from one context to another without changing their meaning. But sentences in ordinary discourse that contain pronouns often lean on other sentences that contain the antecedents of those pronouns. Moreover, some words in our language—and they are among the most useful, but the trickiest, ones—are so adaptable to their context, like chameleons, that they take most of their character from it, and when they are considered apart from any context, they have only the most indefinite meaning. Words like "efficient," "dangerous," "internal," "successful," "free," tell us very little unless we are told, for example, the *purpose* for which it is efficient, or the *standards* in terms of which the success is judged. Contexts like "freehanded," "free lunch," "free love," "free will," "freeborn," "free association," help to limit the word "free" to a somewhat more definite range of meaning, but even in such cases we often feel that we don't know exactly what the word "free" means unless the context provides answers to the questions: "Free *from* what?" "Free *for* what?" "Free *to do* what?"

Another thing that shows the importance of context is the fact that when people use the wrong word we sometimes know what word should have been used. When Mrs. Malaprop says, "I would by no means wish a daughter of mine to be a progeny of learning. . . . I would have her instructed in geometry, that she might know something of the contagious countries," we understand what she thought she was saying because the context so clearly tells us what words are called for if the sentences are to make sense. A malapropism is a word that is wrongly used in a sentence in place of another word that sounds somewhat like it. And if we couldn't tell from the context what the appropriate word would be, we could never recognize a malapropism.

But of course it would be a mistake to overemphasize contextual influence and say that a word *never* has the same meaning in two different contexts. If this were true, language would be even more difficult to manage than it is now. A person who says, "I believe in the dictionary" and later "I believe in the Bible" is presumably using the word "believe" in the same sense in both contexts. Perhaps sometimes when we say that a word is used twice in the same sense we ignore slight differences that could be important for one purpose or another. It is a good idea to keep in mind that a change in context *may* make a change in the sense, but it doesn't seem that it *must*. In the present paragraph the word "context" has, up to this point, been used three times, in three slightly different (immediate) contexts; but it has about the same meaning each time.

It is only when the context is considerably different that the meaning is likely to change. A person who says, "I believe in the dictionary," and, later, "I don't believe in ghosts," is using the word "believe" in two very different senses. But in each of these contexts it can have only one possible meaning, and when the whole context is taken into account there *may* be no question what the meaning is. "I believe in a federal world government" means about the same as "I believe *there should be* a federal world government." "I believe in extrasensory perception" means about the same as "I believe *there is such a thing as* extrasensory perception." "I believe in woman's intuition" means about the same as "I believe *that some of the things that* women intuit *are true.*"

When a word can have different meanings in different kinds of context, we can say that it has **variable** meaning. Its meaning *varies*, and it therefore has a variety of senses when it appears in the dictionary. Some words are more variable than others. But the variable meaning of words doesn't ordinarily give us any trouble so long as there is enough contextual control. The trouble arises when the context is not complete enough to rule out all but one possible meaning. If I say, "Henry rents the house," there is no way for you to tell from the sentences itself whether Henry rents the house *from* someone or *to* someone. When a word can have one (but not both) of two (or more) meanings in a certain context, we shall say that the word is **ambiguous** *in that context*.

The ambiguity of a word is always relative to a context; no word is ambiguous *in itself*. Some words like "freedom," "religion," "democracy," are ambiguous in quite a few contexts, and that is why you have to be careful in interpreting and in using them. Sometimes such words are said to be "meaningless," but the trouble with them is just the opposite: they have so many subtly different meanings that it takes a good deal of skill—more than most writers command—to keep their meanings well under control. And when the writer fails in this task, it is up to the reader. Other words, such as the common nouns, are variable in meaning but are hardly ever ambiguous. It takes a good deal of ingenuity to write a medium-sized sentence in which the word "foot" is ambiguous.

A case of ambiguity, as we have defined it, is a case where there is some *doubt* about the way a discourse is to be interpreted, and you have to choose between alternative readings. Unfortunately, this is not the way the word "ambiguity," is always used. When A. E. Housman, in his poem "To an Athlete Dying Young," writes,

> Home they brought him, shoulder high,
> Townsman of a stiller town,

the word "town" has at least two meanings: the young man's village is quieter for the funeral than it was on the day everyone cheered his victory, and also he is now among the noiseless dead. But "town" is not ambiguous here. It has *both* meanings at once, and there is no uncertainty about them at all.

This sort of double meaning, or **multiple meaning** as it may be called, is also characteristic of one type of pun. There is the old pun, for example, about the two women leaning out of their windows across an alley and shouting at each other angrily: they can never come to an agreement because they are arguing from different premises. Another type of pun is built on *homonyms*, that is, words that have the same sound but different senses ("boy," "buoy"; "recede," "reseed"; "bier," "beer"; "air," "heir"). If you want to call homonyms the same word because they have the same sound, you would then have to say that such words have an even more variable meaning than we supposed. On the whole, we may as well call them different words if they are spelt differently, and then we shall not need to say any more about homonyms, except to note that they can give rise to the sort of pun made by Macbeth when he says he will plant circumstantial evidence on the grooms:

> "If he do bleed,
> I'll *gild* the faces of the grooms withal,
> For it must seem their *guilt*."

This sort of double entendre, whether in pun or poem, is sometimes called "ambiguity," but it is a very different thing from ambiguity in the sense in which we are using the term. The important thing at the moment is to note that there is a difference. The high-pressure context of a poem can squeeze many senses, all at once, out of some of its words; this is the multiple meaning of poetic discourse. But we have ambiguity, in the strict sense, when the context is too loose and flabby to hold the words steadily to any definite sense. The poet has managed to say several things at once; the ambiguous writer has not quite succeeded in saying anything.

Questions and Exercises

1. A. N. Whitehead has said that the important part of language is its "unapprehended background." Explain why a dictionary cannot include this part of the meaning of words in a definition. It may help you, in making this explanation, to read Dominick A. Barbara's "The Role of the Ear in Psychic Life," *Today's Speech*, January, 1957.
2. Beardsley's essay is almost entirely devoted to verbal contexts —the language settings in which words appear. What other kinds of contexts give meaning to a word? What kind of contexts are discussed by Dale Warren in "Aunt Lizzie's Lexicon"? By Rollo May in "The Experience of Becoming a Person"? By Mario Pei in "The Geography of English"?
3. Use the following words in two or more contexts to demonstrate their various meanings: *billion, cat, democracy, skyscraper, cynical, baste, speak, youngster, standard.*
4. Charles W. Cooper in *Preface to Drama*, New York, 1955, pp. 9–10, discusses the ambiguity of the word *drama*. Read this discussion and construct sentences which contain the word drama in its various senses.
5. Find a word in the context of Beardsley's essay which is employed in an unusual sense. Is this sense defined in the dictionary?
6. Consider the following pairs of sentences. Does the italicized word or phrase in each pair have the same meaning in both sentences?

a. I have some *money* in my pocket.
   It takes *money* to go to school.
b. I *believe* in universal education.
   I *believe* in the divine inspiration of the Bible.
c. He told me his *plans* for the future.
   He showed me the *plans* for the new auditorium.
d. The United States is a *political* entity.
   The faculty of the college is having a *political* hassle.
e. Grande Coulee is a *triumph* of foresight and organization.
   Hamlet is a *triumph* of dramatic art.
f. In our experience it is Sammy who is *ubiquitous* with his
   assumptions that Knowledge is to be passively absorbed,
   not found out and mastered. The snakes were not *ubiquitous* as I had expected, but I saw one often enough to keep
   my anxiety alive.

7. Define each of the italicized words in this context. (For suggestions on the definition of words, see Lionel Ruby's *The Art of
   Making Sense*, chapter 4.)
   "Planning" is a highly *popular* word abroad. To the European and Asian, it carries *echoes* of order, of economic justice, of faster progress than their *ramshackle* variety of "free
   enterprise" can ever offer. But in the American language,
   "planning" means a *nasty* habit, like selling *dirty* postcards
   or eating snails. Such things must be expected of those de-
   plorable *foreigners*—but for any *clean-cut* American boy they
   would be unthinkable.
   —*Harper's Magazine*, May, 1955, p. 16.
8. Explain which word in this context is ambiguous and why:
   "Government correspondence costs the taxpayers up to $300
   per letter."
9. Notice that the word *college* has a very special meaning in the
   essay "Colleges Don't Make Sense," by Marion Walker Alcaro.
   Find other examples in this anthology of words which are used
   in specialized senses.
10. Consider the word *full* in the following context and explain its
    nature in the light of Beardsley's discussion:
    "Here lies the emptiest of mortals; he was full of himself."
11. Read James Mackaye's "Ambiguity and Its Avoidance," quoted
    in Irving J. Lee's *The Language of Wisdom and Folly*, and list
    the steps one must take in order to avoid confusing two mean-
    ings of a given word.

◆ ◆ ◆

The Reconstruction of Hidden Value Judgments

FELIX S. COHEN

I.   LOCATING PREJUDICES

WHAT I can do in society depends pretty much on what my neighbors will tolerate. Or, to put the matter more abstractly, the limits of my liberty are the limits of my neighbors' tolerance. Prejudice is the chief enemy of tolerance and therefore the chief enemy of freedom. In order to eliminate prejudice we must identify it. But here we are met by the threshold difficulty that none of us can easily recognize his own prejudices.

For some years I have been asking my students whether any of them had any prejudices, and I have not by this method of inquiry found anybody who had any prejudices and admitted to having them. I can think of only three possible explanations of this fact: (1) that my students have prejudices and know they have them, but are attempting to conceal this fact from me; (2) that my students are actually without prejudices; and (3) that it is normal for people not to see their own prejudices.

As my students are, generally speaking, of the highest moral character, I must reject this first alternative theory of conscious deception. And as my students are a fair cross-section of humanity, I must reject the second alternative, the possibility that my students are in fact unprejudiced. This leaves me with the third alternative theory, at least as a working hypothesis, the theory, namely, that prejudice is something that we are more apt to recognize in others than in ourselves.

Reprinted from *Symbols and Society* edited by Lyman Bryson, Louis Finkelstein and Robert M. MacIver. Copyright 1954 by the Conference on Science, Philosophy and Religion in Their Relation to the Democratic Way of Life, Inc. Reprinted by permission of Harper & Brothers.

In this respect prejudice is not unique. Take the relation, for instance, of *fact* to *theory*, of *reverence* to *idolatry*, of *orthodoxy* to *heterodoxy*, of *common sense* to *metaphysics*. Generally, the theories we believe we call *facts*, and the facts we disbelieve we call *theories*; the attitude of respect for objects we respect we call *reverence*, the attitude of respect for objects which we hold in contempt we call *idolatry*; we are all familiar, of course, with the observation that *orthodoxy* is my doxy and *heterodoxy* is the other fellow's doxy.

Less familiar, perhaps, is the reflection that ways of looking at the universe to which we are habituated we generally call *common sense*, while ways of looking at the universe that are unfamiliar to us we are apt to call *metaphysics*. Even the recognition that the world is not divided between Americans and foreigners, but that Americans are themselves foreigners in most of the world, requires a degree of sophistication which few members of Congress ever consistently attain. For example, in June of 1952, it was not possible to find one-third of either house of Congress willing to support the President's veto of the McCarran-Walter Omnibus Immigration Act, which sets up a new and drastic regime for the stranger in our land. And the sponsors of this law were nearly all professed believers in the infallibility of the Bible, which again and again insists that we should not vex the stranger, but should have one law alike for the home-born and the stranger in our midst, ". . . for remember that ye were strangers in the land of Egypt."

In order to avoid confusing ourselves with the center of the universe, it is necessary to recognize that statements about *strangers* or *strange ways*, or *prejudice*, or *idolatry*, or *things foreign*, involve certain points or reference and lines of direction, and that different minds may operate with different points of reference and different lines of direction. Thus what is the core of life's wisdom and experience and the basis of all reason to me may be seen as the extreme of prejudice by somebody else, and *vice versa*.

Skipping, for the time being, the question of how we can determine which of two divergent moral standpoints is right, and concentrating on the more elementary question of how we can determine whether two moral views are divergent, we face the difficulty that people of the most diverse moral outlooks will often express exactly the same abstract value judgments, that is to say, they will prefer courage to cowardice, justice to injustice, and good to evil. Such preferences may be considered, in effect, verbal conventions. Moral divergences are generally reflected not by challenges to these conventions, but by disagreements as to the content or denotation of such value concepts as courage, justice, and goodness. Such disagreements as to the content of value concepts are commonly reflected in our application of honorific or pejorative terms to a given set of circumstances or persons.

It is hoped that this hypothesis may serve to illumine the divergences of value attitude that are the sources of prejudice and may suggest a technique for locating such sources capable of wider and more scientific application.

As the field of racial and national feeling is generally conceded to be a field in which prejudice plays a major role, it may be helpful to examine some of the semantic data in this field to see what light such data may throw upon the problem of prejudice identification.

II.   THE SEMANTICS OF PREJUDICE

Perhaps the simplest way to recognize racial or national prejudice (in others) is to notice the ways in which people refer to other people. A person who uses the common contemptuous or patronizing terms, *nigger, coon, darkie, redskin, paleface, Chink, Jap, Wop, Spick, Dago, Hunkie, Kraut, Siwash, half-breed, Gook, Frog,* etc., may be quite unaware of the value overtones of these terms, but the sensitive listener, especially if he has been sensitized in a particular direction by repeated impact of these barbed words against his own skin, immediately spots the attitude of contempt that these terms convey. Of course, the user of such terms, when challenged, may reply that these are the terms in common usage in his group, and that he means no offense by them. "He didn't know it was loaded." Almost all of us repeatedly

offend others by a word, a tone, or a gesture, without being aware
of the fact. It is reasonable to suppose, however, that one who
takes up, however innocently, from his environment various word
usages that offend others also commonly takes up, perhaps just
as innocently, the implicit racial and national attitudes of sepa-
rateness, distance, and direction that prevail in that environment.
Why, one may ask, should the use of these terms indicate an
attitude of contempt? In some cases, this question is easily answered. The name itself may indicate association with something
mean or revolting or contemptible in the experience of the name
caller, perhaps with something that typifies the basic avoidance
reaction which human and other animals exhibit toward various
forms of filth and danger.

Such is the case, for instance, with words associating the eating
habits of a racial group with some cheap or, to the word user,
bad-smelling or repelling food, as, for example, *Frog*, *Kraut*,
Spick, or *Greaser*. In other cases the name itself has a downward-
pointing direction, e.g., *coon* (likening a person to a sub-human
animal), or *half-breed* (animals breed; humans marry and bear
children), or *Siwash* (a corruption of *sauvage*).

In still other cases, the name identifies a human being with
what he justly regards as a trivial aspect of himself such as his
skin color, as in the terms, *Negro*, *darkie*, *redskin*, or *paleface*.
The moral overtone of the designation is: the person so designated is peculiar; his outstanding characteristic is the abnormality
of his skin. Such overtones may be created by repeated usage. The
practice of most American newspapers of referring to arrested or
suspected criminals as "Negro" or "alien," if they are either, but
not as "White" or "seventh generation American," or "Protes-
tant," or "freckled," is a technique that builds popular impressions as to the criminality of Negroes or aliens which are often
very far removed from the facts. What may be called "the technique of the irrelevant adjective" is a smear technique that is
difficult to answer. When a New York Congressman objected to
Congressman Rankin's referring to him as a "Jewish Congressman from New York," Congressman Rankin's answer was, in

effect: "Well, you are Jewish, aren't you? Why be ashamed of it?"

The real issue here is not whether a racial or religious adjective is accurately descriptive of an individual but whether the adjective is properly relevant to the context in which it is used. The adjective, *Negro*, may be entirely relevant to a discussion of the medical effects of sunburn, and the adjective, *Jewish*, may be entirely relevant to a discussion of religious ritual. The relevance of these adjectives to a report of a crime wave, however, may depend upon the inarticulate premise that Negroes or Jews are especially disposed to criminal activity. Such inarticulate premises make the difference between sympathetic and unsympathetic accounts of the same event.

In some other instances it is more difficult to understand why the racial designation should be felt as a term of disparagement. (To say that this is so because the term has been used historically in a disparaging way only pushes our question one stage back.) *Dago*, for example, began apparently as a shortening of the honored Italian name, *Diego*, and *wop* as an abbreviation of *guapo* (meaning handsome), yet both terms now carry definitely disparaging overtones, as do such originally harmless abbreviations as *Jap*, *Chink*, and *Hunkie*.

Is there something about the sound of certain words that makes them carry overtones of contempt? (Is it merely a coincidence that the English language uses one-syllable words ending in *unk* to designate so many unhonored objects—*e.g.*, *bunk, chunk, dunk, drunk, flunk, hunk, junk, punk, sunk, skunk, slunk, stunk?*) Does a one-syllable word that can be uttered in less time than it takes to think, perhaps, carry an overtone of contempt more easily than a polysyllabic word or a precise phrase (*e.g.*, *American of Chinese descent*, instead of *Chink*)?

Or is there a more subtle difference between racial terms that are nouns and those that are adjectives? Would this explain why *Chinaman* is so offensive a term to most Chinese, why *Scotchman* is so offensive to most Scots, and why a boy who is Jewish normally resents being called "Jew boy"? Is it that the adjective by its form reminds us that there is always more to be said on the subject, perhaps something more important to say than has yet been said, while the noun, by its form, seems to equate an individual with a single distinguishing characteristic, so that if the chosen characteristic is trival the individual is thereby labeled as a trival individual?

I ask these questions not rhetorically, but in hopes that some answers may emerge. Such answers might help us to extend the bits of empirical knowledge that we have all acquired, from time to time, in this field of discourse, and make it possible to develop a more comprehensive and scientific understanding of the semantics of prejudice.

III. SEMANTIC EGOCENTRICISM

What my revered teacher, Ralph Barton Perry, has called the egocentric predicament shows itself with particular clarity in the language of comparative religion. Almost every religious group has a special term, generally carrying a downgrading connotation, by which it refers to outsiders. Thus to the Mohammedan, the outsider is an infidel; to the Mormon a Gentile; to the Jew a Gentile or pig-eater; and to the Christian an unbeliever or heathen. Thus, if somebody calls me a Gentile, I can be pretty sure that he is a Mormon. A man who calls me an infidel I can generally classify as a Mohammedan. And if I am referred to as an unbeliever I can generally assume that the person who so refers to me is of a Christian faith. These terms when applied to me do not give me information about myself; they do give me information about the speaker. The use of "outsider" terms thus helps to reveal the religious perspective of the user, in so far as it reflects the true believer's estimate of the relation of his own to other faiths.

If we follow Bentham's division of words into the eulogistic, dyslogistic, and neutral, we may note whether a religious reference to a particular group is sympathetic, neutral, or disparaging, by noting the word choice used in such reference. If we take four of the Western world's leading faiths and list for each faith the "insider's" eulogistic or upgrading term for his own faith as "U," list the neutral or middle term as "M," and list the "outsider" dyslogistic or downgrading term as "D," we get the following scheme:

	1	2	3	4
U	Believer	True Believer	Christian	True Christian
M	Jewish	Moslem, Mohammedan	Catholic	Protestant
D	Kike Christ-killer	Heathen, etc.	Romanist, Papist, etc.	Atheist

IV. THE TONGUE'S SECOND DIMENSION

What is important to note is that the choice between columns 1, 2, 3, and 4 on the same horizontal line, referring to four different objects, purports to tell us something about the object of discourse, while the choice of terms in any given vertical line between columns U (up, eulogistic), M (middle, neutral), and D (down, dyslogistic), all relating to the same object, tells us something about the person who is discoursing, perhaps something he did not intend to tell us, in the same way that a fossil skelton tells us something about the animal of which it was a part. Ordinarily people are trained to observe the horizontal or denotative distinctions in discourse. The anthropologists, however, have developed a special listening technique in order to note the vertical or connotative distinctions which mark out the value perspectives of the speaker. Thus, when an anthropologist listens to a native discourse on ghosts or witches, he may be learning a great deal, not about ghosts or witches, but about the value judgments of his informant.

This is a technique of observation that may be equally useful in analyzing the inarticulate moral premises of judges or legislators, who often strenuously and sincerely insist that they have no moral theories but are merely carrying out the "spirit of the Constitution," the "common law," the "dictates of precedent," or the "will of the people." Indeed, whenever a court announces, "This is a court of law and not of morals," the careful reader of judicial opinions must be prepared for a vigorous application of some moral theory as to what judges ought to do. And the more vigorously a court insists that it cannot accept social theories, no matter how plausible, the more certain we can be that the court is embarking upon a social theory that must be kept secret even from its most devoted supporters because if it were recognized as a theory, and exposed therefore to criticism, it would fade in the sunlight of open discussion.

A judge's denial of the relevance of morality or social policy may thus serve as a good indicator of his own views of morality or social policy if we read his opinion with special attention to the choices he makes between upgrading and downgrading terms.

V. THE CONJUGATION OF IRREGULAR ADJECTIVES

Bertrand Russell has called attention to the possibility of conjugating value-weighted adjectives in such form as:

1. I am firm.
2. You are obstinate.
3. He is a pig-headed fool.

More generally, we can say that almost any human characteristic may be described either in honorific or in pejorative terms. Consider, for example, how the choice between upgrading, downgrading, and neutral words to describe a given human trait or inclination may reflect a speaker's value judgment in any of the following cases:

Eulogistic	In-Between	Dyslogistic
Discreet	Cautious	Cowardly
Loyal	Obedient	Slavish
Careful	Meticulous	Fussy
Devoted	Self-subordinating	Fanatical
Kind	Soft	Mawkish
Warmhearted	Sentimental	Mushy
Tolerant	Non-discriminating	Nigger-lover, Indian-lover, etc.
Generous	Liberal	Spendthrift

Eulogistic	In-Between	Dyslogistic
Courageous	Bold	Reckless, Foolhardy
Mature	Old	Decayed
Youthful	Young	Immature
Sound	Conservative	Reactionary
Openminded	Liberal	Unsound
Practical	Aware of material factors	Mercenary
Realistic	Suspicious	Cynical
Humanitarian	Idealist	Do-gooder

VI.   VERB AND NOUN CHOICES AS VALUE INDICATORS

More subtle than the choice of adjectives (and therefore more useful in tracking down concealed value perspectives) is the value orientation that is involved in the choice of a noun or a verb to describe a given activity, operation, or institution, or to identify the position of an individual in society. Consider, for example, the varying connotations of respect or disrespect involved in the choice among the following ways of describing the position of a given individual:

Eulogistic	In-Between	Dyslogistic
Official	Office-holder	Bureaucrat
Statesman	Policy-maker	Politician
Officer	Policeman	Cop
Investigator	Detective	Flatfoot
Governess	Nursemaid	Servant
Business Executive	Employer	Boss
Financial Leader	Banker	Moneylender
		Moneychanger
Doctor	Druggist	Shopkeeper
Pilgrim	Migrant, Refugee, Immigrant	Alien
Orator	Influential Speaker	Rabblerouser

While deferential forms of speech have not attained the same high-development in Western society as in the Orient, a considerable part of our vocabulary of polite intercourse consists in using to a person's face words we do not use behind his back (*e.g.*, your Honor, your Excellency, Dear Sir, "you all"). In Vienna, for example, where politeness is carried to a high degree, it used to be (perhaps still is) customary to address a policeman by a title two grades above his actual rank.

Peculiar individual tastes have relatively little permanent impact upon a social institution like language. But where many individuals in a society share a common value standard, it is natural for them to develop a common code. Such a professional or political code will ordinarily embody, and by constant reiteration will reinforce, the standards that are implicitly held by the group in question.

These codes become particularly important in a political campaign. Our candidates may *inspire*; they never *inflame*, as do the other fellow's candidates. Our candidates may *demonstrate*; only the opposing candidates *allege*. Our candidates may *clarify*; only their opponents will *admit error*. Our candidates may *discern, enlighten, assist, serve, catalyze, counsel*, or *coöperate*. On no account will they *theorize, propagandize, abet, interfere, instigate, incite*, or *conspire*.

California's Governor Warren is reported to have made the sage observation: "When government does something for us, that's social progress; when it does something for the other fellow, that's Socialism." Political oratory may thus offer a wealth of enlightenment to the careful listener, not about the events discussed but about the value-system of the orator. Perhaps this is what was in the mind of the Talmudist who, when asked to define "a wise man," replied: "A wise man is a man who can learn from anybody."

Thurman Arnold has pointed out that the professional jargon of judges and lawyers has influenced the American mind to a point where a whole shift of vocabulary takes place when a judicial function is transferred to an administrative agency: *Procedure* becomes *red tape*; the *rule of law* yields to *bureaucratic discretion*; *precedent* disappears and *force of habit* takes its place, and so on down the line.

The language of colonial administrators offers a particularly impressive exhibition of double bookkeeping in the political field, for here professional and political value standards are largely reinforced by racial or national prides and prejudices. Even in the United States today, where at least lip service must be paid to the traditional American dislike for colonialism, a highly developed system of administrator's double-talk has made it possible for our colonial officials to profess a firm resolve to liquidate their jobs, and allow their so-called wards (for example, American Indians) full rights of citizenship, while in practice they press steadily for increased powers and increased appropriations. Under this system of double-talk, colonial officials "assist," "counsel," "serve," and "enlighten" natives, while other persons never *assist*, but only *abet*, never *advise* but only *incite*, never *serve* but only *interfere*, never *enlighten* but only *propagandize*. When native chiefs or councils make decisions for themselves, this is called *politics*; when decisions are made by colonial officials, that is called *policy-making*. When decisions are put into practice by natives, this is called *manipulation*; when colonial officials handle such matters the preferred term is *administration*. When native property is handled so as to increase its productive yield, this is called *development* if colonial officials or their licensees are doing the handling, and *exploitation* if some one else is doing the handling. When natives take advice from the colonial officials this is called *coöperation*; when they take advice from others this is called *conspiring*. By carefully keeping the two vocabularies distinct it is generally possible for a professionally trained group of administrators to persuade the public that pays its salaries that its "wards" are not yet fit to run their own businesses, manage their own lands, hold their own free elections, make their own contracts, or even decide when to go to bed and when to get up in the morning, and that increasing appropriations and powers should be granted to white officials to enable them to make such decisions for their non-white subjects.

Any white man who speaks up in defense of native freedom and thus impedes the power-drive of the colonial office is officially classified as either a "crank" or a "grafter" or a "paid agitator"— a "grafter" if the natives pay him for his help, a "paid agitator" if white sympathizers pay him, and a "crank" if nobody pays him.

When the white officialdom uncovers acts of dishonesty among its employees, this is called "raising the level of government service"; when an outsider uncovers such acts, this is called "undermining confidence in the Government."

The same semantic techniques are used on a much larger scale in the Communist world, where the "withering away of the state" is the justifying slogan for a vast increase in state power.

The following table of social action words could be expanded indefinitely if time and space permitted. It covers only a few of the key word-choices that, when applied to any given subject matter of a controversial character, may help us to identify the moral or political standpoint of the word-user:

Eulogistic	In-Between	Dyslogistic
Discern	Think	Theorize
Demonstrate	Assert	Allege
Cooperate	Act in concert	Conspire
Assist	Aid	Abet
Clarify	Retract	Admit Error
Serve	Control	Interfere
Administer	Manage	Manipulate
Service, Administration	Office	Bureau
Ownership, Property	Power to exclude	Monopoly
Develop	Create value increment	Exploit
Enlighten	Report	Propagandize
Inspire	Motivate	Inflame
Catalyze	Stir to action	Instigate
Counsel	Recommend	Incite
Social Progress	Expansion of Public Service	Socialism
Orderly Procedure	Procedure	Red tape

VII. "WE" WORDS AND "THEY" WORDS

Generally speaking, words of the first column in the foregoing three tables may be classes as "we" words. They are words which we customarily apply to our own actions and to the actions of those for whom we have a strong fellow feeling. Words of the third column, on the other hand, are "they" words, used to describe the actions of those from whom we are inclined to separate ourselves. Sometimes the relation between "we" words and "they" words involves no more than the addition of the three-letter perjorative suffix, "ism." Thus one who disapproves of peace, or psychology, or social progress, or isolation, is likely to sound much more persuasive if he denounces *pacifism, psychologism, Socialism, progressivism,* or *isolationism.* In other cases the relation of upgrading "we" words to downgrading "they" words is subtler and more difficult to delineate. But generally it is conducive to clarity to ask of any word: Is this a term I would apply to myself?

Just as the choice between "we have sinned" and "you have sinned" so often may mark the difference between effective shared effort at reform and the kind of preaching that moves only the preacher, so the subtler choice between "we" words and "they" words can often reveal moral premises of which the speaker himself may be quite unaware.

When, for example, a court begins an opinion in an Indian property case by referring to Indians moving from one place to another as *roaming, wandering,* or *roving,* we can be pretty sure that it will end up by denying the claimed property rights of the Indians. For these words are words that are commonly applied to buffalo, wolves, or other subhuman animals. They suggest that the relation of an Indian to land was a purely physical relation and not a social relation. There are plainly "out-grouping" or "they" words to describe movements which most of us, thinking of ourselves, would describe by means of such words as *traveling, vacationing,* or *commuting,* words that we would not apply to animals, words that are distinctively human. These latter words connote purpose in movement. Only when we regard a person as strange or perhaps subhuman do we customarily impute aimless motion to him. Thus, if I or a friend should move from one place to another, this physical motion will ordinarily either be described in "we" terms or be assimilated into a more highly descriptive term. We might speak of ourselves as transporting merchandise, or surveying, or berry-picking, or selling life insurance, or settling the West, depending on the occasion and purpose of the physical motion. An unfriendly Indian might disregard all these nuances and describe our action in "they" terms as *trespassing* or *invading the Indian country.* And, conversely, white judges, or white settlers who do not consider Indians quite human will be apt to disregard the purposes and occasions of Indian travel and refer to any moving Indian as a *nomad,* thereby implicitly justifying the taking of Indian lands and homes by more civilized "settlers" or corporations.

More generally, we may say that we are, each of us, likely to place ourselves and those to whom we are especially attached closer to the top than to the bottom of our value worlds. This means that "we" words will generally have a higher value direction than "they" words. For example, when a white judge refers to a defendant as a Negro, Indian, or savage, he is using an "out-grouping" line of demarcation that separates himself from the defendant. On the other hand, a judge who refers to the same defendant as a citizen, a taxpayer, a father, a husband, or a veteran, is using an "in-grouping" delineation that includes himself or honored friends. Perhaps the most significant effort of the attorneys on opposite sides of a case is the effort to persuade the judge or the jury or both to think of the defendant in "we" terms or "they" terms. This, however, is not yet part of what is generally taught in law schools. Certainly a large part of what is involved in this analysis is not yet understood by the present writer. That is why this paper is submitted, in this tentative form, in the hope that it may provoke all possible destructive criticism. . . .

X. CONCLUSION

The technique of semantic analysis will not eliminate human prejudice. It will not even provide a touchstone for distinguishing between truth and prejudice. It will not prove or disprove the hypothesis that there is an absolute relativism of values (*i.e.*, that any value system is absolutely as good as any other system). But the technique of semantic analysis, if it can be developed beyond the bare rudiments here sketched, may help us to uncover the inarticulate value premises of others and even of ourselves and thus to understand the similarities and dissimilarities that exist between any two value perspectives. Such understanding may itself lead to greater tolerance of cultural diversities. At the same time, it may help us to see more clearly the moral implications of our human egocentric limitations. Having achieved such understanding of our own limitations and distortions, we may be in a better position to help others to see theirs. To that extent, semantic analysis may help us to identify and eliminate prejudice, and thus aid us, in the long run, to achieve a greater degree of tolerance and freedom in our society.

Questions and Exercises

1. State the author's hypothesis (paragraph 7) in your own words. How has Cohen proposed to test this hypothesis?
2. To what extent has Cohen supported his thesis and argued his conclusions by the use of objective, empirical data?
3. What does the semantic variability of words like *belief, theory, fact*, and *common sense* suggest concerning the meanings words have for individuals?
4. Cohen's discussion of subjectivity is largely confined to emotionally toned words. What other devices may reveal a subjective or prejudicial perspective?
5. Distinguish between *egocentrism* and *ethnocentrism*, and give an example of each.
6. If you have difficulty understanding what is precisely meant by "value judgments," read Ralph B. Winn's discussion of "The Problem of Values," in *American Philosophy*, Philosophical Library, 1955. Construct a definition of *value judgment* that reflects Winn's thinking.
7. Compare Cohen's classification of prejudices with the classification presented by Vernon A. Langille in "Prejudice: Its Dy-

namics and Consequences," *Journal of Communication*, Autumn, 1956.

8. The author suggests that certain words tell us more about an observer than they do about the thing or event observed. Which of the categories—eulogistic, neutral, or dyslogistic—may be called most subjective? Which most objective?
9. What kind of language does Cohen himself use in speaking of his teacher, Ralph Barton Perry? Eulogistic, neutral or dyslogistic?
10. Considering what Cohen suggests about reading between the lines of a piece of writing, what would you say is Dale Warren's attitude toward commercial advertisers as revealed in "Aunt Lizzie's Lexicon"?
11. How does H. I. Phillips reveal his valuation of dictators in "Little Red Riding Hood"? How does Mark Twain reveal his valuation of *Deerslayer* in "Fenimore Cooper's Literary Offenses"?
12. What is meant by slanting? How does Loy E. Davis slant his judgment of freshmen students in "The Fable of the Man Who Read the Papers"?
13. Find as many examples as you can from your own language experiences, and from your reading, of what Cohen calls "double bookkeeping." (See Alex Bavelas' "How to Talk to the Boss," *Harper's Magazine*, July, 1955.)
14. How are eulogistic terms related to what propaganda analysts refer to as "the yes technique"?
15. Point out any place you can in the essay where Cohen uses black-and-white thinking—the either-or fallacy.
16. Anthropologists affirm that some primitive tribes have two words for "man": one word to describe themselves; another word to describe all others. How may this primitive language custom be observed among people in modern times?
17. Read Vera Micheles Dean's "A Basic Fallacy in Our View of Others," New York *Times Magazine*, May 8, 1955. How does this idea compare with Cohen's thesis?
18. S. I. Hayakawa has said: "Widespread co-operation through the use of language is the fundamental mechanism of human survival. . . . When the use of language results, as it so often does, in the creation of disagreements and conflicts, there is something wrong with the speaker, the listener, or both." What would Cohen say is this "something" that is wrong?
19. Point out the slanting apparent in the following passage and identify the techniques used to achieve it:

"You are victims of an elaborate system of make-believe under which you have an illusion that you are choosing your government. The whole system of so-called English Democracy is a fraud. England is in the hands of a small group of money lords. Do men like Churchill, Camrose, and Pothmere have at heart the well-being of the people of England? Until England is ruled by men who share the feelings of the ordinary peace-loving Englishman—the wage earning man and the home-making woman, the people of the streets and the fields—until your press is controlled by you yourselves and not by a gang of international gamblers, the peace of Europe cannot be assured."

Aunt Lizzie's Lexicon

DALE WARREN

It was from the compressed lips of my Great Aunt Lizzie that I first heard the expression "little pitchers have big ears." I was at one or the other of my two favorite listening posts, at the top of the stairs or behind the plush portieres, and Great Aunt Lizzie was talking to Cousin Hattie, who had come to call. I can see her now, in her habitual black, sitting in the old rocker before the tall French windows which gave onto a clump of lilac and syringa, and beyond which rose the graceful white spire of the Unitarian Church.

I think it was the tone of voice, accompanied by the knowing look, rather than the words themselves, that conveyed their

Reprinted from *The Saturday Review*, December 5, 1953, by permission of Dale Warren and *The Saturday Review*. Copyright 1953 by The Saturday Review, Inc.

meaning to me. Yet the rebuff itself merely whetted my curiosity and sharpened my aptitude for eavesdropping. Unwittingly Great Aunt Lizzie gave me my first lessons in etymology and etiquette. Her phraseology was as picturesque as her convictions were positive.

Where have they gone, these old familiar phrases? The rocker has become a curio, a period piece, and is probably relegated to somebody's attic if it hasn't been split up for kindling wood. And the same holds for Great Aunt Lizzie's choice collection of aphorisms. Hers was a high standard of conduct up to which few of her friends, even relations, were able to measure. I can hear her saying: "The trouble with your uncle is that he simply has no git up and git," or "If you ask me Cousin Hattie is turning into a crashing bore" (obviously the result of her recent trip to England), or "What would you expect of old Farmer Brown? He's just plain ornery," or "I wouldn't trust him for a minute; he's only a fair-weather friend, a Good Time Charlie," or with sly innuendo, "Well, if you believe all you hear she's really no better than she should be."

Not all of her remarks were derogatory, as she was as quick to cast praise as blame. Whenever she spotted a good deed in a naughty world "Blood will tell" was her ready comment. Occasionally this might be varied by "It's easy to see that he is to the manner born" or "born to the purple."

She was also fond of saying that people were "out of the top drawer" or that they were "all wool and a yard wide." Intriguing catch-phrases and equally intriguing concepts all of them to a pair of ten-year-old ears, big or otherwise. Over the word "patrician" she rolled her tongue with obvious relish, and she gave to "plebeian" an altogether different accent, for Great Aunt Lizzie, secure in her black-and-white world, was definitely on the side of the Uncommon Man.

When she said that Mr. Smith was all things to all people it was not as complimentary as it sounded. What she really implied was that he was nothing to anybody. But when she declared that Mr. Hatch's word was every bit as good as his bond you had a feeling you could always rely on Mr. Hatch even if you didn't quite know what a bond actually was. She used to say of her brother-in-law that he was content to be a big frog in a little pond, but you couldn't quite picture Great Uncle Erastus splashing around the pond where you went swimming, however much his jowls did make him look something like a frog.

And it was amusing to try to visualize one of the big mill owners as having been "born with a silver spoon in his mouth" and to picture the lesser fry "kowtowing" to his uppity wife or set on "keeping up with the Joneses." "Small potatoes" was a term she readily attached to those who appeared to her as lacking in ambition. Why potatoes? you wondered. Again it might be "warm beer" or "just tepid brew." Young people she expected to "toe the line." A person without any roots she designated as a "fly-by-night."

The language of the day included a whole galaxy of words which have since fallen into disuse or disrepute, and many of them referred to a standard of excellence toward which it was considered well for the human race to aspire. In Great Aunt Lizzie's lexicon, the Fifth Freedom was obviously the freedom to choose.

Value connoted intrinsic worth, not merely your money's worth as in the present pecuniary vogue. Quality, in the abstract sense, had a similar connotation and was used broadly enough to have spiritual, intellectual, or social implications. It has now been largely appropriated by the manufacturers and merchandisers, having reference merely to goods and commodities, a fiction supported all the way down the line from copywriter to sales lady.

"He was a man of prodigious capacity" used to mean a capacity for hard work, rewarding play, or allround achievement. It was seldom used in the present "bibulous" connection, any more than a Man of Distinction meant a man who was merely particular about what he poured into his highball glass. "Distinguished" can still occasionally be used in polite company without attracting a raised eyebrow, but the much maligned M. of D. has gone over lock, stock, and brimming barrel to the distilling interests.

Once on a time "culture" was used in a complimentary sense, and so was "poise," as "he was a man of culture" or "she was a woman of poise." Nowadays, in our climate of "Anything Goes," "culture," if not strictly medical or scientific, is mostly to be found in the researches of the historians and anthropologists or in the conversation of the intellectuals. To say that a man is cultured is almost the same as saying that he wears purple socks and tie and handkerchief to match. "Poised for flight" has become one of our most overworked clichés, but you seldom come across the word "poise" anymore unless you read the Arthur Murray advertisements.

"We think it is a lot of fun but we don't think it is everything," quipped the Midwesterner to the inbred Bostonian when the subject of "breeding" was introduced. "Breeding," which once was used as a yardstick, accurate or not, for taking human measurements has generally been regulated to the animal kingdom. Otherwise the ready smirk or wisecrack. And everybody knows the metamorphosis of "discriminate," "discriminating," and "discrimination," although no one can quite tell you how they have come to lose face or why they have teamed up with the word "against." To discriminate, if you consult a dictionary, still means "to distinguish accurately." The ability to do so, in the eclectic sense, was once considered a virtue. To "murder the King's English" used to be regarded as little short of a crime, but if today there are fewer indictments on this charge it may be because it is so much easier simply to change the meaning.

"Genteel" has become outmoded as the gentility of *Godey's Lady's Book*, "Elite" has gone as well, except when applied to the latest line of hosiery or footwear. The adjective "exclusive," formerly restricted to clubs, resorts, and finishing schools, is now practically the exclusive property of restaurants, hotels, haberdashery stores, dress shops, imported goods, and suburban real-estate developments. "Selective" has been taken over by the military, as in Selective Service Act, while Select, as well as Genuine, is now coupled with Brand. "Refined," having become confused in the popular mind with effete, has dropped from most vocabularies. Sugar and wheat may still be refined, but you would think twice before using it to characterize your best friend. No more would you think of calling him "cultivated." Gardens may still be cultivated (does anybody still read "Candide"?) but not people. "Aristocratic" carries a full load of reproach; yet the seed catalogues boldly proclaim their delphiniums to be the true aristocrats of the perennial kingdom.

"Sophisticated," in modern American usage, has come to mean affected, and "cosmopolitan," even if considered proper for a club or a magazine, is seldom used to describe one who has got the straw out of his hair. "Stylish" has gone over to the advertising fraternity, and the society editor has taken a strangle hold on "fashionable," which she prefixes to any and all references to weddings. "Subtle" has subtly come to take on the meaning of devious, and if you say of someone that he is "astute" you must have a ready answer to "What's his angle?" "Temperament" used to be considered an asset, as it was analogous to spirit, whether applied to man or horse, but if you happen to say that someone is temperamental it is immediately assumed that he is unstable or unreliable. "Imaginative" is only rarely interpreted in the creative sense; in contemporary terminology it has come to mean that you are beginning to imagine things and are probably headed for a psychiatrist.

"Boy, she's got class!" was considered a fit epithet for the flapper of the Scott Fitzgerald decade, whereas the whistling wolf of today is content with such bebop understatement as "she sends me." The flapper returned the compliment by proclaiming: "He's a prince." Bobby-soxer, or older, now settles for "a good Joe," and "date" does double duty as both personalized noun and verb. "Classy" was a distinction applied with equal enthusiasm to a girl, a night club, an automobile, or a job, and "Ritzy" was then spelled with a capital "R."

The days of the swell and the dandy are gone beyond recall, but the adjectives are apparently here to stay.

"High hat" was a term guaranteed to put the snob in his place, but high hats, even if not stocked with white rabbits, are now as hard to visualize as to procure, if only for the still lingering, if only occasional, Fancy Dress. "White collar," and "stiff-necked" along with it, has also lost ground in competition with the ubiquitous open-neck, tail-free sport shirt—which is really nothing more than a glorified pyjama top. "Stuck up" has also become obsolete, and "ostentatious" has turned into "putting on the dog."

"Snob appeal," and whatever it may connote, has a heady attraction for the advertiser and copywriter. Otherwise how account for converting the lowly mothball into Para-Dichloro Benzene? It's smart to be in the know, so wrap everything up in fancified language and the consumer will beat a path to your door. The morning newspaper urges one in need of a fresh tube of tooth paste to ask for "Pepsodent's exclusive oral detergent." How fancy can you get?

"High brow," as the language becomes purged, is fast giving away to "egghead," and in certain circles liberal has come to mean pink if not downright red. Tradition has become synonymous with reaction. Classical music is now denoted as long-hair, and the drama comes under the heading of Show Biz. Boob, distinct from boor, had a meaning of its own back in the Twenties when Mencken went a step further and coined his much-quoted "booboisie." "Jerk" is the word in today's vernacular—and even "bourgeoisie" has scuttled right out of the American language, together with other shocking French phrases such as "noblesse oblige," "jeunesse dorée," "laissez faire," "nouveau riche," "dernier cri," "tout bien ou rien," "au courant," "comme il faut," "en masse," "succès d'estime," "de trop," "de rigueur," "haut monde," "savoir faire," and "crème de la crème." With valet and chauffeur, debutante and even divorcee beginning to slip, it would seem that "hors d'oeuvres," however it may be pronounced, has alone survived transplanting.

The language of a period, we are told by the semantics

specialists, is an index of its "culture"—or the lack of it. Frederick L. Allen has isolated and dissected "The Big Change" which has set 1950 at several removes from 1900. The Century of Henry Wallace has run half its course and we are living in what Krutch and others have come to accept as the Age of the Common Man, a leveling off which, according to D. W. Brogan, has brought with it "the new democratic snobbery." In an era of shifting standards and values, mass production has assumed the spoon-feeding of the mass mind through the media of mass communication. As a descriptive adjective "mass" has managed to save face, but the populace, once disrespectfully designated as the masses, has now become individualized and personalized. The Common Man is used in the singular and spelled with capital letters and, having supplanted the common herd, carries its own special inflection. One has to keep jumping to catch up with the gyrations of the once so-called vulgar tongue.

The accepted colloquialisms of the time were never questioned by Great Aunt Lizzie, and their meaning, plain as a pikestaff she would have said, was so clear and so precise that she had no need for recourse to the French or any other foreign language. The only occasions on which I can recall her stepping out of line—hers was the day of the much-prized Classical Education— were those on which she said her piece about (the) Hoi Polloi. Although the phrase has persisted for an eon or two, and is written with capitals as well, it survives only in the lingo of Jimmy Durante, where it is always good for a laugh. The explanation obviously lies in the fact that Jimmy Durante is *sui generis* (excuse the Latin) and that the redoubtable Jimmy has cagily twisted it into Hoi Pollou.

Questions and Exercises

1. The author says "Great Aunt Lizzie gave me my first lessons in etymology and etiquette." What precisely is *etymology*? Supply the authors and titles of at least three dictionaries of etymology.

2. What is the etymology of the following words? *kowtow, pecuniary, metamorphosis, genteel, sophisticated, scuttle, populous.*
3. Define the following words which appear in the essay. Use a good college dictionary if you need to.

aphorism	pecuniary	eclectic
innuendo	derogatory	redoubtable
galaxy	connotation	maligned
prodigious	bibulous	metamorphosis
ubiquitous	gyrations	lingo

4. What is meant by the phrase "black-and-white world" in the fifth paragraph?
5. What influence in society has altered the meaning and connotation of the word *distinguished?* What other words have been similarly affected?
6. What is revealed about dictionary definitions in the discussion of *discriminate?* Why cannot lexicographers keep up with changes in the language?
7. What is the meaning of the italicized words in the following phrases or expressions? "advertising *fraternity*," "whistling *wolf*," "*glorified* pyjama top," "*spoon-feeding* of the mass mind," "*vulgar* tongue."
8. What does Warren say of the monetary value to advertisers of using "fancy language"? Do you think this may be taken as a fixed and established rule? Can you find exceptions? What words frequently used by advertisers offend rather than impress you?
9. What French expressions have survived "transplanting" that Warren has overlooked?
10. Explain how the following passage from *Harper's Magazine*, May, 1955, supports the idea developed by Warren in his essay.
"What this country needs is a good five-cent word to describe itself. We have invented a new social system—perhaps the most interesting social contraption since Mumtaz Mahal invented the brassiere in 1608—but we haven't yet thought up a name for it. So we keep on trying to describe it with a set of labels which were devised long ago to fit something entirely different. . . . The new society . . . obviously is quite different from anything the world has ever seen. It doesn't resemble the 'capitalism' of Adam Smith any more than a Super-Constellation resembles a prairie schooner. It certainly isn't 'free enterprise' as Andrew Carnegie used that phrase—

or as some of his mental contemporaries, such as Senator
Homer E. Capehart, still use it. . . ."

11. Show how the word *snobbery* is affected by its context in the
expression "democratic snobbery." In this connection read the
essay in this volume "Meaning and Context," by Monroe C.
Beardsley.

12. Select ten of the familiar expressions, like "plain as a pikestaff,"
which appear in this essay, and determine by referring to one or
more of the dictionaries prepared on historical principles (OED,
DAE, DA) the earliest recorded usage for the expression.

13. By referring to your handbook of composition or communication, or a recent textbook on the history and development of
English, specify five different kinds of semantic change that alter
word meanings from one time to another. Supply five examples
of each type of change.

14. Write a 150–250-word paper on the subject "Words Use Men"
in which you cite several examples of how people are influenced by words, slogans, or stereotyped expressions.

The Geography of English

MARIO PEI

As is invariably the case with all tongues, great and small,
English has succumbed to the inherent centrifugal tendency
of language to break up into local varieties or dialects. This
tendency was responsible for the original fractionalizing of Indo-
European into its various groups (Germanic, Celtic, Slavic,
Italic, Greek, Indo-Iranian, etc.). Continuing to operate unin-
terruptedly, it led to the division of Germanic into Gothic,

From *The Story of English* by Mario Pei. Copyright 1952 by Mario Pei. Published by J. B. Lippincott Company. Reprinted by permission of the publisher.

Scandinavian and West Germanic, the last of which ultimately split up into German, Dutch and English. We have already seen that Anglo-Saxon showed dialectal divisions into Northumbrian, Mercian, Kentish and West Saxon, and that Middle English continued this dialectal division with a Northern, a Southern, and two Midland forms.

Today the dialectal divisions of English continue in part these traditional splits on English soil. But new varieties have sprung up, owing to the departure of the language from its homeland. English speakers from different or the same dialect areas, moving to new lands in the Western Hemisphere, Australia, New Zealand and South Africa, have in the course of time differentiated themselves from those who remained on the British Isles, with the result that one may speak of a "British" English, subdivided into various dialects; of an "American" English, which in the course of three brief centuries has nevertheless had time to evolve varieties of its own; of "Australian," "New Zealand" and "South African" English, in which local dialectal forms are not yet outstanding; and of an entire series of English sub-varieties and Pidgins, born of the attempt on the part of native colonial populations to adapt Imperial or Federal English to their own speech-habits.

There are on British soil at least twenty-four separately identifiable local varieties of speech, most of which are far more divergent among themselves than are corresponding varieties of American speech. To a large extent the English dialects still group themselves around the traditional Middle English divisions (North, South, East Midland, West Midland), with the addition of Scottish, Welsh and Irish adaptations. To some degree, the British dialects are matters of intonation. As one extremely keen American observer, writing for the *Christian Science Monitor*, puts it, "In the west country, you will hear a rich and leisurely burr; in Wales, a melodious attack in the speech, which lends itself to singing; in London, a sharp-witted staccato Cockney; in East Anglia, an odd, almost shy lilt; in the Midlands, a deliberate down-to-earth quality which matches the great central plain; in the North, a hard, vigorous utterance full of dialectal words; in the Northeast, surprisingly, a tongue as soft and gracious as a southern wine; in Scotland and Ireland, a dozen associated accents and dialects, so marked and evocative that you will probably remember them long after the sights that went with them have faded from the mind. . . ."

The divergence of American from British English was first noticed around 1750, and by 1800 the first acrimonious discussions had arisen. There were half-hearted attempts on both sides of the ocean to make the divorcement between the two speech-forms complete, but they were, luckily, dismal failures. As late as 1933 the *Shorter Oxford Dictionary* specifically disclaims making allowance for dialectal, colonial or "American" pronunciations, reflecting the uncompromising stand of speakers of the King's English in this matter. Our own dictionaries on the other hand, mostly favor a New England pronunciation, which is closest to that of England.

In matters of phonology, it may be remarked that American generally preserves more of a spelling-pronunciation than does English (the influence, perhaps, of schoolmarms and spelling bees). It neglects the obscuring of unstressed vowels and the drastic lopping off of unstressed syllables which is characteristic of British speech. As a by-product, we have secondary stress in long words where the British have none (*interésting* vs. *int'resting, legislátive* vs. *législative, dictionáry* vs. *díctionary*). This may offend British ears, but it is less disconcerting than pronouncing *Cholmondeley* as *Chumley, Beauchamp* as *Beecham*, and *Leicester* as *Lester*. It also, incidentally, proves the power of the written language over the spoken.

The British may not approve of our pronunciation, but they usually subscribe to our vocabularly innovations, perhaps to a greater degree than we subscribe to theirs. It is in vain that the Fowlers protest against such rank Americanisms as *back of, anyway, standpoint, right along* and *just,* for the British now use them too.

It is probable, though not proved, that more vocabulary

innovations have come into the language from American than from British sources in the course of the last three centuries. Baugh, in a long list of American words, gives us the key to this phenomenon. On the one hand, new physical conditions in a new continent call for new words (*clearing, underbrush, garter snake, groundhog, land office, apple butter, sidewalk, hitch-hike, low-down, have an axe to grind, fly off the handle, bury the hatchet*). On the other hand, Americans were in contact with foreign languages more than their British cousins during the period of colonization and wholesale immigration. The Indians gave us *porgy, terrapin, tomahawk, wigwam, sachem*, and such loan-translations as *warpath, paleface* and *medicine man*. From the French we got *portage, chowder, cache, bayou, levee*; from the Dutch *coleslaw, cookie, boss* and *scow*; from the Germans *noodle, pretzel* and *sauerkraut*; from the Negroes *banjo, hoodoo, jazz*; from the Chinese *kowtow, fantan, tong* and *yen*; from the Jews *kosher* and *mazuma*. Our own coinage gave us *nickels* and *dimes* and *dollars* and *eagles* after eighteenth-century *marks* and *quints* had disappeared. M. M. Mathews, who has gathered in his *Dictionary of Americanisms* no less than fifty thousand words and terms, has traced the history of most of those American contributions to the common language, showing, among other things, that Admiralty Island Indians (Hutsnuwus tribe) gave rise to a crude firewater called, after them, *kootznehoo*, and later *hooch*; that *appendicitis*, and *moron* were born on American soil; and that we too, despite the briefness of our national history, can render words obsolete. Many reputed Americanisms, when tracked down, have been found to be of British origin. Mathews, for example, discovered that the term *cracker* as applied to poor whites in the South has the original meaning of "boaster," "braggart," which is a Scottish usage. *Ain't*, of course is found on English soil at least as far back as Shakespeare, and the same applies to *without* for *unless*.

Intriguing as are the dialects of Old World English, those of American are at least as fascinating. Twenty-four major varieties have been listed, and Linguaphone recordings of them have been duly made under the direction of Columbia University phoneticians. (These recordings are said to be of special practical value to travelling salesmen.) The scientific study of American dialects began in 1889 with the American Dialect Society, and its principal milestones are Mencken's *American Language* of 1919, the quarterly *American Speech*, G. P. Krapp's monumental *English Language in America* of 1925, the University of Chicago's *Historical Dictionary of American English*, and the *Linguistic Atlas of the United States*, directed by Hans Kurath and numerous associates.

Insofar as it is possible to condense the mass of findings accumulated by these scholars, it may be said that American speech-forms have three major groupings, an Eastern, a Southern and a Midwestern or General American; but within each group variations are numerous and profound, and large cities like New York, Boston and Philadelphia have developed many local peculiarities.

The work of the *Linguistic Atlas* in particular has revealed interesting by-facts, such as the migration routes of our earliest settlers, and the existence of focal or "prestige" areas whose speech is admired and imitated in the surrounding country. Characteristic of the first is the cattle-call *chay*, used around Williamsburg, South Carolina, and duplicated only in County Antrim, Ireland, from which the original Williamsburg settlers must have come; the *pavement* (sidewalk) of Philadelphia, betraying the conservatism of that city in keeping the British word; the *smearcase* of Pennsylvania (from the German *Schmierkäse*) as opposed to the Hudson Valley *potcheese* (from Dutch *potkaas*), and the western New England Dutch *cheese*, an evident coinage.

Both New England and the South drop final -*r*, which the West retains. This parallels the development of the Southern British dialects as against the North of England, and would seem to fit the area migration theory. Clark, however, advances the possibility that final -*r* may at one time have been universal in American speech, and that the South and East, being in touch with southern England, may have dropped it in imitation of the official pronunciation of the home country, while the Midwest, which had lost its overseas contacts, firmly retained the -r. New England, however, inserts a parasitic r in such expressions as I sawr'im, which the South generally does not do. The open sound of o appears in the New England pronunciation of fog, hot, coffee, long, the broad a-sound in ask, grass, bath, the short sound of u in proof. The South, on the other hand, tends to drop final consonants in words like find and kept, and to diphthongize open e (fin', kep', yais, aigg). Other vowel distinctions separate the West from both East and South (typical key words are wash, fog, daughter, house, bird, and now the notorious merry, Mary, marry, where a threefold distinction prevails east of the Alleghanies, but not to the west).

But the main American dialectal distinctions are in vocabulary. An extreme case reported by the Linguistic Atlas is the name of the insect generally known as a "dragon-fly"; in New England it is a devil's darning needle, in parts of New Jersey a spindle, in the Pennsylvania German country a snake waiter, in the Appalachians a snake feeder, while in other parts of the South it is a snake doctor or mosquito hawk. Closet, outhouse, bull are words to be avoided in certain areas of the United States; for the last, there is an entire series of euphemisms: he-brute, stock cow, even gentleman cow and preacher cow. Evening is synonymous with afternoon in some Southern rural districts. Imaginative are chicken hollerin' time for early morning and greenup time for Spring. One generally parks a car, but in Trenton he ranks it, and in southern Delaware he files it. The differences between bag, sack and poke are geographical; so are those between carry and tote, (city) block and square, calling up and phoning up. In South Dakota you don't belong to get up till 9 A.M. A grocery-store sign advertising mangoes in the Midwest does not imply an offer of tropical fruit, but only of green peppers. A heavy rain is a gulley-washer, frog-strangler or chunk-floater, depending on your location, and Midwestern weather bureaus have been known to speak of "slow and gentle sizzle-sozzle" instead of "continued rain" (the South would probably call it *falling weather*). Oklahoma requests you not to "*cabbage on to me* every time I pass," and Philadelphia food-stores have a widely advertised *hoagy* which on investigation turns out to be a real he-man sandwich. New York uses the Dutch *stoop* for something resembling a porch, while the Texas term is *gallery*. *Get shut of* and *jin* are still occasionally heard in the Midwest for "*get* rid of" and "do odd jobs." West Virginia describes a Ph.D. as a "*teach-doctor*, not a real doctor."

In connection with the American dialects, the less said about grammar the better. One grammatical feature of general interest is the so-called "generous plural," represented in the South by *you-all* (for which there is Biblical precedent in Job 17:10), in eastern cities by *youse*, with an intermediate *you-uns*, and a localized *mongst-ye* heard on Albemarle Sound and in Norfolk. The humorous features of American dialectal grammar are illustrated by Uncle Remus' "You er what you is, en you can't be no is-*er*"; by the spurious weather report "It blew and snew and then it thew, and now, by jing, it's friz"; and by the seemingly authentic apology of a farmer who was being chided for driving past a friend on the highway without any sign of recognition: "If I'd knowed it wuz you, I'd a retch out an' wove!"

The Linguaphone Institute once conducted a poll to ascertain where, from the standpoint of diction, the best English in America is spoken. The three winners were Washington, Nashville and Boston, with New York proudly holding last place.

This naturally leads us to a discussion of the linguistic situation in the nation's greatest metropolis, and particularly in its most picturesque and best-loved borough, Brooklyn. To begin with, Brooklynites are accused of sharing with County Kerry Irishmen the characteristic of never answering a question directly, but only by asking another ("Do you think the Dodgers will win the pennant?" "Why shouldn't they?"; "What do you think of the Korean situation?" "What am I, a radio commentator?").

The three major criticisms levelled against untutored Brooklyn phonology are (1) the double substitution of *er* for *oi* and *oi* for *er*, as in *Soiving the Erster*, or *Let us adjoin to the adjerning room*; (2) the intrusion of a parasitic hard *g* after *ng* and before a vowel, as in *Long Guyland*, or *getting gout*; (3) the substitution of *d* for the *t* and voiced *th* sounds in *city, little, the, them*, etc., and of *t* for unvoiced *th* in *threw, third*. In grammar, there are such triple negatives as "an' I don' never git no breaks." It may be remarked that these features are by no means restricted to Brooklyn, or even to Greater New York.

These and similar characteristics have led a Representative from Texas to remark that New York "isn't an English-speaking place," a statement which drew not merely hot retorts from New York language authorities, but also a jocular *Voyager's Language Guide* containing such expressions as *Pahrmee* (described as a translation from the French *pardonnez-moi*), *lemeawf* (an expression said to be often helpful in debarkation from the subway) and *aniainfoolin* (interpreted as "This, I want you to understand, is an order").

Defenders of the New York speech and its Brooklyn subvariety were at pains to point out that *goil* is a better rendering than the *gel* or *gairl* of Britain, that an "ultimate *r*" gets added to the Oxford and Harvard as well as to the Brooklyn pronunciation of *India* and *law*, and that Brooklyn contractions of the type of *gumnt* and *jeet* for *government* and *did you eat* go *pari passu* with Britain's syncopated *Chumley* and *Lester*.

"Brooklynese," said Dr. Bender, "is no upstart. It has a fine tradition going back to the early Dutch burghers. Despite its age, it is still virile and is spreading." Bronx Borough President Lyons, riding forth gallantly to the defense of the New York–Brooklyn speech, charged that "some Texans speak a language no one understands."

But this, too, is an exaggeration. Practically all Americans understand one another, even if, according to the Linguaphone survey, "their speech-patterns are typical of the lazy South," as in Atlanta, or "they sound as though they are being chased by gangsters," as in Chicago; or "they speak as if they had hot potatoes in their mouths," as in Los Angeles.

What is more, they generally manage to understand their British, Canadian, Australian, South African and New Zealand cousins. The English language is fundamentally one, and one it will remain while the institutions of the English-speaking world stand. The language is one of empire—not the empire of physical domination and brute force, but the empire of individual freedom and achievement, of tolerance and consideration for others; in one word, of what a great political leader has chosen to call "the Empire of the Mind."

Questions and Exercises

1. Modern standard English, both British and American, developed from the Mercian dialect. Do whatever research is necessary to discover how and why this dialect became the currency of communication for most English-speaking people, the world over.
2. Noah Webster, the famous American lexicographer, predicted that in the course of 200 years the British and American people would not be able to communicate without benefit of translator. Mention several reasons why his prediction was wrong.
3. H. W. Horwill, in *An Anglo-American Interpreter*, has presented a list of outstanding divergenicies between British and American English. H. L. Mencken, in *The American Language: Supplement One*, included a somewhat similar list. Study these lists and write a short paper in which you characterize some of the essential differences between British and American English.
4. To what extent do you think that the differences between British and American English are increasing or decreasing? Explain.
5. Stephen Leacock was a Canadian. What evidence do you find in his essay "Anyone Can Learn to Write" of peculiarities of style which differ from American usage?
6. Pei says that "our own dictionaries mostly favor a New England pronunciation." Determine to what extent the following three college dictionaries agree on "approved" pronunciation:
   American College Dictionary
   Webster's New World Dictionary
   Webster's New Collegiate Dictionary

7. Look up one of the listed words in Hans Kurath's *A Word Geography of the Eastern United States,* and report to the class on the regional variations you can discover. Can you add to Kurath's list?

   living room, porch, picket fence, pail, faucet, kerosene, sidewalk, corn bread, doughnut, pancake, cottage cheese, midwife.

8. Linguists say that there is no such thing as standard English, only varieties of English. By what standard do you suppose it was determined that in Washington, Nashville, Boston, and New York the "best" English in America is spoken?

9. Is there any relationship between regional varieties in English and cultural or class distinctions? Read Clifton Fadiman's "Party of One," in *Holiday,* October, 1956.

10. What differences in vocabulary, grammar, pronunciation, accent, etc., do you detect between the way you employ language and the way most other members of your class do? Who is right? Read "Do You Talk Good American?" *Changing Times,* January, 1957.

11. Account for the fact that American English contains more innovations than British English. Read "Hallmarks of American" in H. L. Mencken's *The American Language: Supplement One,* and list the principal features of American English which Mencken discusses. Supply current expressions which offer examples of as many of these categories as you can.

12. Explain the fact that there are more noticeable regional differences in the way English is spoken than in the way it is written.

13. Write a paper entitled "The Empire of the Mind" in which you elaborate on the author's thought in the last paragraph of of the essay.

14. What specific forces in American society today tend to eliminate regional differences in language? Why is it more and more difficult to make an accurate recording of existing differences?

15. Explain how regional variations in language record the social history of a region. Cite specific examples to support this thesis.

16. What point made by Donald J. Lloyd in "Snobs, Slobs and the English Language" is the subject of this essay?

IV. FOCUS ON IDEAS

Whenever people engage in verbal communication, they exchange, not words and sentences, but thoughts and ideas. Words are merely the vehicle by which the ideas are transported or conveyed. Too much attention to the words themselves, or to purely mechanical matters of structure and syntax, may actually blur and obfuscate the ideas they are expected to carry. In order to successfully determine the precise meaning of any verbal passage, either written or spoken, one must discover the central idea—the nucleus of the thought intended.

The unfolding of an idea is the initial act in the process of communication. An idea is a thought or insight created in the face of desire by the intellect and emotions acting on the facts of experience. No one knows exactly what happens in the brain and nervous system when an insight flashes into consciousness. But this much is clear: unless words start the machinery of reflective thinking, they are nothing more than meaningless stabs in the dark. When a reader or listener is able to recreate in his own mind the ideas conceived by a writer or speaker, successful communication has been established.

Perhaps the easiest way to understand the nature of ideas is to consider them as solutions to recognized problems. This means simply that if you want to corner the idea in a given selection all you need to do is determine what problem the author is concerned with, and then find his solution to it, or his disposition of it. The essays in this section of the anthology, selected for their emphasis on ideas, offer opportunity for such treatment. In some of the essays the idea is stated in clear, positive, and direct language. In others, the idea is implied and must be determined by examination of the style of writing, the organization of details, and the association and juxtaposition of verbal images.

Two of the essays in this section are directly concerned with problems of education. Robert M. Hutchins and Marion Walker Alcaro present opposing views regarding the kind of education which may best prepare students for domestic, civic, and professional life. The other essays focus on various significant problems of our society. John A. Kouwenhoven, in "What's American about America?" attempts to find a single unifying thread which will unite the diverse elements which make up American society and culture. Mark Twain, in "Huck and Jim on the Raft," presents a sensitive and sympathetic study of the problem of individual rights versus the powers of the state. Loren C. Eiseley, in "The Bird and the Machine," is concerned with the basic freedoms of individuals in a highly complex and overregulated society. And James Thurber, in "Oliver and the Other Ostriches," points out some of the implications of majority rule in the safeguarding of individual rights and privileges of citizens in a democracy.

◆ ◆ ◆

Why Go to College?

ROBERT M. HUTCHINS

MOST AMERICAN parents want to send their children to college. And their children, for the most part, are anxious to go. It is an American tradition that there is something about a college that transforms an ordinary infant into a superior adult. Men and

Reprinted from *The Saturday Evening Post*, January 22, 1938. Copyright 1938 by The Curtis Publishing Company. Reprinted by permission of George T. Bye, author's representative.

women who have been to college sometimes suspect that this is not the case, but they seldom say so. They are alumni, and, as such, it is their life work to maintain the tradition that college—their college anyway—is the greatest place in the world.

College is the greatest place in the world for those who ought to go to college and who go for the right reasons. For those who ought not to go to college or who go for the wrong reasons, college is a waste of time and money.

Who should go to college? In order to answer this question, we might well begin by deciding who should not. My experience with college, as student, teacher and commencement orator, convinces me that the following persons should not go to college:

Children whose parents have no other reason for sending them than that they can afford to.

Children whose parents have no other reason for sending them than to get them off their hands for four years.

Children whose characters are bad and whose parents believe that college will change them for the better.

Children who have no other reason for going to college than to avoid work or have a good time for four years.

Children who have no other reason for going to college than to have a stadium in which to demonstrate their athletic ability.

Children who have no other reason for going to college than the notion that it will help them achieve social or financial success in later life.

These children should be kept at home, or they should be sent to a country club, a trade school, or a body-building institute. There is, or should be, no place for them in an institution whose only excuse for existing is the training of the mind.

If we may then proceed to the original question—"Who should go to college?"—I submit the following answer:

Anyone should go to college who has demonstrated both an aptitude and a desire for more education than he has been able to get in elementary and high school. And I may add that to deprive any such person of a college education because his parents cannot afford to give him one is to commit an offense not only against the individual but also against society at large.

One of the surprising aspects of American society is its indifference to poor men's sons and daughters who give promise of leadership in the national life. It is true that we have scholarships and devices for self-support of college students. But our scholarships are too few to begin to accommodate those who deserve them. And self-support means that a college student who needs all his time to get an education has to devote half of it to earning a living.

There is something of true nobility about the boy—or girl— who works his way through school. To such young people as these, education is an opportunity, not a ritual. It means the sacrifice of gaiety at the age when gaiety is prized highest. It means work, work and more work. The individual who survives this grueling experience is likely to display a high order of industry and courage his life long. But it is precisely because the self-supporting student is likely to be the worthiest student that he should be relieved of the burden of self-support. If, instead of holding down a job from four to eight hours a day, he is able to devote those hours to the development of his mind, our country might produce more Michelsons, Holmeses and Deweys.

In England, a country which has produced more than its share of the world's leaders, the number of scholarships is such that almost no boy or girl who deserves a college education goes without one. It is said that half the students at Oxford and Cambridge are there on scholarships. The Scotch have the world's most comprehensive system for discovering promising young people and supporting them in college. Hence the Scotch rule England.

Those who should go to college should go to get an education. Because the colleges of the United States have allowed themselves to be used for purposes other than education, it has never been easier than it is today, for those who can afford it, to get into college. Nor has it ever been easier to stay in college and be graduated. The only thing that is really difficult to do is get an education. If, however, a young person came to me and told me he wanted to get an education, I would preach him a sermon somewhat as follows:

You can get an education in college if you try. But you must bring three things with you: A certain minimum intellectual equipment, habits of work, and an interest in getting an education. Without them, you can still get into college and stay there for four years. You can have a good time; you can keep out of trouble; you can get a degree and become a full-fledged alumnus with a proprietary interest in all subsequent football scores; but you cannot get an education.

With them, you can get an education and become an enlightened human being. Every college library contains the world's great books. They will not be out when you ask for them. And there is scarcely a college in America that does not have on its faculty at least a few men who have refused to let themselves be used for purposes other than education. It will not be difficult to find them. They will familiarize you with the leading ideas in their own fields. They will interest you in the relations between their own and other fields. And they will suggest how, when you have fulfilled the comparatively easy requirements of your courses, you can educate yourself.

Unless you find these men and listen to them, unless you find the books you should read and read them, you will find college, aside from social life and athletics, a dull place. You will find that college, like the rest of the educational system, is set up for what is known as the "average" student. When you apply for admission, no one will ask you, "What do you know?" You will be asked instead, "How many years have you spent in school?" Your high-school credits will be examined, and if you have succeeded in obtaining "average" grades by bringing the teacher an apple, or by memorizing the dates of Shakespeare's birth and death, you will be admitted to the Elysian fields of the higher learning. The occasional college which has some additional criteria for admission does not demand much more.

Then, you will find that in college, as in high school, you have only to study the professors and memorize some more information.

You will be filled with countless useless facts, 60 per cent of which you will have to repeat to pass countless tests. You may find your intellectual interest stifled by the hopeless prospect of acquiring all the miscellaneous information you are told you must possess. You will tread your weary round, picking up a fragment here and a fragment there, until you have been examined on fragment after fragment and served your time.

This is the fate that awaits you unless you are determined to hew your way through the underbrush of mediocrity and get an education. When you come to college determined to get one, you will find yourself confused at the beginning. Your previous schooling has done little more than teach you, in a broad way, how to read and write; it takes a person ten or twelve years to learn how to do those two things well. When you come to college, you will be interested in acquiring an understanding of the leading ideas in each great field of knowledge. It will require hard work on your part to master these ideas, but students before you have mastered them and few of them were geniuses. So you will not let the appearance of confusion confuse you; you will buckle down to the business at hand and avoid, in so far as it is possible, the pleasant distractions of the campus.

At the end of your first semester or your first year, you will return home to visit your parents. They will want to know what you have learned, and you will try to tell them. Even if you have been determined to get an education, you will be only partly educated, so what you tell them may disturb them. Being only partly educated, you may be most excited by the ideas which, when you have become fully educated, you will realize were among the least important you encountered. If your parents are wise, they will wait until you are fully educated before they decide whether your education has been worth the expense.

Wise as your parents may be, they may have been influenced

by the traditional American attitude toward college. They may want to know whether you made the freshman team, the college paper, or a "good" fraternity. Perhaps you have had the agility to get on the team, the time to try out for the paper, or the money and clothes to get into a "good" fraternity. Perhaps you have had none of these prerequisites for extra-curricular achievement. Perhaps you have had some or all of the prerequisites, but have discovered that getting an education requires all your agility and all your time. In any case, you will inform your misguided parents that much as you hate to disappoint them, you came to college to get an education and cannot be held accountable for failing to get anything else.

You will return to college at the end of your first semester or your first year and pursue your studies. They will get harder as you go along. You will have to think harder and work harder. And the college which you are attending may make it hard to stick to the business of getting an education. For the college you are attending will probably be one that is distinguished for its financial resources, its athletic facilities and its social advantages; most American colleges are. You will have comfortable quarters and good food. Gentlemen purchased at what, for the teaching profession, are good salaries will exhort themselves to keep you amused. Gentlemen purchased at even higher salaries will exert themselves to keep you employed in the gymnasium and on the athletic field. Your associates will be gentlemen. You will like them and they will like you. If you expend no more effort on your courses than you have to, you will find little difficulty in passing them, for they are adjusted to the ability of the average student. This is the unrippled stream of "college life" down which you may meander if you want to.

Do you want to? My classmates and I did. We went to college to go through the formalities, to become college men, to get to know the fellows. The fellows we got to know were those who provided us with the gayest amusements and the most profitable relationships and who afterward formed a great brotherhood ready and willing to help out, socially, politically and financially, those of the brethren who were down on their luck.

The stock of prejudices we brought with us to college remained largely unimpaired when we left it. If we had our corners knocked off, and thus got a kind of education, it was largely because we were associated with a lot of bright young men who took peculiar pleasure in jumping on people for the slightest deviation from the normal. We didn't care to be jumped on, so we never deviated from the normal after we found out what it was.

It was not normal then to depart from the traditional apparel. We all wore the same kind of clothes, just as you are expected to, the only difference being that our coat and pants had to match and yours must not. It was not normal to be sentimental about the college, except in song, nor was it normal to be friendly in conversation unless our remarks were prefaced by enough insults to show that we were manly.

We gradually grew into the likeness of one another, and a rather pleasant likeness we thought it was too. We had the conviction that the society of the great world would welcome us. And so it did, on the whole. The ideals of our era were conformity and "getting ahead." We had already achieved conformity, and we looked as if we would "get ahead," so the world welcomed us.

It made the mistake of believing we were educated. It did not take the trouble, nor did it know how, to discover that we were not. How could we be? College life had offered us a great many things, including education. We had imbibed deeply of those features that were pleasantest and most admired by the outside world. We had not insisted on getting an education, and college had not insisted that we either get one or get out and make room for people who wanted one.

Now that we are old and kicking around in a world which is worse off than it was before we entered it, we wonder if we might not have acquired the social and physical graces by spending four years in the Y.M.C.A. or the Elks. These bodies have high ideals, they are organized for mutual improvement and good fellowship, and their dues are lower than the tuition our parents laid out for our college education.

If you ignore your opportunity as we ignored ours, the world may not let you off as easily as it did us. If you go to college, you will do well to insist on getting an education, as we did not.

As I look around me from the vantage point of my advanced years, I am unconvinced, unlike many of my colleagues, that it is any easier to get a real education today than it was in the Gay 20's. The depression no more sobered the colleges and the universities than it sobered the nation at large. With the return of material prosperity to certain areas of the population, our institutions of higher learning are as much concerned with the social and physical welfare of their students as they were before the crash. This concern may please parents whose ideals remain the ideals of the 20's, but it interferes with giving and getting an education.

Fraternity houses and stadiums are again filled. College and university presidents are setting the pace for the students by promoting programs of expansion and beautification which have little to do with education. Education and scholarship can be carried on in ramshackle buildings. As a university president, I should not expect a university to refuse gifts of beautiful and useful buildings. As a sociable human being, I should not expect a college or university to ignore the social side of life. I should insist, however, that colleges and universities place first things first. The emphasis on the non-intellectual aspects of college life can only stimulate students everywhere to emphasize fraternities, good manners and athletics. This emphasis the country does not need.

As one who has been a "fraternity man" in his day, I think I appreciate the advantages and the evils of this ancient form of comradeship. On the credit side, it may be said that no fraternity ever made a bum of a man. The man who leaves college a bum brought his taste for being a bum to college with him. His character or lack of it, was already crystallized when he arrived at the age of eighteen. If he had the impulse to "bull" all day and play poker all night, he devoted himself to these arts whether his base of operation was a fraternity house, a dormitory or a saloon. On the debit side, it may be said that fraternities—and, of course, sororities—emphasize external possessions such as money, and trivialities such as appearances or "family." Their tradition of snobbishness inflates the ego of ordinary individuals who "make" them and too often breaks the hearts of those who do not. Fraternities are neither a menace nor a boon, and parents and students would both be better off if they regarded them as unimportant.

I have never been a college athlete, but I have been a soldier, and as soldiery and athletics demand much the same things of a young man, I feel qualified to have some opinions on athletics. Moreover, I have attended many football games, addressed many athletic banquets and examined many athletic budgets. The result of my contact with athletics is my conviction that athletics have a place in college, but only up to the point where they interfere with giving and getting an education. Many years ago, long before the football era was well under way, Thorstein Veblen said, "Football has no more to do with culture than bullfighting has to do with agriculture."

College should make a man manly. It can do this by developing his courage and perseverance in the realms of thought. Just as much courage, and courage of a higher sort, is required to tackle a 200-pound idea as to tackle a 200-pound fullback. As long as athletics is recreation, it will do neither the student nor the college any harm and may do them good. When it becomes the chief interest of the student and a major source of income for the college, it will prevent the student from getting an education and the college from giving one. A college which subsidizes athletes as such degrades its educational efforts. A college which is interested in producing professional athletes is not an educational institution.

Some three-hundred college and university presidents recently answered a questionnaire in which they were asked to list, in the order of importance, what they regarded as the purposes of their institutions. Mental discipline, which ranked first sixty years ago, according to a recent analysis of the college catalogues of that day, now ranks twenty-second among the twenty-five avowed purposes of our institutions of higher learning. It is preceded by such objects of higher education as good manners. "Good manners" have no place in the program of higher education. "Personality" has no place in the program of higher education. "Character" has no place in the program of higher education. College develops character by giving young people the habits of hard work and honest analysis. If it tries to teach character directly, it succeeds only in being boring.

An expensively dressed lady once approached the head of a school where I was a teacher and said, "My boy is eighteen years old, and I'm afraid he has been spoiled. I want you to take him and make a man out of him." The head of the school, who was one of the nation's wisest educators, lifted a line from the classics by way of reply: "Late, late, too late—ye cannot enter now."

Why, then, go to college? If the social graces and athletic proficiency can be obtained elsewhere and for less money, if it is too late to alter profoundly the character of a boy or girl of eighteen, perhaps the reason for going to college is to learn how to get into the higher income tax brackets.

This is the reason why a large proportion of our young people go to college. This is one of the reasons why the colleges and universities of the United States provide every imaginable type of specialized course. The thought of the colleges in offering specialized education instead of general education is that any student, by being submitted to imitations of experiences he may have in later life, will be able to make a million dollars by repeating those experiences in the outside world.

The student who has had a general education, who has mastered the fundamental principles of the sciences and the arts, can adjust himself to the world. He can acquire specific techniques in a few weeks or a few months. A college graduate who has concerned himself with the whole field of physics and has achieved an understanding of the relation of the ideas that underlie physics need not worry about getting a job if television should suddenly become a major industry. Nor need he worry if television is replaced by something else.

To this extent college education helps a student earn a living. To this extent it prepares him for the unpredictable variety of unpredictable experiences with which he may be confronted. College is not the place to learn how to make a million dollars, although it will help a student to earn a living by teaching him to use his head, and to use it on whatever problems may confront him.

College is a place to learn how to think. A college graduate who has not learned how to think may make a million dollars, but he will have wasted his time going to college.

I have not been able to discover that the present college generation is much different from my own. We are told that times are different since the crash of 1929. We are told that a new seriousness is sweeping the colleges. The old campus policeman, who has seen generations of them come and go, is quoted as observing that college students are wearing frowns and even scowls. He is quoted as complaining that the red lamp over the open manhole has not been stolen for several years now.

Perhaps he is right. I, too, have observed, like the old policeman, that the students are not so frivolous as I was. But I am not convinced that the new seriousness is meritorious in itself. It is not so important to be serious as it is to be serious about important things. The monkey wears an expression of seriousness which would do credit to any college student, but the monkey is serious because he itches. The depression, which is credited with having brought on the new seriousness in the colleges, merely intensified the conviction of students and their parents that it is important to make money. The new seriousness is a seriousness about the financial future of the individual, reflected in his determination to get some kind of training that will guarantee him what he calls security.

For decades people have been writing articles to show that college graduates make more money than their fellow men. This pious hope is more vehemently expressed today than ever before. As long as our people cling to the illusion that nothing is as important as making money, our colleges and universities will continue to try to teach young people how to make money. They will try to be what we want them to be. They will try to do what we insist they do. And they will fail to give youth the one thing it can get nowhere else, and that is an intellect rigorously trained for the happiness of the individual and the salvation of the world.

At the risk of lapsing into my Commencement Oration manner, I want to suggest that if the goal of life is happiness, you who are going to college should seek the training of the intellect. I repeat: If the goal of life is happiness, you should seek the training of the intellect. Does this sound meaningless? Do you doubt that happiness and the intellect have anything to do with each other?

A trained intellect may increase your earning capacity. On the other hand, it may not. But this it will do—it will provide you with the joy of understanding. And if you have understanding, you will have character. For you cannot be good without being wise. You cannot be right without knowing what is right and what is wrong.

Character, even if it is well grounded by the habits and conventions of early life, may collapse in later years if understanding is not present to support it. For as you grow older you will confront corrupting influences. You will confront "easy" ways to make money and "easy" ways to drown your sorrows. Against such pressures as these, habits and conventions will not prevail unless your reason convinces you that they should.

Nor can you be wise without being good. Your wisdom will enable you to select the means by which you may attain the ends you seek. If you seek the wrong ends, you may turn out to be a wise murderer. Since it is not wise to be a murderer, not even a wise murderer, you will recognize the impossibility of trying to be wise without being good. One of the reasons our age is bewildered and unmoral is that we have tried to separate wisdom and goodness.

So you will want both understanding and character. Some of our people believe, or at least live as if they believed, that it is not understanding and character which determine happiness but the external possessions one acquires, such as money, fame and power. They believe that happiness can be bought. I submit that it cannot.

In the first place, there is no sure way to get money, fame and power. They are goods of chance. Hence, while any man who wants them will work as hard as possible, any man who has attained them, must admit that his success may be largely an accident. The accidents of birth, location, and friendship have led more men to wealth and glory than the practice of the virtues. Many of the men whose lives serve as examples to succeeding generations lived poor and died penniless.

As there is no sure way to get these possessions, so there is no sure way to keep them.

In our own time we have seen fortunes, reputations and thrones swept away overnight. You may lose these possessions through no fault of your own. No one blames the people who lost their savings in the recent depression. Most of these people worked hard and were honest. Yet they lost their possessions.

But even if you are lucky enough to get these things and keep them, they will become monotonous. You will get tired of too many houses and too much food. Some of the wealthiest people in the world are bored. I have known rich men who were so bored that they even wanted to be college professors.

The possession of beautiful things does not in itself guarantee their enjoyment. There is small choice between the man who owns a library and the man who cannot afford a book, if neither of them appreciates literature. Monotony overtakes them both.

Finally, when you have dedicated your lives to the acquisition of money, fame and power, you have become the slaves of insatiable masters. Some men say, "Let me make a lot of money, then I will turn to higher things." I have known many such men, and they never lived long enough to turn to higher things, although some of them lived very long.

The question that was asked twenty-five hundred years ago is still unanswerable: "How can that be wealth of which a man may have a great abundance and yet perish with hunger, like Midas in the fable, whose insatiable prayer turned everything that was set before him into gold?"

If the goal of life is happiness, and if you cannot buy happiness, you will seek it in wisdom and goodness. You will willingly surrender the goods outside of you for the goods of the mind and the goods of the character. These are the main constituents of any abiding happiness. These alone survive every change of fortune. These alone can be won and retained by any man.

You can devote yourselves to the virtues of the mind and the character, and still lead a satisfying, even an exciting life. There is no monotony in the world of the mind and the character. Here the variety of possible experiences is unlimited. Books, people, places take on meaning for you. You will live on a more complex, and, therefore, more interesting level. You can converse with your fellow men, and, since there is no end of ideas in the world, conversation will never pall. You will be able to solve your problems, and you will be able to have peace.

I have said that these goods differ from external goods in that they can be won and retained by any man. The future holds out the promise of increasing time for leisure, so that the man who in the past has been too tired at the end of the day to do anything but sleep or go to the movies will have the time and the energy to develop his mind. When you have these things you can never lose them. They are not listed on the stock exchanges. You cannot be sold out.

Marcus Aurelius said: "Understand that a man is worth just so much as the things are worth about which he busies himself." If you busy yourselves only with animal comforts, you will not know the dignity and importance of being a man. You may be only as happy as the most contented cow. Only if you busy yourselves with the affairs of the mind and the spirit will you know the higher happiness of the creature which differs from the rest of the beasts.

College education in the United States is still restricted to a fraction of the nation's young people. It falls short of providing even that fraction with the understanding which produces the moral and intellectual excellence which, in turn, is the mark of a free man and a free people. A nation which cherishes the freedom of its citizens will try to give all its children an education. It will try to give them the kind of education that leads to understanding.

Questions and Exercises

1. Point out a basic fallacy in the thinking of most people about the nature of a college, as suggested by Hutchins in the first paragraph of this essay. Can you think of other fallacies which regulate people's attitude toward higher education?

2. Do you think that the kind of education Hutchins endorses will prepare a man or woman for a business career? Read in this connection an editorial, "Should a Businessman Be Educated?" *Fortune*, April, 1953. Are the editors of *Fortune* and Mr. Hutchins agreed about the type of education which is most important?

3. E. A. Cross, in "A New College for General Education," *School and Society*, December 27, 1952, suggests the following courses of study for college students. Criticize these suggestions in the light of Hutchins' ideas.

   ". . . I would suggest, first of all: reading, speaking, writing, and listening—the group of subjects educators call 'communication.' Then there should be courses on the college level in general mathematics, in general science, in geography and history (national and world), in art and music, in the social studies (government, economics, sociology, etc.), in languages (French, Spanish, Italian, and such others as individual desires and the local situation call for). . . ."

4. Mr. Cross, in the essay referred to in question 3, defines "general education as follows. Compare this definition with the concept presented by Mr. Hutchins. What differences in emphasis do you detect?

"By general education, I mean those areas of learning that mark the individual as one having a working familiarity with those phases of knowledge that any intelligent, good citizen in a progressive community should have. Or to put it another way, I mean all the phases of learning the educated men and women of a community should have in addition to their occupational, trade, or professional education and training."

5. What arguments does Hutchins advance in this essay that may be used to refute the thesis supported by Mrs. Alcaro in "Colleges Don't Make Sense"? Which of the two authors has the better argument? Explain.

6. Lawrence C. Lockley, University of Southern California, believes that if educators would prepare young people for positions of responsibility in management, they must accept four major responsibilities. Consider these four assignments (listed below), and suggest college courses that may be expected to achieve the desired effects.

a. Teach students to recognize and accept social responsibility.
b. Teach students to accept and follow ethical standards.
c. Lay the groundwork for the ability to manipulate workers, processes, and materials. Focus on thinking.
d. Teach students to recognize problems and seek the solution to them.

7. What types of evidence does Hutchins use in an attempt to convince you of the soundness of his conviction? Can you find examples of deductive reasoning? What are some of the premises on which the arguments are founded? Are these premises sound?

8. To what extent do you think the educational situation in America has changed since Hutchins wrote this essay? What facts presented need to be brought up to date?

9. Select a number of Hutchins' unsupported statements, such as, "The student who has had a general education, who has mastered the fundamental principles of the sciences and the arts,

can adjust himself to the world." Discuss these statements in class. Supply evidence which will support them or refute them.

10. Survey the curricular offerings of the college you are attending, and determine to what extent the offerings are in harmony with the demands made by Hutchins for a liberal education. What courses do you find which are examples of overspecialization?

11. What does Hutchins mean by "the best books"? Explain the theory of education which makes use of the idea of reading certain approved masterpieces of literature. How does this theory differ from that advanced by John Dewey and his followers?

12. Following are five aims of a liberal education. Criticize these aims in the light of Hutchins' ideas. What aims suggested by Hutchins are omitted from the list? What aims listed are not discussed by Hutchins?

   a. To offer a kind of mental discipline which will influence a student's ability to learn, to concentrate, and to reflect.
   b. To contribute to the continuity of the stream of culture which is our heritage.
   c. To develop the student's aesthetic susceptibilities.
   d. To contribute toward the student's orientation to the world in which he lives by leading him to develop areas of knowledge concerning parts of it.
   e. To develop for the student the skills of communication.

13. Write a paper on the subject "General or Specialized Education?" in which you employ arguments presented by Hutchins or Alcaro. Attempt to reconcile the two points of view with a sound proposal for your own educational future.

14. Student attitudes toward general education were surveyed and reported by John W. Kidd, and others, in *Journal of Higher Education*, vol. XXV, April, 1954. These attitudes are arranged in rank order as evaluated by the students interviewed. Study this list and determine the importance attached by students to the objectives outlined in question 12. To what extent do the students interviewed recognize the need for a broad, general education? How important do the students consider emphasis on thinking and communication?

15. What agreements and disagreements do you find between Hutchins' ideas on education and Jameson's ideas as advanced in "How to Stay in College"?

◆ ◆ ◆

Colleges Don't Make Sense

MARION WALKER ALCARO

THE DAY I graduated from college I believed—modestly, and yet with a nice warm glow of conviction—that I was an educated young woman. I had salted away an impressive supply of miscellaneous information. My mind, after constant limbering up with fancy mental gymnastics, was as supple as a ballerina. I was all set to deal with Life. One year later, at close grips with two very elemental problems of living—marriage and motherhood—I was beginning to suspect that I was poorly equipped to handle either one. Now, after ten years, I know that for a girl who was earmarked for domesticity from the time she diapered her first doll, college was a criminal waste of time.

Let me hasten to explain—before the feminists and the sentimentalists and many of my own classmates rise in wrath—that I am not an advocate of any back-to-the-cradle-and-kitchen movement. And I have no quarrel with our colleges when it comes to the preparation they give the potential career girl. They turn out brilliantly trained teachers, artists, and professional women. But the girl who is destined to be primarily a woman is shortchanged. The girl who during her college years is obviously marking time before marriage—and there's nothing wrong with that, by the way—is given the same fare as the girl who is going "to make something of herself." The former is dished out great hunks of obsolete literature, gobs of history that she won't remember, scoops of science that she won't remember either, dibs and dabs of philosophy and psychology, and a smattering of languages thrown in for seasoning. She is

Reprinted from *Woman's Day*, May, 1946, by permission of Marion Walker Alcaro and *Woman's Day*. Copyright 1946 by Woman's Day, Inc.

given a B.A. for swallowing the mixture, but nothing in this time-honored goulash has any use or meaning in her post-graduate life.

A degree has come to have tremendous snob appeal. A college graduate may belong to university clubs, and college women's clubs, and revel in class reunions. But these privileges are dearly bought at the price of four years of intellectual doodling. Since about 80 per cent of the alumnae of women's colleges marry and raise families, it seems to me that their alma maters have as great a responsibility toward the girl whose destiny is marriage as they have toward her career-minded classmates. It seems to me that she should get something more out of college than a few friendships and the satisfaction of leaping some stiff intellectual hurdles. And yet her needs are either bungled, ignored, or looked down upon.

The root of the trouble is that education for women started out with a chip on its shoulder. It had to fight the Battle of the Sexes; but after proving conclusively that women are the mental equals of men it has maintained the competition long after the original issue has become ancient history. Women's colleges are slavishly patterned after men's colleges, on the belligerent theory that if the gander can take it so can the goose. Any deviation from the masculine formula, any purely feminine innovation, would be considered a loss of academic prestige. In their desire to show the men a thing or two, women's colleges have urged their students to rise above the chores that have been traditionally a woman's lot, ignoring the facts that those chores still have to be done and that women have to do them. Marriage and motherhood are not represented as professions demanding skill and training, but as humble sidetracks. As a result, the college girl who marries is not only poorly prepared for her role in life but vaguely apologetic about it. "I have nothing interesting to report," wrote one graduate in response to a questionnaire sent out for her tenth reunion. "I have a husband and three children."

Make no mistake—I know that to suggest the lowly domestic arts invade the ivy-covered walls of our snootier colleges for women—on the same footing with Beowulf—would be like shaking a bee tree. But all the same, for the girl who marries, there should be some relation between the hours spent in classroom and laboratory and library and the demands of post-graduate life.

Take my own case. Shortly after graduation I married a young doctor just beginning his internship. Let's take a look at the qualifications of the wife to whom this lucky guy turned over the responsibility for his physical well-being, his house, his bank account, his children, and to a large extent his career itself. I was as informed as all get out when it came to the significance of revolution and romanticism. I could chatter about the minor English poets of the sixteenth century. I had studied Anglo-Saxon grammar. I knew all about the love life of the earthworm. But I couldn't cook a decent meal. I couldn't manage a house. Pregnancy amazed me. Babies scared me. And my knowledge of finance was limited to what-shall-I-do-until-my-allowance-comes.

Oh, I learned all right. I learned the hard way. My college professors would say that because my mind had been conditioned by the study of the liberal arts I had learned to grasp a problem, analyze it, seek out the proper references, and then proceed to solve it. Don't you believe it! I learned because I jolly well had to, and I learned slowly and painfully by the method of trial and error—mostly error.

The preparation of undergraduates for marriage should be a vibrant challenge to the liberal arts college. If domestic arts were taught as brilliantly, as scientifically, as exhaustively, and on the same scale as the belles lettres, they could assume a respected place in the college curriculum. The need exists—a need which is not filled later by quick courses in cooking schools, or schools for brides, or courses for expectant mothers. With imagination and some bold pioneering, our colleges could meet it adequately.

Some standard college courses need only a change of focus

or emphasis. For instance, look at the methods of teaching the sciences and of teaching what we call "hygiene." When I was in college I was exposed to one year of zoology. The class spent the first six weeks dissecting pickled frogs. The class did—I didn't. I spent my time on the fire escape trying to keep from losing my lunch. From there we progressed to the amoeba, the crayfish, and the earthworm. We studied them all in detail. We dissected, we drew diagrams, we squinted into microscopes, we peered into test tubes—for two long laboratory and three lecture periods every week. For the one member of the class who studied medicine this undoubtedly proved useful. The majority of us could have done with far less concentration on lowly creatures and far more information about pregnancy, childbirth, prenatal care, the menopause, and sex. These matters were taken care of in a one-semester, one-hour-a-week hygiene course consisting of some sketchy lectures by the college physician (unmarried) and an embarrassed physical education instructor (also unmarried).

When a cat has her first litter of kittens, nature thoughtfully provides her with the knowledge of how to bring them up. With humans it doesn't work that way. When my first son was born, I came out of the anaesthetic knowing no more about how to take care of him than I did before. After I got him home I spent most of my time with my nose in a book on babies. He yelled—I ran for the book! He didn't yell—I ran for the book! How much wear and tear on both of us would have been avoided if I could have studied child care as painstakingly as I studied French drama. I came across my drama notebook the other day—pages and pages of meticulous notes on musty plays by musty playwrights. If I had had as elaborate a notebook on child care to refer to during the crises of the past nine years, motherhood would have been a snap.

No matter what her domestic setup may be, necessarily the woman who marries spends time and thought on food. The college which holds its academic nose at the mention of anything which smacks of the culinary misses an opportunity to explore a fascinating subject which could be approached from many angles. Think what the combined forces of the departments of history, science, and economics could do with the study of food and nutrition—if they put their minds on it! Working with food would be high adventure for a college graduate if she were given some scholarly groundwork in its chemistry, its romance, and its role as world force and determinant of history. There are those—among them me—who would go even further and suggest that expert cookery could take its place among the fine arts with apologies to no one. But that is probably an earthy point of view.

Money matters are designated in the minds of most women as Great Mysteries. And yet many women at some time in their lives are forced to manage their own incomes. And many women marry doctors and clergymen and other babes in the woods of finance. How about a course in the fundamentals of investment, insurance, taxation, and managing a budget? Nothing elaborate—one semester would do. It seems to me that the department of mathematics could, without losing face, sandwich one in somewhere.

My roommate took history of art—ancient, Renaissance, modern, and contemporary. Unofficially I took it too; after drilling her for quizzes for two years, I felt like an authority. This came in handy when I went to Florence. I wasn't lost in the Pitti and the Uffizi. But I was lost in a furniture store when I chose the furnishings for my first house. What a conglomeration I picked out for my family to live with! It has taken years to replace that junk, and there are still a few horrors around the house to remind me of my youth and ignorance. If colleges for women would offer courses in architecture for home owners and in interior decoration—including the study of modern and traditional furniture, china, glassware, silver, and fabrics—they would earn the gratitude of the husbands of their alumnae.

The most progressive step in education for women that has been made in recent years is a course in personal grooming offered by a junior college in the Middle West. The colleges which have hailed it with lofty amusement or out-and-out sneers would do well to take another look at some of their own frowzy undergraduates. Or at some of their own finished products, for that matter. The mental giantess who looks like a scarecrow is intellectually lopsided. The woman who knows how to make the most of her appearance stands a far better chance of achieving well-balanced personal development. Training in the selection of clothes, and in personal grooming, and in the use of cosmetics, may seem frivolous to the devotees of Shakespeare, but it adds up to sound preparation for living.

Colleges rationalize the adherence to their moth-eaten curricula by insisting that a liberal arts education according to the stereotyped formula introduces a girl to intellectual vistas that will enrich the rest of her life. That sounds dandy. Unfortunately the argument doesn't hold water. The average bachelor of arts who marries is so totally unprepared to meet the demands of her new life that she is lucky if she finds time to read Dick Tracy. If she had some practical training along with the academic hardtack, she could step into her role as a professional woman instead of a bungling amateur—and then, yes, she would have a chance to develop the intellectual tastes acquired in college. Our colleges for women point with pride to the few celebrities which they produce—the scientists, the artists, the politicians, the prima donnas of business. When they can produce many women who know the business of womanhood and who have been taught to respect its dignity, then the cap-and-gown crowd will have real cause for self-congratulation.

Questions and Exercises

1. What theory of education does Mrs. Alcaro's argument best support? Is the author an advocate of John Dewey's instrumentalism? Or is she an advocate of Robert M. Hutchins' rationalism or essentialism? Explain.

2. What is Mrs. Alcaro's principal objection to a liberal education? Find in her essay the best argument you can which attacks Hutchins' views as set forth in "Why Go To College?"

3. What types of argument does the author make use of in defending her thesis? Point them out in the text of the essay. Can you refute any of these arguments on the basis of your own experience or the course offerings of the college you are attending?

4. Ralph Waldo Emerson, in the first five paragraphs of "The American Scholar," expresses the idea that overspecialization makes "monsters" of men. How does Mrs. Alcaro refute this idea?

5. What specific methods of explanation—examples, illustration, statistics, analogy, comparison and contrast, etc.—does the author use in clarifying her idea?

6. What does Mrs. Alcaro mean by "academic hardtack"? What course of study offered by your college might be properly designated as such?

7. Consider the essay as an example of problem-solution argument. What is the problem, and what is the author's solution to the problem? Point out the passages in the essay on which you base your answer.

8. What are the essential characteristics of the author's style of writing? How does this style support the thesis proposed?

9. Find ten examples of emotionally toned or loaded words used by the author in defending her argument. What other devices does she employ to persuade you to her way of thinking?

10. What is the relationship if any between Mrs. Alcaro's apologetic attitude toward domestic life and what Rollo May says about "The Experience of Becoming a Person"?

11. Consider the analogy the author draws between a cat caring for her kittens and a human mother for her children? Does the analogy make a forceful argument? Does it satisfactorily prove the thesis?

12. Consider the author's statement: "My college professors would say that because my mind had been conditioned by the study of the liberal arts I had learned to grasp a problem, analyze it, seek out the proper references, and then proceed to solve it." To what extent were the professors right, judging by Mrs. Alcaro's organization of the essay?

13. Compare Mrs. Alcaro's ideas about colleges for women with the ideas presented by Mirra Komarovsky in "What Colleges

Should Teach Women," *Harper's Magazine*, November, 1949; and by Louis William Norris in "How To Educate a Woman," *The Saturday Review*, November 27, 1954. Point out similarities and differences in the several points of view. Which of the ideas do you think is most tenable and why?

◆ ◆ ◆

The Bird and the Machine

LOREN C. EISELEY

I SUPPOSE their bones have years ago been lost among the stones and winds of those high glacial pastures. I suppose their feathers blow eventually into the piles of tumbleweed beneath the straggling cattle fences and rotted there in the mountain snows, along with dead steers and all the other things that drift to an end in the corners of the wire. I do not quite know why I should be thinking of birds over the *New York Times* at breakfast, nor particularly of the birds of my youth half a continent away. It is a funny thing what the brain will do with memories and how it will treasure them and finally bring them into odd juxtapositions with other things, as though it wanted to make a design, or get some meaning out of them, whether you want it or not, or even see it.

It used to seem marvelous to me, but I read now that there are machines that can do these things in a small way, machines that can crawl about like animals, and that it may not be long now until they do more things—maybe even make themselves

"The Bird and the Machine" from *The Immense Journey* by Loren C. Eiseley. Copyright 1956, 1957 by Loren C. Eiseley. Reprinted by permission of Random House, Inc. Originally published in *Harper's Magazine*, January, 1956.

—I saw that piece in the *Times* just now—and then they will, maybe—well, who knows—but you read about it more and more with no one making any protest, and already they can add better than we and reach up and hear things through the dark and finger the guns over the night sky.

This is the new world that I read about at breakfast. This is the world that confronts me in my biological books and journals, until there are times when I sit quietly in my chair and try to hear the little purr of the cogs in my head and the tubes flaring and dying as the messages go through them and the circuits snap shut or open. This is the great age, make no mistake about it; the robot has been born somewhat appropriately along with the atom bomb, and the brain they say now is just another type of more complicated feedback system. The engineers have its basic principles worked out; it's mechanical, you know; nothing to get superstitious about; and man can always improve on nature once he gets the idea. Well, he's got it all right and that's why, I guess, that I sit here in my chair, with the article crunched in my hand, remembering those two birds and that blue mountain sunlight. There is another magazine title on my desk that reads, "Machines Are Getting Smarter Every Day." I don't deny it, but I'll stick with the birds. It's life I believe in, not machines.

Maybe you don't believe there is any difference. A skeleton is all joints and pulleys, I'll admit. And when man was in his simpler stages of machine building in the eighteenth century, he quickly saw the resemblances. "What," wrote Hobbes, "is the heart but a spring, and the nerves but so many strings, and the joints but so many wheels, giving motion to the whole body?" Tinkering about in their ships it was inevitable in the end that men would see the world as a huge machine "subdivided into an infinite number of lesser machines."

The idea took on with a vengeance. Little automatons toured the country—dolls controlled by clockwork. Clocks described as little worlds were taken on tours by their designers. They were made up of moving figures, shifting scenes, and other remarkable devices. The life of the cell was unknown. Man, whether he was conceived as possessing a soul or not, moved and jerked about like these tiny puppets. A human being thought of himself in terms of his own tools and implements. He had been fashioned like the puppets he produced and was only a more clever model made by a greater designer.

Then in the nineteenth century, the cell was discovered, and the single machine in its turn was found to be the product of millions of infinitesimal machines—the cells. Now, finally, the cell itself dissolves away into an abstract chemical machine— and that into some intangible, inexpressible flow of energy. The secret seems to lurk all about, the wheels get smaller and smaller, and they turn more rapidly, but when you try to seize it the life is gone—and so, it is popular to say, the life was never there in the first place. The wheels and the cogs are the secret and we can make them better in time—machines that will run faster and more accurately than real mice to cheese.

I have no doubt it can be done, though a mouse harvesting seeds on an autumn thistle is to me a fine sight and more complicated, I think, in his multiform activity, than a machine "mouse" running a maze. Also, I like to think of the possible shape of the future brooding in mice, just as it brooded once in a rather ordinary mousy insectivore who became a man. It leaves a nice fine indeterminate sense of wonder that even an electronic brain hasn't got, because you know perfectly well that if the electronic brain changes it will be because of something man has done to it. But what man will do to himself he doesn't really know. A certain scale of time and a ghostly intangible thing called change are ticking in him. Powers and potentialities like the oak in the seed, or a red and awful ruin. Either way, it's impressive; and the mouse has it, too—or those birds, I'll never forget those birds, though I learned the lesson of time first of all. I was young then and left alone in a great desert— part of an expedition that had scattered its men over several hundred miles in order to carry on research more effectively. I learned there that time is a series of planes existing superficially in the same universe. The tempo is a human illusion, a subjective clock ticking in our own kind of protoplasm.

A CANYON BETWEEN WORLDS

As the long months passed, I began to live on the slower planes and to observe more readily what passed for life there. I sauntered, I passed more and more slowly up and down the canyons in the dry baking heat of midsummer. I slumbered for long hours in the shade of huge brown boulders that had gathered in tilted companies out on the flats. I had forgotten the world of men and the world had forgotten me. Now and then I found a skull in the canyons and these justified my remaining there. I took a serene cold interest in these discoveries. I had come, like many a naturalist before me, to view life with a wary and subdued attention. I had grown to take pleasure in the divested bone.

I sat once on a high ridge that fell away before me into a waste of sand dunes. I sat through hours of a long afternoon. Finally glancing by my boot an indistinct configuration caught my eye. It was a coiled rattlesnake, a big one. How long he had sat with me I do not know. I had not frightened him. We were both locked in the sleep-walking tempo of the earlier world, baking in the same high air and sunshine. Perhaps he had been there when I came. He slept on as I left, his coils, so ill discerned by me, dissolving once more among the stones and gravel from which I had barely made him out.

Another time, I got on a higher ridge, among some tough little wind-warped pines half covered over with sand in a basinlike depression that caught everything carried by the air up to those heights. There were a few thin bones of birds, some cracked shells of indeterminable age, and the knotty fingers of pine roots bulged out of shape from their long and agonizing grasp upon the crevices of the rock. I lay under the pines in the sparse shade and went to sleep once more.

It grew cold finally, for autumn was in the air by then, and the few things that lived thereabouts were sinking down into an even chillier scale of time. In the moments between sleeping and waking I saw the roots about me and slowly, slowly, a foot in what seemed many centuries, I moved my sleep-stiffened hands over the scaling bark and lifted my numbed face after the vanishing sun. I was a great awkward thing of knots and aching limbs, trapped up there in some long patient endurance that involved the necessity of putting living fingers into rock and by slow, aching expansion bursting those rocks asunder. I suppose, so thin and slow was the time of my pulse by then, that I might have stayed on to drift still deeper into the lower cadences of the frost, or the crystalline life that glisters pebbles or shines in a snow flake, or dreams in the meteoric iron between the worlds.

It was a dim descent but time was present in it. Somewhere far down in that scale the notion struck me that one might come the other way. Not many months thereafter, I joined some colleagues heading higher into a remote windy tableland where huge bones were reputed to protrude like boulders from the turf. I had drowsed with reptiles and moved with the century-long pulse of trees; now, lethargically, I was climbing back up some invisible ladder of quickening hours. There had been talk of birds in connection with my duties. Birds are intense, fast-living creatures—reptiles—I suppose one might say—that have escaped out of the heavy sleep of time, transformed fairy creatures dancing over sunlit meadows. It is a youthful fancy, no doubt, but because of something that happened up there among the escarpments of that range, it remains with me a life-long impression. I can never bear to see a bird imprisoned.

We came into that valley through the trailing mists of a spring night. It was a place that looked as though it might never have known the foot of man, but our scouts had been ahead of us and we knew all about the abandoned cabin of stone that lay far up on one hillside. It had been built in the land rush of the last century and then lost to the cattlemen again as the marginal soils failed to take to the plow.

There were spots like this all over that country. Lost graves marked by unlettered stones and old corroding rim-fire cartridge cases lying where somebody had made a stand among the boulders that rimmed the valley. They are all that remain of the range wars; the men are under the stones now. I could see our cavalcade winding in and out through the mist below us: torches, and lights reflected on collecting tins, and the far-off bumping of a loose dinosaur thigh bone in the bottom of a trailer. I stood on a rock a moment looking down and thinking what it cost in money and equipment to capture the past.

We had, in addition, instructions to lay hands on the present. The word had come through to get them alive, birds, reptiles, anything. A zoo somewhere abroad needed restocking. It was one of those reciprocal matters in which science involves itself. Maybe our museum needed a stray ostrich egg and this was the payoff. Anyhow, my job was to help capture some birds and that was why I was there before the trucks.

The cabin had not been occupied for years. We intended to clean it out and live in it, but there were holes in the roof and the birds had come in and were roosting in the rafters. You could depend on it in a place like this where everything blew away and even a bird needed some place out of the weather and away from coyotes. A cabin going back to nature in a wild place draws them till they come in, listening at the eaves, I imagine, pecking softly among the shingles till they find a hole and then suddenly the place is theirs and man is forgotten.

Sometimes of late years I find myself thinking the most beautiful sight in the world might be the birds taking over New York after the last man has run away to the hills. I will never live to see it, of course, but I know just how it will sound because I've lived up high and I know the sort of watch birds keep on us. I've listened to sparrows tapping tentatively on the tin of the air conditioners when they thought no one was listening, and I know how other birds test the vibrations that come up to them through the television aerials.

"Is he gone?" they ask, and the vibrations come up from below, "not yet, not yet."

Well, to come back, I got the door open softly and I had the spotlight all ready to turn on and blind whatever birds were there so they couldn't see to get out through the roof. I had a short piece of ladder to put against the far wall where there was a shelf on which I expected to make the biggest haul. I had all the information I needed just like any skilled assassin. I pushed the door open with the hinges only squeaking a little after the oil was put on them. A bird or so stirred—I could hear them—but nothing flew and there was a faint starshine through the holes in the roof.

I padded across the floor, got the ladder up, and the light ready, and slithered up the ladder till my head and arms were over the shelf. Everything was dark as pitch except for the starlight at a little place back of the shelf near the eaves. With the light to blind them, they'd never make it. I had them. I reached my arm carefully over in order to be ready to seize whatever was there and I put the flash on the edge of the shelf where it would stand by itself when I turned it on. That way I'd be able to use both hands.

Everything worked perfectly except for one detail—I didn't know what kind of birds were there. I never thought about it at all and it wouldn't have mattered if I had. My orders were to get something interesting. I snapped on the flash and sure enough there was a great beating and feathers flying, but instead of my having them, they, or rather he, had me. He had my hand, that is, and for a small hawk not much bigger than my fist he was doing all right. I heard him give one short metallic cry when the light went on and my hand descended on the bird beside him; after that he was busy with his claws and his beak was sunk in my thumb. In the struggle I knocked the lamp over on the shelf and his mate got her sight back and whisked neatly through the hole in the roof, and off among the stars outside. It all happened in fifteen seconds and you might think I would have fallen down the ladder, but no, I had a professional assassin's reputation to keep up and the bird, of course, made the mistake of thinking the hand was the enemy and not the eyes behind it. He chewed my thumb up pretty effectively and lacerated my hand with his claws, but in the end I got him, having two hands to work with.

He was a sparrow hawk and a fine young male in the prime of life. I was sorry not to catch the pair of them, but as I dripped blood and folded his wings carefully, holding him by the back so he couldn't strike again, I had to admit the two of them might have been a little more than I could have handled under the circumstances. The little fellow had saved his mate by diverting me, and that was that. He was born to it, and made no outcry now, resting in my hand hopelessly, but peering toward me in the shadows behind the lamp with a fierce, almost indifferent glance. He neither gave nor expected mercy and something out of the high air passed from him to me, stirring a faint embarrassment.

I quit looking into that eye and managed to get my huge carcass with its fist full of prey back down the ladder. I put the bird in a box too small to allow him to injure himself by struggle and walked out to welcome the arriving trucks. It had been a long day and camp still to make in the darkness. In the morning that bird would be just another episode. He would go back with the bones in the truck to a small cage in a city where he would spend the rest of his life. And a good thing, too. I sucked my aching thumb and spat out some blood. An assassin has to get used to these things. I had a professional reputation to keep up.

THE CRY OF THE HAWK

In the morning with the change that comes on suddenly in that high country, the mist that had hovered below us in the valley was gone. The sky was a deep blue and one could see for miles over the high outcroppings of stone. I was up early and brought the box to which the little hawk was imprisoned out onto the grass where I was building a cage. A wind as cool as a mountain spring ran over the grass and stirred my hair. It was a fine day to be alive. I looked up and all around and at the hole in the cabin roof out of which the other little hawk had fled. There was no sign of her anywhere that I could see.

"Probably in the next county by now," I thought cynically, but before beginning work I decided I'd have a look at my last night's capture.

Secretively, I looked again all around the camp and up and down and opened the box. I got him right out in my hand with his wings folded properly and I was careful not to startle him. He lay limp in my grasp and I could feel his heart pound under the feathers but he only looked beyond me and up.

I saw him look that last look away beyond me into a sky so full of light that I could not follow his gaze. The little breeze blowed over me again, and nearby a mountain aspen shook all its tiny leaves. I suppose I must have had an idea about then of what I was going to do, but I never let it come up into consciousness. I just reached over and laid the hawk on the grass.

He lay there a long minute without hope, unmoving, his eyes still fixed on that blue vault above him. It must have been that he already was so far away in heart that he never felt the release from my hand. He never even stood. He just lay with his breast against the grass and my eye upon him.

In the next second after that long minute he was gone. Like a flicker of light, he had vanished with my eyes full on him, but without actually seeing even a premonitory wing beat. He was gone straight into that towering emptiness of light and crystal that my eyes could scarcely bear to penetrate. For another long moment there was silence. I could not see him. The light was too intense. Then from far up somewhere a cry came ringing down.

I was young then and had seen little of the world, but when I heard that cry my heart turned over. It was not the cry of the hawk I had captured; for, by shifting my position against the sun, I was now seeing further up. Straight out of the sun's eye, where she must have been soaring restlessly above us for untold hours, hurtled his mate. And from far up, ringing from peak to peak of the summits over us, came a cry of such unutterable and ecstatic joy that it sounds down across the years and tingles among the cups on my quiet breakfast table.

I saw them both now. He was rising fast to meet her. They met in a great soaring gyre—that turned to a whirling circle and a dance of wings. Once more, just once, their two voices, joined in a harsh wild medley of question and response, struck and echoed against the pinnacles of the valley. Then they were gone forever somewhere into those upper regions beyond the eyes of man.

I am older now, and sleep less, and have seen most of what there is to see and am not very impressed any more, I suppose, by anything. "What Next in the Attributes of Machines?" my morning headline runs. "It Might be the Power to Reproduce Themselves."

I lay the paper down and across my mind a phrase floats insinuatingly: "It does not seem that there is anything in the construction, constituents, or behavior of the human being which it is essentially impossible for science to duplicate and synthesize. On the other hand . . ."

All over the city the cogs in the hard, bright mechanism have begun to turn. Figures move through computers, names are spelled out, a thoughtful machine selects the fingerprints of a wanted criminal from an array of thousands. In the laboratory an electronic mouse runs swiftly through a maze toward the cheese it can neither taste nor enjoy. On the second run it does better than a living mouse.

"On the other hand . . ." Ah, my mind takes up, on the other hand the machine does not bleed, ache, hang for hours in the empty sky in a torment of hope to learn the fate of another machine, nor does it cry out with joy nor dance in the air with the fierce passion of a bird. Far off, over a distance greater than space, that remote cry from the heart of heaven makes a faint buzzing among my breakfast dishes and passes on and away.

Questions and Exercises

1. This essay is included in the anthology because of the author's focus upon an idea. What is that idea? Write a paragraph in which you state clearly the idea suggested to you.
2. Explain fully by what method Eiseley brings his idea into focus.
3. Man is said to learn about himself by analogy with the machines he creates. The more intricate the machines become, the more man knows about himself. Considering the latest scientific inventions of human beings, what do men reason is the probable make-up and operation of the brain? How does this idea compare with George R. Harrison's "How the Brain Works," *The Atlantic*, September, 1956?
4. Explain why the author freed the bird he had taken so much pains to capture. How is this action related to Mark Twain's "Huck and Jim on the Raft"?
5. What is the essential thing contained in the human brain that is lacking in an electronic one?
6. What qualities does Eiseley discuss of birds that he deplores the lack of in modern man?
7. Compare Eiseley's experience with a rattlesnake with that of Mrs. Rawlings in "An Ancient Enmity." How does this experience support the idea of the other?
8. Explain how the context in which the birds are discussed helps to promote the author's thought.
9. Explain how this essay demonstrates Perry's and Whitlock's notion of reading as an active rather than a passive activity, as explained in "The Right to Think—Through Reading."
10. Considering some of the specific opinions Eiseley expresses in the essay, what would you say are his principal criticisms of the modern world?
11. What is the unifying impression made in the four paragraphs beginning "We came into that valley through the trailing mists . . ."?
12. Compare Eiseley's thesis in this essay with Thurber's thesis in "Oliver and the Other Ostriches," or with Paul Fisher's thesis in "A Forgotten Gentry of the Fourth Estate."
13. What connection do you see between Eiseley's thought in this essay and Saroyan's story "The Circus"? Explain fully.
14. How might you apply Eiseley's thesis to the present plight of the American Indian? What other applications can you think of?

15. Consider the author's supposition that birds are reptiles escaped out of the heavy sleep of time. What does this suggest about the progress of man toward freedom?
16. What use does the author make of the seasons, the weather, and the facts of the physical world to create the impression he wants to make?
17. What specific devices can you detect in the essay by which the author makes an emotional appeal to his readers?
18. Compare Eiseley's thesis in this essay with Thomas H. Ferril's thought in "Western Half-Acre," *Harper's Magazine*, July, 1946.

Huck and Jim on the Raft

MARK TWAIN

WE SLEPT most all day, and started out at night, a little ways behind a monstrous long raft that was as long going by as a procession. She had four long sweeps at each end, so we judged she carried as many as thirty men, likely. She had five big wig-wams aboard, wide apart, and an open campfire in the middle, and a tall flag-pole at each end. There was a power of style about her. It *amounted* to something being a raftsman on such a craft as that.

We went drifting down into a big bend, and the night clouded up and got hot. The river was very wide, and was walled with solid timber on both sides; you couldn't see a break in it hardly ever, or a light. We talked about Cairo, and wondered whether we would know it when we got to it. I said likely we wouldn't, because I had heard say there warn't but about a dozen houses there, and if they didn't happen to have them lit up, how was we going to know we was passing a town? Jim said if the two big rivers joined together there, that would show. But I said maybe we might think we was passing the foot of an island and coming into the same old river again. That disturbed Jim—and me too. So the question was, what to do? I said, paddle ashore the first time a light showed, and tell them pap was behind, coming along with a trading-scow, and was a green hand at the business, and wanted to know how far it was to Cairo. Jim thought it was a good idea, so we took a smoke on it and waited.

There warn't nothing to do now but to look out sharp for the town, and not pass it without seeing it. He said he'd be mighty sure to see it, because he'd be a free man the minute he seen it, but if he missed it he'd be in a slave country again and no more show for freedom. Every little while he jumps up and says:

"Dah she is?"

But it warn't. It was Jack-o'-lanterns, or lightning-bugs; so he set down again, and went to watching, same as before. Jim said it made him all over trembly and feverish to be so close to freedom. Well, I can tell you it made me all over trembly and feverish, too, to hear him, because I begun to get it through my head that he *was* most free—and who was to blame for it? Why, *me*. I couldn't get that out of my conscience, no how nor no way. It got to troubling me so I couldn't rest; I couldn't stay still in one place. It hadn't ever come home to me before, what this thing was that I was doing. But now it did; and it stayed with me, and scorched me more and more. I tried to make out to myself that *I* warn't to blame, because *I* didn't run Jim off from his rightful owner; but it warn't no use, conscience up and says, every time, "But you knowed he was running for his freedom, and you could 'a' paddled ashore and told somebody." That was so—I couldn't get around that no way. That was where it pinched. Conscience say to me, "What had poor Miss Watson done to you that you could see her nigger go off right under your eyes and never say one single word? What did that poor old woman do to you that you could treat her so mean? Why, she tried to learn you your book, she tried to learn you your manners, she tried to be good to you every way she knowed how. *That's* what she done."

I got to feeling so mean and so miserable I most wished I was dead. I fidgeted up and down the raft, abusing myself to myself, and Jim was fidgeting up and down past me. We neither of us could keep still. Every time he danced around and says, "Dah's Cairo!" it went through me like a shot, and I thought if it *was* Cairo I reckoned I would die of miserableness.

Jim talked out loud all the time while I was talking to myself. He was saying how the first thing he would do when he got to a free state he would go to saving up money and never spend a single cent, and when he got enough he would buy his wife, which was owned on a farm close to where Miss Watson lived; and then they would both work to buy the two children, and if their master wouldn't sell them, they'd get an Ab'litionist to go and steal them.

It most froze me to hear such talk. He wouldn't ever dared to talk such talk in his life before. Just see what a difference it made in him the minute he judged he was about free. It was according to the old saying, "Give a nigger an inch and he'll take an ell." Thinks I, this is what comes of my not thinking. Here was this nigger, which I had as good as helped to run away, coming right out flat-footed and saying he would steal his children—children that belonged to a man I didn't even know; a man that hadn't ever done me no harm.

I was sorry to hear Jim say that, it was such a lowering of him. My conscience got to stirring me up hotter than ever, until at last I says to it, "Let up on me—it ain't too late yet—I'll paddle ashore at the first light and tell." I felt easy and happy and light as a feather right off. All my troubles was gone. I went to looking out sharp for a light, and sort of singing to myself. By and by one showed. Jim sings out:

"We's safe, Huck, we's safe! Jump up and crack yo' heels! Dat's de good ole Cairo at las', I jis knows it!"

I says:

"I'll take the canoe and go and see, Jim. It mightn't be, you know."

He jumped and got the canoe ready, and put his old coat in the bottom for me to set on, and give me the paddle; and as I shoved off, he says:

"Pooty soon I'll be a-shoutin' for joy, en I'll say, it's all on accounts o' Huck; I's a free man, en I couldn't ever ben free ef it hadn't ben for Huck; Huck done it. Jim won't ever forgit you, Huck; you's de bes' fren' Jim's ever had, en you's de *only* fren' ole Jim's got now."

I was paddling off, all in a sweat to tell on him; but when he says this, it seemed to kind of take the tuck all out of me. I went along slow then, and I warn't right down certain whether I was glad I started or whether I warn't. When I was fifty yards off, Jim says:

"Dah you goes, de old true Huck; de on'y white genlman dat ever kep' his promise to ole Jim."

Well, I just felt sick. But I says, I *got* to do it—I can't get *out* of it. Right then along comes a skiff with two men in it with guns, and they stopped and I stopped. One of them says:

"What's that yonder?"

"A piece of raft," I says.

"Do you belong on it?"

"Yes, sir."

"Any men on it?"

"Only one, sir."

"Well, there's five niggers run off to-night up yonder, above the head of the bend. Is your man white or black?"

I didn't answer up promptly. I tried to, but the words wouldn't come. I tried for a second or two to brace up and out with it, but I warn't man enough—hadn't the spunk of a rabbit. I see I was weakening; so I just give up trying, and up and says:

"He's white."

"I reckon we'll go and see for ourselves."

"I wish you would," says I, "because it's pap that's there, and maybe you'd help me tow the raft ashore where the light is. He's sick—and so is mam and Mary Ann."

"Oh, the devil! we're in a hurry, boy. But I s'pose we've got to. Come, buckle to your paddle, and let's get along."

I buckled to my paddle and they laid to their oars. When we had made a stroke or two, I says:

"Pap'll be mighty much obleeged to you, I can tell you. Everybody goes away when I want them to help me tow the raft ashore, and I can't do it by myself."

"Well, that's infernal mean. Odd, too. Say, boy, what's the matter with your father?"

"It's the—a—the—well, it ain't anything much."

They stopped pulling. It warn't but a mighty little ways to the raft now. One says:

"Boy, that's a lie. What *is* the matter with your pap? Answer up square now, and it'll be the better for you."

"I will, sir, I will, honest—but don't leave us, please. It's the—the—Gentlemen, if you'll only pull ahead, and let me heave you the headline, you won't have to come a-near the raft—please do."

"Set her back, John, set her back!" says one. They backed water. "Keep away, boy—keep to looard. Confound it, I just expect the wind has blowed it to us. Your pap's got the smallpox, and you know it precious well. Why didn't you come out and say so? Do you want to spread it all over?"

"Well," says I, a-blubbering, "I've told everybody before, and they just went away and left us."

"Poor devil, ther's something in that. We are right down sorry for you, but we—well, hang it, we don't want the smallpox, you see. Look here, I'll tell you what to do. Don't you try to land by yourself, or you'll smash everything to pieces. You float along down about twenty miles, and you'll come to a town on the left-hand side of the river. It will be long after sun-up then, and when you ask for help you tell them your folks are all down with chills and fever. Don't be a fool again, and let people guess what is the matter. Now we're trying to do you a kindness; so you just put twenty miles between us, that's a good boy. It wouldn't do any good to land yonder where the light is—it's only a wood-yard. Say, I reckon your father's poor, and I'm bound to say he's in pretty hard luck. Here, I'll put a twenty-dollar gold piece on this board, and you get it when it floats by. I feel mighty mean to leave you; but my kingdom! it won't do to fool with smallpox, don't you see?"

"Hold on, Parker," says the man, "here's a twenty to put on the board for me. Good-by, boy; you do as Mr. Parker told you, and you'll be all right."

"That's so, my boy—good-by, good-by. If you see any runaway niggers you get help and nab them, and you can make some money by it."

"Good-by, sir," says I; "I won't let no runaway niggers get by me if I can help it."

They went off and I got aboard the raft, feeling bad and low, because I knowed very well I had done wrong, and I see it warn't no use for me to try to learn to do right; a body that don't get *started* right when he's little ain't got no show—when the pinch comes there ain't nothing to back him up and keep him to his work, and so he gets beat. Then I thought a minute, and says to myself, hold on; s'pose you'd 'a' done right and give Jim up, would you felt better than what you do now? No, says I, I'd feel bad—I'd feel just the same way I do now. Well, then, says I, what's the use you learning to do right when it's troublesome to do right and ain't no trouble to do wrong, and the wages is just the same? I was stuck. I couldn't answer that. So I reckoned I wouldn't bother no more about it, but after this always do whichever come handiest at the time.

I went into the wigwam; Jim warn't there. I looked all around; he warn't anywhere. I says:

"Jim!"

"Here I is, Huck. Is dey out o' sight yit? Don't talk loud."

He was in the river under the stern oar, with just his nose out. I told him they were out of sight, so he come aboard. He says: "I was a-listenin' to all de talk, en I slips into de river en was gwyne to shove for sho' if dey come aboard. Den I was gwyne to swim to de raf' agin when dey was gone. But lawsy, how you did fool 'em, Huck! Dat *wuz* de smartes' dodge! I tell you, chile, I 'spec it save' ole Jim—ole Jim ain't going to forgit you for dat, honey."

Then we talked about the money. It was a pretty good raise— twenty dollars apiece. Jim said we could take deck passage on a steamboat now, and the money would last us as far as we wanted to go in the free states. He said twenty mile more warn't far for the raft to go, but he wished we was already there.

Questions and Exercises

1. Henry Steele Commager, in *Living Ideas in America*, calls this chapter from *Huckleberry Finn* "not only an enthralling story, but a sermon as well." What is the central idea of the sermon, as you see it? Why did Commager include the story in his book of ideas?

2. Charles Kaplan, in a critical comparison of *Huckleberry Finn* and *Catcher in the Rye* (*College English*, November, 1956), has this to say of the incident of this chapter:

   "Huck's tortured decision not to 'turn in' Jim is made on the basis of his own feelings, which he automatically assumes to be sinful since they have so often put him at odds with society. His personal moral code seems always to run counter to his duty to society, a conflict which serves to confirm him in the belief that wickedness is in his line, 'being brung up to it.' In the crucial moral act of the novel, Huck must 'decide, forever, betwixt two things, and I knowed it. I studied a minute, sort of holding my breath, and then says to myself, *all* right, then I'll *go* to hell!' Huck's humanity overcomes the so-called duty to society."

   Make a list of the conflicts that plague American youth today. Does the conflict between individual conscience and social action, or legal compulsion, exist among us now? Explain.

3. Explain Huck's pangs of conscience in terms of Rollo May's "The Experience of Becoming a Person" or of Susanne Langer's "Language and Creative Thought."

4. Compare Mark Twain's thesis in this chapter with Thoreau's thesis in *Civil Disobedience*. Is Mark Twain's narrative as forceful as Thoreau's exposition? Analyze its specific appeals.

5. What loss would Mark Twain's thesis suffer if the language of the chapter were corrected according to the codified rules of grammar and syntax? Do you think Mark Twain would have endorsed Donald Lloyd's thoughts on usage, as presented in "Our National Mania for Correctness," or in "Snobs, Slobs, and the English Language"?

6. Find an example in this chapter of thinking based on what A. E. Mander calls "groundless beliefs." How many similar beliefs can you think of which reveal a strong racial prejudice? To what extent do you think this belief is still cherished by Americans after 100 years?

7. Discuss Huck Finn as a propagandist in this story. What human motives did he appeal to in controlling the thoughts of the two men who questioned him?

8. Discuss the validity of the slogan "honesty is the best policy" with reference to Huck's liberties with the "truth." Using this as a case study, engage in class discussion on the question: "To what extent should custom, fashion, or public opinion govern individual thinking and action?"

9. This chapter describes life along the Mississippi in the 1850's. Point out examples of specific language usages which are no longer current today. What is the meaning of *wigwam* in this context?

10. Stuart Chase, in "The Luxury of Integrity," says: "You and I, and Americans generally, have a personal standard of honorable conduct." Assuming that Huck Finn had such a personal standard, and was justified in his action, what are the implications for people who defy social regulation today?

11. Bertrand Russell says: "It is sympathy that has produced the many humanitarian advances of the last hundred years." With respect to the Negro, what precisely are these advances? What possibilities exist for further advancement? What does Huck's attitude toward Jim suggest for the present desegregation problem in American society?

12. How does Mark Twain create a unified impression in the story? How is this impression related to the theme or thesis of the

story? How is the author's style of writing related to the total effect produced by the incidents narrated?

13. The following statement is from a lecture given by Woodrow Wilson when he was a professor at Princeton University: Consider the statement in connection with Huck Finn's dilemma. "Morality is a great deal bigger than law. The individual morality is the sense of right or wrong of one man. The social morality must strike an average. This is where reformers make their tragic mistake. There can be no compromise in individual morality; but there *has* to be a compromise, an average, in social morality. There is indeed an element of morality in the very fact of compromise on *social* undertakings."

14. Define the words *statism* and *individualism* as they concern Huck Finn's conflict of values. In this connection, read chapter 6 of Huston Smith's *The Purposes of Higher Education*, New York, 1955, entitled "The Individual Versus the State."

◆ ◆ ◆

What's American About America?

JOHN A. KOUWENHOVEN

THE DISCOVERY of America has never been a more popular pastime than it is today. Scarcely a week goes by without someone's publishing a new book of travels in the bright continent. The anthropologists, native and foreign, have discovered that the natives of Middletown and Plainville, U.S.A. are as amazing and as interesting as the natives of such better known communities as the Trobriand Islands and Samoa. Magazines here and abroad provide a steady flow of articles by journalists, historians, soci-

Reprinted from *Harper's Magazine*, July, 1956, by permission of John A. Kouwenhoven. Copyright 1956 by Harper & Brothers.

ologists, and philosophers who want to explain America to itself, or to themselves, or to others.

The discoverers of America have, of course, been describing their experiences ever since Captain John Smith wrote his first book about America almost 350 years ago. But as Smith himself noted, not everyone "who hath bin at Virginia, understandeth or knowes what Virginia is." Indeed, just a couple of years ago the Carnegie Corporation, which supports a number of college programs in American Studies, entitled its Quarterly Report "Who Knows America?" and went on to imply that nobody does, not even "our lawmakers, journalists, civic leaders, diplomats, teachers, and others."

There is, of course, the possibility that some of the writers who have explored, vicariously or in person, this country's past and present may have come to understand or know what America really is. But how is the lay inquirer and the student to know which accounts to trust? Especially since most of the explorers seem to have found not one but two or more antipodal and irreconcilable Americas. The Americans, we are convincingly told, are the most materialistic of peoples, and, on the other hand, they are the most idealistic; the most revolutionary, and, conversely, the most conservative; the most rampantly individualistic, and, simultaneously, the most gregarious and herd-like; the most irreverent toward their elders, and, contrariwise, the most abject worshipers of "Mom." They have an unbridled admiration of everything big, from bulldozers to bosoms; and they are in love with everything diminutive, from the "small hotel" in the song to the little woman in the kitchen.

Maybe, as Henry James thought when he wrote *The American Scene*, it is simply that the country is "too large for any human convenience," too diverse in geography and in blood strains to make sense as any sort of unit. Whatever the reason, the conflicting evidence turns up wherever you look, and the observer has to content himself with some sort of pluralistic conception. The philosopher Santayana's way out was to say that the American mind was split in half, one half symbolized by the skyscraper, the other by neat reproductions of Colonial mansions (with surreptitious modern conveniences).

"The American will," he concluded, "inhabits the skyscraper; the American intellect inherits the Colonial mansion." Mark Twain also defined the split in architectural terms, but more succinctly: American houses, he said, had Queen Anne fronts and Mary Ann behinds.

And yet, for all the contrarieties, there remains something which I think we all feel to be distinctively American, some quality or characteristic underlying the polarities which—as Henry James himself went on to say—makes the American way of doing things differ more from any other nation's way than the ways of any two other Western nations differ from each other.

I am aware of the risks in generalizing. And yet it would be silly, I am convinced, to assert that there are not certain things which are more American than others. Take the New York City skyline, for example—that ragged man-made Sierra at the eastern edge of the continent. Clearly, in the minds of immigrants and returning travelers, in the iconography of the ad-men who use it as a backdrop for the bourbon and airplane luggage they are selling, in the eyes of poets and of military strategists, it is one of the prime American symbols.

Let me start, then, with the Manhattan skyline and list a few things which occur to me as distinctively American. Then, when we have the list, let us see what, if anything, these things have in common. Here are a dozen items to consider:

1. The Manhattan skyline
2. The gridiron town plan
3. The skyscraper
4. The Model-T Ford
5. Jazz
6. The Constitution
7. Mark Twain's writing
8. Whitman's *Leaves of Grass*

9. Comic strips
10. Soap operas
11. Assembly-line production
12. Chewing gum

Here we have a round dozen artifacts which are, it seems to me, recognizably American, not likely to have been produced elsewhere. Granted that some of us take more pleasure in some of them than in others—that many people prefer soap opera to *Leaves of Grass* while others think Mark Twain's storytelling is less offensive than chewing gum—all twelve items are, I believe, widely held to be indigenous to our culture. The fact that many people in other lands like them too, and that some of them are nearly as acceptable overseas as they are here at home, does not in any way detract from their obviously American character. It merely serves to remind us that to be American does not mean to be inhuman—a fact which, in certain moods of self-criticism, we are inclined to forget.

What, then, is the "American" quality which these dozen items share? And what can that quality tell us about the character of our culture, about the nature of our civilization?

SKYLINES AND SKYSCRAPERS

Those engaged in discovering America often begin by discovering the Manhattan skyline, and here as well as elsewhere they discover apparently irreconcilable opposites. They notice at once that it doesn't make any sense, in human or aesthetic terms. It is the product of insane politics, greed, competitive ostentation, megalomania, the worship of false gods. Its products, in turn, are traffic jams, bad ventilation, noise, and all the other ills that metropolitan flesh is heir to. And the net result is, illogically enough, one of the most exaltedly beautiful things man has ever made.

Perhaps this paradoxical result will be less bewildering if we look for a moment at the formal and structural principles which are involved in the skyline. It may be helpful to consider the skyline as we might consider a lyric poem, or a novel, if we were trying to analyze its aesthetic quality..

Looked at in this way, it is clear that the total effect which we call "the Manhattan skyline" is made up of almost innumerable buildings, each in competition (for height, or glamor, or efficiency, or respectability) with all of the others. Each goes its own way, as it were, in a carnival of rugged architectural individualism. And yet—as witness the universal feeling of exaltation and aspiration which the skyline as a whole evokes—out of this irrational, unplanned, and often infuriating chaos, an unforeseen unity has evolved. No building ever built in New York was placed where it was, or shaped as it was, because it would contribute to the aesthetic effect of the skyline—lifting it here, giving it mass there, or lending a needed emphasis. Each was built, all those now under construction are being built, with no thought for their subordination to any over-all effect.

What, then, makes possible the fluid and ever-changing unity which does, in fact, exist? Quite simply, there are two things, both simple in themselves, which do the job. If they were not simple, they would not work; but they are, and they do.

One is the gridiron pattern of the city's streets—the same basic pattern which accounts for Denver, Houston, Little Rock, Birmingham, and almost any American town you can name, and the same pattern which, in the form of square townships, sections, and quarter sections, was imposed by the Ordinance of 1785 on an almost continental scale. Whatever its shortcomings when compared with the "discontinuous street patterns" of modern planned communities, this artificial geometric grid—imposed upon the land without regard to contours or any preconceived pattern of social zoning—had at least the quality of rational simplicity. And it is this simple gridiron street pattern which, horizontally, controls the spacing and arrangement of the rectangular shafts which go to make up the skyline.

The other thing which holds the skyline's diversity together is the structural principle of the skyscraper. When we think of individual buildings, we tend to think of details of texture, color, and form, of surface ornamentation or the lack of it. But as elements in Manhattan's skyline, these things are of little consequence. What matters there is the vertical thrust, the motion upward; and that is the product of cage or skeleton, construction in steel—a system of construction which is, in effect, merely a three-dimensional variant of the gridiron street plan, extending vertically instead of horizontally.

The aesthetics of cage, or skeleton, construction have never been fully analyzed, nor am I equipped to analyze them. But as a lay observer, I am struck by fundamental differences between the effect created by height in the RCA building at Radio City, for example, and the effect created by height in Chartres cathedral or in Giotto's campanile. In both the latter (as in all the great architecture of the past) proportion and symmetry, the relation of height to width, are constituent to the effect. One can say of a Gothic cathedral, this tower is too high; of a Romanesque dome, this is top-heavy. But there is nothing inherent in cage construction which would invite such judgments. A true skyscraper like the RCA building could be eighteen or twenty stories taller, or ten or a dozen stories shorter without changing its essential aesthetic effect. Once steel cage construction has passed a certain height, the effect of transactive upward motion has been established; from there on, the point at which you cut it off is arbitrary and makes no difference.

Those who are familiar with the history of the skyscraper will remember how slowly this fact was realized. Even Louis Sullivan—greatest of the early skyscraper architects—thought in terms of having to close off and climax the upward motion of the tall building with an "attic" or cornice. His lesser contemporaries worked for years on the blind assumption that the proportion and symmetry of masonry architecture must be preserved in the new technique. If with the steel cage one could go higher than with loadbearing masonry walls, the old aesthetic effects could be counterfeited by dressing the façade as if one or more buildings had been piled on top of another—each retaining the illusion of being complete in itself. You can still see such buildings in New York: the first five stories perhaps a Greco-Roman temple, the next ten a neuter warehouse, and the final five or six an Aztec pyramid. And that Aztec pyramid is simply a cheap and thoughtless equivalent of the more subtle Sullivan cornice. Both structures attempt to close and climax the upward thrust, to provide something similar to the *Katharsis* in Greek tragedy.

But the logic of cage construction requires no such climax. It has less to do with the inner logic of masonry forms than with that of the old Globe-Wernicke sectional bookcases, whose interchangeable units (with glass-flap fronts) anticipated by fifty years the modular unit systems of so-called modern furniture. The bookcases were advertised in the 'nineties as "always complete but never finished"—a phrase which could with equal propriety have been applied to the Model-T Ford. Many of us remember with affection that admirably simple mechanism, forever susceptible to added gadgets or improved parts, each of which was interchangeable with what you already had.

Here, then, are the two things which serve to tie together the otherwise irrelevant components of the Manhattan skyline: the gridiron ground plan and the three-dimensional vertical grid of steel cage construction. And both of these are closely related to one another. Both are composed of simple and infinitely repeatable units.

THE STRUCTURE OF JAZZ

It was the French architect, Le Corbusier, who described New York's architecture as "hot jazz in stone and steel." At first glance this may sound as if it were merely a slick updating of Schelling's "Architecture . . . is frozen music," but it is more than that if one thinks in terms of the structural principles we have been discussing and the structural principles of jazz.

Let me begin by making clear that I am using the term jazz in its broadest significant application. There are circumstances in which it is important to define the term with considerable precision, as when you are involved in discussion with a disciple of one of the many cults, orthodox or progressive, which devote themselves to some particular subspecies of jazz. But in our present context we need to focus upon what all the subspecies (Dixieland, Bebop, Swing, or Cool Jazz) have in common: in other words, we must neglect the by no means uninteresting qualities which differentiate one from another, since it is what they have in common which can tell us most about the civilization which produced them.

There is no definition of jazz, academic or otherwise, which does not acknowledge that its essential ingredient is a particular kind of rhythm. Improvisation is also frequently mentioned as an essential; but even if it were true that jazz always involves improvisation, that would not distinguish it from a good deal of Western European music of the past. It is the distinctive rhythm which differentiates all types of jazz from all other music and which gives to all of its types a basic family resemblance.

It is not easy to define that distinctive rhythm. Winthrop Sargeant has described it as the product of two superimposed devices: syncopation and polyrhythm, both of which have the effect of constantly upsetting rhythmical expectations. André Hodeir, in his recent analysis of *Jazz: Its Evolution and Essence*, speaks of "an unending alternation" of syncopations and of notes played *on* the beat, which "gives rise to a kind of expectation that is one of jazz's subtlest effects."

As you can readily hear, if you listen to any jazz performance (whether of the Louis Armstrong, Benny Goodman, or Charlie Parker variety), the rhythmical effect depends upon there being a clearly defined basic rhythmic pattern which enforces the expectations which are to be upset. That basic pattern is the 4/4 or 2/4 beat which underlies all jazz. Hence the importance of the percussive instruments in jazz: the drums, the guitar or banjo, the bull fiddle, the piano. Hence too the insistent thump, thump, thump, thump, which is so boring when you only half-hear jazz —either because you are too far away, across the lake or in the next room, or simply because you will not listen attentively. But hence also the delight, the subtle effects, which good jazz provides as the melodic phrases evade, anticipate, and return to, and then again evade the steady basic four-beat pulse which persists, implicitly or explicitly, throughout the performance.

In other words, the structure of a jazz performance is, like that of the New York skyline, a tension of cross-purposes. In jazz at its characteristic best, each player seems to be—and has the sense of being—on his own. Each goes his own way, inventing rhythmic and melodic patterns which, superficially, seem to have as little relevance to one another as the United Nations building does to the Empire State. And yet the outcome is a dazzlingly precise creative unity.

In jazz that unity of effect is, of course, the result of the very thing which each of the players is flouting: namely, the basic 4/4 beat—that simple rhythmic gridiron of identical and infinitely extendible units which holds the performance together. As Louis Armstrong once wrote, you would expect that if every man in a band "had his own way and could play as he wanted, all you would get would be a lot of jumbled up, crazy noise." But, as he goes on to say, that does not happen, because the players know "by ear and sheer musical instinct" just when to leave the underlying pattern and when to get back on it.

What it adds up to, as I have argued elsewhere, is that jazz is the first art form to give full expression to Emerson's ideal of a union which is perfect only "when all the uniters are isolated." That Emerson's ideal is deeply rooted in our national experience need not be argued. Frederick Jackson Turner quotes a letter written by a frontier settler to friends back East, which in simple, unself-conscious words expresses the same reconciling of opposites. "It is a universal rule here," the frontiersman wrote, "to help one another, each one keeping an eye single to his own business."

One need only remember that the Consitution itself, by providing for a federation of separate units, became the infinitely extendible framework for the process of reconciling liberty and unity over vast areas and conflicting interests. Its seven brief articles, providing for checks and balances between interests, classes, and branches of the government establish, in effect, the

underlying beat which gives momentum and direction to a political process which Richard Hofstadter has called "a harmonious
system of mutual frustration"—a description which fits a jazz
performance as well as it fits our politics.

The aesthetic effects of jazz, as Winthrop Sargeant long ago
suggested, have as little to do with symmetry and proportion as
have those of a skyscraper. Like the skyscraper, a jazz performance does not build to an organically required climax; it can
simply cease. The "piece" which the musicians are playing may,
and often does, have a rudimentary Aristotelian pattern of beginning, middle, and end; but the jazz performance need not. In
traditional Western European music, themes are developed. In
jazz they are toyed with and dismantled. There is no inherent
reason why the jazz performance should not continue for another
12 or 16 or 24 or 32 measures (for these are the rhythmic cages
which in jazz correspond to the cages of a steel skeleton in
architecture. As in the skyscraper, the aesthetic effect is one of
motion, in this case horizontal rather than vertical.

Jazz rhythms create what can only be called momentum.
When rhythm of one voice (say the trumpet, off on a rhythmic
and melodic excursion) lags behind the underlying beat, its four-
beat measure carries over beyond the end of the underlying beat's
measure into the succeeding one, which has already begun. Conversely, when the trumpet anticipates the beat, it starts a new
measure before the steady underlying beat has ended one. And
the result is an exhilarating forward motion which the jazz trumpeter Wingy Manone once described as "feeling an increase in
tempo though you're still playing at the same tempo." Hence
the importance in jazz of timing, and hence the delight and
amusement of the so-called "break," in which the basic 4/4 beat
ceases and a soloist goes off on a flight of rhythmic and melodic
fancy which nevertheless comes back surprisingly and unerringly
to encounter the beat precisely where it would have been if it
had kept going.

Once the momentum is established, it can continue until—
after an interval dictated by some such external factor as the

conventional length of phonograph records or the endurance of dancers—it stops. And as if to guard against any Aristotelian misconceptions about an end, it is likely to stop on an unresolved chord, so that harmonically as well as rhythmically everything is left up in the air. Even the various coda-like devices employed by jazz performers at dances, such as the corny old "without a shirt" phrase of blessed memory, are harmonically unresolved. They are merely conventional ways of saying "we quit," not, like Beethoven's insistent codas, ways of saying, "There now; that ties off all the loose ends; I'm going to stop now; done; finished; concluded; signed, sealed, delivered."

TWAIN AND WHITMAN

Thus far, in our discussion of distinctively "American" things, we have focused chiefly upon twentieth-century items. But the references to the rectangular grid pattern of cities and townships and to the Constitution should remind us that the underlying structural principles with which we are concerned are deeply embedded in our civilization. To shift the emphasis, therefore, let us look at item number 7 on our list: Mark Twain's writing.

Mark's writing was, of course, very largely the product of oral influences. He was a born storyteller, and he always insisted that the oral form of the humorous story was high art. Its essential tool (or weapon), he said, is the pause—which is to say, timing. "If the pause is too long the impressive point is passed," he wrote, "and the audience have had time to divine that a surprise is intended—and then you can't surprise them, of course." In other words, he saw the pause as a device for upsetting expectations, like the jazz "break."

Mark, as you know, was by no means a formal perfectionist. In fact he took delight in being irreverent about literary form. Take, for example, his account of the way *Pudd'nhead Wilson* came into being. It started out to be a story called "Those Extraordinary Twins," about a youthful freak consisting, as he said of "a combination of two heads and four arms joined to a single body and a single pair of legs—and I thought I would write an ex-

travagantly fantastic little story with this freak of nature for hero
—or heroes—a silly young miss [named Rowena] for heroine,
and two old ladies and two boys for the minor parts."

But as he got writing the tale, it kept spreading along and other
people began intruding themselves—among them Pudd'nhead,
and a woman named Roxana, and a young fellow named Tom
Driscoll, who—before the book was half finished—had taken
things almost entirely into their own hands and were "working
the whole tale as a private venture of their own.".

From this point, I want to quote Mark directly, because in the
process of making fun of fiction's formal conventions he employs
a technique which is the verbal equivalent of the jazz "break"—
a technique of which he was master.

When the book was finished, and I came to look round to see
what had become of the team I had originally started out with—
Aunt Patsy Cooper, Aunt Betsy Hale, the two boys, and Rowena
the light-weight heroine—they were nowhere to be seen; they had
disappeared from the story some time or other. I hunted about
and found them—found them stranded, idle, forgotten, and permanently useless. It was very awkward. It was awkward all around;
but more particularly in the case of Rowena, because there was a
love match on, between her and one of the twins that constituted
the freak, and I had worked it up to a blistering heat and thrown
in a quite dramatic love quarrel [now watch Mark take off like a
jazz trumpeter flying off on his own in a fantastic break] wherein
Rowena scathingly denounced her betrothed for getting drunk, and
scoffed at his explanation of how it had happened, and wouldn't
listen to it, and had driven him from her in the usual "forever"
way; and now here she sat crying and brokenhearted; for she had
found that he had spoken only the truth; that it was not he but the
other half of the freak, that had drunk the liquor that made him
drunk; that her half was a prohibitionist and had never drunk a
drop in his life, and, although tight as a brick three days in the
week, was wholly innocent of blame; and, indeed, when sober was
constantly doing all he could to reform his brother, the other half,
who never got any satisfaction out of drinking anyway, because
liquor never affected him. [Now he's going to get back on the basic
beat again.] Yes, here she was, stranded with that deep injustice
of hers torturing her poor heart.

Now I shall have to summarize again. Mark didn't know what to do with her. He couldn't just leave her there, of course, after making such a to-do over her; he'd have to account to the reader for her somehow. So he finally decided that all he could do was "give her the grand bounce." It grieved him, because he'd come to like her after a fashion, "notwithstanding she was such an ass and said such stupid, irritating things and was so nauseatingly sentimental"; but it had to be done. So he started Chapter Seventeen with: "Rowena went out in the back yard after supper to see the fireworks and fell down the well and got drowned."

It seemed abrupt, [Mark went on] but I thought maybe the reader wouldn't notice it, because I changed the subject right away to something else. Anyway, it loosened up Rowena from where she was stuck and got her out of the way, and that was the main thing. It seemed a prompt good way of weeding out people that had got stalled, and a plenty good enough way for those others; so I hunted up the two boys and said they went out back one night to stone the cat and fell down the well and got drowned. Next I searched around and found Aunt Patsy Cooper and Aunt Betsy Hale where they were aground, and said they went out back one night to visit the sick and fell down the well and got drowned. I was going to drown some of the others, but I gave up the idea, partly because I believed that if I kept that up it would arouse attention, . . . and partly because it was not a large well and would not hold any more anyway.

That was a long excursion—but it makes the point: that Mark didn't have much reverence for conventional story structure. Even his greatest book, which is perhaps also the greatest book written on this continent—*Huckleberry Finn*—is troublesome. One can scarcely find a criticism of the book which does not object, for instance, to the final episodes, in which Tom rejoins Huck and they go through that burlesque business of "freeing" the old Negro Jim—who is, it turns out, already free. But, as T. S. Eliot was, I think, the first to observe, the real structure of *Huck Finn* has nothing to do with the traditional form of the novel—with exposition, climax, and resolution. Its structure is like that of the great river's steady flow and the eccentric superimposed rhythms of Huck's flights from, and near recapture by, the restricting forces of routine and convention.

It is not a novel of escape; if it were, it would be Jim's novel, not Huck's. Huck is free at the start, and still free at the end. Looked at in this way, it is clear that *Huckleberry Finn* has as little need of a "conclusion" as has a skyscraper or a jazz performance. Questions of proportion and symmetry are as irrelevant to its structure as they are to the total effect of the New York skyline.

There is not room here for more than brief reference to the other "literary" items on our list: Whitman's *Leaves of Grass*, comic strips, and soap opera. Perhaps it is enough to remind you that *Leaves of Grass* has discomfited many a critic by its lack of symmetry and proportion, and that Whitman himself insisted: "I round and finish little, if anything; and could not, consistently with my scheme." As for the words of true poems, Whitman said in the "Song of the Answerer"—

> They bring none to his or her terminus or to be
>   content and full,
> Whom they take they take into space to behold the
>   birth of stars, to learn one of the meanings,
> To launch off with absolute faith, to sweep through
>   the ceaseless rings and never be quiet again.

Although this is not the place for a detailed analysis of Whitman's verse techniques, it is worth noting in passing how the rhythm of these lines reinforces their logical meaning. The basic rhythmical unit, throughout, is a three-beat phrase of which there are two in the first line (accents falling on *none, his,* and *term . . . be, tent,* and *full*), three in the second and in the third. Superimposed upon the basic three-beat measure there is a flexible, nonmetrical rhythm of colloquial phrasing. That rhythm is controlled in part by the visual effect of the arrangement in long lines, to each of which the reader tends to give equal duration, and in part by the punctuation within the lines.

It is the tension between the flexible, super-imposed rhythms of the rhetorical patterns and the basic three-beat measure of the underlying framework which unites with the imagery and the logical meaning of the words to give the passage its restless, sweeping movement. It is this tension, and other analogous aspects of the structure of *Leaves of Grass* which give to the book that "vista" which Whitman himself claimed for it. If I may apply to it. T. S. Eliot's idea about *Huckleberry Finn*, the structure of the *Leaves* is open at the end. Its key poem may well be, as D. H. Lawrence believed, the "Song of the Open Road."

As for the comics and soap opera, they too—on their own frequently humdrum level—have devised structures which provide for no ultimate climax, which come to no end demanded by symmetry or proportion. In them both there is a shift in interest away from the "How does it come out?" of traditional story telling to "How are things going?" In a typical installment of Harold Gray's *Orphan Annie*, the final panel shows Annie walking purposefully down a path with her dog, Sandy, saying: "But if we're goin', why horse around? It's a fine night for walkin' . . . C'mon, Sandy . . . Let's go . . . " (It doesn't even end with a period, or full stop, but with the conventional three dots or suspension points, to indicate incompletion.) So too, in the soap operas, *Portia Faces Life*, in one form or another, day after day, over and over again. And the operative word is the verb *faces*. It is the process of facing that matters.

AMERICA IS PROCESS

Here, I think, we are approaching the central quality which all the diverse items on our list have in common. That quality I would define as a concern with process rather than with product—or, to re-use Mark Twain's words, a concern with the manner of handling experience or materials rather than with the experience or materials themselves. Emerson, a century ago, was fascinated by the way "becoming somewhat else is the perpetual game of nature." And this preoccupation with process is, of course, basic to modern science. "Matter" itself is no longer to be thought of as something fixed, but fluid and ever-changing. Similarly, modern economic theory has abandoned the "static equilibrium" analysis of the neo-classic economists, and in philosophy John Dewey's instrumentalism abandoned the classic philosophical interest in final causes for a scientific interest in "the mechanism of occurrences"—that is, process.

It is obvious, I think, that the American system of industrial mass production reflects this same focus of interest in its concern with production rather than products. And it is the mass-production system, *not* machinery, which has been America's contribution to industry.

In that system there is an emphasis different from that which was characteristic of handicraft production or even of machine manufacture. In both of these there was an almost total disregard of the means of production. The aristocratic ideal inevitably relegated interest in the means exclusively to anonymous peasants and slaves; what mattered to those who controlled and administered production was, quite simply, the finished product. In a mass-production system, on the other hand, it is the process of production itself which becomes the center of interest, rather than the product.

If we are aware of this fact, we usually regard it as a misfortune. We hear a lot, for instance, of the notion that our system "dehumanizes" the worker, turning him into a machine and depriving him of the satisfactions of finishing anything, since he performs only some repetitive operation. It is true that the unit of work in mass production is not a product but an operation. But the development of the system, in contrast with Charlie Chaplin's wonderful but wild fantasy of the assembly line, has shown the intermediacy of the stage in which the worker is doomed to frustrating boredom. Merely repetitive work, in the logic of mass production, can and must be done by machine. It is unskilled work which is doomed by it, not the worker. More and more skilled workers are needed to design products, analyze jobs, cut patterns, attend complicated machines, and co-ordinate the processes which comprise the productive system.

The skills required for these jobs are different of course, from those required to make handmade boots or to carve stone ornaments, but they are not in themselves less interesting or less human. Operating a crane in a steel mill, or a turret lathe, is an infinitely more varied and stimulating job than shaping boots day after day by hand. A recent study of a group of workers on an automobile assembly line makes it clear that many of the men object, for a variety of reasons, to those monotonous, repetitive jobs which (as we have already noted) should be—but in many cases are not yet—done by machine; but those who like such jobs like them because they enjoy the process. As one of them said: "Repeating the same thing you can catch up and keep ahead of yourself . . . you can get in the swing of it." The report of members of a team of British workers who visited twenty American steel foundries in 1949 includes this description of the technique of "snatching" a steel casting with a magnet, maneuvered by a gantry crane running on overhead rails:

In its operation, the crane approaches a pile of castings at high speed with the magnet hanging fairly near floor level. The crane comes to a stop somewhere short of the castings, while the magnet swings forward over the pile, is dropped on to it, current switched on, and the hoist begun, at the same moment as the crane starts on its return journey. [And then, in words which might equally be applied to a jazz musician, the report adds:] The whole operation requires timing of a high order, and the impression gained is that the crane drivers derive a good deal of satisfaction from the swinging rhythm of the process.

This fascination with process has possessed Americans ever since Oliver Evans in 1785 created the first wholly automatic factory; a flour mill in Delaware in which mechanical conveyors —belt conveyors, bucket conveyors, screw conveyors—are interlinked with machines in a continuous process of production. But even if there were no other visible sign of the national preoccupation with process, it would be enough to point out that it was an American who invented chewing gum (in 1869) and that it is the Americans who have spread it—in all senses of the verb—throughout the world. An absolutely non-consumable confection, its sole appeal is the process of chewing it.

The apprehensions which many people feel about a civiliza-tion absorbed with process—about its mobility and wastefulness as well as about the "dehumanizing" effects of its jobs—derive, I suppose, from old habit and the persistence of values and tastes which were indigenous to a very different social and eco-nomic system. Whitman pointed out in *Democratic Vistas* more than eighty years ago that America was a stranger in her own house, that many of our social institutions, like our theories of literature and art, had been taken over almost without change from a culture which was not, like ours, the product of political democracy and the machine. Those institutions and theories, though some (like collegiate gothic, of both the archi-tectural and intellectual variety) are less widely admired than formerly.

Change, or the process of consecutive occurrences, is, we tend to feel, a bewildering and confusing and lonely thing. All of us, in some moods, feel the "preference for the stable over the precarious and uncompleted" which, as John Dewey recognized, tempts philosophers to posit their absolutes. We talk fondly of the need for roots—as if man were a vegetable, not an animal with legs whose distinction it is that he can move and "get on with it." We would do well to make ourselves more familiar with the idea that the process of development is universal, that it is "the form and order of nature." As Lancelot Law White has said, in *The Next Development in Man:*

Man shares the special form of the universal formative process which is common to all organisms, and herein lies the root of his unity with the rest of organic nature. While life is maintained, the component processes in man never attain the relative isolation and static perfection of inorganic processes. . . . The individual may seek, or believe that he seeks, independence, permanence, or perfection, but that is only through his failure to recognize and accept his actual situation.

As an "organic system" man cannot, of course, expect to achieve stability or permanent harmony, though he can create (and in the great arts of the past, has created) the illusion of them. What he can achieve is a continuing development in response to his environment. The factor which gives vitality to all the component processes in the individual and in society is "not permanence but development."

To say this is not to deny the past. It is simply to recognize that for a variety of reasons people living in America have, on the whole, been better able to relish process than those who have lived under the imposing shadow of the arts and institutions which Western man created in his tragic search for permanence and perfection—for a "closed system." They find it easy to understand what that very American philosopher William James meant when he told his sister that his house in Chocorua, New Hampshire, was "the most delightful house you ever saw; it has fourteen doors, all opening outwards." They are used to living in grid-patterned cities and towns whose streets, as Jean-Paul Sartre observed, are not, like those of European cities, "closed at both ends." As Sartre says in his essay on New York, the long straight streets and avenues of a gridiron city do not permit the buildings to "cluster like sheep" and protect one against the sense of space. "They are not sober little walks closed in between houses, but national highways. The moment you set foot on one of them, you understand that it has to go on to Boston or Chicago."

So, too, the past of those who live in the United States, like their future, is open-ended. It does not, like the past of most other people, extend downward into the soil out of which their immediate community or neighborhood has grown. It extends laterally backward across the plains, the mountains, or the sea to somewhere else, just as their future may at any moment lead them down the open road, the endless vistaed street.

Our history is the process of motion into and out of cities; of westering and the counter-process of return; of motion up and down the social ladder—a long, complex, and sometimes terrifyingly rapid sequence of consecutive change. And it is this sequence, and the attitudes and habits and forms which it has bred, to which the term "America" really refers.

"America" is not a synonym for the United States. It is not an artifact. It is not a fixed and immutable ideal toward which citizens of this nation strive. It has not order or proportion, but neither is it chaos except as that is chaotic whose components no single mind can comprehend or control. America is process. And in so far as people have been "American"—as distinguished from being (as most of us, in at least some of our activities, have been) mere carriers of transplanted cultural traditions—the concern with process has been reflected in the work of their heads and hearts and hands.

Questions and Exercises

1. What single thread does Kouwenhoven suggest ties together the Manhattan skyline, jazz, the Constitution, chewing gum, and soap operas?
2. When the author talks of Americans as "abject worshippers of 'Mom,'" is he suggesting, as some sociologists have, that this country is essentially a matriarchy?
3. To what extent is Kouwenhoven's idea about America in process an explanation of the pragmatic philosophy of William James?
4. Where in the essay does the author pose the central question to be focused upon? Where do you find a succinct answer to the question?
5. Which of the twelve most characteristic things about America, listed by the author, would you reject, or replace? What would you substitute?
6. Defend the conviction that the American language should have been included as one of the principal characteristics of the American people.
7. Melville said in *Moby Dick*: "This whole book is but a draught—nay, but the draught of a draught." How does this statement make Melville's work an appropriate item for Kouwenhoven's list? Can you suggest other qualities of *Moby Dick* that argue its process nature? What about the chapter "Of the Monstrous Pictures of Whales" (included in this volume)?

8. How does scientific empiricism demonstrate Kouwenhoven's notion of incompleteness and open-endness?

9. "We would do well," says Kouwenhoven, "to make ourselves more familiar with the idea that the process of development is universal, that it is the 'form and order of nature.' " What does this suggest about the applicability of codified rules of grammar for modern American language usage? Explain with reference to specific usages.

10. What are the implications for education, politics, economy, religion, or government of Kouwenhoven's idea of flux and change?

11. Read Crevoceur's *Letters from an American Farmer* (1782), and determine to what extent he recognized America as an institution in process.

12. "We've finished Scripture," says a girl in a child's school; "we had it last year." Stephen Leacock, in "Education Is Eating Up Life" from *Too Much College,* uses this example to show that there is too much emphasis in education on finishing, or getting done with courses of study. This would seem to be an especially futile attitude to assume toward courses in reading, writing, speaking, or listening. Explain why, and suggest ways of combatting this pernicious tendency in our schools.

13. A famous educator once said: "An ideal, like democracy, does not lend itself to simple definition, nor can it be confined within any definition, for, if it is a genuine ideal, it is always being enriched, extended, broadened." How does this statement match Kouwenhoven's idea of America in process?

14. Explain the following statement in terms of Kouwenhoven's idea:
    "For the proper execution of the professional duty of any member of the faculty of a liberal arts college, no prescribed 'method' or 'approach' is either necessary or possible."

15. Clifton Fadiman in one of his essays speaks of "mind-man" and "thing-man." Kouwenhoven has said little in his article about man's intellect. Read Daniel J. Bourstin's "The Place of Thought in American Life," *The American Scholar,* Spring, 1956, and suggest the feasibility of nominating "ideas" as a symbol of the American people.

16. Mark Twain once said: "When I stop writing for the day, I always leave off in the middle of a sentence. This is so I can begin again the next morning right off, without having

to read back to refresh my memory. It saves a lot of time."
You may question the time saved by this device. What merit,
if any, does it have?

◆ ◆ ◆

Oliver and the Other Ostriches

JAMES THURBER

An austere ostrich of awesome authority was lecturing
younger ostriches one day on the superiority of their species to
all other species. "We werc known to the Romans—or, rather,
the Romans wcre known to us," he said. "'They called us *avis
struthio,* and we called them Romans. The Greeks called us
strouthion, which means 'truthful one,' or, if it doesn't, it
should. We are the biggest birds, and therefore the best. Anything any bird can do, we can do better."

All his listeners cried "Hear! Hear!" except a thoughtful one
named Oliver. "We can't fly backward like the hummingbird,"
he said aloud.

"The hummingbird is losing ground," said the old ostrich.
"We are going places, we are moving forward."

"Hear! Hear!" cried all the other ostriches except Oliver.

"We lay the biggest eggs and therefore the best eggs," continued the old lecturer.

"The robin's eggs are prettier," said Oliver.

© 1956 The New Yorker Magazine, Inc.; in *Further Fables for Our Time* (Simon
and Schuster). Reprinted by permission of The New Yorker Magazine, Inc.

"Robins' eggs produce nothing but robins," said the old os-trich. "Robins are lawn-bound worm addicts."

"Hear! Hear!" cried all the other ostriches except Oliver.

"We get along on four toes, whereas Man needs ten," the elderly instructor reminded his class.

"But Man can fly sitting down, and we can't fly at all," com-mented Oliver.

The old ostrich glared at him severely, first with one eye and then the other. "Man is flying too fast for a world that is round," he said. "Soon he will catch up with himself, in a great rear-end collision, and Man will never know that what hit Man from behind was Man."

"Hear! Hear!" cried all the other ostriches except Oliver.

"We can make ourselves invisible in time of peril by sticking our heads in the sand," ranted the lecturer. "Nobody else can do that."

"How do we know we can't be seen if we can't see?" de-manded Oliver.

"Sophistry!" cried the old ostrich, and all the other ostriches except Oliver cried "Sophistry!," not knowing what it meant.

Just then the master and the class heard a strange alarming sound, a sound like thunder growing close and growing closer. It was not the thunder of weather, though, but the thunder of a vast herd of rogue elephants in full stampede, frightened by nothing, fleeing nowhere. The old ostrich and all the other os-triches except Oliver quickly stuck their heads in the sand. Ol-iver took refuge behind a large nearby rock until the storm of beasts had passed, and when he came out he beheld a sea of sand and bones and feathers—all that was left of the old teacher and his disciples. Just to be sure, however, Oliver called the roll, but there was no answer until he came to his own name. "Oli-ver," he said.

"Here! Here!" said Oliver, and that was the only sound there was on the desert except for a faint, final rumble of thunder on the horizon.

Moral: Thou shalt not build thy house, nor yet thy faith, upon the sand.

Questions and Exercises

1. State the central idea of this fable in one. succinct, declarative sentence.
2. Consider the satirical elements in the fable. Identify as many specific criticisms of American ways or attitudes or institutions as you can.
3. What is the relationship, if any, between Thurber's fable and Rollo May's "The Experience of Becoming a Person"?
4. What is Thurber's conviction regarding national, racial, or cultural superiority? Explain.
5. How does reading this fable demonstrate the creative and active aspects of the receptive skills, as discussed by Stuart Chase in "Are You Listening?" and by Perry and Whitlock in "The Right to Think—Through Reading"?
6. Compare Thurber's thought in this fable with Shelley's "Ozymandias" or with Carl Sandburg's "Four Preludes on Playthings of the Wind," from *Smoke and Steel*. To what extent is the idea a prediction of America's future?
7. Show how this fable illustrates Susanne Langer's idea about the use of symbols in creating thoughts, as discussed in "Language and Creative Thought."
8. Compare the technique used by Thurber in this fable with that employed by Phillips in "Little Red Riding Hood." Which author in your opinion is more subtle? Which more caustic?
9. What is the relation between Thurber's idea and the idea expressed by Steinbeck in "How to Tell Good Guys from Bad Guys"? Between Thurber's idea and that expressed by Eiseley in "The Bird and the Machine"?
10. How can you account for the divergent ideas different people get from reading a given poem, drama, or novel, such as *Moby Dick* or *Hamlet*? Read in this connection Theodore Morrison's "Dover Beach Revisited," *Harper's Magazine*, February, 1940.
11. Compare the idea in this fable with Mark Twain's idea in "Huck and Jim on the Raft." How does Thurber's point of

view differ from Mark Twain's? Which author's treatment is more persuasive?

12. What political or social problems in America are suggested by the fable? State one of these problems in the form of a question and limit it in such a manner as would make it suitable for scientific investigation or research.

13. Contrast and define the kinds of thinking employed by Oliver and any one of the other Ostriches.

V. GETTING AT THE TRUTH

The principal function of facts in oral or written discourse is to support and defend ideas. If words can be compared to ships, ideas are the cargo. Purpose is the rudder that keeps the ship on course. And facts are the ballast that insures the effectiveness of the propelling power.

A fact is a datum of experience that can pass the most rigid tests of repeated examination. A report is a statement of fact that can be confirmed and verified by any number of qualified observers. Many of the statements which pass for reports are actually nothing more than casual statements of opinion. Instead of revealing the true nature of facts, such statements pass judgment on them and exhibit these judgments as truth.

Many of the principles by which people regulate their lives are what A. E. Mander calls "Groundless Beliefs"—beliefs not only ungrounded but actually contrary to observable facts. Evan Jones, in "Pick and Shovel Sherlock Holmes," demonstrates from personal experience how facts can be honestly discovered. Herman Melville's chapter from *Moby Dick* is a kind of satire on the widespread ignorance of people generally, including so-called scientists. Melville stresses the impossibility of ever arresting a fact in process. Jean Mayer, in his criticism of college textbooks and scientific treatises, lifts the curtain on a kind of mass hallucination which people have about the world and themselves. Wendell Johnson empha-

261

sizes personal responsibility in getting at the truth for ourselves by making appropriate use of the senses with which we are equipped.

One of the best indications of intellectual maturity is one's capacity to challenge his own basic assumptions and to distinguish between truth and falsehood, between facts and inferences from facts, and between reports and judgments. Successful communication, both in the transmission and the reception of meaning, requires the ability to suspend judgment until all the facts pertaining to a particular problem are discovered and taken into account. We must accept the counsel once offered by T. H. Huxley: "Sit down before a fact as a little child, be prepared to give up every pre-conceived notion, follow humbly wherever and to whatever abysses nature leads, or you shall learn nothing."

Groundless Beliefs

A. E. MANDER

IN FUTURE we are going to follow the practice—until it becomes a habit ("second nature")—of classifying propositions according to their grounds. Of every statement we come across, we shall ask: "HOW DO WE KNOW THAT? WHAT REASON HAVE WE FOR BELIEVING THAT? ON WHAT 'GROUNDS' IS THAT STATEMENT BASED?" Probably we shall be astonished at the number of propositions met with in everyday life—propositions usually accepted blindly, without question, as a matter of course—which we shall find it necessary to class as groundless. They rest upon mere tradition, or on somebody's bare assertion unsupported by even a shadow of proof. . . .

It may be a belief which we originally accepted as a result of simple "suggestion," and we have continued to hold it ever since. It has now become one of our regular habits of thought. *Perhaps somebody—somewhere—sometime—told us a certain thing, and quite uncritically we accepted and believed it. Perhaps it was away back in our early childhood—before we had even developed the power of questioning anything that might be told to us.* Many of our strongest convictions were established then; and now, in adult life, we find it most difficult even to question their truth. They seem to us "obviously" true: we feel that even to question them would be "absurd."

But if the staunchest Roman Catholic and the staunchest Presbyterian had been exchanged when infants, and if they had been brought up with home and all other influences reversed, we can have very little doubt what the result would have been. It is consistent with all our knowledge of psychology to conclude that each would have grown up holding exactly the opposite beliefs to those he holds now . . . and each would then have felt as sure of the truth of his opinion as he now feels—of the truth of the opposite opinion. The same thing is true, of course, of many beliefs other than those of a religious nature. If we had grown up in a community where polygamy or head-hunting, or infanticide, or gladiatorial fighting, or duelling, was regarded as the normal and natural thing—then we should have grown up to regard it as "obviously" natural and perfectly moral and proper. If we had been bred by criminals amongst criminals in one of those quarters of a great city where criminals dwell—then we should have grown up with a set of moral standards quite different from those we have. Or if an English baby had been adopted and brought up in a German home, and had grown up with no knowledge that his parents were English, all the sentiments and beliefs of that person would be "German" and not "English." Many of our beliefs—many of our most deeply-rooted and fundamental convictions—are held simply as a result of the fact that we happen to have been "brought up" to them.

Of course we do not cease, when we cease to be children, to adopt new beliefs on mere suggestion. We continue doing it, more or less unconsciously all our lives: hence, to take only the most striking examples, the enormous influence of newspapers and the effectiveness of skilful advertising. *Much of what passes as such is not, strictly, thinking at all. It is the mere "parroting" of ideas picked up by chance and adopted as our own without question. Most people, most of the time, are mere parrots.* But as we leave childhood, we tend to accept only such new ideas as fit in with the ideas we already hold; and all conflicting ideas seem to us "obviously" absurd.

Propositions that are accepted simply because "everybody says so," must be classed under the same heading. The dogma may not be that of any particular individual: it may be a dogmatic statement which has been passed from one person to another, from generation to generation, perhaps for hundreds— perhaps for thousands—of years. It may be part of the traditional belief of the people or the race. In that case, it is part of our social inheritance from some period in the past. But we should fully face the fact (already stated) that beliefs which are merely inherited from the past must have originated at a time when men knew much less than they know today. So the fact that a belief is "old" is no argument in its favour.

We need especially to be on our guard when we come across propositions which seem to be "obviously" true—so obviously that it seems impossible to doubt them.

When we find ourselves entertaining an opinion about which there is a feeling that *even to enquire into it* would be *absurd, unnecessary, undesirable,* or *wicked*—we may know that that opinion is a non-rational one.   —TROTTER

When we are tempted to say that any general truth is so "obvious" that it would be absurd even to question it, we should remember that the whole history of the development of human thought has been full of cases of such "obvious truths" breaking down when examined in the light of increasing knowledge and reason. For instance, for ages nothing could have seemed more obvious, more utterly beyond question, than the proposition that slavery was natural, reasonable, necessary, and right. Some kinds of men were "obviously" "slaves by nature." To doubt it was impossible.

Again, for more than two thousand years, it was "impossible to conceive" the planets as moving in paths other than circles. The circle was "obviously" the perfect figure; and so it was "natural" and "inevitable" to suppose that the planets moved in circles. The age-long struggle of the greatest intellects in the world to shake off that assumption is one of the marvels of history.

It was formerly "obvious" that the heart—and not the brain —was the organ of consciousness. To most people today (even apart from proof) it seems equally "obvious" that we think with our brains. Many modern persons find it very difficult to credit the fact that men can ever have supposed otherwise. Yet —they did. And, what is more, the "truth" that we think with our hearts seemed to them so "obvious" that it was absolutely impossible for them to doubt it.

That the earth must be flat, formerly seemed so obvious and self-evident that the very suggestion of any other possibility would have been—and was—regarded as a joke.

It was for two thousand years "taken for granted" as "obvious" that a heavy weight must fall faster than a light one. An assumed or dogmatic proposition which had been universally accepted as "obvious"; and which, when challenged, was supported by reference to a dogma of Aristotle. Until Galileo actually demonstrated the contrary, nothing could have seemed more beyond possibility or doubt.

Propositions which are accepted blindly, without question, on the grounds of mere assumption or dogma, need to be frankly recognized as such. Progress in human thought seems to consist mainly in getting rid of such ideas.

Other beliefs are held through self-interest. Modern psychology leaves us no room for doubt on this point. We adopt and cling to some beliefs because—or partly because—it "pays" us to do so. But, as a rule, the person concerned is about the last person in the world to be able to recognize this in himself. Indeed, he would probably be highly indignant if told of what anyone familiar with modern psychology can recognize so plainly. It would be quite wrong to attribute all opinions—even political opinions—to self-interest. But it would be equally wrong to deny that this is one potent factor.

"Self-interest" is to be understood first in the ordinary sense, as referring to a man's way of earning his livelihood and acquiring wealth. But we may extend the term to cover also his interest in social position; popularity with his fellows (at least his own "set"); the respect and goodwill of those whose respect and goodwill he values; agreeable associations with the people of a particular party, church, or social set, from which he would be excluded if his opinions were changed. It covers his interest in his own career; in whatever prestige he enjoys as one of the leaders—or at least as a valued supporter—of some movement or institution, some political party, some religious body, some other kind of society or group. There is many a man who is unconsciously compelled to cling to a belief because he is a "somebody" in some circle—and if he were to abandon that belief, he would find himself nobody at all.

Putting it broadly, we should always suspect any of our opinions when we recognize that our happiness depends, directly or indirectly, upon our continuing to hold them—when we might lose anything, material or otherwise, by changing our opinion.

Somewhat similar is the acceptance of an opinion through the desire—probably not recognized by the person concerned —to justify his own nature, his own position, or his own behaviour. The coward can so easily adopt a philosophy which seems to justify cowardice—though, of course, "cowardice" is not the name he gives it! The lazy and bungling person can adopt a set of opinions which prove to his satisfaction that "the grapes are sour"—the "grapes" being the rewards that more energetic and competent men can win. And many a preacher and propagandist is like the fox that lost his tail. (There is much wisdom in Aesop!)

Many groundless opinions are held through sentimental associations. The thought is associated with memories—pleasant or unpleasant as the case may be—of particular persons who held similar opinions. It is found that many a man who in childhood was hostile to his father, in after life is always prejudiced against whatever opinions his father used to express. And conversely in the case of one who has pleasant recollections of his father, his mother, a teacher perhaps, or some other person who played a big part in his early life.

In adult life, as we have often observed, a bitter quarrel may change a man's opinion entirely. Antagonism to a man usually produces some antagonism to his opinions; and the bitterness felt against the man usually spreads to the idea for which he stands. What keen satisfaction we find in belittling the opinions, or attacking the opinions, of somebody of whom we are jealous, or of somebody against whom we bear a grudge! But, on the other hand, it is equally true that friendly feelings to a man have an effect in disposing us to feel friendly to his views.

Other opinions again are determined by what we may best call Fashion. To take one example: how largely our opinions on the merits of certain authors, or poets, or composers, are dictated merely by fashion! But the effect of fashion is very much wider than that: we trace it almost everywhere, in every field of thought. *We tend very strongly to feel and to believe as others are feeling and believing. Not all others, perhaps; but others of our own set.*

But we do not, as a rule, continue all our lives changing our sentiments and opinions with every change of fashion. Sooner or later our minds become fixed. Many a man holds his opinions today—because they happened to be in fashion ten, twenty, thirty, forty, or fifty years ago.

Once an opinion is accepted, whatever be the cause of its acceptance, it has a strong tendency to persist. Every time we think along a particular thought-pattern, it makes it easier for us to think the same way again. It is quite legitimate to speak of "habits" of thought. The "brain path" becomes so well worn; the pattern of brain-centres becomes so well connected up by continual use, that the nerve current finds a route of practically no resistance, and so it always takes almost exactly the same course.

We all know the person who has a string of stock anecdotes. We all know too the person who has certain stock arguments and opinions which he expresses, almost in the same words, whenever he receives the "cue." We all know men and women whose minds work like gramophones. Put them on to the "record" about the good old days; or about prohibition; or about the wicked capitalists; or about the lazy and improvident workers; or about their illnesses (the tale of their troubles and the number of operations they have undergone); or about some holiday they once spent; or about the country going to the dogs; or about the modern girl; or some long, tedious anecdote about what I said to him, and what he said to me, and I said . . . and he said . . . *and then I told him straight* . . . *!* All we have to do is to start him off—and nothing on earth can stop him—until the "record" has run out!

The same thing is true of opinions and beliefs of all kinds. After they have been held a certain length of time, they become, as it were, so stamped in by continual use that it is almost impossible now to change them. While we are young, we are continually taking in new ideas, altering our thought-patterns, "making up our minds" afresh. As we grow older, we become less and less able to accept any new idea which will not fit in with our existing thought-pattern. Thus we become, in James's term, Old Fogeys. Sometimes our thought-patterns set while we are still quite young. In a few rare cases they remain open or alterable even into old age. An Old Fogey may have become such at seventeen—or seventy. We are Old Fogeys from the moment when we become unable to accept any new fact, any new idea, which would necessitate changing our established habits of thought. "I am almost afraid to say so (says James), but I believe that in the majority of human beings Old Fogeyism begins at about the age of twenty-five."

Yet when full allowance has been made for all these non-rational factors in the determination of opinion, there remains— not in all minds, not in most minds, but in some—a desire to discover the facts; to think things out in a clear and rational way; to get at the truth at all costs, whatever it may turn out to be! For such minds this . . . is written.

Questions and Exercises

1. Mander lists six principal sources for what he calls "groundless beliefs." Cite several examples of each kind of belief he discusses.
2. To what extent are "groundless beliefs" cherished by twentieth-century Americans? You may want to check the results of a polling agency to determine the answer to this question. See, for example, Eugene E. Levitt's "Superstitions: Twenty-five Years Ago and Today," *American Journal of Psychology*, July, 1952, pp. 443–449.
3. What objective (verifiable) evidence can you point to that testifies of the influence of groundless beliefs on human behavior? (How many hotels in this country, for example, have a thirteenth floor?)
4. Find five examples in commercial advertising of groundless beliefs used for promoting an item of merchandise.
5. How does Mander's discussion of "self-interest" complement and reinforce what Cohen says about "we" and "they" in "The Reconstruction of Hidden Value Judgments"? About prejudice?
6. Many important questions, according to Mander, were once settled by dogma. To what extent does Brenda Ueland depend on this kind of evidence to support her thesis in "Walk a Thousand Miles This Year"?
7. Before a man is accepted as an authority on a given subject, we have a right to know as much as possible about his qualifica-

tions. Test some recognized authority (on a particular subject) by finding answers to the following questions:

   a. Does the authority actually exist? Is he accessible? Or is he an abstraction, like "reliable sources," or "informed opinion"?
   b. Is the authority qualified to report accurately and to draw valid conclusions? Is he a specialist in the subject under consideration?
   c. Is the authority conversant with the most recent discoveries in the field of investigation?
   d. Does the authority present an objective, impartial, unbiased, unprejudiced opinion about his subject?

8. For each of the truisms listed below, who would be likely to justify his behavior by quoting or citing it?

   a. Business is business.
   b. Haste makes waste.
   c. First come, first served.
   d. The customer is always right.
   e. Travel is broadening.
   f. All work and no play makes Jack a dull boy.
   g. A classic is a book everyone wants to have read and no one wants to read.
   h. Luck is 99 percent pluck.
   i. Like father, like son.
   j. Lucky in cards, unlucky in love.
   k. You get what you pay for.
   l. In wine there is truth.

9. By what method does Robbins in Evan Jones' "Pick and Shovel Sherlock Holmes" put groundless beliefs in their proper place?

10. During the next few days, make a point of listening for unsupported statements of alleged facts in the conversation of your friends and acquaintances. Challenge the statements by asking for proof or evidence, and see how many groundless beliefs you can uncover.

11. Occasionally what might be taken for a groundless belief turns out, on close inspection, to be a verifiable fact. Recently some investigators in a state department of health became interested in the St. Johnswort plant when they read it was used to

"drive out witches." Tests showed that the plant contains a substance that acts strongly against bacteria, killing infection or "driving out witches." This clue led the researchers to a new antibiotic which—in its unpurified state—has one-tenth the potency of penicillin. Can you cite other examples of this kind?

◆ ◆ ◆

Seeing What Stares Us in the Face

WENDELL JOHNSON

THE STORY has been told of how a professor came to be dismissed from the faculty of a university during the Middle Ages: in the course of prolonged dispute concerning the number of teeth there are in a horse's mouth, he brought in a horse!

The hero of this forlorn footnote to human history symbolizes both the basic method of genius and the hazards of its use.

The hazards vary, of course, with one's circumstances—and prudence—but the method does not lend itself to compromise. It is, as we have seen, a method that involves four steps—question, observation, report, conclusion—and they are to be performed in that order, and over and over again. Without questions that require observations, and throw a steady beam into the places where they might be undertaken, either no observations will be made, or, if they are, nothing will be made of them. And as soon as clear questions have been asked, we have no choice but to set about making the observations they require—

except as we may cherish our ignorance and conspire with ourselves to preserve it.

The alternatives to asking answerable questions, and then making honest attempts to find answers to them, are clear—and disgraceful. We can ask no questions at all, either out of stupor or as a display of arrogance. We can ask questions that are misleading, or vague, or meaningless—to be answered, respectively, by mountebanks, the confused, and the very naïve. Or, we may ask clear questions and then refuse to acknowledge them, as a gesture of fear, smugness, or irresponsibility.

The one form of human behavior that is consistently honest by conscious design is that behavior which is scientific. If you really believe that honesty is the best policy then you will strive to behave as scientifically as possible. If you try it you may decide against it, but then at least you will know that, by so far, you prefer dishonesty. In that case you are likely to be comforted by the arguments advanced by Mr. Stefansson in favor of "the standardization of error" (in an unforgettable book by that title) on the ground that generally agreed-upon error would be—that is, in fact—more convenient than truth. For one thing, truth tends to change as the restless atoms weave anew and anew the shimmery fabric of fact. Error, on the other hand, agreed upon and firmly fixed in legend and in law, is something one can count upon from day to day, even from century to century.

And there are other considerations. Truth peeks from behind the most unlikely hedges at the most embarrassing moments. It discredits the old—to the corrupting delight of the young. It tarnishes brass hats and soils vestments. Error, standardized and sanctified, is, by contrast, discreet and reassuring. It gilds our incompetence with the arresting luster of honor. It gives to our accepted foolishness the iridescent glow of wisdom, and in a thousand other ways as well confirms our benevolent conviction that we are wiser than we seem. If these you take to be advantages then all is clear.

If, however, you feel compelled to reject these appeals to the comfort and convenience of deceit, you will be relieved to find a method for the madness of your honesty. We have examined the first requisite of the method: the fashioning of questions that can be answered by means of observations that can be made. It is time now we considered the honest ways of making these observations.

The most important thing to know about an observation is that it has to be made more than once, by more than one person, before it can be entered with confidence in the ledger of fact. Truth is never private.

These, of course, are fighting words. Few other pages of history are so smudged with blood as those on which the masses of men have written—and are writing—their determined declaration of independence from those presumptuous few who claim to know by secret revelation what is best for them. This was the basic issue of the French Revolution—and the American Declaration of Independence. It has ever been the argument, punctuated by gunfire, against the Kings. It is the sword that hangs heavy over the head of every dictator—military, political, industrial, academic, religious, legal, familial, or of any other stripe. It is the justification of democracy.

Science and democracy acknowledge no Stone Tablets, no Sons of Heaven, no Führers, no Medicine Men or Shamans. The truth does indeed make men free—free from the tyranny of Knowers—for there is no truth except as it has been confirmed by those for whom it is intended. In the economical phrase of Carl Sandburg, "The people, yes."

Precisely because an observation is the act of an individual, there is no way of knowing whether it is true—dependable, that is—until at least one other individual has made it, too. And this holds regardless of who makes it first. The first beholder may be a potentate wound round with gold braid, fastened together with medals made from silver soaked in milk drawn from the seventh cow sired by the seventh bull, and blessed by the incantations of seven aged men who never face anywhere but east. It makes no difference. Somebody has to agree with him closely enough to make the observation reliable for practical purposes.

The more other persons there are who agree with him, and the more closely they agree, the better. And it doesn't matter who they are so long as they are independent and properly equipped, trained, and situated to see what he said he saw. If they see it, too, he can be believed accordingly. If they don't, the chances are he is a fraud, and any person of usable wit will hold in reserve this possibility until further notice.

This is the sort of thing scientific workers refer to when they speak about the reliability of their data. They are talking about the limits within which two or more observers, with comparable opportunities for seeing the same thing, agree in what they see. The greater the agreement among qualified observers, working independently of one another, the more reliable the observations they report. This concern for observational agreement is such a fundamental preoccupation of scientists that a large share of their labor goes into the job of devising methods for insuring that their observations, upon which their knowledge and theory depend, shall be as reliable as possible.

In the laboratory this makes for a tremendous amount of work and ingenious invention—and for more and more dependable findings. Outside the laboratory, in the ordinary circumstances of everyday life, it makes for a habit of mind conducive to rigorous honesty and integrity. In the absence of this habit of mind injustices and tragedies of bias tend to be widespread and inevitable. For reliability, in the fundamental scientific sense, is essential to fair play. It is presumed as a prerequisite of democratic legal procedure. This is an issue, therefore, that has tremendous personal and social consequences outside laboratories as well as inside them. The rules of honesty, as they apply to observational reliability, cannot, with honesty, be set aside sometimes. They pass, as it were, through any and all walls, those of marble and mud alike.

In the names of justice, good sportsmanship, and general honesty, it is simply essential that information reported in the public press, in meetings of committees, or across lunch tables be double-checked. In engineering and industry this is a matter of profits or bankruptcy. In medicine it is a matter of life or death. In public affairs and in private life it is a matter of integrity or corruption. In the laboratory it is taken for granted as a necessary and elementary part of scientific behavior.

If you would be reliable, dependable, honest, you may not report as an established fact whatever has not been observed by more than one person—even though you be that one person. And those who verify the observation must be suitably equipped and situated and sufficiently unaffected by suggestion, illusion, or self-interest.

Facts are public, and he who buys a secret gives alms to fraud.

All this is said, of course, with the clear realization that facts arise in experience—and every experience is personal. It is necessarily, in each instance, the experience of some one individual. An act of observation is no exception to this rule. In the case of an observation made by you of something outside your skin, I can verify it. But if you say you feel a pain in your back I cannot feel it too. How, then, am I to establish reliably that you do feel a pain in your back? You may be lying, or malingering, or you may need a psychiatrist.

The fact is that I may not fully verify your reported feeling by myself. For it must be checked by observations of its circumstances and effects, and my own observations of these circumstances and effects are to be checked by at least a second observer, independent and competent. Assuming that they are checked and found to be reliable, these observations are the evidence by which your report is to be judged. It may not be conclusive evidence, but it is the only evidence we can have, and quite often—as in medical practice—it will be dependable enough to be useful. Certainly, if no evidence can be found of any physical reason why there should be a pain in your back, it is to be concluded that probably either you are giving a false report or you are neurotic. And there are observational checks for determining which is more probably the case. If you are neurotic you do have a pain in your back—because of an idea in your head—and proper procedures, observational again, will be more or less likely to reveal what the idea is, and how it can be altered to get rid of the pain.

So it is that even our reports of the observations we make of the goings-on and feelings inside us are to be judged as being more or less reliable, depending on the relevant additional observations that support them or not. To insist, "It's my back and I ought to know," does not in the least degree convince a scientist.

The basic rules of observational reliability are simple, however widely untaught and unlearned they may seem to be. As a matter of fact, we trust them constantly, in certain respects, even though it may not often occur to us that they are the rules we are trusting. We know from common experience, if not from controlled experiment, that as a rule the readings of thermometers, meters, scales, and the like are reasonably reliable, and so we tend to rely generally on our own thermometer readings and observations of speedometers. Whenever we have checked them against the readings made by our companions they have turned out to show considerable agreement and so to be fairly dependable, as a rule. Having established the practical reliability of a particular kind of observation as commonly made, we live with it—at tolerable risk. So it is that, without bothering to check every report by which we are guided, we manage to survive in large numbers, in spite of depths of innocence that are essentially beyond sounding.

Facts—reliable observations—are worth no more to us, however, than our points of view and our philosophies permit us to make of them. There is a kind of fruitless cunning in much of our surviving—a reliance on facts that are, in truth, dependable for purposes of taking breath, together with an equal faith, all too often, in the lies and nonsense that forever frustrate our reachings out for love and peace and wisdom.

Yet, the facts of observation are indispensable to our sanity, and they can and do affect our points of view, our basic attitudes and philosophies. Certainly there is no way for us to look upon the truth, and align our living with it, except as we may learn to see what stares us in the face. For, seeing not what we look at, we see what is not there at all. And holding fast to visions, we consume our lives in fitful struggle with devils of our own invention, encouraged and commanded by the angels that we dream.

It is by learning to see what stares us in the face that we may triumph over self-deception, since it is a kind of learning that depends upon our trusting the testimony of our fellows to challenge and complement our own. For there is a trickery about our senses that makes our seeing all suspect, save as we test it for the stray effects of fancy. And only far more testing than we mostly think to do can make it fancy-free.

Questions and Exercises

1. What are the implications for education in the statement: "There is no truth except as it has been confirmed by those for whom it is intended"?
2. The author of this essay mentions Carl Sandburg's *The People, Yes*. Locate this book in the library and after sampling a few pages of its contents, explain Mr. Sandburg's purpose in writing the book.
3. Stuart Chase, in "The Scientific Method in Action," chapter 2 of his book *Proper Study of Mankind*, discusses ten characteristics of the scientific method. Compare this analysis with Wendell Johnson's four characteristics, explained in this essay. Has Johnson left out any important points that are presented by Chase?
4. The author suggests in this essay that the usefulness of facts depends on an investigator's purpose for collecting them. Select ten facts you have accumulated in your college experience so far, and explain what purpose each serves.
5. Which of the following three questions about automation is what Johnson calls an answerable question? Explain.
   a. Will automation increase unemployment in the United States?

b. Will automation rob humanity of the inalienable right of free choice?

c. What are the effects of automation on industrial production in this country?

6. Considering Johnson's discussion of honesty and integrity in fact finding, how can you explain the anomaly of two or more so-called "scientific reports," on a given question, which arrive at different conclusions? Find examples of such variance?

7. An eminent educator argues that members of a minority race (Negroes, Japanese, Italians) are inferior in intelligence as compared to native-born Americans of North European ancestry. If he employs a standardized intelligence test, with established norms for all age groups, how can you question the validity of his findings?

8. John T. Ruud, in "The Blue Whale," *Scientific American*, December, 1956, shows that Herman Melville was mistaken in thinking that the sperm whale is the largest "fish" in the sea. Which of the points presented by Johnson does this discovery support?

9. What are the basic rules of observational reliability as presented by Johnson? Explain why it is physically impossible for one person to verify another's observation exactly. (For a more technical discussion, see William H. George, "Scientific Observation," in *The Scientist in Action*, New York, 1938.)

10. John Fischer, editor of *Harper's Magazine*, has referred to the battle of the Alamo as one of the "worst military bloopers in American history." Explain with reference to Johnson's discussion of observational reliability why the people of Texas are blind to the "truth" about this affair.

11. Write a definition for a *fact* which harmonizes with Johnson's views on the subject. Support your definition with three examples taken from different areas of observation.

12. Explain why the average person cannot "see what stares him in the face." Cite several instances of this human failure or foible.

13. Johnson says that "if no evidence can be found of any physical reason why there should be a pain in your back, it is to be concluded that probably either you are giving a false report or you are neurotic." Are these the only possible alternatives? What others can you mention? What does Johnson probably mean by *neurotic* in this context?

14. Consider the statement: "Science and democracy acknowledge no Stone Tablets, no Sons of Heaven, no Führers, no Medicine Men or Shamans." Is this literally true? Can you find examples in the history of American democracy that refute the validity of this statement? Is democracy strictly scientific?
15. Can you cite examples of democratic legal procedure that failed to reveal the "truth" about the innocence or guilt of a man tried for murder or treason?
16. This essay originally appeared as a chapter in Wendell Johnson's book *Your Most Enchanted Listener*. What relevancy do you see in this chapter to the subject of listening effectiveness? How does this discussion agree with Stuart Chase's "Are You Listening?"
17. Write a descriptive report of some object in your environment that you come in contact with daily. See how many features you can discover which have hitherto escaped your attention. Report only what you can actually see. Do not pass judgment on the facts you observe.

◆ ◆ ◆

Pick and Shovel Sherlock Holmes

EVAN JONES

Ask the average citizen what an archaeologist is and he'll talk vaguely about a Ph.D. who has spent years in the dustbins of scholarship and who once in a blue moon goes off to dig around Egyptian pyramids or poke among the Aztec ruins of Mexico.

Originally published under the title "Pick and Shovel Historian" in *Collier's*, August 5, 1955. Copyright 1955 by Crowell Collier Publishing Company. Reprinted by permission of Harold Ober Associates.

Yet perhaps the most active archaeologist in this country today is a professional odd-jobman named Roland Wells Robbins. Between house-painting and window-cleaning assignments, he has probably dug out more buried American history than any other single person. His field is not lost civilizations, but the lost landmarks of the formative years of the United States.

A forty-seven-year-old Massachusetts native who had to leave high school in his freshman year to take a job, Robbie is the self-made expert who singlehandedly unearthed the long-forgotten site of Henry David Thoreau's famed Walden Pond retreat, who located the site and supervised the excavation of the Saugus Iron Works, Massachusetts' newest tourist attraction, and who this spring turned up evidence of Thomas Jefferson's birthplace at Shadwell, near Charlottesville, Virginia.

At first glance you'd never suspect Robbie of being either a scientist or a window washer. He looks like a gentle, understanding high-school athletic coach—compact, enthusiastic, weather-seared. Yet he is a titan in one of the mustiest of sciences.

His only tools are a pick, shovel, putty knife, a probing rod which he had a blacksmith make to his own specifications, and occasionally a metal detector—and he has broken most of the rules of textbook archaeology. Nevertheless, his scientific success is already firmly inscribed on a monument at Walden Pond and in the full-scale replicas of his seventeenth-century discoveries at Saugus.

Proud though he may be of his achievements, Robbie would prefer some less solemn-sounding title than archaeologist. Perhaps he is more closely related to the weekend spelunkers who have made a sport of exploring caverns in the bowels of the earth. Although Robbie is a member of the Massachusetts Archaeological Society, he thinks of himself more as a treasure hunter after quarry "more exciting than pirate's gold"—or sometimes as a subterranean detective, a Sherlock Holmes of the sleeping past.

The most recent treasure Robbie has been digging for is Jefferson's first home—a quest inspired by the curiosity of generations of tourists. Although almost 1,000,000 people make the pilgrimage to Charlottesville every year to wander wide-eyed through Monticello, the magnificent estate which the author of the Declaration of Independence designed and built for himself, most leave unsatisfied. They want to see the house in which the Virginian was born. But all there is to show are the barren acres of Shadwell, a mile and a half from Monticello's gate; the house itself was burned to the ground in 1770 and after almost 200 years, during which the site was regularly plowed and planted, all visible signs of the old homestead disappeared.

It was the word "visible" that aroused Robbie. What about the invisible? What about clues to the foundations that might still exist below the surface soil? Last November he left his Lincoln, Massachusetts, home on a five-day sortie to Charlottesville to find the answer.

On a bright fall day Robbie paced the ridge called Shadwell. He had to rely on what instinct a New Englander could muster below the Mason and Dixon's line, plus the efficiency of his probe rod. In blue jeans and sport shirt, he strode all over the ridge, puncturing the turf at intervals. Again and again he came back to the crest, which had a commanding view of the Rivanna River.

On his second day at Shadwell, his rod struck something hard. Nervously digging with his shovel, he unearthed what appeared to be a brick platform. He scurried to a phone, called members of the Thomas Jefferson Birthplace Memorial Park Commission, and some hours later in their presence removed the platform and revealed a small square of brick walls. The square appeared to be filled only with red clay, but Robbie was not satisfied. Why should an unexplained structure like this contain nothing but soil? He dug down to find a deep layer of moldering ashes from which he produced several eighteenth-century bone-handled iron knives and forks, a number of buttons, 339 iron nails and a handful of fragments of window glass buried so long that they had turned iridescent. It was the kind of quick find that has marked all of his pick-and-shovel career.

Robbie was commissioned to make an extensive excavation to prove once and for all whether the shape of Jefferson's birthplace was still preserved underground or had been destroyed in the years of post-Jefferson ownership.

The digging was not scheduled to start until April 1st, however; so Robbie went back to New England to spend his spare time during the cold months digging out clues from books. "Instead of counting sheep," he said, "I used to go to sleep counting the number of people in Jefferson's family." Eight children and two parents lived at one time at Shadwell, and to Robbie this fact was a clue to the size of the house. He read a half-dozen biographies, and in a 25-cent edition of a life of Jefferson he made copious notes. On the flyleaf he wrote: "Important—J. had 83 slaves at time of fire. Where did they live? Were slave quarters burned?" With so little historical record, no clue was insignificant.

This spring Robbie established himself at Shadwell for what may be a lengthy search. In the area in which he had found his first artifacts, he marked off a working grid covering more than an acre and set small wooden stakes at ten-foot intervals. He hired a tractor with a posthole-digger attachment and sent it back and forth across his grid, punching a hole at every stake to sample the evidence that might lie underground. "It's like prospecting for oil," he said. "You can drill, but if there's no oil there's no pay-off. Some of the plantation houses did not have cellars in the eighteenth century. But even so, if we can find fireplace foundations they may provide a good indication of the size of the house."

Undaunted when his network of holes indicated that there had never been a real house-sized cellar at Shadwell, he went to work with his shovel. Just below the depth of a plow blade, he found stones and bricks laid in the shape of a rude hearth. Robbie believes that this was a fireplace at the main house. A four-foot-square brick-lined pit and a slightly larger clay pit were found near the chimney base. They are thought to be root or cooling cellars built beneath the floor of the main house. Not far away he also uncovered a perfectly formed six-foot-square pit, from which he took out broken pieces of clay pipes stained with tobacco, and rusted knife blades—all evidence of eighteenth-century occupation. Were these articles that Jefferson had handled? It was too early for final answers, but Robbie promised to scrape down every inch of Shadwell's surface for clues and the artifacts that would help the Thomas Jefferson Birthplace Memorial Park Commission erect an authentic mecca for tourists who now leave Monticello unsatisfied.

How did an odd-jobman qualify for a job with so much responsibility?

One day in April, 1945, while moving furniture in a Concord house preparatory to painting the living room, Robbie got into conversation with the woman owner. She told him that her father had posed for the arms of Concord's famous Minute Man statue, marking the spot where "once the embattled farmers stood, and fired the shot heard round the world." When he returned home that evening, Robbie decided he'd like to know more about the statue—who else had posed for it, where the idea for it originated, and so on.

"I'm just naturally curious," Robbie says now, "so I started digging on my own in old newspaper files and town records. I was lucky enough to turn up many facts which no one before had related to the story of the Minute Man, and I wrote a little booklet which I tried to sell. I didn't make much money on it, but some people thought it was a pretty good research job. As a matter of fact, when that book appeared I was called an archaeologist for the first time."

Soon afterward, Robbie's natural curiosity led him to nearby Walden Pond for a picnic celebrating the centennial of Henry David Thoreau's retreat to woodland seclusion. And there he found an argument. People who had studied Thoreau for years couldn't agree on the original location of the cabin which the philosopher had made famous. The only thing certain was that the cabin had been moved away and later dismantled. Robbie sat there in the woods and listened. This situation, obviously, called for the same kind of sleuthing he had exercised in the case of the Minute Man. So he was easy bait for members of the Thoreau Society, who had heard about his unsolicited Concord research; they talked him into trying—without payment—to settle the Walden issue.

Robbie started by buying a 95-cent copy of Walden in a Concord bookstore, a 98-cent GI trench shovel, a pocket compass and a couple of pairs of canvas gloves. Then he had an inspiration. He went to a neighboring blacksmith and ordered his first probing rod—36 inches of steel tapering to a point at one end and with a strap-steel handle at the other. With this device, he reasoned, he could poke into the ground for objects like boulders and bricks without having to wear himself out digging.

After several readings of Walden, comparing it line for line with sections of Thoreau's journals, he ransacked all material available in archives. He spent long hours in the Concord and Lincoln libraries poring over nineteenth-century files of Boston newspapers, and he had lengthy sessions with the Middlesex County commissioners, with the superintendent of the Walden Pond State Reservation, and with Thoreau scholars in Massachusetts and in places as far afield as Vermont and North Carolina.

Robbie determined that Thoreau's house had been moved several miles away shortly after its builder vacated in 1847. "Within a few years the action of the elements on sandy soil— the work of erosion—eliminated all surface evidence," Robbie reported. "By 1945, with such evidence lacking, hearsay had developed many legends about the cabin and its fate."

Robbie studied the frontispiece drawing in the first edition of Walden and noted that Thoreau had written, "My house was on the side of a hill . . . half a dozen rods from the pond." He carefully compiled every other phrase Thoreau had used about the house. "With these I painstakingly reconstructed in my mind the scene," his report says, "and taking this mental model out to Walden Pond, I endeavored to locate the spot into which it would fit. The needle in the haystack was what might be left of the foundation of the house chimney, which my research indicated had been covered over along with the cellar hole when the house was moved."

His first day out, accompanied by three intrigued Thoreau Society members, he came across two or three pieces of brick embedded in a path on Thoreau's side of the pond. The find clicked with his library research. "Thoreau was the only one known to have brought brick into this vicinity," he told his friends, and he marked the spot. On his next trip, "in an area eight feet long, three feet wide in its greatest width, and from two to seven inches beneath the surface," he found 100 pieces of brick. He hastened to a Cambridge brickyard to have them analyzed for age. They were found to be water-struck, handmade bricks, at least a century and a half old, and they appeared to be fragments of the "one thousand old bricks" Thoreau reported he had purchased for four dollars. But these pieces showed no mortar, and the neophyte archaeologist still had the chimney foundation to locate.

Robbie was momentarily discouraged. Then he reasoned that Thoreau might have dropped a load in carrying bricks to the house site, a possibility that would account for Robbie's first find. He went out the next Sunday and laid out what he thought was a logical path from the brick chips to the hill Thoreau had mentioned. Probing along this narrow area, he found under a white pine stump chunks of plaster, mortar-covered bricks and "several old, badly rusted handmade square nails. Some of the bricks were smoke-blackened."

At this moment, Robbie heard a young voice say, "What are you digging for?"

Robbie recorded the incident in his report: "Looking up startled, I found two Army sergeants viewing my labors. One of them was a six-foot, rather slender, good-looking young man who seemed unusually interested in what I was doing. Courteously but insistently, he plied me with questions about Thoreau and his life at Walden until, apparently thinking he was annoying me, he apologized.

" 'Sorry to bother you, sir, but you see I'm a distant relative of Henry David Thoreau. I live in California and am on my way home from the war in Europe. I've never been here before—may never get here again—so, naturally, I'm anxious to learn what I can of Walden.'

" 'You mind my asking your name?' I inquired.

" 'I'm Henry David Thoreau, Jr.,' he replied."

Astounded, Robbie scrambled out of his hole and brushed the soil of Walden off his pants. Then with an inward grin, he asked young Thoreau for his dog tags—and he still has one as evidence. "I knew then I couldn't miss," he said. "It was such a colossal coincidence that it had to mean something."

But the realist in Robbie pooh-poohed even colossal coincidence. The fact was that he had found some evidence embedded in the roots of an old tree, and the fact called for a specialist. He summoned his friend, John Lambert, of the Massachusetts Department of Conservation, Division of Forestry, and together they established the age of the white pine stump at "eighty-eight, a year one way or the other." Robbie pushed back his duck-billed cap and beamed. Here was proof that the tree had been seeded and had grown *after* the hut had been moved away; it had taken root on what must have been the very site.

Two Sundays later, the spare-time archaeologist found more nails, pieces of window glass and, two feet below the surface, boulders bound together by mortar. "By evening," he wrote in his casebook, "earth that for nearly a century had covered the remains of the chimney's foundation was removed, revealing the answer to the true location of Thoreau's Walden house. We had put an end to all the legends and to the years of disagreements among scholars as to the exact site."

So satisfied were the scholars with Robbie's discovery that the spot has been marked with a line from one of Thoreau's poems:

"Go thou my incense upwards from this hearth." On a nearby granite slab is the inscription, "Site of Thoreau's Cabin, Discovered November 11, 1945, by Roland Wells Robbins." In addition, Professor Walter Harding of the University of Virginia, secretary of the National Thoreau Society, wrote, "He authenticated the exact site of the cabin so that we are now far more certain of just where Thoreau dwelt than on which boulder the Pilgrims landed at Plymouth beach."

Here was heady eulogy for a window washer, but it failed to deter Robbie from his appointed rounds. There were plenty of storm sashes to be cleaned and hung that fall, floors to be scraped and refinished during the winter, screens to be put on in the spring. Robbie is a good business-man and he respected his reputation as the most dependable handy man on Boston's western periphery. He continued to earn a good living for his wife and three children until archaeology again caught up with him in the fall of 1948.

Twenty miles away in Saugus, The First Iron Works Association had been formed. It owned the ancient ironmaster's house on Central Street and had discussed some sort of restoration which would do justice to the site of an ironworks built in 1646–1647. The association people called in Robbie because of the fame he had won at Walden.

"They were willing to pay me what I knew I could earn at my window and painting business," Robbie says, "plus a limited amount for pick-and-shovel men. Nobody thought the project would last more than a few weeks, but they felt a pass ought to be made at seeing if any remnant of the place was left underground. I had my regular customers to take care of, so I agreed to use what time I could until the middle of October, when I knew the storm-window rush would come."

Driving to the ironmaster's house one day, Robbie came across a couple of laborers digging a sewer trench—and promptly signed them on to work in their off hours. In the time that he himself could spare from his odd-job contracts, he put his trusty probe rod into action. Almost immediately he located a pile of cinders which could have been left only by operation of the colonial foundry. Taking rough directions from this pile, he probed with his rod until he struck boulders, and before the month was out he and his awed helpers had uncovered a disintegrating rock pile which still showed the shape of the blast furnace foundation. Next to it he unearthed the base of the giant bellows which had fanned the long-dead furnace fire.

Robbie's immediate success caused the Iron Works Association to report the findings to the American Iron and Steel Institute—with the result that this manufacturers' group agreed to finance the further digging and reconstruction of the foundry in its seventeenth-century form. Robbie was hired for the duration.

Still no one sensed how much colonial life lay buried in the overgrown bank of the little Saugus River, and for many months Robbie continued to surprise everyone by unearthing 300-year-old items as diverse as workmen's eating utensils, nails and rust-encrusted castings.

Then one day he appeared at a Saugus town meeting with a strange request. "If you'll only reroute Central Street," he told the people of Saugus, "we can excavate to the exact location of the water wheel which powered America's first assembly line."

Somebody in the meetinghouse guffawed. "You're talking about three hundred years ago! Water wheels are made of wood. Buried timber don't last that long."

Robbie, steel-springed and persuasive, endeavored to explain. He knew that normally wood rots away when buried so long in the earth, but he had figured out on paper that 22½ feet below the Central Street pavement was the site of a water wheel which had furnished power for the ironworks. He didn't expect to find the wheel itself, but he had to get permission to dig out three centuries of fill if the final restoration was to be accurate.

"I kept saying I was talking about the site, not the wheel itself," Robbie recalls, "but you should have seen the expressions on the faces of the sidewalk engineers the day we actually found a big segment of the sixteen-foot water wheel. The pieces had been miraculously preserved by an underground water table, and all of a sudden I was a prophet."

To some of Robbie's admirers this find was even more astounding than the witnessing of the Walden discovery by young Thoreau.

Robbie's Saugus tour of duty lasted five years, ending in August, 1953. In September, 1954, the Saugus Iron Works Restoration, complete to the last major detail, was formally dedicated. It is tucked away on the edge of the twentieth-century village of Saugus, a mile off U.S. Route 1 and ten miles north of Boston. As the result of Robbie's work, today's tourist can go back in history as suddenly as he hits the fence that now severs Central Street. First to catch his eye will be the rebuilt blast furnace, beyond it the forge building, the slitting mill and the wharf. In spring, summer and fall water splashes over seven giant water wheels, spilling through replicas of seventeenth-century sluices. Above the blast furnace and next to the ironmaster's house is a museum containing tons of artifacts which Robbie retrieved—everything from calipers to a 500-pound hammer used for refining red-hot iron.

Robbie would be the last to say that such success is built solely on luck. His muscles tingle with too many memories of pick-and-shovel excavations. He still thinks of himself as a detective who goes underground "for clues that aren't in the books." And his face is alive with enthusiasm when he talks about any of his projects. As this is written, he is still hard at work on the Shadwell-Jefferson excavation. When he finishes that, he will direct the research for excavation of early Du Pont powder mills in Wilmington, Delaware.

"My work just helps to show what can be done with archaeology in the United States," Robbie says. "We're a country that has grown too fast and been too careless of our landmarks. The pages of our history, young as it is, are spotted with blanks and contradictions. Yet most of the answers are available, waiting to be dug from the earth. Your own yard may hide a clue that could rewrite an entire chapter."

Questions and Exercises

1. Explain how Robbins' discoveries can be called "scientific successes," in the face of the fact that "he had broken most of the rules of textbook archaeology." How does this anomaly support the contention of Jean Mayer in "The Case of the Disrespectful Mice"?
2. What specific qualifications did Robbins possess which made it possible for him to uncover the truth where others had repeatedly failed?
3. In the light of the facts reported in this essay, make a list of the personal qualities which are necessary for scientific discovery.
4. Read Henry David Thoreau's "Where I Lived, and What I Lived For," and point out the clues it contains that may have helped Robbins in locating the site of Thoreau's Walden Pond hut.
5. Comment on the scientific attitude revealed in the statement: "It was such a colossal coincidence that it had to mean something." How does Susanne Langer explain the significance of such a statement in "Language and Creative Thought"?
6. Make a detailed list of the steps Robbins took in establishing the "truth" about Walden Pond, from the time he accepted his assignment to the time of his final decision regarding the validity of his find.
7. Point out an instance in this report in which Robbins verified a theory or hypothesis by empirical methods.
8. Historians talk about two kinds of evidence: primary evidence and secondary evidence. Primary evidence is based on direct observation of facts. Secondary evidence is based on a report or reports of the facts. To what extent did Robbins depend on each of these kinds of evidence in establishing the "truth"?
9. What does this essay suggest about the accuracy of standard history books? Can you point out any of the "blanks and contradictions" with which the pages of our history are said to be spotted?
10. How does Robbins dramatize the theory of A. E. Mander regarding "Groundless Beliefs"?
11. Read Marchette Chute's essay "Getting at the Truth," *The Saturday Review*, September 19, 1953, and show how her explanation of how biographical truth is distorted applies to the question of the exact location of Thoreau's Walden Pond hut.

12. Find examples in this essay of each of the following:

   a. Defining a problem.
   b. Drawing inferences from facts.
   c. Testing a hypothesis.
   d. Making use of documentary evidence.
   e. Verification of facts.
   f. Making predictions from factual observations.
   g. Drawing conclusions from observed facts.
   h. Inductive reasoning.
   i. Cause and effect argument.
   j. Groundless belief.

Of the Monstrous Pictures of Whales

HERMAN MELVILLE

I SHALL ere long paint to you as well as one can without canvas, something like the true form of the whale as he actually appears to the eye of the whaleman when in his own absolute body the whale is moored alongside the whale-ship so that he can be fairly stepped upon there. It may be worth while, therefore, previously to avert to those curious imaginary portraits of him which even down to the present day confidently challenge the faith of the landsman. It is time to set the world right in this matter, by proving such pictures of the whale all wrong.

It may be that the primal source of all those pictorial delusions will be found among the oldest Hindoo, Egyptian, and Grecian sculptures. For ever since those inventive but unscrupulous times

Reprinted from *Moby Dick* by Herman Melville.

when on the marble panellings of temples, the pedestals of stat-
ues, and on shields, medallions, cups, and coins, the dolphin was
drawn in scales of chain-armor like Saladin's and a helmeted head
like St. George's; ever since then has something of the same sort
of license prevailed, not only in most popular pictures of the
whale, but in many scientific presentations of him.

Now, by all odds, the most ancient extant portrait anyways
purporting to be the whale's, is to be found in the famous cavern-
pagoda of Elephanta, in India. The Brahmins maintain that in
the almost endless sculptures of that immemorial pagoda, all the
trades and pursuits, every conceivable avocation of man, were
prefigured ages before any of them actually came into being. No
wonder then, that in some sort our noble profession of whaling
should have been there shadowed forth. The Hindoo whale referred to, occurs in a separate department of the wall, depicting
the incarnation of Vishnu in the form of Leviathan, learnedly
known as the Matse Avatar. But though this sculpture is half man
and half whale, so as only to give the tail of the latter, yet that
small section of him is all wrong. It looks more like the tapering
tail of an anaconda, than the broad palms of the true whale's
majestic flukes.

But go to the old Galleries, and look now at a great Christian
painter's portrait of this fish; for he succeeds no better than the
antediluvian Hindoo. It is Guido's picture of Perseus rescuing
Andromeda from the sea-monster or whale. Where did Guido get
the model of such a strange creature as that? Nor does Hogarth,
in painting the same scene in his own "Perseus Descending,"
make out one whit better. The huge corpulence of that Ho-
garthian monster undulates on the surface, scarcely drawing one
inch of water. It has a sort of howdah on its back, and its dis-
tended tusked mouth into which the billows are rolling, might be
taken for the Traitors' Gate leading from the Thames by water
into the Tower. Then, there are the Prodromus whales of old
Scotch Sibbald, and Jonah's whale, as depicted in the prints of
old Bibles and the cuts of old primers. What shall be said of
these? As for the bookbinder's whale winding like a vinestalk

round the stock of a descending anchor—as stamped and gilded on the backs and title-pages of many books both old and new—that is a very picturesque but purely fabulous creature, imitated, I take it, from the like figures on antique vases. Though universally denominated a dolphin, I nevertheless call this bookbinder's fish an attempt at a whale; because it was so intended when the device was first introduced. It was introduced by an old Italian publisher somewhere about the 15th century, during the Revival of Learning; and in those days, and even down to a comparatively late period, dolphins were popularly supposed to be a species of the Leviathan.

In the vignettes and other embellishments of some ancient books you will at times meet with very curious touches at the whale, where all manner of spouts, jets d'eau, hot springs and cold, Saratoga and Baden-Baden, come bubbling up from his unexhausted brain. In the title-page of the original edition of the "Advancement of Learning" you will find some curious whales.

But quitting all these unprofessional attempts, let us glance at those pictures of Leviathan purporting to be sober, scientific delineations, by those who know. In old Harris's collection of voyages there are some plates of whales extracted from a Dutch book of voyages, A.D. 1671, entitled "A Whaling Voyage to Spitzbergen in the ship Jonas in the Whale, Peter Peterson of Friesland, master." In one of those plates the whales, like great rafts of logs, are represented lying among ice-isles, with white bears running over their living backs. In another plate, the prodigious blunder is made of representing the whale with perpendicular flukes.

. Then again, there is an imposing quarto, written by one Captain Colnett, a Post Captain in the English navy, entitled "A Voyage round Cape Horn into the South Seas, for the purpose of extending the Spermaceti whale, drawn by scale from one killed on the coast of Mexico, August, 1793, and hoisted on deck." I doubt not the captain had this veracious picture taken for the benefit of his marines. To mention but one thing about it, let me say that it has an eye which applied, according to the accompanying scale, to a full grown Sperm Whale, would make the eye of that whale a bow-window some five feet long. Ah, my gallant captain, why did ye not give us Jonah looking out of that eye!

Nor are the most conscientious compilations of Natural History for the benefit of the young and tender, free from the same heinousness of mistake. Look at that popular work "Goldsmith's Animated Nature." In the abridged London edition of 1807, there are plates of an alleged "whale" and a "narwhale." I do not wish to seem inelegant, but this unsightly whale looks much like an amputated sow; and, as for the narwhale, one glimpse at it is enough to amaze one, that in this nineteenth century such a hippogriff could be palmed for genuine upon any intelligent public of schoolboys.

Then, again, in 1825, Bernard Germain, Count de Lacépedé, a great naturalist, published a scientific systemized whale book, wherein are several pictures of the different species of the Leviathan. All these are not only incorrect, but the picture of the Mysticetus or Greenland Whale (that is to say, the Right Whale), even Scoresby, a long experienced man as touching that species, declares not to have its counterpart in nature.

But the placing of the cap-sheaf to all this blundering business was reserved for the scientific Frederick Cuvier, brother to the famous Baron. In 1836, he published a Natural History of Whales, in which he gives what he calls a picture of the Sperm Whale. Before showing that picture to any Nantucketer, you had best provide for your summary retreat from Nantucket. In a word, Frederick Cuvier's Sperm Whale is not a Sperm Whale, but a squash. Of course, he never had the benefit of a whaling voyage (such men seldom have), but whence he derived that picture, who can tell? Perhaps he got it as his scientific predecessor in the same field, Desmarest, got one of his authentic abortions; that is, from a Chinese drawing. And what sort of lively lads with the pencil those Chinese are, many queer cups and saucers inform us.

As for the sign-painters' whales seen in the streets hanging over the shops of oil-dealers, what shall be said of them? They are generally Richard III whales with dromedary humps, and very savage; breakfasting on three or four sailor tarts, that is whaleboats full of mariners: their deformities floundering in seas of blood and blue paint.

But these manifold mistakes in depicting the whale are not so very surprising after all. Consider! Most of the scientific drawings have been taken from the stranded fish; and these are about as correct as a drawing of a wrecked ship, with broken back, would correctly represent the noble animal itself in all its undashed pride of hull and spars. Though elephants have stood for their full-lengths, the living Leviathan has never yet fairly floated himself for his portrait. The living whale, in his full majesty and significance, is only to be seen at sea in unfathomable waters; and afloat the vast bulk of him is out of sight, like a launched line-of-battle ship; and out of that element it is a thing eternally impossible for mortal man to hoist him bodily into the air, so as to preserve all his mighty swells and undulations. And, not to speak of the highly presumable difference of contour between a young sucking whale and full-grown Platonian Leviathan; yet, even in the case of one of those young sucking whales hoisted to a ship's deck, such is then the outlandish, eel-like, limbered, varying shape of him, that his precise expression the devil himself could not catch.

But it may be fancied, that from the naked skeleton of the stranded whale, accurate hints may be derived touching his true form. Not at all. For it is one of the more curious things about this Leviathan, that his skeleton gives very little idea of his general shape. Though Jeremy Bentham's skeleton, which hangs for candelabra in the library of one of his executors, correctly conveys the idea of a burly-browed utilitarian old gentleman, with all Jeremy's other leading personal characteristics; yet nothing of this kind could be inferred from any Leviathan's articulated bones. In fact, as the great Hunter says, the mere skeleton of the whale bears the same relation to the fully invested and padded animal as the insect does to the chrysalis that so roundingly envelopes it. This peculiarity is strikingly evinced in the head, as in some part of this book will be incidentally shown. It is also very curiously displayed in the side fin, the bones of which almost exactly answer to the bones of the human hand, minus only the thumb. This fin has four regular bone-fingers, the index, middle, ring, and little finger. But all these are permanently lodged in their fleshy covering, as the human fingers in an artificial covering. "However recklessly the whale may sometimes serve us," said humorous Stubb one day, "he can never be truly said to handle us without mittens."

For all these reasons, then, any way you may look at it, you must needs conclude that the great Leviathan is that one creature in the world which must remain unpainted to the last. True, one portrait may hit the mark much nearer than another, but none can hit it with any very considerable degree of exactness. So there is no earthly way of finding out precisely what the whale really looks like. And the only mode in which you can derive even a tolerable idea of his living contour, is by going a whaling yourself; but by so doing, you run no small risk of being eternally stove and sunk by him. Wherefore, it seems to me you had best not be too fastidious in your curiosity touching this Leviathan.

Questions and Exercises

1. Melville's classification of the monstrous pictures of whales reveals three principal categories: historical, popular, and scientific. Which of these classes of pictures would you expect to be most accurate? Why?
2. Melville says: "The living whale, in his full majesty and significance, is only to be seen at sea in unfathomable waters. . . . his precise expression the devil himself could not catch." If we assume that the whale symbolizes truth, what does the statement suggest with regard to the facts of the universe? What precautions did Melville take in *Moby Dick* to present the whole truth?
3. What parallel do you see between Melville's focus on the flux of nature and Kouwenhoven's thesis in "What's American about America?"
4. How does this chapter from *Moby Dick* support the contentions of A. E. Mander in "Groundless Beliefs"?

5. Melville says: "And the only mode in which you can derive even a tolerable idea of [the whale's] living contour, is to go a whaling yourself." What admonition for all researchers is contained in this simple announcement?

6. Considering the shortcomings of the scientific pictures, described by Melville, what does the author imply about scientific truth generally? How does this agree with Mayer's thesis in "The Case of the Disrespectful Mice"?

7. Read the article by Loren C. Eiseley "Was Darwin Wrong about the Human Brain?" in *Harper's Magazine*, November, 1955, which mentions the exploded Piltdown hoax. What other scientific myths may be nothing more than "monstrous pictures of a whale"?

8. What is the significance of the allusion to Richard III in this chapter?

9. If a whale's skeleton "gives very little idea of his general shape," what hint do we have regarding the precise nature of prehistoric mammals?

10. Determine Melville's meaning of the following words which appear in the chapter: *hippogriff, fastidious, stove, full-length, bow-window, quarto, antediluvian, vignette.*

11. What parallel to Melville's "half-man, half-whale" may be found in the legends, myths, and tall tales of the American frontier?

12. Who wrote "The Advancement of Learning" and what is Melville's probable purpose in mentioning it in his discussion of error?

13. If, as Melville suggests, some points of view give more accurate pictures of the whale than others, what lesson can we learn for the business of getting at the truth in reporting?

14. Norman Cousins' "History Is Made By Headlines," *The Saturday Review*, July 25, 1954, is a discussion of distortion in the news. What other examples of Melville's thesis can you cite?

15. Read the following passage by Wolfgang Langewiesche, and discuss its relationship to Melville's thought in this chapter:

> "The air view is an honest view: 'You can't kid *me*' is your attitude as you look down. 'So *that's* how it is.' For example, the great, famous dams—Hoover, Norris, Grand Coulee. In the ground view, the thing you marvel at is how big they are. The glamour photographs show them that way—small human figures, dwarfed by the gigantic wall behind them. Well, from the air, it's the other way round. It strikes you how small they are. Hoover Dam especially—it's actually

hard to find! The eye sweeps all over the naked rock and the shores of Lake Mead before you find it—hidden down in a gulch. It makes you smile. Some boy has jammed a rock into this stream at just the right spot—and has managed to dam up one hell of a big lake. Small cause, big effect: clever little devil. And that, I'm sure, is the correct view. An engineer would say so. He would always try to build the smallest possible dam, not the biggest."

◆ ◆ ◆

The Case of the Disrespectful Mice

JEAN MAYER

I SPEND much of my time studying disrespectful mice. Sometimes it looks as though these mice do not actually aim to show disrespect for widely publicized expert opinions and that their sins are mostly of ignorance. They have not read the right books and they just don't know. And yet at other times anyone watching them would feel that they *have* read the textbooks and that they *are* downright malicious when they misbehave. This is very disconcerting to many experts who, on the basis of their knowledge of physiology, psychology, nutrition, or medicine, feel they ought to be able to predict how these mice should react in at least a number of situations. It would be upsetting to me, too, if by now I had not come always to expect the worst from them. If you develop this viewpoint, these mice will rarely disappoint you.

Appropriately enough, this steady series of scientific paradoxes can be traced to a catastrophe. A few years ago, a forest fire started on Mount Desert Island and, just as everyone thought it had died down, suddenly jumped out of control. By the time it was over, it had ruined a large part of Bar Harbor and destroyed, not only a number of baroque hotels and Victorian houses, but also the Jackson Memorial Laboratory.

This unique institution, famous the world over among biologists, is for specialists of the genetics of mammalian species the equivalent of what the Louvre and the British Museum combined would be for archaeologists. Founded by Dr. C. C. Little, a scholar and an administrator who enjoys the almost unique distinction of still being a productive scientist after having been president of two universities, the Jackson Laboratory was (and, in its new plant, is) devoted to the study of hereditary processes in mice. Lest this appear to stern utilitarians a somewhat futile pastime, let it be pointed out that it is difficult for an animal to study the genetics of its own species, because by the time it has seen two or three generations appear the observer is dead. Biblical observers, who, according to the scriptures, very much outlived the commonly allotted three score and ten, and who did pay close attenton to genealogy, do not seem to have made use of their fine opportunity to study human genetics. On the other hand, mice become of marriageable age in a few weeks, and observations of hereditary processes in the little creatures have taught us more in a few years than we could have learned if the ancient Egyptians had taught the human race to count blue and brown eyes instead of stars.

Furthermore, there are no limitations, among experimental mice, about who can be bred to whom. Even in societies which do not leave the choice of a mate to chance and romantic love, such practices as brother-sister or mother-son marriages are discouraged. It may be that one of the reasons for the strong taboos which universally forbid choosing a parent, or a brother or sister, for a spouse is precisely the reason why this type of mating is such a useful tool in genetics; it brings to light and allows one to recognize and study hitherto hidden genetic characteristics which, in the case of the human race, might profitably remain in a discreet shadow.

In the hands of the geneticists of Bar Harbor, the systematic use of incest as the only basis for producing new generations (or perhaps "halfgenerations" in some cases) has taught us much about the heredity of disease. In particular, we have learned something about the heredity of skeletal malformation and other "congenital" abnormalities, of susceptibility to infection, and of the so-called degenerative conditions, often characteristic of old age, like kidney diseases. Above all the mice have taught us a great deal about the hereditary factors in cancer and about the way in which environmental influences interplay with constitutional traits to cause or prevent the appearance of tumors.

But to get back to the fire and to the mischievous mice. As often after upheavals of societies, one of the consequences of the disaster was a number of unscheduled matings. The colony was being reconstituted from a few escapees rescued from the flames, as well as from the progeny of the native Bar Harbor mice which had been sent to outside institutions, and in the course of this process a "V" male was crossed with a "Black 57" female. (There are some more picturesque genetic designations, such as nonagouti, fuzzy, leaden, or—as we shall see—waltzing.) Among their descendants, in a proportion which—for once—conformed to the rules for a "Mendelian recessive" gene (about one fourth), there appeared animals which, as they developed, became grossly obese, weighing two, three, sometimes four times as much as their normal-weight brothers and sisters; round, soft, placid little balls of mouse-fat, shorter lived than average, but seemingly contented.

Let me hasten to add that although these obese animals—the disrespectful mice of this story—dutifully conformed to the laws of genetics, we faced a practical difficulty: they did not reproduce. Still they could be obtained, slowly at first, by finding out, by trial marriages, which ones among the thin male and female mice carried the "obese" gene, and by mating males and females who were both carriers. When two dozen or so of the obese mice had been produced, a little over two years ago, some of them were sent to us to study, in our laboratory at the Nutrition Department of the Harvard School of Public Health. We had been interested for a long time in what makes animals and people eat, what makes them stop eating, and why some of them don't stop and become fat; and now with the aid of funds from a number of industrial concerns, which came to us through the Nutrition Foundation of New York, and from the U.S. Public Health Service, we began some specific investigations. Here were real challenge and real opportunity.

II

It must be noted that by their very existence, these obese mice contradict a great many authoritative teachings. As overweight is not only unbecoming but actually bad for one, physicians, nutritionists, and health authorities have justifiedly preached reducing to the extra plump. We know, in fact (if the truth be for once told), extraordinarily little about why people get fat. The one thing which is well established in this field is the old law of conservation of matter and energy, which in this context means that fat does not materialize out of thin air. To become fat, you must have absorbed more energy, as food, than you have expended as heat and as muscular work. (The "you" is used in the oratorical, not the personal, fashion.) Conversely, if we starve you, you will lose weight. Once again, this is just about all we know on the subject, and it leaves unanswered the real question, which is, "Why do some people eat more than they require?" Perhaps understandably, most therapeutists seem to fear that if they give the slightest consideration to search for causes of this overeating, overweight patients will seize upon it as an excuse for avoiding self-starvation. If the victims of obesity are led to think that there may be a physiologic basis for their condition, they may cease to struggle and simply blame destiny.

However, not a few laymen (among whom, perhaps, the reader himself may be numbered) have noted that corpulence often "runs" in families. They have concluded, not unnaturally, that there is an hereditary factor in obesity. According to many textbooks of nutrition, medicine, public health, etc., they could not be more wrong. These textbooks are all the more emphatic in that they bring forth no convincing evidence on the subject, only pompous statements. For example, a well-known treatise on clinical nutrition comes forth in its twenty-eighth chapter, "Obesity," with some typical pronouncements. Besides stating once and for all that "Body build is inherited; obesity is not," it adds that "Pains must be taken to explain . . . that while shape is inherited, obesity is an acquired characteristic." Pains indeed! (The only honest way to describe the situation is probably to say that while a tendency to eat more than the body requires, and hence to obesity, may be inherited, one still has to do the actual overeating to become fat; if one doesn't, one may remain thin, but it may be at the cost of spending one's whole life feeling hungry.)

If you get one of the more sophisticated proponents of the view that genetic factors must be ruled out to agree that there *are* families which show an unusually high proportion of plump members, he will quickly explain that this is because of the socio-cultural familial enviroment, which stresses large meals and rich foods. He is left undisturbed by the fact that you can't make normal experimental animals obese by varying the composition of their diet. He also ignores whatever evidence has been collected by students of human genetics.

In spite of the difficulties of the subject there are a few geneticists who have concentrated on observing human beings. Scientists such as Von Verschuer and Newman have noted such simple facts as the extreme similarity of the weights of identical twins through life, even when they have been reared and have been living in different environments. Other observers, such as Julius Bauer, Rony, Angel, and Gurney, have studied more devious matters such as the number of children and the proportion among these of obese individuals in the marriages of the various possible combinations of obese and normal-weight men and women. (This means, more clearly, of thin men with fat women, fat men and thin women, and the assorted pairs.) Out of all this enough material has been gathered to support tolerably well the suggestion that there *are* several genes which control obesity in man. In fact a couple of these geneticists are so sure of themselves that they are not afraid to describe one of . these genes as dominant and another by the rather formidable characterization of "sex-linked and recessively lethal." However, catch a "health educator" believing all that. He will go on insisting that there is no heredity in obesity.

But meanwhile here are our obese mice, triumphantly Mendelian, moving around for all the world to see in the same sociocultural environment as their thinner siblings.

Another distressing trait of the obese mice is their attitude toward exercise. Orthodox teaching holds that exercise is no way to reduce. You may have contrasted, in juvenile fantasies, the hard, lean Indian scout, warrior, or explorer with the roly-poly banker seated at his desk. Nonsense, say the experts. You should know that the more you rise from your armchair, the more your appetite will increase. Eighteen holes of golf on a cool crisp fall morning would not offset the effect on your weight that a supplementary Hershey bar (or whisky sour) would have. Well, the mice have never heard of all this. The thin mice are in perpetual motion. Put them in a squirrel cage equipped with a counter and you will find that the wheel will turn several thousand times a day if there is a thin mouse in the cage, almost not at all if the inhabitant is a fat mouse.

Worse than this, we have already mentioned the fact that there is such a thing as a "waltzing" gene. The unfortunate mice which display this hereditary characteristic are doomed to perpetual motion, round and round in their cage. if they see anything they want, they can only approach it after following a series of circles. They will pause for food, water, sleep, and other basic physiologic needs, but the rest of the time they are bent on their apparently aimless errand, in a manner reminiscent of Dante's Inferno or, more appropriately perhaps, of athletic practice. If an obese mouse is also a waltzing mouse, he may not stay quite as thin as a "non-obese" mouse, but he reaches only about half the weight of an ordinary fat mouse. Arthur Murray please note. If you are tempted to the conclusion that perhaps exercise *is* a reducing aid provided it is practiced daily and in moderation (*not* in sudden and violent weekend and summer vacation bouts), you may find by personal experience or observation that you were justified in your guess, expert opinion notwithstanding.

I shall pass lightly over several other low blows to the specialist, the extreme offensiveness of which might not be apparent to the layman. For example, textbooks say that obese subjects should display a normal "basal metabolic rate." The fat mice do no such thing; their basal metabolic rate is low and may be down to minus fifty. Their endocrine glands misbehave. They develop a form of diabetes which is superbly unaffected by doses of insulin that would shake a horse, and which may be due to a hitherto undescribed hormone. They are unable to burn their fat properly. Also, if you place them in the cold, in spite of their enormous paddings of fat they will die within a couple of hours while the thin mice survive indefinitely. Similar examples of "deviationism" could be enumerated for an hour.

But these heresies are trivial compared to what is yet to come. For what is yet to come is acquiescence, not disagreement. Submissiveness, not revolt. And unfortunately this perfect agreement is with the one branch of science and medicine which might not appreciate it, to wit, psychiatry. It is in this respect that the fat mice show themselves naked for what they are: ruthless, vicious iconoclasts.

III

Psychiatric textbooks and articles and lecturers with knowledge in such things generally agree that obesity is a psychosomatic disorder. Obese patients, they say, have remained at the "oral" stage of personality development. That is, they have not transferred their "sexual" interest from maternal milk—and food in general—to more adult preoccupations. They are, as a result, still using food as a substitute for newer forms of release—hence their obesity. In addition, they show other infantile traits: lack of initiative and of will power, need for approval and affection, and often an outwardly lethargic—even though inwardly insecure—attitude. Often they have been subjected in their early childhood to the excessive attention of an overprotective mother. Their only redeeming feature is that, according to life-insurance statistics, obese people are less prone to suicide than thin people.

This is where it is going to hurt. The obese mice overeat. Furthermore, if you put them in a "cafeteria" situation, where they can freely select the components of their diet, they will compose themselves a diet very different from that chosen by ordinary mice. Strangely enough, in the diet they so select, the proportion of fat, protein, and sugar resembles that of milk.

As for libido, the obese mice just won't mate. Their sex organs are, as far as the most competent anatomists and histologists can tell me, quite normal. In fact, if an egg formed by the ovary of an obese female is transplanted into a thin mouse and properly fertilized, it will give a perfectly good mouse (this is the way obese mice are actually mass-produced nowadays). Similarly, the male sperm seems fit for active duty. Yet an obese male and an obese female, thrown together, won't mate. They won't mate with thin partners either, which seems to eliminate purely aesthetic considerations. They are just not interested in sex.

Also the fat mice have no initiative, no curiosity. Put a thin mouse in a new cage and he will run and explore it. But not the fat mouse. Sometimes he will sit and eat and sometimes he will just sit. After a while he will eat.

The fat mice do like to be patted on the back. They crane their necks to be carressed and they nestle in your hand. By contrast, try to catch a thin mouse. He will run like mad to elude you. If finally cornered, he will turn around and bite (I speak from long and bitter experience). Or in desperation he will jump from the table, even if the three-foot drop is going to kill him. But not the fat mouse. He will only ask for more fondling.

As for overprotective mothers, it is hard to say who has them and who hasn't. But there can be little doubt that mother mice, whatever their color, their weight, or their genetic composition, are overprotective. If you so much as look from a distance at a mother mouse, she will collect all her litter and hide it in the darkest corner of the cage. She hides the future thin mice and the future fat mice too. But then many thin people have had solicitous mothers.

If you reduce the obese mice by fasting them, they will become active, though still not quite so active as non-obese mice. They will exhibit more initiative and more curiosity in their search for food. They act as if they felt better. On the other hand, so far in our experience, their loss of weight leaves unchanged both the predilection for fat and the lack of interest in sex. And of course, if the slimmed mice are left free again to decide on their own caloric intake, they will quickly eat their way back to obesity.

I think you will now agree that the obese mice have an "oral" personality. It goes with the tendency to obesity. You can't separate it from the obesity no matter what breeding schemes you try. But does it really cause obesity, or is it simply, like obesity, a visible symptom of a deeper, more primitive genetic lesion? Like, for example, the fact that these little pieces of fatty acids won't let themselves get completely oxidized, but stubbornly build up again. Or do you care to go deeper still and place the primary lesion at the confines of Mind and Matter, in a faulty arrangement of the "probable" positions and movements of the atoms which constitute the elementary components of genes? No matter where you choose to stop, however, look and see what happened to all these learned theories on obesity.

Well, now you know why the mice are turning me into something of a skeptic. But, don't forget, while they have made a hash of human explanations and predictions, they have been very scrupulous with the laws of nature. The conservation of energy still holds. If your cousin eats less, she won't grow so fat. And, if need be, the same would be true for you. And remember, the thin mice bury their fat brothers and sisters whose libido never grew up.

Questions and Exercises

1. Considering that the case study of the obese mice constitutes evidence in support of a thesis, what is the author's thesis, or central idea?

2. How does Mayer support the ideas proposed by Mander in "Groundless Beliefs"?

3. What logical fallacy may the "experts" who write textbooks on obesity be accused of? What groundless belief puts readers of these texts at the mercy of the authors?

4. Bergen Evans in "Wolf, Wolf" from *The Natural History of Nonsense* offers further evidence of the gullibility of educated people, scholars, and professional men of our day. Compare the nature of the groundless beliefs in this and Evans' essay.

5. Mention at least one instance in which "intelligent" people have been taken in by a groundless belief. (The discovery of the hoax in connection with the "Piltdown man" is one example.) Relate the incident to your classmates.

6. A few years ago there was a great furor in certain education circles because of "un-American" tendencies in college textbooks. What do you think Mayer would criticize in a textbook? Which of the two types of criticism is in the best interests of a college student?

7. What are some of the dogmatic statements made by "scientists" that come under Mayer's critical scrutiny?

8. In what part of the essay does Mayer lean heavily on authority in order to establish his point? Name the authorities.

9. Define the following words used in the essay: *deviationism, oral personality, histologist, libido, genetic lesion, sibling, oratorical you, genetics, congenital, abnormality, baroque hotel.*

10. Wendell Johnson in "Seeing What Stares Us in the Face" has much to say about reliability of personal observation. To what extent is authority unreliable, as suggested by Mayer? How can authoritative statements be validated?

11. Anthony Standen in his book *Science Is a Sacred Cow* has this to say of the science of physics:

    "Physics is *not* a body of indisputable and immutable Truth; it is a body of well-supported probable opinion only, and its ideas may be exploded at any time. This ought to be more generally known, and should be widely publicized. Perhaps it would be hardly in human nature to expect physicists to do this for themselves, but somebody else ought to do it for them."

Redefine the word *truth*, as it applies to findings in the field of physics, in harmony with Mr. Standen's remarks.

VI. PURPOSEFUL COMMUNICATION

Without a definite purpose, discourse either written or spoken becomes a mere exercise in word spinning. If a person doesn't know where he is going, how can he hope to arrive? The lack of a real purpose for communication probably accounts for the large percentage of unsatisfactory attempts to communicate meaning successfully, and for the overabundant examples of dull, vapid, insipid "nonsense" that are exhibited by students in fulfillment of specific assignments in writing and speaking.

A person must not only have a controlling purpose for transmitting ideas; he must also have a definite purpose for receiving them. This is well brought out in the essay by Perry and Whitlock in Section I of this anthology. These authors contend, you will remember, that reading comprehension cannot be measured unless a well-defined purpose for reading has been established.

Purposes for communicating ideas may be conveniently arranged into six general classes: to create (to solve problems), to inform (to report facts), to direct (to explain processes and give directions), to entertain (to amuse and divert), to criticize (to pass judgment), and to persuade (to inspire, convert, or activate). The essays in this section of the anthology offer examples of each of these general purposes. Some of the essays fit into more than one of the six categories, and it is not always clearly apparent which of several purposes actually controlled the author's efforts.

You will notice that in some of the essays the author's purpose is not stated directly. The reader's task in such instances is to weigh the significance of style of writing, emotional toning of words, organization of elements, association of ideas, suggestion, and analogy, in the hope that they will point up the author's intended purpose and his meaning. While there is nothing particularly subtle about some of the essays, the fables by H. I. Phillips and by Loy E. Davis and the critical study by Mark Twain are indirect and present a definite challenge to a reader's ingenuity.

The essay by Paul Fisher is an example of a documented report and is included here as a model of a well-organized research paper. Miss Ueland's essay on walking shows how various types of evidence may be mustered in defense of a thesis or idea. Mr. Highet's discussion of persuasion supplies an excellent example of explanation and direction as a type of discourse.

◆ ◆ ◆

The Art of Persuasion

GILBERT HIGHET

A STRANGE enterprise, persuasion.

What makes us think that we can change another man's mind, simply by talking to him? Surely it argues a great deal of confidence in our own powers, in his malleability, and ultimately in the force of speech, or reason, or both. It is tricky enough to try to persuade an individual—a wife or husband, a friend or partner, a business prospect, a rebellious daughter, an angry police-man. But how difficult is it to influence a group of people—a hall full of wildcat strikers, a meeting of creditors, a mutinous crew, or a jury?

Hard it is, surely. Yet it is done, and done constantly. When it is well done, the patient scarcely feels it. Usually he thinks that he has made his own decision, or that he has, through his own perspicacity, managed to discover the truth. Once when Lord Brougham, the brilliant nineteenth-century lawyer, had won a difficult case, one of his juniors fell into conversation with a jury-man leaving the courtroom. "Heavens," said the juryman, "what a wonderful lawyer that Mr. Savage is, to be sure! He does make a noble speech!" Brougham's assistant heard this with astonish-ment, for Savage had appeared on the losing side. "Well now," he said, "I should have thought Lord Brougham was the better lawyer. Didn't he win the verdict?" "Oh yes," said the juryman, "but then you see it was easy enough for him, he had all the right on his side."

That was a perfect example of persuasion, smoothly applied and painlessly concluded. As long as he lived, that juror would be convinced that he and his peers had merely looked at the facts on both sides and assessed their weight. He would never realize that Lord Brougham had persuaded him to think one set of facts heavier than the other.

Very few of us can have such power as that. Yet we all spend much of our lives *trying* to persuade other people to do things for our sake. Parents attempt to influence children; young men woo girls and vice versa; husbands and wives are continually en-deavoring to persuade each other, although a lot of their effort is wasted and some of it backfires. And what is business but per-suading the public to buy? What is politics but persuading the public to vote for this and support that and endure these for the promise of those?

If that is so, then how is persuasion, really skillful and effective persuasion, managed? If it is a fundamental activity, it must have a few basic principles.

It looks as though there were two different types of persuasion. One is the ordinary type, which we all try to do. The other is more mysterious and less logical, hard to resist and hard to understand. Suppose we look at the ordinary type first.

Anyone who wishes to win over an individual or a group must have something to offer. He can not bargain unless he has something to bargain with. Therefore, before starting, he should be quite clear what inducement he intends to put before his victim. It need not be large. It need not be lasting. But it must be attractive. The biggest and simplest mistakes are usually made at this stage. Sometimes the operator starts talking without having an exact idea of the size and scope of his own offer. He may realize too late that he hasn't offered enough, and then try to increase the bid, and meet a resistance which has grown inflexible. Sometimes he talks himself into offering far too much, and loses on the deal. (This is Reverse Persuasion.) Often he attempts to negotiate without offering anything tangible or interesting, and thinks he has been unjustly treated when the persuadee refuses.

An even commoner mistake is made by those unfortunates who choose the wrong inducement. A hook baited with clam will catch a sea bass, but if you drop it into a trout stream, you will get no trout. So, first, you should make up your mind about the nature of your inducement. And, second, you should think about it in connection with your patient, until you are quite sure it will really attract him. If it leaves him cold, you lose. If it repels him, the result may be disastrous.

For instance, when husbands and wives try to persuade each other, the chief consideration they have to offer is continued happiness in marriage. "You ought to do this, darling, because it will make us both happy—even happier than we are now." That is the standard married argument, and it is most effective when it is put like that. But there are difficult points in marriage at which such inducements have no real meaning. A wife or a husband sometimes begins to reflect that marriage is no good anyhow, so that it is useless to go on tinkering with it. At this point, bad persuasion will cause an explosion. A wife will say to her young husband, "If you go out drinking again next Saturday, I'll leave you and take the baby." The husband inwardly shouts, "Good, that's exactly what I wanted." What started him drinking was the new discomfort of home with a baby in it, and the new responsibilities. Now he is presented with a new escape from them all.

The abruptness and violence of these failures always surprise both parties. There is another reason for the failures. It is *hurry*. No important job of persuasion can be done quickly. Few important jobs of persuasion can be done in one stage. To be effective, persuasion must be slow, gradual, easy, patient.

That is how the best propagandists work—those who get lasting results. Think of the many Christian ministers who have converted ferocious savages, world-weary Chinese mandarins, fanatical Communist officials, glum peasants, and vain, flippant young noblemen. One of St. Teresa's operational rules was "Much can be done by patience." The most remarkable conversions of the Jesuit missionaries were planned years in advance and took many years to execute. It is the chief mistake made by American publicists, teachers, and statesmen, to think that if they point out the right course, everyone will at once follow it. Here is Democracy, we say. Look at it. It's good, isn't it? Well, adopt it. But . . . no. Without preparation, no conversion will last. Rapid-fire persuasion is almost sure to fail.

The second rule of persuasion, then, is that it must be gradual. And the third rule develops out of that. The third rule is that it must work on the emotions as well as on the mind. Human beings were suffering fear and anger, enjoying hope and pleasure, long before they were able to think clearly. Their emotions still lie deeper than their reason, sometimes work against their reason, and, for satisfactory action, should always be harmonized with their reason. Persuasion will be most effective when it begins with the emotions. Therefore we ought to start persuading—before introducing any arguments—by calming and smoothing, pleasing and flattering the patient. Surgery never begins until the patient is anæsthetized. Persuasion should never start until the patient has been made receptive.

This, then, is the technique of the ordinary type of persuasion.

First, select the inducement. Second, establish a welcoming atmosphere. Third, argue gently, and slowly, and gradually.

We can all do that. But there is a much more difficult type of persuasion which seems to have no rules at all. Yet, when it works, it is far more effective. We often hear of a man who has been able to persuade hardheaded businessmen or wary old hardhearted dowagers that he is in direct communication with God, that he knows the hiding place of Kubla Khan's treasure, that he can foretell the stock market through magnetic rays, that he is the child of a multimillionaire, kidnapped in infancy, or the reincarnation of Paracelsus, or the Master of the Elements. Vast sums of money, limitless trust and adoration are lavished on these persuaders by their victims. And yet they have no real inducement to offer. Often they do not argue. Their emotional appeal is strong, but it is so absurd that we, standing outside, can scarcely understand how anyone could succumb to it. Casanova persuaded the Duchess d'Urfé that he could help her to be reborn as a male child, after a mystical marriage presided over by the Sylphs and the Moon. She was to appoint him guardian of her new baby-self and leave him all her money in trust; the operation failed only at the last moment through a slip of Casanova's roving attention. Saint-Germain persuaded numbers of experienced statesmen that he was two thousand years old and knew the Secrets of the Spheres. The Tichborne claimant persuaded Lady Tichborne that she was his mother.

Of the same order, though in a different group, are the great diplomats. We know their names—Bismarck, Disraeli, Richelieu, Franklin—but we do not know their methods. The biographies tell us the facts of their careers, but seldom explain *how* they contrived their marvellous successes. For instance, how did Bismarck persuade the king of the German states to accept the king of Prussia as German Emperor, and to stand behind his throne while he was crowned? Not just by pointing the guns of the Prussian Army at them. It was a long process, so tortuous, so varied, and made of so many subtle touches that it has never been adequately described; but one thing is sure about it, that it was mainly the work of persuasion. Yet it was persuasion of a special type, depending little on the ordinary methods, something far more like the art of the man who holds three deuces and persuades his opponent, with a 5–6–7–8–9 straight, to throw in his hand.

It would be easier to understand the art of persuasion if these geniuses did not exist. But they do, and most of us are at their mercy. And they have no technique that we can describe, no rules, no—on the contrary, they are always incalculable, bold and random, could it be "inspired"?

Yet they do have a few traits in common, which are basic. The chief of these is will-power and concentration. If you really want to persuade people that you are St. John the Baptist returned to life, or the future ruler of Europe, you must first be 1000% determined to do so. You need not believe it yourself. But you must concentrate on making others believe it. Every act, every word, every gesture must serve that purpose. Most people have weak wills and wandering minds. If they meet someone with concentrated conviction, they believe he is what he appears to be. If they meet someone with a strong will, they feel they must sooner or later give way to him; and sooner or later most of them do.

Another trait of many great persuaders (outside diplomacy) is this. They are not logical. They do not make clear, reasonable plans and enlist their victims in carrying them out. Often they talk nonsense. They make us believe myths. They make dreams more real than daily life. Why they should do so is a hard question. Perhaps the cold truth about daily life is so grim that few of us can face it; we welcome a myth, if it is only strong enough. But the great top-level persuaders have usually been Quixotes who could make us, like poor Sancho Panza, ride on behind them, simply because they seemed to know where they were going, even if it was towards the Kingdom of Micomicon. A splendid example of this has recently appeared in the United States: the Armenian mystic Gurdjieff's *All and Everything*, twelve hundred pages of absolute nonsense, which looks from time to time as though it were about to make some kind of higher sense, and then shoots off into the circumambient gas.

But on this level one essential technique of persuasion remains valid. It is that persuasion must be gradual. People will believe anything, however absurd. But they will swallow it only in small doses. When Alice told the White Queen "One can't believe impossible things," the Queen replied "I daresay you haven't had much practice. When I was your age I always did it for half an hour a day. Why, sometimes I've believed as many as six impossible things before breakfast."

Therefore a high-level persuader will begin by hints, and rich stimulating morsels, and tantalizing glimpses into the Luminous Void. Slowly, slowly, almost reluctantly, he will lead his Sanchos further into the Impossible. Soon they will be pushing bravely ahead, jumping the chasms between Inexplicables, swinging freely across the ravines of the Incomprehensible, glissading upwards on the slopes of the Unutterable. Sometimes, dizzy with the thin air, they will pull their master gaily ahead into the unknown, and even if he tries to restrain them they will link arms and swing him out over the edge of sanity. Yet even then, the adventure of persuasion began slowly, slowly; patiently; quietly; slowly.

These, then, are the two kinds of persuasion. One is simple and reasonable. The other is weird and incalculable. Many can do the first, few the second. Just once or twice in our lives we may be able to exercise persuasion of the second type—once or twice at a tremendous crisis, when we feel that everything, *everything* depends on what the girl will answer, or when we see the crowd warming up and a chance sentence seems to draw it together and make it our instrument, or when the tough old man asks us what we have to offer, and sits back and listens. At such times, with luck, we feel the flood flowing through us, we guide it and master it and see the others carried away by it.

Such a triumph may come only once. If it comes again, if we can recall it and strengthen it, we may become masters of persuasion. (Madame Pompadour began by being a girl who found

she could twist one man round her little finger, and then a
second man, and then. . . .)

But if not, we can do what is calmer and safer: we can settle
for reason. We want not opposition, but harmony. Not conflict,
but control. The friendly face, the calm voice. Quietness, gentleness, cheerfulness to relieve the tension. And then, slowly, the
persuasion should begin. Kindness, real or imitated. Then reason,
real or imitated. Even the imitation of kindness and of reason
will draw people together, and will help, in time, to create the
real virtues.

Questions and Exercises

1. Highet's analysis of persuasion, on the basis of form, reveals
   two distinct types. Analyze persuasion according to functional
   types (the purposes served) and list as many types as you can.
2. If persuasion is both a science and an art, which of Highet's
   classifications concerns its scientific aspects? Which the artistic? Explain.
3. Define the essential difference between persuasion and propaganda. See William Albig's discussion of "Propaganda," in
   Modern Public Opinion, p. 291.
4. Cite a personal example of what Highet calls "reverse persuasion." To what extent do you think Voorhis' "Advice to Forlorn Freshmen" may be an example?
5. What techniques employed by Hitler, Stalin, and such dictators place them in either of the two categories discussed by
   Highet?
6. Select two speech textbooks at random and determine to what
   extent the authors discuss the second of Highet's types of persuasion.
7. Consider the three principal requirements for effective persuasion advanced by Highet. What use does Brenda Ueland make
   of these principles in "Walk a Thousand Miles This Year"?
8. Select three commercial advertisements in magazines and analyze the persuasive techniques employed. What human motives
   are appealed to? What lures are offered? How is the "proper
   atmosphere" created?

9. Make a list of ethical principles by which persuasion should be judged. Supply several examples of what you might call unethical persuasion.

10. Many discussions of persuasion distinguish between logical appeals and psychological, or emotional, appeals. Highet makes little if any mention of this distinction. In your opinion, what is the persuasive value of verifiable facts or inferences from facts? Can you find examples in commercial ads of this kind of persuasion? Can you find examples of pseudoscientific appeals?

11. The purpose of this essay is to explain kinds of persuasion and to show how they operate. How well does the author achieve this purpose for you?

12. Using the following guide, write a paper or give a talk in which you explain a process or give directions for accomplishing a specified task.
   a. Present ideas and facts in a logically ordered sequence.
   b. Give complete information. How much you include will depend on how much the reader is expected to know already.
   c. Clarify new ideas or processes by describing their characteristics or properties, and by answering such questions as who? what? when? where? and how?
   d. Define unfamiliar terms and terms with special or unique meanings.
   e. Be specific as to who are the doers and who the recipients of action.
   f. Include examples, drawings, flow charts, and other means of amplifying and clarifying your directions.

13. Analyze and discuss the persuasive elements in Mrs. Alcaro's "Colleges Don't Make Sense." To what extent are you convinced of her idea?

14. Highet says: "Persuasion will be most effective when it begins with the emotions." Explain this statement with reference to Rollo May's "The Experience of Becoming a Person" or to Felix Cohen's "The Reconstruction of Hidden Value Judgments."

15. Discuss the nature of the persuasion employed by Orson Welles as explained in the following passage:
   "Although it has been some time now since Orson Welles scared his countrymen with his dramatized on-the-spot news broadcast of the men from Mars landing in South Jersey, words continue to use men and often make fools of them. Even

though the actor Welles bellowed 'Hallowe'en!' to his radio listeners, many of them left their homes to satisfy their curiosity and look for the space ship. Even a college professor equipped with a torch and a geologist's hammer journeyed out in search of meteorites."

What other examples of the confusion of words and facts can you mention?

16. Many discussions of persuasion analyze the process into three steps: inspiration, conversion, and activation. Define these three varieties of persuasion and determine to what extent Highet's treatment of the subject includes or ignores them.

17. The next time a salesman tries to persuade you to purchase an item he represents, listen carefully to his techniques of persuasion. To what extent were you persuaded by his words? How can you account for the success or failure of his attempts?

18. Give a persuasive speech in class, using the first of Highet's two types of persuasion. Choose your own subject. Pay close attention to matters discussed in this essay.

19. The very sound of words gives them a persuasive power. Make a list of "persuasive words" that you hear on TV commercials.

A Forgotten Gentry of the Fourth Estate

PAUL FISHER

IN THE days before typesetting machines and time studies, when steam beer went at a nickel a pint and railroads had not found all the valleys, in these days the American tramp printer had

Reprinted from *Journalism Quarterly*, Spring, 1956, by permission of Paul Fisher and the *Journalism Quarterly*. Copyright 1956 by The Association for Education in Journalism.

his time in the sun. The sun never shone brighter for the tramp than during those years after Appomattox and before Ottmar Mergenthaler's Linotype, when the printing industry grew great with the nation's press and all type composition was done by hand. In these days the legend of the tramp printer was formed.

Printers had always been peripatetic gentlemen. Their wander years were sometimes of their own choosing and sometimes not. John Gutenberg was still alive when a religious controversy at Mainz sent his disciples onto all roads leading from that city, many to the warmer, kinder Italian climate. During the centuries printing remained under political and religious controls, countless practitioners of the Art Preservative discovered that only by keeping steadily on the move could they preserve their heads.

The break-up of the guild system, resulting in a progressive deterioration of apprenticeship controls and standards, brought complete chaos in the 19th century. The apprentice refused to "bury the wife," that is, complete training under a master. Domination was easily escaped by footing it down the road where he could pass himself off as a journeyman to unsuspecting printers and editors. Once on the road, the self-declared "jour" never lacked for company.

Tramp printers—sometimes called "prints," "tourists," "roadsters," even *"rara aves"* and *"haute beaux"*—were in plentiful supply in the later 19th century for many reasons. Some were on the road out of necessity. Seasonal fluctuations in the industry forced those lacking seniority to hike about hoping to "catch on" where the "biz" was better. There were fugitives from financial and marital miscues. (Tramps tended to talk little of their pasts.) Old age, alcoholism and pride contributed to the flow. It was a time of many labor abuses by urban printing management, and there were those men who refused to bear them.

To illustrate with one abuse, type sizes were shaved, minion becoming minionette. Pay, always on piece rate, continued on the basis of the larger point size. The compositor thus set more type for less money. And this in a period when it took a good typesetter, all things fair, to make 25 cents as an hourly average.

Still, the best guess would be that most of the prints were on the road because that was where they wanted to be. The West was calling during these years. Out yonder there was much to be seen. Printers were not alone in wanting to see it.

Calling, too, were the numerous marginal weekly newspapers and job shops following in the wake of the rapid westward expansion. Foundry supply houses were lenient with credit, and contentious communities readily supported contentious editors, politically if not in a monetary way. So there was a glut of country editors who welcomed tramp assistance for a few days. The editors could not have afforded more either financially or physically. Editors often enjoyed drinking stints with their visitors, who were vital sources of communication, and the stints were not short.

The tramp is generally pictured as a very rapid typesetter. The inevitable exceptions aside, this is short of the truth. Many were adept only at distribution for this reason. Country shops, short of time and labor, pushed aside forms to be killed, letting them stand until the tramp print made his appearance. It worked out nicely for all hands but for none more than the non-union traveler who could not catch on in the organized city shops but who could depend on type awaiting distribution in hamlets along midwestern and western roads.

Formation in 1852 of the National Typographical Union (becoming today's International in 1869) gave the wandering printer an all-powerful pass to any clime: the union card. Railroadmen were engaged in the struggles of unionism and this proof of union membership to a railroad brakeman assured unmolested passage by boxcar. Indeed, possession of an ITU "ducat" invited offers to ride the cushions at no obligation. The card could be passed around among a shop's regulars (called "home guards" or sometimes, contemptuously, "homesteaders") for donations, a practice some would call panhandling but referred to by tramps as "raising the wind." Constables inclined to jug seedy travelers as vagrants accepted the card as visible means of support. The card lightened considerably the insecurity of travel.

So, for many reasons, the tramp printer established himself as a figure to be reckoned with on the American printing scene. He had his own jargon, his own laws and customs and his own prejudices. The late Jay E. House, who gained familiarity with the tramping gentry when he was an editor on the Topeka *Capital*, recalled the old print in this wise:[1]

If he slept at night on the floor of the composing room, he first spread a clean newspaper upon it. A soiled newspaper did not fit his sense of the aesthetic. If he caught work, he stayed a day or a week, but seldom more than a month. He was not a lady's man in the accepted sense of the word. A woman meant a home, and a home meant bondage. Usually he was well read and often he was well educated. He had a competent and understanding grasp of matters and affairs. He liked to call attention to errors of fact, grammar and construction written or passed by the editor, and what he thought of reporters wasn't fit to print.

There is no doubt but that the tramp was pretty much the prodigious drinker he generally has been pictured as being. It was Andrew J. ("Muskogee Red") Redmond who, when advised by a friend to bite an apple whenever the urge for liquor came over him, replied: "And who in the hell wants to carry a bushel of apples around on his shoulder!" Along with alcoholism there seems to have been a fair use of narcotics. Two well known prints, Sloan and Jarbeau (both were "Kid"), were users.

The tramp printer played strengths against weaknesses. He brought the tricks of a hundred shops. He could kick any press, pour faultless rollers, mix a paste that would not sour, a glue that would stick and not melt. No one could match the stories he could tell. Little wonder that to the country printer, as William Allen White recalled for the 1900 convention of the United Typothetae, his arrival meant "what the coming of a new star means to an astronomer."[2]

Not uncommonly the traveling typesetters had means of earn-

[1] Jay House, "The Old Tramp Printer," *The Saturday Evening Post*, CCVI:34 (February 17, 1934), p. 23.
[2] William Allen White, "The Tramp Printer," *The American Printer*, XXXI:3 (November, 1900), p. 170.

ing a dollar outside the trade. Many of them did vaudeville acts or traveled lecture circuits at favorable times of the year. Sam Leffingwell was an occasional actor, and Elmer Bascom never put scissors to hair or beard so he could model as a Biblical character for the artists of religious printing houses. Impromptu revivals and selling patent medicines were also the resort of tramps when the trade offered thin pickings.

The print who did not know his Bible and Shakespeare seems to have been the exception. Mark ("Lazarus") Hansen for decades delighted Scandinavian settlements in Wisconsin and Minnesota with Norse translations of Shakespeare. A bar served as stage for Lazarus. Timothy ("Professor") Stiles has been recalled by Hubert Canfield as "an authority on the lays of ancient Rome. Wherever Suetonious felt uncertainty about an event in Roman history, Timothy could set him straight. . . ."[3] Isaac ("Colonel") Busby, who restricted his travels to Missouri and Iowa, regularly assumed management of country papers while editors took vacation. Deeds of their accomplishments are easily multiplied. No doubt, many of the prints were men of parts.

By 1880, so deep was the respect for the tramp, employing printers were inclined to the belief that the only finished printer was one who had travel experience. (It is still considered valuable in northern European countries.) Once the apprentice received his journeyman's card, he was expected to take a post-graduate course on the road. Suggestions were made to the ITU and the UTA that a system be set up to facilitate the travel of young journeymen, but suggestions were never acted upon. This must have been a relief to the tramps who were findings jobs harder to come by as the century rolled up its last years.

For a man not without inconsistencies, the print showed a remarkable uniformity in the routes he traveled. He might make the same shops for years, never varying his schedule, and such country printers as he favored could judge within a week or so when he would knock on the door, ask for breakfast or "gate"

---

[3] Hubert Canfield, "My Recollections of Four Tramp Printers," *The Colophon* (New Graphic Series), III (September, 1939), p. 68.

money and, breakfast eaten, return to peg or throw in type. While the true *"rara aves"* migrated with wildfowl to favorable climates, many tramps never left a single state or geographical region. The aristocrats of the brethren were transcontinental travelers, the "coast-to-coasters," and they were relatively few. It is very improbable that the tourist abroad qualifies as a true tramp. Many, on approved leaves of absence, undertook their "Grand Tours" of foreign lands (the more foreign, the better) in the spirit of a stunt, writing letters back to the trade periodicals that appeared under such titles as "In a Fiji Printing Office," "A Peruvian Print Shop" and "Night Work in Finland."

In the dying days of oldstyle tramping, just before the introduction of the Linotype, the wanderers seem to have concentrated in two areas. One was the Pacific Northwest, where "Weary Willie" Waterhouse, "Oldstyle" Jones and "Thin Space" Jones, "Pica" Shaefer and "One-Finger" Shaefer, and "Old Slugs" Biggsby and "Easy Pickings" Stewart ambled off into oblivion. (Some say Weary Willie was last seen in Texas around 1928.) The central plain states made up the other area, and the regions near the Mississippi, Ohio and Missouri rivers were especially favored. A group of tramps known as the "Missouri River Pirates" were still making towns between St. Louis and Sioux City when the new century was ushered in.

The rivers, of course, furnished cheap and interesting travel. Not infrequently a company of printers would lash together a raft and float where the river took them, jugging for "cat" as they drifted. Jefferson City, capital of Missouri and rich in state printing and sin, was a regular port of call. When the legislatures convened, midwestern state capitals could expect an influx of tramps to handle the overflow of printing.

River larks aside, however, the railroad was the accepted mode of travel. If the tramp printer ever had a hero, he must have been the railroad man. Some prints imitated railroad engineers in their dress. If the tramp missed his train connections, he would walk up the tracks to the next town, railroad beds regularly being in better condition than country roads. Jack Jordan, a tourist who got elected to the Arkansas legislature, once proposed a bill that would force railroads to sink crossties a normal pace apart to facilitate the tramp's ambulations.

They began to knell the death of the tramp as the Linotype commenced to come on the market in some quantity in the mid-1890s. (Some thought it would be the death—from starvation—of all printers.) As John Gordon remembered it, when he privately printed his memorial to the tramp printer:[4]

In 1893 the Linotype came over the typographical horizon, sending most of the old Birds scurrying to some other business. Some died of grief, a few bought a cow and tried to swap her in the Stock Exchange for Oil Stock, others preached Temperance Sermons and used themselves as Horrible Examples to affright their audiences into sobriety.

This would appear to be short of the truth.

The fact is that the change from handset composition temporarily swelled the ranks of the tramp prints. There simply were not enough Linotypes in the cities, especially in the East, for available compositors.

Grieve though they did, printers, particularly the younger ones, saw the handwriting on the composing stone. The machine had come to stay, and they had to learn it. So they "barnstormed," as they expressed it, to "steal the trade." The modus operandi was quite different from that of the old handset tramp.

The barnstormer applied for work wherever there was a dark "Merg." His job lasted until his ignorance was noticed, often not an hour. The Linotype was the mysterious pearl of the shop, to be entrusted only to the gentlest and most skilled of hands. Still, as he gathered stolen hours of self-instruction, the barnstormer's competence increased. He was not to be denied. "What are you giving me?" roared a foreman of the New Orleans Picayune, noted as a "barnstormer's paradise," pointing to John Motley's handful of slugs for an evening's work. Replied Motley,

---

[4] John Gordon, A Memorial to the Tramp Printer (South Brewer, Me.: Gordon Press, 1927), p. 54.

"Just what you and ten thousand other foremen are going to get until I learn this damned thing."

The barnstormer's day was short. It was done as soon as the industry had trained a corps of machine operators sufficient to its needs. The barnstormer was happy to harbor in a permanent "sit," which certainly differentiates him from the oldstyle tramp.

The flowering of tramp printing was done. A slow withering set in. There were many causes other than the Linotype, Henry Ford's horseless carriage among them. The automobile centralized trading areas, some towns in an area booming while others decayed. By 1910 many print shops in the neglected towns had shut their doors. Weeklies folded by the hundreds. Life in the boom towns grew more efficient, more regulated—to a tramp, complicated. It was a time-clock punching existence that was building up, an impossible existence for a group of men who were wont to boast, "When my coat's buttoned, my trunk's packed." "Poor old typographical errors," William Allen White sighed, "they were cast before the days of the point system and they have been thrown into the hell-box of oblivion."[5] This, in 1900.

The climate of opinion had changed. Road experience was no longer recommended to the apprentice. Here is a wall motto widely displayed in composing rooms at the time of White's sigh:

Don't tramp as long as you can avoid it. That is to say, do not throw up a situation where you are making a good living, and start out in search of more lucrative or pleasant employment. There is no place on earth where you will not find Printers in abundance, with every advantage of prior claims of work to be done. If you are making a good living where you are, you can surely save something if you will, and go farther by staying than by tramping.

Surely, enough to curdle the blood of a true tramp. But the true tramps were getting fewer, ever fewer. Much of the old respect for the gentry was gone.

[5] White, *loc. cit.*

The trade's leading periodical, *The Inland Printer*, editorialized in 1910: "A tramp printer is a simple vagrant, and deserves nothing but our detestation." A distinction was made between the tramp and the tourist, the latter traveling "because circumstances compel him to, or because he loves to travel and see what's to be seen." And finally, with Christian charity, "We do not for a moment forget that within the rugged and illy-clad breast of (the tramp) . . . beats the heart of one who might have been a better man. . . ."[6]

A country whose West had been settled by people of tramping blood began to look on itinerants as bums, people to be distrusted rather than be given, as in times past, a room in the attic or privileges of the loft or composing room floor for the night. The drum of regularity, as persistent as the whir of the Linotype, was heard everywhere. The ITU president told the 1902 convention: "The trend in the printing trade is toward permanency in the office staff, both regulars and substitutes."[7] The rank-and-file of the union liked the development.

In 1915 the union dealt the tramp a body blow. Many papers were seven-day publications, only six of which by union law the regular could work. The regular could lay off any shift he chose, and he chose whatever shift might benefit a tramp. The body blow came in a new ruling that the regular take his day off on a certain day each week. The papers, appreciating this efficiency, then hired more regular hands to cover the days off. The tramp, thus, could place only a shaky dependence in extra work, and this the foreman preferred to give to local substitutes.

The ruling hurt the more because from earliest times the tramp printer had bound his destiny with that of the newspaper and the newspaper's methods of production. Very few tramps were book or job workers, these quieter, more staid divisions of the industry being beneath their contempt. The pace and excitement

---

[6] Anon., "The Old-Time Tramp Printer," *The Inland Printer*, XLVI:3 (December, 1910), p. 436.

[7] George A. Tracy, *History of the Typographical Union* (Indianapolis: International Typographical Union, 1913), p. 690.

of newspaper production suited them well. Unhappily in these later years the tramp did not suit the newspaper well.

Prohibition further depleted the thinning ranks, for when they took away the gin mills they took away a powerful solace for the lonely men.

A few tramps continued on in the oldstyle tradition. Muskogee Red was still active in the 1920's, still building tales of derring-do. As an old man, his periphery so contracted that he could be expected through Topeka three times yearly, this making him virtually a resident printer by old standards. Once Muskogee went to a doctor complaining of chest pains. The doctor advised him to sleep with his windows open. "Hell, doc," Muskogee replied, "I'm sleeping under a wagon now. What do you want me to do? Kick out a few spokes?" As a veteran of the Grand Army of the Republic, Muskogee lived out his last days on a union pension of eight dollars a week. He was buried in his home town of birth that was often never seen after early manhood.

Another print in the grand old style who traveled through many meager, newstyle years was William R. ("Kokomo Joe") Phillips, who carried his personal belongings in a cigar box (a satchel would have subjected him to the ridicule of "carrying a turkey"). Kokomo Joe's gnomish figure was known to the composing rooms of most states. He preferred hitchhiking ("goosing the ghost") to hopping the rattlers, a preference that would never have been understandable to his illustrious tramping ancesters. No one is sure what happened to Kokomo Joe, a teller of towering tales. There was once the one about the bear he wrestled one night in the Georgia woods. . . . He disappeared in the late 'twenties, maybe the early 'thirties. The stories vary.

The tales oldtimers can tell of the old tramp printers are often droll and sometimes suspect. Said Kid Sloan (like many, his given name was worn from memory by his monicker) as he prepared to depart an office after an embroilment with the editor: "I notice the editor rolls down his desk top at quitting time. Well, I'm quitting and I'm rolling down *my* desk top." Whereupon he pulled his upper case over his lower case, cascading the font into pi. Many other prints are credited with the same declaration and act. Again, there are at least half a dozen versions of how Reeves (no given name surviving either) got his monicker, "Gadget."

In the tales they tell the tramp printer is always a hell-raiser, always independent, generally a witty drunk. He was something more. While too many years have passed accurately to assess the total contribution made by the American tramp printer to his trade, there is no doubt it was considerable and on many levels. He was a teacher of young printers at a time when no adequate texts or courses of instruction in printing existed. Unlike the traditional journeyman, close with the tricks of the trade, the tramp gloried in sharing his knowledge long before the Printing House Craftsmen coined the motto "Share your knowledge." There is every reason to believe that the tramp felt a kindness to the apprentice, possibly prompted by the lad's admiration, when few in the industry did.

As a card carrier and journeyman, the tramp's efforts in behalf of his union were tremendous. Eddie ("Captain") Rivers had it this way: "The only design in life I have favored is the design of the union label." In the ITU's first quarter-century, tramps did far more than the state deputy organizers in establishing locals, many of which exist today because a tramp came into the backshop to spread the gospel. Foremen were as often hired for brawn as for brain, and they were ready to handle very roughly men with the union gospel. "Square men," the gospel men were called.

No service in behalf of the union was too mean. The tramp, unknown to local foremen and superintendents, could get work in a struck shop where he functioned as a spy and saboteur. During the labor difficulty with Rand-McNally in 1900, it was a tramp who shifted a few figures in the forms of a railroad time schedule just before they went on the press for a run into the hundreds of thousands. Emery dust in press gears guaranteed a slow-down. Any evidence of corruption on the part of the foreman, that strong and early enemy of unionism, was forwarded posthaste to the foreman's boss.

The tramp printer was probably as big a boom to the **country** journalist as he was a bane to the city journalist. The tramp took off some of the burden in the country, but in the city he put on pressure for unionism. The tramps made up a mobile working force when country editors needed them most, when they could not have afforded other. There was more to it than that. Many of the nation's prosperous midwestern and western newspapers owe their beginnings to tramp printers, "those itinerant crusaders to the sparsely inhabited and semi-civilized localities of the continent."[8] A few reformed tramps even ended their days as editors. But more often where establishment of a paper was involved, the tramps were content to get it under way and then to transfer the mortgage. No editorial sanctum for them.

But the tramp's greatest contribution, impossible to weigh, probably lies in the simple fact of his being. He came into the shops with the breath of the bottle and unwashed clothes—and with the breath of fresh air and freedom. His impertinence in the face of authority and his fierce independence were a tonic to men locked in permanent situations, standing 12 hours a day to the drudgery of the case. If the regulars could not follow him down the road, they could treasure the accounts and embroider on the recountings of the tramp's escapades on his last visit. "Did you hear what he told the Old Man when. . . ."

Tramp printing, in the freest definition, is not dead in America, though few who drift today think of themselves as tramps. It is just that they change jobs frequently. Tramping today (1956) differs in many respects from tramping as it was practiced, say, from 1865 to 1915. It lacks the urgency and compulsion of the older days; it lacks the color, the daring, the stringency. Modern tramp printing—"floating"—lacks the honor or half-honor, respect or half-respect, the oldstyle tramp print knew. "No drifters," "no floaters" caution the situations open classifieds in the trade press. They took in the welcome mat a long time ago, and there is no "gate" money today.

Printers now on the road are of the stream of development

---

[8] M. J. Carroll, "The Tramp Printer," *The Inland Printer*, VI:7 (April, 1889), p. 583.

reaching back to incunabular years. They may be in the line of the tradition forged in the hard and bumptious years of the late 19th century. But they are not part of the legend of the American tramp printer, not as it is popularly entertained, not as it has been entertained here.

PARTIAL BIBLIOGRAPHY

I am in debt for the bulk of the material to nearly 50 printers, once upon a time tramps, who have corresponded with me. I am especially in debt to W. L. ("Bull") Gibson for the loan of his unpublished memoirs of tramping life and to R. C. ("Shorty") Thomlinson, a voluminous correspondent.

Albert, C. H., *A Brief History of Oklahoma City Typographical Union No. 283, 1894–1948.* Oklahoma City, Okla.: Bert Beals, 1948. Unpaginated.

Anonymous, *Diamond Jubilee, 1852–1927, Indianapolis Typographical Union No. 1.* Indianapolis, Ind.: Hollenbeck Press, 1927. Unpaginated.

Barnett, George E., "The Printers: A Study in American Trade Unionism," *American Economic Association Quarterly*, X (October, 1909), pp. 1–387.

Gordon, John, *A Memorial to the Tramp Printer.* South Brewer, Me.: Gordon Press, 1927. 79 pp.

Graham, J. B., *Handset Reminiscences.* Salt Lake City, Utah: Century Printing Co., 1915. 307 pp.

Hansen, Mark L. (Lazarus), *The Passing of "Lazarus."* Galt, Calif.: Published by the author at the office of the Galt *Herald*, 1934. 12 pp.

Harris, Dwight Thacher, and Souders, Clifford V., *Fifty Years of History: Topeka Typographical Union No. 121, 1882–1932.* Topeka, Kan.: Topeka Typographical Union No. 121, 1932. 88 pp.

Hicks, John Edward, *Adventures of a Tramp Printer, 1880–1890.* Kansas City, Mo.: Midamericana Press, 1950. 285 pp. (Ostensibly a purely biographical piece of work, this is, in fact, just a fanciful weaving of tramp printer tales.)

Moore, John W., *Historical Notes on Printers and Printing.* Concord, N.H.: Republican Press Assn., 1886. 604 pp.

Sams, John Walters, *Stray Leaves from the Journal of a Wandering Printer.* Duncan, Indian Territory: Eagle Publishing Rooms, 1904. 144 pp. (Last signatures missing.)

Stevens, George A., *New York Typographical Union No. 6: A Study of a Modern Trade Union and Its Predecessors.* Albany, N.Y.: J. B. Lyons Co., 1913. 717 pp.

Tracy, George A., *History of the Typographical Union.* Indianapolis, Ind.: International Typographical Union, 1913. 1144 pp.

Weaver, William D., *Tramp Printers.* Washington, D.C.: Government Printing Office, 1941. 20 pp.

Questions and Exercises

1. The central idea of this essay might differ somewhat with different points of view of the reader. What is of central significance to a folklorist, or a student of cultural anthropology? To a student of mass communication?

2. Study the etymology of "jour." What words are derived from it, and what are their literal meanings? What is the meaning of the word in this essay?

3. Make a list of the words in the essay that are from the specialized vocabulary of tramp printing. How many of these words are still current in the jargon of journalism?

4. This essay might properly be called a "report of reports." Explain the nature of the evidence mustered by the author. How close did Fisher get to what is known as "primary evidence"? How does this type of investigative paper differ from one concerned with a topic from the natural sciences?

5. To what extent does the author evaluate the evidence or pass judgment on the facts he employs? What methods of slanting do you detect?

6. To what extent could this investigative report be called scientifically objective? Point out any evidence you find of subjectivity.

7. What characteristics of bona fide folk characters were possessed by "Kokomo Joe" or "Muskogee Red"?

8. Explain what is meant by "oral tradition." Compare the emphasis placed on it in this essay with McLuhan's comments in "Sight, Sound and the Fury."

9. A documented report is one in which the evidence is pinned down to specific cases which have been recorded in history or literature. To what extent does this report qualify as a well-documented report?

10. How does Fisher's conclusion about the effect of the tramp printer on journalism support the idea expressed by Rollo May in "The Experience of Becoming a Person"?
11. Study the organization and structure of the essay. What are the main divisions of thought? List them in outline form, keeping your labels or sentences parallel.
12. How does Fisher's statement "Printers now on the road are of the stream of development reaching back to incunabular years" exemplify Kouwenhoven's idea of America in process in "What's American about America?"
13. Define the word *legend* as it is used in this essay, referring to tramp printing.
14. Write an investigative report, or research paper, of about 1500 words, in which you focus your attention on some problem of current concern to society, and bring evidence to bear on this problem in such a way as to allow you to draw logical conclusions. Document your report, using the style sheet recommended by your instructor. Include a bibliography of the books and periodicals you made use of in writing the report.

◆ ◆ ◆

Fenimore Cooper's Literary Offenses

MARK TWAIN

The Pathfinder and *The Deerslayer* stand at the head of Cooper's novels as artistic creations. There are others of his works which contain parts as perfect as are to be found in these, and scenes even more thrilling. Not one can be compared with either of them as a finished whole.

The defects in both of these tales are comparatively slight. They were pure works of art.—PROF. LOUNSBURY.

From *In Defense of Harriet Shelley and Other Essays* by Mark Twain. Copyright 1918 by The Mark Twain Company; copyright 1945 by Clara Clemens Samossoud. Reprinted by permission of Harper & Brothers.

The five tales reveal an extraordinary fullness of invention.
. . . One of the very greatest characters in fiction, Natty
Bumppo. . . .

The craft of the woodsman, the tricks of the trapper, all the delicate are of the forest, were familiar to Cooper from his youth up.—
PROF. BRANDER MATTHEWS.

Cooper is the greatest artist in the domain of romantic fiction yet
produced by America.—WILKIE COLLINS.

It seems to me that it was far from right for the Professor of
English Literature in Yale, the Professor of English Literature in
Columbia, and Wilkie Collins to deliver opinions on Cooper's
literature without having read some of it. It would have been
much more decorous to keep silent and let persons talk who
have read Cooper.

Cooper's art has some defects. In one place in *Deerslayer*,
and in the restricted space of two-thirds of a page, Cooper has
scored 114 offenses against literary art out of a possible 115.
It breaks the record.

There are nineteen rules governing literary art in the domain
of romantic fiction—some say twenty-two. In *Deerslayer* Cooper
violated eighteen of them. These eighteen require:

1. That a tale shall accomplish something and arrive somewhere. But the *Deerslayer* tale accomplishes nothing and arrives
in the air.

2. They require that the episodes of a tale shall be necessary
parts of the tale, and shall help to develop it. But as the *Deerslayer* tale is not a tale, and accomplishes nothing and arrives
nowhere, the episodes have no rightful place in the work, since
there was nothing for them to develop.

3. They require that the personages in a tale shall be alive,
except in the case of corpses, and that always the reader shall
be able to tell the corpses from the others. But this detail has
often been overlooked in the *Deerslayer* tale.

4. They require that the personages in a tale, both dead and
alive, shall exhibit a sufficient excuse for being there. But this
detail also has been overlooked in the *Deerslayer* tale.

5. They require that when the personages of a tale deal in conversation, the talk shall sound like human talk, and be talk such as human beings would be likely to talk in the given circumstances, and have a discoverable meaning, also a discoverable purpose, and a show of relevancy, and remain in the neighborhood of the subject in hand, and be interesting to the reader, and help out the tale, and stop when the people cannot think of anything more to say. But this requirement has been ignored from the beginning of the *Deerslayer* tale to the end of it.

6. They require that when the author describes the character of a personage in his tale, the conduct and conversation of that personage shall justify said description. But this law gets little or no attention in the *Deerslayer* tale, as Natty Bumppo's case will amply prove.

7. They require that when a personage talks like an illustrated, gilt-edged, tree-calf, hand-tooled, seven-dollar Friendship's Offering in the beginning of a paragraph, he shall not talk like a negro minstrel in the end of it. But this rule is flung down and danced upon in the *Deerslayer* tale.

8. They require that crass stupidities shall not be played upon the reader as "the craft of the woodsman, the delicate art of the forest," by either the author or the people in the tale. But this rule is persistently violated in the *Deerslayer* tale.

9. They require that the personages of a tale shall confine themselves to possibilities and let miracles alone; or, if they venture a miracle, the author must so plausibly set it forth as to make it look possible and reasonable. But these rules are not respected in the *Deerslayer* tale.

10. They require that the author shall make the reader feel a deep interest in the personages of his tale and in their fate; and that he shall make the reader love the good people in the tale and hate the bad ones. But the reader of the *Deerslayer* tale dislikes the good people in it, is indifferent to the others, and wishes they would all get drowned together.

11. They require that the characters in a tale shall be so clearly defined that the reader can tell beforehand what each will

do in a given emergency. But in the *Deerslayer* this rule is vacated.

In addition to these large rules there are some little ones. These require that the author shall

12. *Say* what he is proposing to say, not merely come near it.
13. Use the right word, not its second cousin.
14. Eschew surplusage.
15. Not omit necessary details.
16. Avoid slovenliness of form.
17. Use good grammar.
18. Employ a simple and straightforward style.

Even these seven are coldly and persistently violated in the *Deerslayer* tale.

Cooper's gift in the way of invention was not a rich endowment; but such as it was he liked to work it, he was pleased with the effects, and indeed he did some quite sweet things with it. In his little box of stage-properties he kept six or eight cunning devices, tricks, artifices for his savages and woodsmen to deceive and circumvent each other with, and he was never so happy as when he was working these innocent things and seeing them go. A favorite one was to make a moccasined person tread in the tracks of the moccasined enemy, and thus hide his own trail. Cooper wore out barrels and barrels of moccasins in working that trick. Another stage-property that he pulled out of his box pretty frequently was his broken twig. He prized his broken twig above all the rest of his effects, and worked it the hardest. It is a restful chapter in any book of his when somebody doesn't step on a dry twig and alarm all the reds and whites for two hundred yards around. Every time a Cooper person is in peril, and absolute silence is worth four dollars a minute, he is sure to step on a dry twig. There may be a hundred handier things to step on, but that wouldn't satisfy Cooper. Cooper requires him to turn out and find a dry twig; and if he can't do it, go and borrow one. In fact, the Leatherstocking Series ought to have been called the Broken Twig Series.

I am sorry there is not room to put in a few dozen instances of the delicate art of the forest, as practised by Natty Bumppo and some of the other Cooperian experts. Perhaps we may venture two or three samples. Cooper was a sailor—a naval officer; yet he gravely tells us how a vessel, driving toward a lee shore in a gale, is steered for a particular spot by her skipper because he knows of an *undertow* there which will hold her back against the gale and save her. For just pure woodcraft, or sailorcraft, or whatever it is, isn't that neat? For several years Cooper was daily in the society of artillery, and he ought to have noticed that when a cannon-ball strikes the ground it either buries itself or skips a hundred feet or so; skips again a hundred feet or so— and so on, till finally it gets tired and rolls. Now in one place he loses some "females"—as he always calls women—in the edge of a wood near a plain at night in a fog, on purpose to give Bumppo a chance to show off the delicate art of the forest before the reader. These mislaid people are hunting for a fort. They hear a cannon-blast, and a cannon-ball presently comes rolling into the wood and stops at their feet. To the females this suggests nothing. The case is very different with the admirable Bumppo. I wish I may never know peace again if he doesn't strike out promptly and *follow the track* of that cannon-ball across the plain through the dense fog and find the fort. Isn't it a daisy? If Cooper had any real knowledge of Nature's way of doing things, he had a most delicate art in concealing the fact. For instance: one of his acute Indian experts, Chingachgook (pronounced Chicago, I think), has lost the trail of a person he is tracking through the forest. Apparently that trail is hopelessly lost. Neither you nor I could ever have guessed out the way to find it. It was very different with Chicago. Chicago was not stumped for long. He turned a running stream out of its course, and there, in the slush in its old bed, were that person's moccasin tracks. The current did not wash them away, as it would have done in all other like cases—no, even the eternal laws of Nature have to vacate when Cooper wants to put up a delicate job of woodcraft on the reader.

We must be a little wary when Brander Matthews tells us

that Cooper's books "reveal an extraordinary fullness of invention." As a rule, I am quite willing to accept Brander Matthews's literary judgments and applaud his lucid and graceful phrasing of them; but that particular statement needs to be taken with a few tons of salt. Bless your heart, Cooper hasn't any more invention than a horse; and I don't mean a high-class horse, either; I mean a clotheshorse. It would be very difficult to find a really clever "situation" in Cooper's books, and still more difficult to find one of any kind which he has failed to render absurd by his handling of it. Look at the episodes of "the caves"; and at the celebrated scuffle between Maqua and those others on the tableland a few days later; and at Hurry Harry's queer water-transit from the castle to the ark; and at Deerslayer's half-hour with his first corpse; and at the quarrel between Hurry Harry and Deerslaver later; and at—but 'choose for yourself; you can't go amiss.

If Cooper had been an observer his inventive faculty would have worked better; not more interestingly, but more rationally, more plausibly. Cooper's proudest creations in the way of "situations" suffer noticeably from the absence of the observer's protecting gift. Cooper's eye was splendidly inaccurate. Cooper seldom saw anything correctly. He saw nearly all things as through a glass eye, darkly. Of course a man who cannot see the commonest little everyday matters accurately is working at a disadvantage when he is constructing a "situation." In the *Deerslayer* tale Cooper has a stream which is fifty feet wide where it flows out of a lake; it presently narrows to twenty as it meanders along for no given reason, and yet when a stream acts like that it ought to be required to explain itself. Fourteen pages later the width of the brook's outlet from the lake has suddenly shrunk thirty feet, and become "the narrowest part of the stream." This shrinkage is not accounted for. The stream has bends in it, a sure indication that it has alluvial banks and cuts them; yet these bends are only thirty and fifty feet long. If Cooper had been a nice and punctilious observer he would have noticed that the bends were oftener nine hundred feet long than short of it.

Cooper made the exit of that stream fifty feet wide, in the first place, for no particular reason; in the second place, he narrowed it to less than twenty to accommodate some Indians. He bends a "sapling" to the form of an arch over this narrow passage, and conceals six Indians in its foliage. They are "laying" for a settler's scow or ark which is coming up the stream on its way to the lake; it is being hauled against the stiff current by a rope whose stationary end is anchored in the lake; its rate of progress cannot be more than a mile an hour. Cooper describes the ark, but pretty obscurely. In the matter of dimensions "it was little more than a modern canal-boat." Let us guess, then, that it was about one hundred and forty feet long. It was of "greater breadth than common." Let us guess, then, that it was about sixteen feet wide. This leviathan had been prowling down bends which were but a third as long as itself, and scraping between banks where it had only two feet of space to spare on each side. We cannot too much admire this miracle. A low-roofed log dwelling occupies "two-thirds of the ark's length"—a dwelling ninety feet long and sixteen feet wide, let us say—a kind of vestibule train. The dwelling has two rooms—each forty-five feet long and sixteen feet wide, let us guess. One of them is the bedroom of the Hutter girls, Judith and Hetty; the other is the parlor in the daytime, at night it is papa's bedchamber. The ark is arriving at the stream's exit now, whose width has been reduced to less than twenty feet to accommodate the Indians— say to eighteen. There is a foot to spare on each side of the boat. Did the Indians notice that there was going to be a tight squeeze there? Did they notice that they could make money by climbing down out of that arched sapling and just stepping aboard when the ark scraped by? No, other Indians would have noticed these things, but Cooper's Indians never notice anything. Cooper thinks they are marvelous creatures for noticing, but he was almost always in error about his Indians. There was seldom a sane one among them.

The ark is one hundred and forty feet long; the dwelling is ninety feet long. The idea of the Indians is to drop softly and secretly from the arched sapling to the dwelling as the ark creeps along under it at the rate of a mile an hour, and butcher the family. It will take the ark a minute and a half to pass under. It will take the ninety-foot dwelling a minute to pass under. Now, then, what did the six Indians do? It would take you thirty years to guess, and even then you would have to give it up, I believe. Therefore, I will tell you what the Indians did. Their chief, a person of quite extraordinary intellect for a Cooper Indian, warily watched the canal-boat as it squeezed along under him, and when he had got his calculations fined down to exactly the right shade, as he judged, he let go and dropped. *And missed the house!* That is actually what he did. He missed the house, and landed in the stern of the scow. It was not much of a fall, yet it knocked him silly. He lay there unconscious. If the house had been ninety-seven feet long he would have made the trip. The fault was Cooper's, not his. The error lay in the construction of the house. Cooper was no architect.

There still remained in the roost five Indians. The boat has passed under and is now out of their reach. Let me explain what the five did—you would not be able to reason it out for yourself. No. 1 jumped for the boat, but fell in the water astern of it. Then No. 2 jumped for the boat, but fell in the water still farther astern of it. Then No. 3 jumped for the boat, and fell a good way astern of it. Then No. 4 jumped for the boat, and fell in the water *away* astern. Then even No. 5 made a jump for the boat—for he was a Cooper Indian. In the matter of intellect, the difference between a Cooper Indian and the Indian that stands in front of the cigar-shop is not spacious. The scow episode is really a sublime burst of invention; but it does not thrill, because the inaccuracy of the details throws a sort of air of fictitiousness and general improbability over it. This comes of Cooper's inadequacy as an observer.

The reader will find some examples of Cooper's high talent for inaccurate observation in the account of the shooting-match in *The Pathfinder.*

A common wrought nail was driven lightly into the target, its head having been first touched with paint.

The color of the paint is not stated—an important omission, but Cooper deals freely in important omissions. No, after all, it was not an important omission; for this nail-head is *a hundred yards from* the marksmen, and could not be seen by them at that distance, no matter what its color might be. How far can the best eyes see a common house-fly? A hundred yards? It is quite impossible. Very well; eyes that cannot see a house-fly that is a hundred yards away cannot see an ordinary nail-head at that distance, for the size of the two objects is the same. It takes a keen eye to see a fly or a nail-head at fifty yards— one hundred and fifty feet. Can the reader do it?

The nail was lightly driven, its head painted, and game called. Then the Cooper miracles began. The bullet of the first marksman chipped an edge of the nail-head; the next man's bullet drove the nail a little way into the target—and removed all the paint. Haven't the miracles gone far enough now? Not to suit Cooper; for the purpose of this whole scheme is to show off his prodigy, Deerslayer - Hawkeye - Long - Rifle - Leatherstocking - Pathfinder - Bumppo before the ladies.

"Be all ready to clench it, boys!" cried out Pathfinder, stepping into his friend's tracks the instant they were vacant. "Never mind a new nail; I can see that, though the paint is gone, and what I can see ·I can hit at a hundred yards, though it were only a mosquito's eye. Be ready to clench!"

The rifle cracked, the bullet sped its way, and the head of the nail was buried in the wood, covered by the piece of flattened lead.

There, you see, is a man who could hunt flies with a rifle, and command a ducal salary in a Wild West show to-day if we had him back with us.

The recorded feat is certainly surprising just as it stands; but it is not surprising enough for Cooper. Cooper adds a touch. He has made Pathfinder do this miracle with another man's rifle; and not only that, but Pathfinder did not have even the advantage of loading it himself. He had everything against him, and yet he made that impossible shot; and not only made it, but did it with absolute confidence, saying, "Be ready to clench." Now a person like that would have undertaken that same feat with a brickbat, and with Cooper to help he would have achieved it, too.

Pathfinder showed off handsomely that day before the ladies. His very first feat was a thing which no Wild West show can touch. He was standing with the group of marksmen, observing —a hundred yards from the target, mind; one Jasper raised his rifle and drove the center of the bull's-eye. Then the Quartermaster fired. The target exhibited no result this time. There was a laugh. "It's a dead miss," said Major Lundie. Pathfinder waited an impressive moment or two; then said, in that calm, indifferent, know-it-all way of his, "No, Major, he has covered Jasper's bullet, as will be seen if any one will take the trouble to examine the target."

Wasn't it remarkable? How *could* he see that little pellet fly through the air and enter that distant bullet-hole? Yet that is what he did; for nothing is impossible to a Cooper person. Did any of those people have any deep-seated doubts about this thing? No; for that would imply sanity, and these were all Cooper people.

The respect for Pathfinder's skill and for his *quickness and accuracy of sight* [the italics are mine] was so profound and general, that the instant he made this declaration the spectators began to distrust their own opinions, and a dozen rushed to the target in order to ascertain the fact. There, sure enough, it was found that the Quartermaster's bullet had gone through the hole made by Jasper's, and that, too, so accurately as to require a minute examination to be certain of the circumstance, which, however, was soon clearly established by discovering one bullet over the other in the stump against which the target was placed.

They made a "minute" examination; but never mind, how could they know that there were two bullets in that hole without digging the latest one out? for neither probe nor eyesight could prove the presence of any more than one bullet. Did they dig? No; as we shall see. It is the Pathfinder's turn now; he steps out before the ladies, takes aim, and fires.

But, alas! here is a disappointment; an incredible, an unimaginable disappointment—for the target's aspect is unchanged; there is nothing there but that same old bullet-hole!

"If one dared to hint at such a thing," cried Major Duncan, "I should say that the Pathfinder has also missed the target!"

As nobody had missed it yet, the "also" was not necessary; but never mind about that, for the Pathfinder is going to speak.

"No, no, Major," said he, confidently, "that *would* be a risky declaration. I didn't load the piece, and can't say what was in it; but if it was lead, you will find the bullet driving down those of the Quartermaster and Jasper, else is not my name Pathfinder."
A shout from the target announced the truth of this assertion.

Is the miracle sufficient as it stands? Not for Cooper. The Pathfinder speaks again, as he "now slowly advances toward the stage occupied by the females":

"That's not all, boys, that's not all; if you find the target touched at all, I'll own to a miss. The Quartermaster cut the wood, but you'll find no wood cut by that last messenger."

The miracle is at last complete. He knew—doubtless *saw* —at the distance of a hundred yards—that his bullet had passed into the hole *without fraying the edges*. There were now three bullets in that one hole—three bullets embedded processionally in the body of the stump back of the target. Everybody knew this—somehow or other—and yet nobody had dug any of them out to make sure. Cooper is not a close observer, but he is interesting. He is certainly always that, no matter what happens. And he is more interesting when he is not noticing what he is about than when he is. This is a considerable merit.

The conversations in the Cooper books have a curious sound in our modern ears. To believe that such talk really ever came out of people's mouths would be to believe that there was a time when time was of no value to a person who thought he had something to say; when it was the custom to spread a two-minute remark out to ten; when a man's mouth was a rolling-mill, and busied itself all day long in turning four-foot pigs of thought into thirty-foot bars of conversational railroad iron by attenuation; when subjects were seldom faithfully stuck to, but the talk wandered all around and arrived nowhere; when con-

versations consisted mainly of irrelevancies, with here and there a
relevancy, a relevancy with an embarrassed look, as not being
able to explain how it got there.

Cooper was certainly not a master in the construction of
dialogue. Inaccurate observation defeated him here as it defeated
him in so many other enterprises of his. He even failed to notice
that the man who talks corrupt English six days in the week
must and will talk it on the seventh, and can't help himself.
In the *Deerslayer* story he lets Deerslayer talk the showiest kind
of booktalk sometimes, and at other times the basest of base
dialects. For instance, when some one asks him if he has a
sweetheart, and if so, where she abides, this is his majestic
answer:

"She's in the forest—hanging from the boughs of the trees, in a
soft rain—in the dew on the open grass—the clouds that float about
in the blue heaven—the birds that sing in the woods—the sweet
springs where I slake my thirst—and in all the other glorious gifts
that come from God's Providence!"

And he preceded that, a little before, with this:

"It consarns me as all things that touches a fri'nd consarns a fri'nd."

And this is another of his remarks:

"If I was Injun born, now, I might tell of this, or carry in the scalp
and boast of the expl'ite afore the whole tribe; or if my inimy had
only been a bear"—[and so on].

We cannot imagine such a thing as a veteran Scotch Com-
mander-in-Chief comporting himself in the field like a windy
melodramatic actor, but Cooper could. On one occasion Alice
and Cora were being chased by the French through a fog in the
neighborhood of their father's fort:

"*Point de quartier aux coquins!*" cried an eager pursuer, who seemed
to direct the operations of the enemy.
"Stand firm and be ready, my gallant 60ths!" suddenly exclaimed
a voice above them; "wait to see the enemy; fire low, and sweep the
glacis."
"Father! father!" exclaimed a piercing cry from out the mist; "it
is I! Alice! thy own Elsie! spare, O! save your daughters!"

"Hold!" shouted the former speaker, in the awful tones of parental agony, the sound reaching even to the woods, and rolling back in solemn echo. "'Tis she! God has restored me my children! Throw open the sally-port; to the field, 60ths, to the field! pull not a trigger, lest ye kill my lambs! Drive off these dogs of France with your steel!"

Cooper's word-sense was singularly dull. When a person has a poor ear for music he will flat and sharp right along without knowing it. He keeps near the tune, but it is *not* the tune. When a person has a poor ear for words, the result is a literary flatting and sharping; you perceive what he is intending to say, but you also perceive that he doesn't *say* it. This is Cooper. He was not a word-musician. His ear was satisfied with the *approximate* word. I will furnish some circumstantial evidence in support of this charge. My instances are gathered from half a dozen pages of the tale called *Deerslayer*. He uses "verbal" for "oral"; "precision" for "facility"; "phenomena" for "marvels"; "necessary" for "predetermined"; "unsophisticated" for "primitive"; "preparation" for "expectancy"; "rebuked" for "subdued"; "dependent on" for "resulting from"; "fact" for "condition"; "fact" for "conjecture"; "precaution" for "caution"; "explain" for "determine"; "mortified" for "disappointed"; "meretricious" for "factitious"; "materially" for "considerably"; "decreasing" for "deepening"; "increasing" for "disappearing"; "embedded" for "enclosed"; "treacherous" for "hostile"; "stood" for "stooped"; "softened" for "replaced"; "rejoined" for "remarked"; "situation" for "condition"; "different" for "differing"; "insensible" for "unsentient"; "brevity" for "celerity"; "distrusted" for "suspicious"; "mental imbecility" for "imbecility"; "eyes" for "sight"; "counteracting" for "opposing"; "funeral obsequies" for "obsequies."

There have been daring people in the world who claimed that Cooper could write English, but they are all dead now—all dead but Lounsbury. I don't remember that Lounsbury makes the claim in so many words, still he makes it, for he says that *Deerslayer* is a "pure work of art." Pure, in that connection, means faultless—faultless in all details—and language is a detail. If Mr. Lounsbury had only compared Cooper's English with the English which he writes himself—but it is plain that he didn't; and so it is likely that he imagines until this day that Cooper's is as clean and compact as his own. Now I feel sure, deep down in my heart, that Cooper wrote about the poorest English that exists in our language, and that the English of *Deerslayer* is the very worst that even Cooper ever wrote.

I may be mistaken, but it does seem to me that *Deerslayer* is not a work of art in any sense; it does seem to me that it is destitute of every detail that goes to the making of a work of art; in truth, it seems to me that *Deerslayer* is just simply a literary *delirium tremens*.

A work of art? It has no invention; it has no order, system, sequence, or result; it has no life-likeness, no thrill, no stir, no seeming of reality; its characters are confusedly drawn, and by their acts and words they prove that they are not the sort of people the authors claims that they are; its humor is pathetic; its pathos is funny; its conversations are—oh! indescribable; its love-scenes odious; its English a crime against the language.

Counting these out, what is left is Art. I think we must all admit that.

Questions and Exercises

1. At the beginning of this essay, Mark Twain quotes three eminent critics of his day regarding the merits of Cooper's fiction. Look up the reputation of these men in the *Dictionary of American Biography*, and decide how acceptable their criticism should be.
2. Mark Twain once announced that *Joan of Arc* was his greatest work. Read this book, and apply to it the tenets of criticism the author used on Cooper's works. Write a paper in which you criticize *Joan of Arc* as a work of art.
3. Mark Twain criticizing Ruskin's prose once exclaimed, "It reminds me of a cat having a fit in a platter of tomatoes!" Read

brief criticisms of Ruskin's literary works in the *Cambridge History of English Literature* and one other reference work, and decide how valid was Mark Twain's flippant estimate.

4. Many of Mark Twain's critical statements are little more than personal opinions made with no standard of judgment in mind other than bias and prejudice. This essay is an exception. Explain the nature of criticism employed here.

5. Of the eighteen rules set forth for writing in this essay, which ones would you select as guiding principles for a course in communication skills? Defend your choices.

6. Find three reviews of a book you have read recently and compare the methods of the reviewers. To what extent does each employ a recognizable standard of judgment? (Use the *Book Review Digest* to locate the reviews.)

7. In rule number 8, mentioned by Mark Twain in this essay, what is meant by "crass stupidities"?

8. What is the rhetorical principle set forth in rule 2 in the essay?

9. Rule number 17 says: "Use good grammar." Judging by Mark Twain's own writing in this essay and in "Huck and Jim on the Raft," how well does the author agree with Donald J. Lloyd's notion of "Our National Mania for Correctness"?

10. What evidence do you find in the essay that Mark Twain was making an issue of a matter that deserved little if any attention? Explain.

11. How would you defend the notion that Mark Twain was not criticizing Cooper at all, but Cooper's critics?

12. Write a paper in which you criticize William Saroyan's "The Circus" employing the eighteen rules set forth by Mark Twain in this essay.

13. Mark Twain says of Cooper: "Cooper's proudest creation in the way of 'situations' suffers noticeably from the absence of the observer's protecting gift." How does this statement agree with Melville's thought in "Of the Monstrous Pictures of Whales"? How was it possible for Mark Twain to know about Cooper's superficial observations?

14. In another place, Mark Twain says: "Cooper was certainly not a master in the construction of dialogue." After reading "Huck and Jim on the Raft," do you think Mark Twain, himself, was superior to Cooper in this respect? Explain.

15. Construct an outline of the specific qualities of Cooper's writing that Mark Twain has selected for his critical study? What qualities did he ignore?

16. One of the problems of Mark Twain scholarship is to determine
    to what extent his literary criticisms may be taken seriously.
    Read his essay "Is Shakespeare Dead?" and decide whether or
    not he was defending or ridiculing the exponents of Baconian
    authorship of the plays.

◆ ◆ ◆

Walk a Thousand Miles This Year

BRENDA UELAND

WE HAVE forgotten the blessings of walking and its many benefits
to body and soul. We have forgotten the fluid, limber, long-
legged physique that endless walking moulds, and the rose-suf-
fused complexion. Now perhaps women can be persuaded to
become walkers—that is to say, to walk three or four miles a day
and occasionally twenty-five or thirty miles—if they knew how
beautiful it would make them. And after a year or two of this—
just as you were congratulating yourself on your astonishing re-
juvenation and comeliness—you might find that you had also
acquired iron health, wonderful feet and a tirelessness, for almost all tiredness is in the legs. And most important of all, you
may find that the walking has brought about an alchemy, a
transfiguration of soul.

First let us consider walking and beauty. Schopenhauer called
women "the short-legged race," a dreadful insult because it is
often true. As a matter of fact the male and female skeletons
have the same proportions, but the legs of living women *look*

Reprinted from *Vogue*, January, 1951. Copyright 1950 The Condé Nast Publications Inc. By permission of Brenda Ueland.

shorter because of steatopygous fat that accumulates around the hips and thighs, and this seems to shorten the legs by three or four inches. But if you will walk for long miles, "striding from peak to peak like a compass," as some one described Thomas Carlyle in the mountains, that horrid padding and quilting may melt away and your legs will seem longer, straighter.

And then walking will give you fresh colour because you are outdoors every day. It will give you fine eyes like those of a sea captain because they can rest on the far horizon at least for an hour a day (eyes were intended for this and not for peering at print). And walking will make you graceful and light and limber. The walker's figure is a broad chest and shoulders, long straight legs close together at the top, that swing in a beautiful arc from the waist, for inevitably after a thousand miles, you will acquire this economy of motion. You just can not help it. You will have an easy, flowing, light-footed stride with utter relaxation except at that tiny point where there is a light spring from the ground. Beautifully coordinated children and panthers have this. Red Indians had it. "And when she turned," said Virgil, "the goddess was known by her stride."

As we grow older the force of gravity gradually pulls the shoulders into a droop and it pulls down our mouths and our chins and our abdomens, alas! so that more and more we take on the outlines of doleful stalagmites; or we begin to resemble birds, you might say: a plump undifferentiated body and thin, unused-looking legs. But if you walk four miles every day properly this can never happen.

Then the walker acquires a tirelessness that seems like phenomenal energy but it is not. It is due merely to underpinnings that never seem to give out.

In Norway, where for centuries men and women have had to ski and walk over wild and endless mountains, they have much health, good nature, endurance and fine physiques; indeed the Scandinavian leg is said to be most like those on the Parthenon.

I knew Colonel Ole Reistad, Commander of "Little Norway," the training camp in Canada during World War II, an all-round athlete and the winner of the Egeberg Trophy in Norway. Colonel Reistad used to tell of a fine game they play in Norway: everybody—men, women, children, admirals, bankers, labourers, university athletes, expectant mothers, elderly school teachers, grandmothers—all gather together. Each person has a compass and a topographical map. They pick out on the map a point ten miles away over fens and mountains and then they all race for it.

Sir Leslie Stephen, the great English biographer, Virginia Woolf's father, concluded after long scholarship that "the literary movement at the end of the 18th Century was obviously due to the renewed practice of walking. . . ." He said that Shakespeare "divined the connection between walking and a 'merry heart.' " One secret of John Wesley's power is not always mentioned. He went on foot to save horse hire and made the great discovery that twenty or thirty miles a day was a wholesome allowance for a healthy man. The fresh air and exercise "put spirit into his sermons." Coleridge speaks of walking forty miles a day in Scotland. Wordsworth walked about 180,000 miles in his life "to which indeed he was indebted for a life of unclouded happiness."

"A remarkable instance of the wholesome influence of walking," wrote Sir Leslie Stephen, "might be given from the case of Scott who in spite of his lameness, delighted in walks of twenty or thirty miles a day, and climbing crags, trusting to the strength of his arms to remedy the stumbling of his foot. The early strolls enabled him to satiate his mind with local traditions, and the passion for walking under difficulties shows the manly nature which has endeared him to three generations."

Carlyle has been called "the patron saint of walking" and that is perhaps why his descriptions of scenery are unsurpassed. He once walked fifty-four miles, from Muirkirk to Dumfries, "the longest walk I ever made," he tells us.

William Blake walked thirty miles in a night: "Nothing can stop the Fury of my Course among the Stars of God & in the Abyss of the Accuser." John Burroughs said: "Indeed, I think it would be tantamount to an astonishing revival of religion if the people would walk to church on Sunday and walk home again."

It is so hard to remember that everyone walked all the time just fifty years ago, and how the reflections of it must have become interwoven into every human soul. In *Grey Eminence* Aldous Huxley describes how Father Joseph, a Capuchin monk and Richelieu's foreign minister, walked on all his diplomatic missions far down into Spain and over the Alps to Rome. "Horny like a savage's from the incessant marching and counter-marching across the face of Europe, his feet splashed through the puddles, stepped unflinchingly on the stones, treading the beat of the reiterated words, 'Love, Christ's love. . . .' "

Here is a little advice about walking itself: do not press. Do not strain your muscles and jerk along with calisthenic grimness. Do not think of destination. On the contrary see how loose, free, easy you can be in all your muscles. Feel light as a dancer. Take long ambling steps, or if you like, take fast ones, but see that they are loose. And to assure yourself of this looseness, dogtrot now and then. Trot as limp as you can. It is a kind of study in relaxation; one should never strain or push; for in my experience fatigue comes into the system only when there is tension and it is this only that makes one feel so terribly drained and pale after much exercise.

To prevent this tension you must remember this: *Never strain any muscle to its utmost.* With this relaxed walking and dog-trotting, all the muscles around the shoulder blades, the pectoral muscles, the flaccid upper arm come to life and begin to show smooth and delicately defined contours.

Thoreau said: "I have met with but one or two persons in the course of my life who understood the art of walking, who had a genius, so to speak, for sauntering: which word is beautifully derived from idle people who roved about the country in the Middle Ages, and asked charity, under pretense of going *à la Sainte Terre*, to the Holy Land, until the children exclaimed, 'There goes a Sainte-Terreur,' a Saunterer, a Holy-Lander."

John Finley called himself one of these Holy Landers or

Saunterers and gave a handsome bronze medal to everybody in New York who would walk a thousand miles a year: "A La Sainte Terre," it was inscribed, with the maxim: "To Our Better Selves." His own walking was chiefly in the busy city streets. "More than once I have walked around Manhattan Island, an afternoon's or day's journey within reach of thousands, keeping as close as possible to the water's edge all the way around. [It is 26 miles.] During the subway strike in New York I saw able-bodied men riding in improvised barges or busses at a slower-than-walking pace because, I suppose, though still possessed of legs, these cliff dwellers had become enslaved by wheels just as the mythical Ixion who was tied to one."

A thousand miles a year! That is hardly three miles a day. Remember that all vision comes out of solitude and space and walking. Walk a thousand miles this year (or two thousand). Perhaps not only your figure but your spirit will be transformed.

Questions and Exercises

1. Analyze the persuasive appeals made by Miss Ueland in this essay. What specific human motives does she capitalize on in pressing her point?
2. Read "The Advocate," chapter 24 of *Moby Dick*, and compare Melville's method of enhancing the whaling industry with Miss Ueland's method of promoting the merits of walking. What use does each author make of prestige?
3. Explain the assertion that "All vision comes out of solitude, and space, and walking." Can you find exceptions to this generalization?
4. Check the dates of the authorities referred to in this essay. How many of the authors are drawn from our own times? How can you account for this?
5. What is the significance of Miss Ueland's thesis as far as education is concerned? Do you think organized sports and physical education courses should suffice for the development of proper physique? Explain.
6. Point out a place in the essay where Miss Ueland makes use of explanations and directions as a method of developing her idea.

7. What are the twin objectives of walking, according to the author? Why is one stressed more than the other?
8. Miss Ueland explains the importance of relaxation while walking. What psychosomatic benefits do you suppose might accrue from relaxed walking?
9. Jean Mayer, in "The Case of the Disrespectful Mice," has something to say of the relation between exercise and obesity. To what extent would he endorse Miss Ueland's suggestions?
10. Compare the methods used by Miss Ueland in this essay with those used by Philip Wylie in "Are We Forgetting How to Walk?" in *This Week*, May 2, 1954 (also in *Reader's Digest*, April, 1957).
11. Write a persuasive paper on a subject of your choice in which you employ some of the techniques and devices used by these authors in trying to sell their idea.
12. Prepare a bibliography of the documents Miss Ueland referred to in the essay.
13. What word in the essay does the author supply the etymology for?

◆ ◆ ◆

The Fable of the Young Man Who Read the Papers

LOY E. DAVIS

THERE WAS a Young Man who didn't like to Work during the Hot Summer Months, and didn't have much Appetite, so he decided to be a Teacher. He could Read and Write, so he decided to teach English.

Reprinted from *AAUP Bulletin*, Summer, 1955, by permission of Loy E. Davis and the American Association of University Professors.

These were the Real Reasons, but he managed to Think Up some that Looked Good on Paper, and after a While he even got so he half Believed Them.

He said that Money Isn't Everything, and it would be Quite Noble to Hold the Lamp of Learning 'Way Up, and let the Gleam go down the Dark Corridors, and keep the Young Truth-Seekers from Falling Over One Another in their Hurry to Get There. All over the Country, Young People were Lying Awake Nights for fear the Alarm wouldn't Go Off, and they might Miss Out on Something they Ought to Know. He said the English Language was a Great Heritage, and had been used Quite a Bit of the Time by some of our Most Illustrious People. He said that all the Students would Greatly Appreciate any little Bit of Information that would help them Achieve Complete Mastery of their Beloved Mother Tongue. And they would of course be Dying to become Intimately Acquainted with the Great Literary Masterpieces that Bejewel the Diadem of the King's English, like *Uncle Tom's Cabin* and *The Psalm of Life.* He would Wind Up with a Quotation from Shelley about Driving his Dead Thoughts over the Universe like Withered Leaves to Quicken a New Birth. The Dead Thoughts was the only part that Fitted In, but it all Sounded Nice.

So he got some Rimless Glasses and a Box of red Verithin Pencils, and Set Up—I mean Sat Up—as Instructor in English on the College Level.

II

In September he Started In with High Hopes and considerable Eagerness, and a Suit of Clothes that was beginning to Wear Through. By October he had begun to Wonder whether Somebody had been Putting Him On, and whether the Real Thing wasn't maybe a bit Different from the Way he had Heard It.

First, that Part about the Money. His Salary looked like What the Boy Shot At. His Pay for Carrying the Lamp wasn't enough to buy the Coal Oil. It was more than he Deserved, but it was Inadequate. Inflation was Striking like Chain Store Lightning all

Around him, but his Pay Check had Lightning Rods on it, and not much Else. Money isn't Everything, but the local Purveyors of Viands had a regular Mania for it, and the Lady who Rented Rooms was downright Mercenary. But by Cutting Out Dessert, and absentmindedly Overlooking a Meal now and then, and Settling for a Room with no Hot Water, he was able to Get By, and find a Small Amount of Melancholy Joy in Suffering for the Common Good. At least that was the Phrase he had seen used in the Books.

Besides the Money, there was that Stuff about the Gleam down the Dark Hallways, and the Young Seekers Falling Over Themselves. This is the Way It Was:

The Alarm Clocks often failed to Wake the Earnest Young People who had finally managed to Get to Sleep just before the alarm Failed to Go Off, after they had Tossed All Night at the Unbearable Thought of not getting there On Time. Sickness was at an all-time Minimum in the City where the Teaching Went On, but back in the Home Towns there were Epidemics of Everything from Chronic Eczema to Avian Leukosis, and Relatives were Dying Off like Flies, especially on Week-Ends. Then there were Football Games, Football Pep Sessions, Football Banquets, Convocations, Movies, Victory Varieties, Dances, Midnight Serenades, Initiations, Bridge Parties, Student Elections, Meetings of the Fraternities, Meetings of the Independent Association, Meetings of Student Fellowship, the Newman Club, the Glider Club, the Camera Club, the Glee Club, etc., etc., etc.

None of the Young Instructor's students ever Attended any of These Things, because they were Trying to Take Advantage of There Opprotunities, so they could Take There Place in the World, and English was There Weakest Subject, and they Knowed how Important it is in this Present Day an Age for a Individual to Speak and Write Good, a Specially in the Business World or Things Along That Line, so they were all Burning the Midnight Oil and Holding There Noses to the Grindstone, and etc. But they seemed to be more Susceptible than most people to Toothaches, Headaches, Earaches, Stomachaches, Touches of the Flu, and Nightblindness, so they wouldn't be able to Take the Test at the Scheduled Time, and the Theme would have to be Handed In Late. In Short, the Young Instructor was running Head On into Human Nature on the College Level.

III

When the Papers came in, he thought he must have Got Hold of the Wrong Batch. They didn't seem to be Talking About the things *he* had been Talking About. He knew the English Language had done a lot of Borrowing, but he didn't know it had borrowed So Much. The Theme Writers often Took Things for Granite, they Preformed Brillantly in Atheletics, they ate their Desert in the Dinning Room while dressed in their Best Cloths, they Behaved like Angles and kept up their Moral, they had, or Could Of had, Expierences with Burgulars, Villians, Phamplets, Prespiration, and Mischevious Members of the Femine Sex. They were Familar with Airoplanes and Similiar Equiptment. They Beleived that one of the Principle Factors of a Person is Undoubtably Enviorment, and that it is a great Tradegy that some Goverments won't leave the Rest of the World live Peacably, without Allways Attacting them. They said that School Work was Druggery, but they would try their Upmost to do it Couragously, Irregardless.

On the Literature Papers he had a Hard Time recognizing the Masterpieces that Bejewel the Diadem. One student said the Autocrat of the Breakfast Table conducted one of the Radio Programs where they gave people Orchids, and the Scarlet Letter was worn by a Girl Yell Leader from Anderson High School. Others talked about the play *Orthello*, and Satin in *Paradise Lost*, and Sherlock in *The Merchant of Venus*, and Thorio's *Waldron*, and *Imitations of Immorality* by William Wadsworth. Others said they had Read the Wrong Assignment.

On the Grammar Test they had Held their Noses so long Preparing for, they gave the Instructor a New Slant on the Terminology. For Instance:

In the sentence "The Instructor's Salary was Raised by the Department Head and the Dean because he Deserved More Money," *Money* was the Object of the Instructor, and *Salary* was an Adjective because it Depended on the Department Head and could be Modified by the Dean. Some Students went on to say that *because he Deserved More Money* was a Non-essential Pharse.

In the sentence "The Closing of her Eyes showed that the Girl enjoyed the Kiss," *the Girl* was Passive, *the Closing of her Eyes* was Reflexive, and *Permission* was Understood.

In the sentence "The Man Put Soda Water in his Whiskey and Drank with Confidence," *Soda Water* was Parenthical because it Could Of been Left Out, and *Confidence* was Misplaced.

And in the sentence "The Baby being too Young to Walk, his Father carried him," *the Baby being too Young to Walk* was Dependent because it couldn't Stand Alone. They said *his Father* was Indefinite, and the Antecedent of *the Baby* was not Clear.

The Young Instructor went to his Room and turned the Basin full of Cold Water and held his Head Under for a Long Time.

MORAL: *Life is a Tough Preposition.*

Questions and Exercises

1. Assuming that the author's purpose in this essay is satirical, who exactly is the target for his criticism? Find a concise definition of satire, and determine to what extent this fable qualifies as an example.
2. What is the precise nature of the criticism in paragraph three, pertaining to effective writing?
3. "To find a Small Amount of Melancholy Joy in Suffering for the Common Good," is an example of a platitude. Can you find

other examples in the essay? What other types of linguistic expression, such as aphorisms, proverbs, slogans, or truisms do you find?

4. Read the essay with an eye to spelling errors and make a list (correctly spelled) of all the misspellings.

5. What similarity do you find between this essay and Voorhis' "Advice to Forlorn Freshmen"? How does Davis demonstrate the results of taking Voorhis' advice?

6. Find five clichés or hackneyed expressions in the fable, and explain how you would alter the context in which each appears, in order to get rid of them.

7. Define a *Malapropism*. Explain the etymology of the word, and find five examples of this type of expression in the essay.

8. Determine the basis of the humor contained in the last five paragraphs of the fable. Who would appreciate this type of humor better, a student who understands the principles of grammar well, or one who knows very little about grammar and syntax? What other types of humor can you identify in the fable?

9. In what respects is Davis' analysis in this fable a hasty generalization from observable facts about language arts courses? How well would his criticism apply to the class in which you are enrolled?

10. Give one good example of stereotyping in the essay. For illumination on this topic, read John Steinbeck's "How to Tell Good Guys from Bad Guys," in Section VII of this anthology.

11. Correct the punctuation of the first paragraph in Section III of the fable. What error in punctuation is most frequent?

12. Make a list of the difficulties Davis thinks show up in student writing. How many of these same difficulties do you experience?

13. A. Whitney Griswold, of Yale University, once wrote: "I know one excellent schoolteacher who spends his summers running a hot-dog stand in an amusement park so that he can afford to stick by his profession the rest of the year." Where in Davis' fable does the author focus on the problem suggested here?

◆ ◆ ◆

Little Red Riding Hood

AS A DICTATOR WOULD TELL IT

H. I. PHILLIPS

ONCE UPON a time there was a poor, weak wolf. It was gentle and kindly and had a heart of gold. It loved everybody and felt very sad when it looked around and saw so much deceit, selfishness, strife, treachery and cunning on the loose. All it wanted was to be let alone.

Now in a cottage near the edge of the forest there lived a little girl who went by the name of Little Red Riding Hood. (It was obviously an alias.) She was a spy, a vile provocateur and an agent of capitalistic interests. Anybody could tell by one look at Little Red Riding Hood that she was full of intrigue. Her golden curls reeked with base designs. Her pink skin showed tyranny in every pigment.

To the casual spectator, perhaps, Little Red Riding Hood might seem just a pretty, little ten-year-old child, but this was a superficial piece of character analysis. The kid was not to be trusted an inch. She was a rattlesnake, a viper and an imperialist. And on top of all that she was not interested in peace or a better world order.

Little Red Riding Hood had a grandmother who lived about two miles away. Grandma was a louse too!

No wolves liked her. They never invited her anywhere.

It came to pass that one day the poor, weak, helpless wolf took an aspirin and some spring tonic, to brace himself up, and then went for a little walk.

Reprinted from *Collier's*, January 20, 1940. Copyright 1940 by The Crowell Collier Publishing Company. By permission of the author H. I. Phillips, columnist, The Associated Newspapers.

When the wolf walked he liked to think things over. He liked to dwell on the unhappiness in the world and to think up ways for ending it and making everybody happy and self-sustaining. This took a lot of concentrating and when he was concentrating the wolf sometimes got lost in thought and didn't know what he was doing. Suddenly, and before he knew what was what, he found himself not only in Grandma's cottage but in her bedroom!

He had kicked down the door.

Grandma was pretty startled and demanded, "What is the meaning of this?"

"I am repulsing an invasion," the wolf explained, scorning all subterfuge.

Grandma was an aggressor. That was clear.

So the wolf ate her up.

It was a counterattack with pursuit.

Then the wolf heard footsteps in the hall. He was terribly frightened by this time. It had been such a harrowing morning.

Suddenly there came a faint knock on the door. The wolf realized at once that he was in for more persecution.

"Who's there?" he asked.

"Little Red Riding Hood," came the reply in a child's voice.

The wolf saw it all now. He was surrounded!

So he put on Grandma's nightgown and nightcap and jumped into bed to do some more thinking. He liked to think in bed. It was next best to thinking when out walking in the woods.

"Come up, my child!" the wolf cried to Little Red Riding Hood, his teeth chattering with fear and apprehension.

Little Red Riding Hood started upstairs, and, oh, what an ordeal that was to the poor little wolf! It seemed that she would never make the top landing, "Clumph, clumph, clumph!" came her footsteps, stair by stair. "Clumph, clumph, clumph!"

The wolf was in terror, but he summoned all his courage and waited.

At last Little Red Riding Hood came striding into the bedroom. She was very overbearing, the big bully!

The wolf watched while she put down her huge basketful of

groceries. "Poisoned food," he thought. The wolf was no fool. The wolf had been around.

"I've brought you some nice goodies, Grannie," said Little Red Riding Hood with a smile that might have fooled the democratic states, but that made no impression on the wolf. He knew that kind of smile. He had seen it on all photographs of international bankers in the newsreels. He saw that he was now in greater danger than ever.

"I don't feel like eating now," he said, "We'll come to that later." He was just stalling for time, of course, as his eyes ran over Little Red Riding Hood from her ankles to her head. "Come, sit over here on the bed!"

Little Red Riding Hood jumped at the invitation. The wolf was now in a panic. Never had he been in such danger.

"Why, Grandma, what big eyes you have!" exclaimed Little Red Riding Hood, after a moment.

"The better to see you with, my dear."

"And, Grandma, what a big mouth you have!"

The wolf didn't like that crack. "The better to kiss you with, my sweet," he stalled.

"And, Grandma, what big teeth you have!" said Little Red Riding Hood.

This was too much. She was getting too personal. In fact she was exhausting the patience of the wolf. And if there was one thing the wolf couldn't stand it was having his patience exhausted.

"Ah, let's quit stalling!" the wolf cried, rebelling against deceit and trickery in any form. "I'm not your grandma. I'm a wolf. I'm a good wolf, a nice friendly wolf. I don't want any trouble with anybody. And what happens? First your grandmother ambushes me . . . and now you try to cut off my retreat!"

"What became of Grandma?" asked Little Red Riding Hood, always looking for trouble.

"I question the propriety of your asking me that question," said the wolf, who was a stickler for international law. "But if you insist, put it in writing and address it to me via the proper diplomatic channels."

"I want to know what happened to Grannie," repeated Little Red Riding Hood, pulling a knife on him.

Well, no self-respecting wolf could stand for a brazen attitude like that. And besides there was the matter of candor and honesty.

"Oh, well, since you want to know, I ate her up," the wolf announced. "I ate her in self-defense."

Little Red Riding Hood got off the bed and stood looking at the wolf now. The wolf watched her weep and wring her hands. She gave way to all these emotions of ferocity, barbarism and hatred.

"Ah," said the wolf, "So now you are going to attack me, too!"

Little Red Riding Hood now got onto the floor on her hands and knees and showed her teeth. She crouched for a spring. She began growling.

There was not a minute to lose. The wolf was in deadly peril. He was encircled. This was a fight for his existence. Leaping from the bed, he struggled with Little Red Riding Hood, using nothing but his superior strength, his long claws, his enormous teeth and his jaws of steel, while the kid used brass knuckles, knockout drops, poison gas, a magnetic bomb, a sledge hammer and a hatchet.

Little Red Riding Hood fought savagely and barbarously, violating all the rules, ignoring all treaties and showing contempt for ethics. It was a terrific struggle. But the wolf won by sheer courage. He tore Little Red Riding Hood to pieces to preserve his dignity and ate her as a matter of principle.

"I'll teach 'em not to terrorize me," said the wolf, resuming his walk through the woods, thinking and thinking.

He was getting his patience back now.

Questions and Exercises

1. What is the author's controlling purpose in writing this fable? What ulterior or secondary purposes may he have had?

2. What is the author's central idea or thesis? State the thesis in one succinct, declarative sentence.
3. What is the nature or design of organization of the fable? Explain in detail.
4. At what specific points in the fable does the author reveal his idea indirectly? How did he alter the traditional story of Little Red Riding Hood in order to achieve his own purposes?
5. Name three historical incidents to which the idea might conceivably apply.
6. How can you determine the specific application intended by the author? Do whatever research is necessary to convince yourself that you have discovered the author's precise intentions. Use the date of publication as a clue.
7. What is the nature of the writing? Is it informative? Critical? Persuasive? Entertaining? Creative? Or a combination of these?
8. What fallacy in straight thinking is the author concerned with in the fable? To what extent does this fallacy operate among Americans? Explain.
9. Find examples in the fable of the following: stereotypes, dramatic irony, rationalization, name-calling, satire, egocentrism or ethnocentrism.
10. Compare the author's technique in this fable with Thurber's technique in "Oliver and the Other Ostriches" and with Davis' "The Fable of the Man Who Read the Papers." Point out similarities and differences.
11. Explain how specific words used in this fable demonstrate Beardsley's idea of "Meaning in Context."
12. Discuss the fable as an example of stereotyped thinking. Read in this connection John Steinbeck's "How to Tell Good Guys from Bad Guys."
13. Make a list of the "we" values and the "they" values in this fable, by referring to Felix Cohen's discussion of "The Reconstruction of Hidden Value Judgments."

VII. THE MASS MEDIA OF COMMUNICATION

Newspapers, magazines, motion pictures, radio, and television are among the most powerful forces of social control in the modern world. Much of the information we acquire of the goings-on of individuals, institutions, communities, and nations comes to us through the channels of mass communication. Furthermore, many of our ideas, opinions, beliefs, attitudes, and tastes are acquired in packaged form through these highly influential mediums. Unfortunately people on the receiving end of such well-established lines of communication are often at the mercy of unscrupulous scalawags who have no intention of safeguarding the interests and welfare of the general public. Unless we are to be eternally victimized by demagogues, charlatans, and rogues, we must devise ways of counteracting the vicious effects of unethical and socially irresponsible uses of language.

Propaganda is purposeful communication of a very special kind. It may be either constructive or destructive. It is usually defined as the deliberate and systematic manipulation of public opinion. When it works against the best interests of society it most always gains its ends by concealing motives, by suppressing facts, and by misrepresenting the truth. It usually makes an appeal to the emotions of readers and listeners rather than to their powers of reason. We need to be especially wary of advertisers and publicity men who are as a rule much more interested in achieving their own objectives than in serving the public which supports them.

Pernicious propaganda generally succeeds best among people who are apathetic, mentally sluggish, or just plain stupid. People who are able to do their own thinking and who have been trained to recognize the various types of special pleading that are used to hypnotize minds and direct and regulate actions are much less likely to be taken in by verbal chicanery. A proper education in the ways of words in human affairs should offset the evil effects of planned dishonesty. Our assumption is that the more people know about the process of propaganda and about how human beings can be motivated, the more likely they are to make intelligent decisions. The truth about propaganda will make one free of its snares and pitfalls. A healthy skepticism is a good indication of intellectual maturity.

The essays in this section of the anthology have been selected because of their concern with the mass media of communication. They focus on both the assets and liabilities of these media with reference to the wants, needs, desires, rights, and liberties of the American people.

◆ ◆ ◆

The Responsibility of the Newspaper Reader

FRANK LUTHER MOTT

THAT MYTHICAL person, "the average reader," has little to interest us. We may suspect that, on the whole, he is a pretty bad reader; but the questions that really concern us are what bad

Reprinted by permission of the publishers from Frank Luther Mott *The News in America*. Cambridge, Mass.: Harvard University Press. Copyright 1952 by The President and Fellows of Harvard College.

reading is and what its effects are and, on the other hand, what good reading can do for us.

Mr. Clifton Fadiman is anxious about "the decline of attention in our time," and particularly "the decline in the ability to read." He qualifies his terms, however, when he describes this modern phenomenon which justly disturbs him and so many other observers as a "paralysis" caused by various pressures, and as "a wholesale displacement" of the attention "away from ideas and abstractions toward things and techniques." Probably there is no contemporary decline of the power of attention, which could result only from widespread physiological change among the people, but rather there are shifts in both interests and the manner of satisfying those interests. At any rate, the faults of modern methods of attention, as shown particularly in habits of reading and thinking, are very serious.

Two of these faults are fairly obvious. The first may be called "fragmentation." The modern American, to be sure, can concentrate his attention over a considerable period of time upon a matter which moves him deeply; but when his desires or curiosities are not strongly enlisted, the multiple pulls and lures of this our modern life divide his time and interest into small bits. Moreover, this fragmentation increases, and bits become smaller bits, so small that they tend to become useless and by their very multiplicity to destroy the effects of each other.

The second prominent fault in our reading and thinking is that we have not learned to fix our attention discriminatingly; we do not concentrate on the matters that are actually of the deepest import to our society and ourselves. This, too, is probably due largely to the whirling confusion of modern life, with its multiple pulls at our curiosities and its quick distribution of fads and popular fancies.

Against these great sins of our popular reading and thinking, against the common faults of attention, American media of communication should themselves lead reformatory crusades. They have responsibilities of leadership in such matters and, instead of catering to popular weaknesses and encouraging bad reading, ought of course to engage in a constant struggle to raise standards. But we cannot avoid the fact that, after all, the fundamental responsibility in these desperately important matters rests upon the reader, the hearer, and the viewer.

It is in the news and the way it is presented in America that we are chiefly interested here; and the newspaper is, historically as well as basically today, our main reliance for the presentation of the news. So let us look for a moment at the reader's relationship to his newspaper, keeping in mind that much of what is said about that medium applies also to the magazine, radio, television, the motion picture, and so forth.

The newspaper is primarily dependent on its readers for its very existence. Circulation is fundamental. It is not upon advertising but upon circulation that the life and prosperity of a newspaper depends. If it has readers, it is in a favorable position to get advertising; but it has to get readers first, and to keep them. Up to about 1890, circulation brought more revenue into most newspaper tills than advertising. Then, in a period of business expansion, advertising had an extraordinary growth in America until, by 1914, it provided two-thirds of the income of many dailies, and by the time of the financial crash of 1929, three-fourths. Thereafter that unreasonable proportion was steadily reduced, until it was back to two-thirds by about 1940. It continues to be reduced, under the influence of increases in subscription rates which are logical and necessary. Today there are many papers, especially outside the metropolitan fields, which receive as much revenue from circulation as from advertising; some receive more. But quite apart from this matter of proportional income, it has always been, and always must be, a fundamental fact that newspaper publication is founded on readership, and that the social, economic, and political functions of a newspaper are performed primarily for the benefit of readers.

That puts a great deal of power over a newspaper into the hands of its readers. They can make or break it. It cannot be said too often that the people as a whole can have very much the kind of newspapers they want. Even in a city with a noncompetitive newspaper situation, editors and publishers are very sensitive to the results when readers begin to turn to the radio or out-of-town papers for their news. They know they are never secure, and that they do not dare to let circulation slip; they know that the paper's prosperity depends on reader acceptance.

This power of the people over their newspapers cannot exist in a dictatorship, in which news as well as editorial policies are controlled by government. Nor is there need in such a state for the people to exercise any control over news policies, since they have no political powers which true information by newspaper would implement.

But in a democracy, the benefits which the people derive from their power over the newspapers are balanced, of course, by responsibilities. That is, the privilege which we enjoy in this country of being informed more fully than any other people in the world about events and situations at home and abroad is balanced by an obligation to maintain and improve our free press.

We take our responsibilities as members of a democratic society rather casually. Our forefathers were stirred by the sense of being part of a great experiment in the history of mankind; we have grown used to our democracy as to an old coat. There is much alarm expressed about the large proportion of qualified voters who do not go to the polls; but perhaps it is just as well that men and women who have failed to inform themselves adequately, and who have little care for the welfare of their information system, do not vote. Both property and literacy qualifications have been used in this country to limit the right to suffrage; but nobody has yet devised an acceptable information test for voters, and of course nobody ever will. We shall have to muddle along, supported by our enduring faith in the intelligence of the people as the best basis for government yet devised.

And we shall be aided and supported also by continuing efforts to make our information system, which is chiefly our news system, more and more effective. In that system—vast, multiform, tireless, efficient—there are many faults, shortcomings, and dangers. . . . For these failures as well as for the great successes of the system the people have a fundamental responsibility because the system is made and operated for them, and is answerable to them.

What can the people do about their news system? Well, to make a beginning, write letters to newspaper editors. Ask for more full texts of important speeches and documents, for more news behind the news, for more analyses by qualified experts of social and economic conditions in special fields. Ask for more foreign news. Complain of slanted presentations by specific by-liners. Complain of the "play" of news in a set political pattern. Similar complaints may be made to radio stations.

Do not despise this kind of direct action. It is your newspaper, your radio station, and the editors know it is. You would be surprised to find how sensitive editors actually are to such comments from readers and hearers. A dozen letters often seem to them to indicate an avalanche of reader reaction. Of course, they disregard what are patently crank letters, but reasonable remonstrances and suggestions have great weight. In these days of expensive and scarce paper, adding certain kinds of news means crowding something else out; but let the editor worry about that. It is his business. And your letters will not be unwelcome if they show some understanding of the news; intelligent coöperation on the part of readers and hearers is valuable, and is generally so recognized.

This direct action may often be carried a step farther. Especially in the smaller cities, readers may utilize personal contacts with editors. In general, they are the most approachable, most lively minded men in the world. They like to talk about newspapers, or radio, and they like to hear what their readers or hearers think about their product. They are used to criticism, which they may resent if it is malicious or hackneyed; but they are critical themselves, and they usually value constructive suggestions offered in good faith and friendly spirit. Few newspapermen would go as far as the publisher of the *Press Democrat*, of Santa Rosa, California, who set up an advisory panel representing chief elements in the community, with which he meets regularly; but readers' views, when well meant and sensible, are commonly welcomed and heeded in a newspaper office.

It is assumed that in such direct action, whether by letters to the editor or personal contacts with him, you are interested in the actual betterment of news service. Pulling wires for selfish ends, trying to get something into the paper for personal reasons, is a type of scheming against which newspapermen are always on guard. Only when it is on the high ground of public service can such direct action as is suggested be effective.

But after all, the chief contribution which readers can make to the cause of maintaining and improving our news system is to do a better job of reading. The "good reading" which was suggested at the beginning of this chapter is bound to have a double effect: it not only improves the general information of the reader, but in the long run it raises the level of the gathering and editing of the news. The former objective should furnish us with a compelling motive for good reading, but the latter is also an important consideration if we have the general welfare at heart. The more general result is a little like the "work of supererogation" of the old theologians—something not necessary to personal salvation, but a praiseworthy performance and not to be forgotten. It works after this fashion. Newspapers, dependent as they are upon readers for their prosperity, watch habits of reading through reader-interest studies and in other ways; then they adapt their offerings to what their audience seems to want. A change in the reading preferences of a single individual would, of course, have no effect, but any considerable shift would soon make itself felt. The individual who adopts a good reading pattern has the benefit of it himself, and the satisfaction of knowing that his weight is counting for the general good. In other words, he is voting right.

What is this "good reading" about which we have been talking?

In the first place, it is systematic. How much time do you devote each day to newspaper reading? Available studies show differences according to the age of the reader, but indicate that at forty years of age he spends forty minutes or more with his week-day paper, and more on Sunday. Certainly forty minutes a day is little enough time for the newspaper; but whatever it is, it should be allocated regularly. It may be spent on a suburban train or a streetcar or bus, or in the living room after dinner, in an office or in a club or (Lord help us!) at the breakfast or luncheon table; but it should be as regular as sleeping or eating. Twenty minutes *every* day is better than an hour or two every second or third day, hit or miss, because without regularity the reader loses the connection and the sense of running events. Casual and cursory methods of "picking up the paper" lead to that fragmentation which is one of the great curses of newspaper reading.

This leads to the suggestion of a technique which is used, consciously or unconsciously, by all good readers—the "follow through" practice. Every series of events in the papers, from a campaign for a public swimming pool to a great war, is a serial story; and it is far more interesting and understandable if it is followed regularly. A young woman will sometimes complain: "Politics! Oh, I can't get interested in politics. It's just too confusing!" It is confusing, of course—until one gets into the current of the story. It is like a mystery novel in which a dozen characters are introduced in the first few pages: you have to read two or three chapters before you get them sorted out. But persistent reading day after day makes the figures of the great statesmen and political leaders emerge as personalities and as the spokesmen for ideologies which are very important to us.

One of the chief principles of good newspaper reading is that it should be comprehensive. What is your own habit on picking up your paper? Do you glance first at the top headlines on page one, and then turn quickly to the financial section? Or the sports pages? Or the women's pages? Or the comics? We shall always follow our special interests, to be sure; but to stop with such an interest or interests is a narrow and short-sighted policy. Explore the inside pages. Theodore M. Bernstein, an editor on the *New York Times*, remarked not long ago that "One of our national maladies might be described as a page-one fixation . . . the fallacious notion that all one need read to be well informed is the front page." Try reading in some field in which you do not now have an interest. Travel is broadening, even when made through the columns of a good newspaper.

Readers of the smaller papers often go through them from beginning to end, but many dwellers in large cities never have read a paper through. Large papers are made to be read much more thoroughly than many of us appreciate. The *Philadelphia Evening Bulletin* printed its issue for June 4, 1928, in the form of a cloth-bound book. It made 307 pages of highly diversified, entertaining, and instructive reading. This did not include the advertising, though readers certainly should not neglect that part of their newspapers.

But the Philadelphia reader of June 4, 1928, was by no means limited to the *Evening Bulletin*, nor is he today. He can easily pick up New York or Washington papers if he prefers them to the local *Bulletin, Inquirer,* or *News.* The point is that a good news reader should choose his newspapers with discrimination, and should get some variety into his news fare. It is true that many cities are now provided with only one paper, but it is an exceptional situation in which out-of-town papers are not easily available. Most good readers receive the local paper for local news and supplement it with news from other sources.

The other sources ought by no means to be neglected. Shop around among the various radio offerings and find the best. Read the news-magazines. Try the Sunday *New York Times* or *Herald Tribune.* Watch the news programs of your television station. In these United States there is a rich and varied service of news and information, it is inexpensive, and it is necessary for intelligent living and citizenship.

And yet, with all these riches, it is easily possible to read in such a casual and haphazard fashion that one may get very little real information of any great importance from it all. This brings us to the crux of the "good reading" problem.

A large part of our newspaper reading is done in situations of relaxation. Father comes home from work tired. He washes up, has a good dinner with his family, feels better. In the living room, the children have turned on the radio, or perhaps the television set. Father settles into his easy chair, takes off his shoes, lights his pipe, picks up his paper. Who can begrudge him *enjoyment* of his paper? He needs enjoyment, relaxation, escape from his daylong worries. That is what comics, sports, and amusing features are for; that is why picture pages, comics, and sports pages (in that order) rank next to front pages in reader-notice surveys.

But good reading of newspapers does not stop with such diverting matters. A mind which is awake to the crucial problems on which the fate of the world depends today wants far more than the answer to such questions as what Stanley Musial's batting average is at the moment, or how Alley Oop is faring in the Roman amphitheater. A lively minded reader looks over the latest dispatches from European and Asiatic capitals; he reads the correspondence from Washington; he must gather the views of the columnists and editorial writers. In other words, a hardheaded reader will always spend a considerable amount of time on "hard" news, leaving concentration on "soft" news to soft heads.

The serious reader will also want enough of a given story to get his teeth into. If the President of the United States or a returned General of the Army or a Nobel prize winner makes a major pronouncement, he will read, if not the whole of it, at least a sizable portion. The newspaper serves all classes of readers and must always be a highly composite miscellany, with thousands of brevities; but a good reader wants significant events, situations, and pronouncements set forth with fullness and detail, and he is willing to give time and effort to reading and studying such stories.

In these days when there is more leisure than ever before, there should be more time for serious reading. If our people will not read seriously, they will not deserve a mature press and radio.

Schools and colleges can do something about it. High school courses in current events which emphasize techniques of newspaper reading and radio-news listening (and now television viewing) are now part of the curricula of all good modern high schools and preparatory schools. In colleges and universities, specialized training of this kind, outside schools of journalism, is likely to be neglected on the theory that the student will keep abreast of the news anyway—perhaps in connection with courses in the social sciences. But neither schools nor colleges should dare to neglect this essential training.

Schools may help, and the press and radio may do much toward the end of the proper reception and appreciation of the news—an important patriotic duty—but we must remember that, after all, the final verdict on good reading and therefore on a good news system rests with us, the people—the readers, hearers, and viewers themselves.

Questions and Exercises

1. What, in Mott's opinion, is the principal weakness of "average readers"? How does this idea compare with the opinions of Perry and Whitlock in "The Right to Think—Through Reading"?
2. Mott mentions an article by Clifton Fadiman, "The Decline of Attention," which appeared in *The Saturday Review*, August 6, 1949. Read this article, and determine to what extent Mott's summary is adequate. How does Fadiman characterize the "new journalism"?
3. Explain how "Our National Mania for Correctness" by Donald J. Lloyd is an example of what Mott calls failure "to concentrate on matters that are actually of deepest import to our society."
4. Compare Mott's ideas about reading newspapers with those presented by Richard D. Altick in *Preface to Critical Reading*, pp. 299–322.
5. Mott says: "A good news reader should choose his newspapers with discrimination." Obviously this requires some kind of standard of judgment or criterion. What are the canons of good journalism generally agreed upon which regulate the contents of a respectable newspaper?
6. List the elements of journalism that Mott suggests we should militate against. What other things make for ineffective or

illegitimate reporting? Read Norman Cousins' "History Is Made By Headlines," *The Saturday Review*, July 25, 1954, and Ken Macrorie's "The Process of News Reporting," *ETC.*, Summer, 1956.

7. Evaluate Mott's suggestions for improving the newspapers of America. What further suggestions should be included?

8. What is meant by "yellow journalism"? What are the characteristics of this kind of journalism? What specific newspapers may be accused of this type of journalistic practice? Read, for example, William Allen White's "Good Newspapers and Bad," *The Atlantic*, May, 1934. Also "Hearst Journalism," in *Life*, August 27, 1951.

9. Write a 200-word paper on the subject "The Newspaper's Responsibility to Society." Make use of the canons of good journalism you itemized for question 6. Read in this connection "Good Newspapers, if Any," by Gerald Johnson, *Harper's Magazine*, June, 1945.

10. Make a list of several ways by which a newspaper can slant a story and present a distorted view of the news. Find an example of each of these ways in a newspaper.

11. Compare the coverage of two or more newspapers on a given story. How much space was the story allotted in each paper? Where did the story appear in each paper? How was the story slanted?

12. To what extent have other of the mass media of communication taken over the functions of the newspaper? Explain by citing actual instances.

13. Compare Mott's ideas on the limitations of the mass media with the ideas presented by McLuhan, Wood, and Albig in this section of the anthology. What is the common denominator of all these essays on reporting?

14. Determine the meanings of the following words as they are used in this essay: *fragmentation, hackneyed, supererogation, cursory, crux.*

15. John Ciardi, poetry editor of *The Saturday Review*, once wrote: "The fastest reader is not the best reader any more than the best conductor of Beethoven is the man who gets through the 'Eroica' in the shortest elapsed time. Why not take a stopwatch to the Symphony, if this is your measure?" Would Mott agree or disagree with this idea? Explain.

◆ ◆ ◆

What's Happening to Our Newspapers?

LOUIS B. SELTZER

NEWSPAPER CIRCULATION is now at all-time peaks. Advertising volume is incredible; the goose hangs high. Profits in spite of costs and taxes are pretty good. We in our business are well fed, well clothed, well sheltered, and anxious to let well enough alone. We think we are good, because business and circulation are good. In the last decades the phenomena of science have thrown mulitple competition at us; not only are we surviving but we are expanding almost everywhere and in some places fabulously. It is quite true that over the years there has been a high mortality rate among newspapers, but even that, at least for the moment, appears to be suspended.

Despite all the happy omens, however, it may be useful to step out of the sunshine for a few minutes in order to observe some scattered clouds.

A lot has happened in the roughly forty years I have been in the business. For one thing, forty years ago newspapers were virtually alone as the principal medium of fact and opinion. There were some magazines, but they were mainly concerned with fiction and entertainment. Newspapers were vital, enterprising, resourceful, audacious. They dug. They tolerated no intermediaries. They went to original sources. They were courageous. They were dedicated, devoted, determined.

Along came Bigness—Bigness begot by mass production. Instantly, as is the way of such things, it affected, influenced, and catalyzed the newspaper business. Gradually, along with almost everything and everybody else, we changed character if not form. Original reporting, crusading, individual investigative reporting began to subside, almost in proportion as features, fiction, comics, departments, and entertainment flowed into our columns. It seemed logical, even inevitable. Circulation was the big thing; increased advertising volume was important. And as costs rose in a fabulously expanding economy there was created an economic cycle. It couldn't have been otherwise. Probably it shouldn't have been otherwise. But this cycle did, nonetheless, produce some changes—and it is with these changes, both good and bad, with which I now propose to deal.

It is a fact, evidence for which literally abounds on newsstands, that, whereas newspapers were once primarily concerned with fact and opinion, and magazines with fiction and features, an abrupt, significant, and interesting reversal has taken place. The magazines of America gradually became the instruments of original reporting, crusading, investigative reporting. The newspapers of America gradually took on the former coloration of the magazines with their fiction, features, crossword puzzles, panels, columnists, comics, and other entertainments.

It is important to consider this shift as between newspapers and magazines. For one thing, in newspaper offices a realignment of relative staff importance has taken place. It is a shift from emphasis upon original and investigative reporting to the columnist or clever, sprightly writer—the personality with turned phrase or ingeniously contrived approach. For another, de-emphasis of what once was the newspaper's essential strength has occurred at precisely the wrong time. When it is needed most its absence is most conspicuously noted and felt. It is especially needed today in order to deal with the big changes of our age.

Across the nation, in every community no matter what size or economic condition, there are sweeping social, economic, political, and physical changes that literally cry out for the attention, leadership, counsel, guidance of American newspapers. If, as I am personally convinced, there is a paradoxical frustration and impotence felt by the individual in America in the presence of unprecedented plenty, then how much more this paradoxical feeling afflicts our communities—overwhelmed as they are by tremendous change, industrial expansion, educational inadequacies, housing shortages, racial frictions, business realignments, deterioration of inner cores, by the fierce sociological and psychological winds which blow across the whole American landscape.

Knowing their present is prosperous, and convinced and believing, therefore, their future relatively secure, too many editors believe their newspapers need not change. It's much easier to hire wire services than to gather, write, and print local news. The wire news is already there, ready to pick up and set. You don't have to hire a lot of men and women to round it up. You don't get into arguments with your readers over it.

Local situations are the conversation pieces for nine-tenths of the talk among newspaper readers. Most papers, however, give nine-tenths of Page One to news from remoter and less controversial areas. They then check with *The New York Times* to see if their judgments are upheld.

When most papers do turn to their local scenes what do they cover? In too many cities and on too many papers it's the easy way out that editors seek. They take the news the press agents bring in. They cover meetings and speeches and good causes that come easy and that no one can find any fault with. They blurb the friend of a friend at the Union Club, where the editor eats his lunch every day.

I take my hat off to the few newspapers in this country whose editors are going out and getting the local stories which are hard to get—and which sometimes loose all hell on the editorial offices—but these papers are very, very scarce. I can count them on the fingers of my two hands, maybe one. It's easy to reprint the police chief's report on how crime has declined each year, but rugged when you set out to document and illustrate how policemen are mooching from the refrigerators of brothels. It's easy to talk about desegregation far away, but not right at home.

The magazines, to repeat, are doing some of the best digging for facts going on in this country today. And newspapers, many of them built to greatness on the tradition of fearless reporting, are only going through the motions of covering beats or waiting for the news releases to be thrown through the transom. I feel certain that big stories, tremendous situations, are lying undiscovered and untouched in almost every large city in the country waiting for alert reporters directed by energetic and fearless editors to dig them out. How much livelier some of our dailies would be, and how much the great majority of readers would love them for it, if these big stories could be brought to the surface.

It takes courage to do that. It takes experienced and competent direction of such assignments, for readers are more sensitive and more vocal than ever if you go off half-cocked on a job of investigative reporting. It takes staff—good men, well-paid, specialized reporters. It takes money. To wait until circulation or advertising revenue drops and then attempt to turn the trend is futile. That would be too much like the advertiser who quits spending money when times are good and wonders why he doesn't survive when trouble hits.

Nobody's going to do the local digging-reporting if newspapers don't. Some of the good magazines may do the job in national or international situations. But they probably won't come into the smaller towns for obvious reasons. Nor will radio and television do it. Their field has settled down to be mostly entertainment (and in the process they have considerably reduced the demand of newspaper readers for entertainment in the paper). All this makes the newspaper more important than ever locally.

Let's move to another area where editors are taking the easy way out in meeting changing conditions. This is in the area of the use of paper—newsprint. What happens when the price of newsprint goes up? The journalistic hierarchy decides to buy a little less by using narrower rolls. And then they absorb the reduced width by cutting out white space, narrowing column rules, shortening lines of type, crowding another column to a page, trimming the height of the page, or one or more of a dozen devices to make the paper look worse which in turn makes it harder to read and makes the reader mad enough to turn his attention to television or a typographically-attractive magazine.

What in the world can be in editors' minds, or business managers', when they believe that papers can prosper forever by allowing the product to deteriorate in content and appearance and vigor and salability at the very point in history when they all face the greatest competition for people's time and attention? People's reading habits are changing. They are spending less time with their daily papers. A story has to be really important to be read if it is long and wordy. Careful selection of material and careful editing to get it down to a length that will be read are more vital than ever. The appeal of good pictures is still on the rise. A paper has got to have eye-appeal as well as good reporting, writing, and editing. It must look good not only on Page One but all through it if the reader is to stay with it more than a minute.

Nine out of ten papers are crowded, lack eye-appeal, crowd too much in too little. The reader isn't spending enough time with it to get his five or ten cents' worth. When money gets scarce in that household there's going to be an easy place for him —or her—to save that five or seven or ten cents.

In these thick and crowded-looking papers not very much help is given the reader in finding what he's looking for. Again there are distinguished exceptions, but mostly editors are letting important pages and departments wander aimlessly around Page One, unanchored and often unfound. Sometimes an index is printed on Page One, but that isn't enough. Is the editor afraid to offend an advertiser by throwing him off the front or back of a section? That's generally the same advertiser who'll be glad to keep buying the additional circulation you'll get by making your paper attractive, easy to read, and easy to find things in.

Readers don't like stories that start on one page and finish on another, no matter what the disguise or allure. How many jumps did the average paper have yesterday? Why can't they be edited out? Readers like easy-to-read type. How many papers are still using seven point, plus a lot of five-and-a-half agate? Even eight-point is being frowned on in many places now, and already abandoned in a few. What is the business doing about color, or is it going to abandon that great area of popular appeal entirely to the magazines and television?

Think for a minute of all the appeals these days to the time and attention of the teen-agers, for instance. Is the local newspaper meeting this competition and getting these young people as readers now, when they should be getting the newspaper habit? Doesn't it all boil down to this: once the reader came to the newspaper because he had few other places to go; now it must go to him. He can't any longer be offered a product in a "take-it-or-leave-it" spirit. He's got to be coaxed, sold. The newspapers must be part of his family. He's got to feel the editor is his friend and not just a big corporation trying to take his money.

Big industries spend millions on public relations, and they'd give millions more to have in the palm of their hands, and listening, just a tiny fraction of the people who read papers. But newspaper promotions tend to be gimmicks to get people to buy a few extra papers to work a puzzle, to fill out a coupon. If newspapers want to appeal to readers by giving them something in addition to news then why don't they spend more money helping young mothers learn how to care for their babies, or show men and women what they can do to find a better home or neighborhood, or how to feed and entertain aged couples who otherwise have few pleasures? This is the circulation that lasts.

Most editors need to get out more and be a part of the town. They stay too much in their offices, visit too much with the some people. Some offices are so inaccessible a person can't get a hearing unless he has influence. A newspaper must have human qualities. It must have understanding and sympathy and know what is really in the hearts of its readers, and it can't get that if the men who run it sit in their offices and read *The New York Times*.

Here are a couple of paragraphs from a recent stirring speech made by a distinguished fellow townsman, Dean Carl F. Wittke of Western Reserve University, one of the country's ablest historians and scholars. Dean Wittke, speaking of the growth of American social conscience, said:

Flexibility has kept our democracy strong and made it stable. We have made mistakes, but the sober common sense of the American people, acting by the democratic process, has triumphed in the end. In this we have faith. We prefer ballots to bullets, and counting noses to breaking them, and because we have been willing to experiment we have proceeded by evolution rather than revolution.

It is for these reasons that the protection of our fundamental civil liberties is so important. We need free enterprise in business and industry, and we need free enterprise in ideas about government and its functions. We need free schools, for they are the lighthouses that chart the course of civilization. They are society's experiment stations, and they provide new dreams and hopes when we are tempted to yield to despair. We need a free, an intelligent, and an independent press, and in an era of mass production of newspapers by great publishing companies we need more William Allen Whites to get off their chest what they really think.

Again Dean Wittke said:

The sober second thought of the American people is overcoming the paralyzing fear and hysteria which led the fainthearted to lose courage and confidence in the American way of life. If we would preserve this land as a place where individual liberty can exercise its invigorating effect; if we would preserve that flexibility which alone can insure orderly progress; if we would keep this a land of promise and hopes, and rugged and high adventure, then we cannot condone interference with any of the channels of information and free debate upon which the progress of this nation depends. Not majority rule but the rights of minorities, as defined in the law, the Constitution, and the courts, is the real test of democracy.

He concluded:

Man's dream-world of justice and brotherhood has been as powerful a motivating force as any material thing in fashioning a moral design for the good life. History is full of records of men and women who have devoted their lives to those who have been hurt and bruised in the human adventure. The essence of all great religions is mercy, and all the virtues are enwrapped in compassion for one's fellow man and devotion to the beloved community.

And for myself, making use of Dean Wittke's phrase "beloved community," I believe that the American newspaper of the future will be made great by reflecting the crazy-quilt pattern of a bewildering and swiftly changing world while remaining close to the "beloved community" for which and in which it is published. And that "beloved community" may either be Eugene, Oregon, or Crestline, Ohio, or Tulsa, Oklahoma, or San Francisco or Chicago or New York or Houston or Cleveland or any community in America—be it counted in the hundreds or in the millions.

Questions and Exercises

1. How can you account for the apparent fact that the audio-visual media of communication have not affected to any marked degree the circulation of newspapers in this country?
2. What does the folding of such magazines as *The American Magazine* and *Collier's* testify about the security of the two channels of communication: newspapers and magazines? Explain.
3. List the author's principal criticisms of the American newspaper.
4. Compare the importance Seltzer attaches to local news with the idea proposed by Mott in "The Responsibility of the Newspaper Reader." What percentage of space in a newspaper should be devoted to local, national, and international news?
5. Why should the judgments of the editors of *The New York Times* constitute a standard for other newspapers to check by?
6. How is the author's phrase "digging for facts" related to Evan Jones' "Pick and Shovel Sherlock Holmes"?
7. Check the concentration on reports of several leading magazines, and make a list of the topics covered. Determine to what extent these same subjects are given adequate treatment in the newspapers.
8. H. A. Overstreet in *The Mature Mind* has argued that America has a vested interest in sensational news. Check the news stories of three different newspapers published the same day and determine what percentage of the coverage may be justifiably called "sensational" in each case.

9. Which of the points made by Mott in "The Responsibility of a Newspaper Reader" about the habits of newspaper readers does Seltzer agrees with?
10. Read Clifton Fadiman's "Decline of Attention," *The Saturday Review,* August 6, 1949, and compare his ideas with Seltzer's plea for more eye appeal in the American newspaper. Do the two authors agree on what should be done?
11. What is meant by editorializing the news? Find specific examples in news stories of the inclusion of editorial judgments of the facts reported.
12. What are the qualifications of a good reporter, according to Seltzer? To what extent does his idea agree with Fisher's thought in "A Forgotten Gentry of the Fourth Estate"?
13. Criticize the quotation in this essay from Dean Carl F. Wittke on the basis of specificity. What devices of language does the Dean employ to promote his idea? What words does he use that are ambiguous because not adequately defined?
14. How does Seltzer's idea in the final paragraph of this essay support the thesis of Kouwenhoven's "What's American about America?"
15. What does Seltzer think about conformity to established dogmas and standards of jounalistic practice? Support your answer by specific statements from the essay.

◆ ◆ ◆

Influence of Magazines on the Reader and the Social Group

JAMES PLAYSTED WOOD

THE INDIVIDUAL, if there was ever a time in which he could, can no longer live in a world bounded by the range of his five senses

From James Playsted Wood—*Magazines in the United States,* Second Edition. Copyright 1956 The Ronald Press Company. Reprinted by permission of the publisher.

and by what information of people and events outside that small realm he can obtain through rumor. The geographical contraction of the modern world, brought about by speeded transport and viciously improved armament, and the speeded tempo of world activity have emphasized the need for full communication. What is happening in Manchuria, in Germany, in Tibet, at the North Pole, in science, in education, in politics, in industry, is now a matter of vital concern to the man or woman in Brooklyn, in San Francisco, and everywhere else in the United States. Whether he likes it or not, the citizen of Cincinnati is now a citizen of the world. He always was, but he did not always realize it until the magazine, the press, the radio, and television, the forces of communication most important today, told him so. These forces have taught him to be aware of the world, have kept him aware of it, and have made the American probably the most copiously informed citizen of any country. . . .

The four major forces affecting and controlling national public opinion, the magazine, the newspaper, the radio, and television, first created the public opinion they affect. It is axiomatic that no public opinion exists where no materials, no facts, no ideas have been provided. They serve a hunger they themselves have aroused. The newspaper is local in circulation. Its influence ends at the boundaries of its distribution. The day's newspaper is discarded upon being read, replaced by tomorrow's editions. Except where a definite crusade has been undertaken and is pressed in a journal's pages day after day over a period of weeks or months, the approach of the newspaper is fragmentary. Active human memory being what it is, the strongest effects of television and the radio quickly fade. The magazine suffers from these limitations less than the other major media. Ideally, the national magazine, prepared weeks ahead of issue date, need not compress, limit, or oversimplify in the presentation of a subject. There is time to deliberate and prepare a full and thoughtful article. The magazine has retained its original characteristics as a *magazine*, a storehouse of varied material. The offerings in every issue—articles, fiction, illustrations, sports, politics, science, economics, fashions, art, music, and all the other subjects covered in the modern magazine—allow reader selection.

The American public spends an appreciable part of its time reading magazines that have been skillfully enough edited and made physically attractive enough to catch and hold its undivided attention. The magazine is usually retained for further reading, for reading by other members of the purchaser's household long after the newspaper has been discarded and the radio program has faded. Reliance is placed on both the editorial and the advertising contents of the magazine in proportion to the repute which the magazine has established and maintains.

All of these contentions have been substantiated by surveys. A Gallup poll of June 14, 1948, asked how many people recognized a famous magazine cartoon character by sight or by association with the place they met her. Some 30,000,000 people correctly identified character and magazine. Another 25,000,000 recognized, by name or by association with a magazine which frequently carries his work, a famous magazine-cover artist. Other surveys discovered that readers spend an average of two hours and twenty-four minutes in actual reading of copies of a famous weekly. Answers to questionnaires placed in 80,000 copies of one periodical showed that current issues of the magazine were kept by the family in places where it would be picked up and reread, and that 66 per cent keep their copies for a month or longer after the issue is published.

Such studies aid in determining something of the social force of a magazine. Postulating a cause-and-effect relationship, the results obtained by a magazine's definite campaign are concrete evidence of its power. Not as easily determined is the sustained force of magazines in moulding and influencing their readers' attitudes toward people and ideas, in conditioning their reactions, in making them, in part, the people that they are.

Lacking this evidence, perhaps the best proof of the ordinary and continued impact of a strong magazine on its readers is the letters to the editor and similar indications of attentive reading that follow on the appearance of each issue. Here it must be remembered that only a small fraction of those who feel tempted to write the editor do write, and that only a small fraction of those moved to strong agreement or disagreement with some statement in an article even consider placing their comments on paper. Examples of this could be multiplied almost at will from the experiences of any of today's reputable and widely circulated periodicals. It is commonplace for a magazine to receive requests for thousands of reprints of a given article.

"—And Sudden Death" by J. C. Furnas, which appeared in *Reader's Digest* in 1935, was probably one of the most widely circulated magazine articles ever published. A highly dramatic story of fatalities from automobile accidents, and a gruesome warning, it was republished again and again in newspapers and in publications other than the *Digest*. *Reader's Digest* distributed thousands and thousands of reprints to civic societies and other organizations alarmed by the growing number of highway fatalities.

Sixty-eight words in the middle of a 1,750-word *Country Gentlemen* article on dogwood trees offered seeds to those requesting them. In less than two weeks 15,000 readers wrote the magazine asking for the seeds; almost 25,000 requested them within a short time, virtually exhausting the supply available for distribution.

Occasionally a magazine article provokes marked and even unexpected results directly traceable to its appearance. Mark Sullivan, while still a student at the Harvard Law School, suggested to William Belmont Parker, an associate editor of *The Atlantic Monthly*, that he do an article on the political corruption in Pennsylvania. Parker approved the idea, and Sullivan wrote a strong indictment of Pennsylvania politics. He attacked Senator Matthew S. Quay, Republican boss of the state; he described bribery and vote-buying, the parceling out of political favors, the oppression of those who refused to conform to demands of the machine. Pennsylvania, he said, wallowed in corruption. Sullivan went further. He drew unpleasant comparisons between the contributions of Pennsylvania and Massachusetts to literature and public life. Bliss Perry bought his article for forty dollars but suggested that, as Sullivan was young and unknown, it be published anonymously. The article appeared as "The Ills of Pennsylvania" by "A Pennsylvanian" in the *Atlantic,* October, 1901. It created a furor. Outraged Pennsylvanians wrote indignant letters to the magazine. The anonymous author was excoriated. The most forceful reply was written by Samuel Whitaker Pennypacker, a very learned judge in Philadelphia. His able defense of both Pennsylvania and Senator Quay brought him into such favorable notice that he was made Quay's nominee for the governorship of Pennsylvania and was elected.

In 1934, *The Saturday Evening Post* published "Schoolhouse in the Foothills." These articles by Alvin F. Harlow told the story of a young teacher's struggles in her school at "Shady Cove" in the Tennessee mountains. Though no solicitation was made, gifts of money, clothes, books, and other equipment poured into the *Post* from every part of the country for transmission to the teacher. To handle the enormous correspondence which resulted from the articles, the magazine had to employ an assistant for the article writer and a secretary for the schoolteacher. The "Shady Cove" school received everything it needed, and so much more that arrangements were made to direct the continuing flow of gifts to schools in other mountain villages.

It is not always by their expressions of approval that readers demonstrate their reactions to a magazine. When *The Atlantic Monthly* published Harriet Beecher Stowe's "The True Story of Lady Byron" in September, 1869, shocked and horrified subscribers hurriedly canceled their subscriptions, and the magazine was made to feel the sting of popular disapproval. James T. Fields, who succeeded James Russell Lowell as *Atlantic* editor in 1861, may have had this experience in mind when he admitted ruefully: "I could double the merit of the articles in the *Atlantic Monthly* and halve my subscription list at the same time." When Edward Bok dared discussion of sex and venereal disease in the *Ladies' Home Journal* the genteel feminine world of the 1890's declared shrilly for his annihilation, and the *Journal* lost hundreds of indignant subscribers. A few years ago one of the larger magazines published an article which was widely misconstrued. Though the magazine received many letters approving the article, it received thousands from others who believed it inaccurate and unjust. So violent was the attack on the magazine that its editor had to explain and apologize in paid space in large city newspapers the intent of his magazine in purchasing and printing the article.

The significance of these last three illustrations is not that magazine audiences disapproved certain editorial items, but that the influence of magazines is strong enough to cause quick and strong expression of opinion. One newspaper in its bitter attack on a magazine for what it considered a biased and intolerant article inadvertently paid unusual tribute to a competitive medium when it said editorially: "Any magazine that reaches 3,000,000 readers is one that is bound to have far-reaching influence on the thinking of the United States."

The potential influence of material appearing in the modern national magazines is not limited to the readers of the magazine and those influenced by the thinking of magazine readers. The vast audience of these magazines is many times multiplied when the same material is later published in book form and when, as often happens with a novel, the book becomes a motion picture. The modern national magazine exerts its power among the experts discussing economic or scientific questions, and affects the adolescent sighing and bubbling bubble gum in a darkened movie house while she lives vicariously the life of her Hollywood heroine.

The magazine pours its stream of facts and ideas into the great well of information and suggestion to which other sources, radio, television, newspapers, speeches, books, also contribute. Given the great number of American magazines, their large circulations, the number and diversity of subjects which they cover, and the important fact that magazines are periodical—that they come out each week or each month, each time with new diversions and new facts, or at least rearrangements of old ones—

their contribution to this pool of knowledge and sentiment for the forming of public and private opinion is immeasurable.

According to the Magazine Advertising Bureau, American magazines are read by nearly seven out of every ten adults of fifteen years of age or older. Eight out of ten families in this country read magazines regularly. *Life* alone claims a total readership for each issue published of over 26,000,000. Others of the most widely distributed magazines claimed proportionately high readership figures, figures running well into the millions. Magazine penetration is deep. Magazine pressure on the American mind is continuous and unrelenting.

These readers are directly subject to magazine influence. The same magazine material, or the sustained editorial attitude of some one magazine or a group of them, may reach others through a lecture, a sermon, a serious discussion, or a newspaper account of something a magazine has published. Whether or not they are acknowledged as the source, magazines have certainly provided the material of countless sermons, books, and lectures.

It is probable that in the Presidential election of 1928 many citizens voted for or against Al Smith because of what he said and the way he said it in *The Atlantic Monthly*. Many whose attitude toward the New Deal, and later toward Russia, was determined by what they read in *The Saturday Evening Post* might not have acknowledged, perhaps had ceased to be aware of, the source of their disapproval; just as others, consciously or unconsciously, had their opinions of Prohibition changed when *Collier's* articles showed that it was not working successfully. The hostess who is complimented on the appearance of her dinner table is not apt to credit the illustration in an advertisement in one of the women's magazines as the inspiration she carefully followed. Thousands of young women today are wearing "Gibson Girl" costumes. Many of them were born almost a quarter of a century after Charles Dana Gibson influenced the dress, manners, and appearance of an earlier generation of American young women by his famous drawings in the old *Life* and then in *Collier's*.

Most individuals find it difficult to isolate the original bases of their opinions, tastes, prejudices, and beliefs. Often they can distinguish no single source. They stem from conversations, from odds and ends remembered of their formal education, from their experience with people and things, sometimes from simple imitativeness. More often than they realize, their conceptions, sometimes their misconceptions, had their ultimate origin in a magazine.

Society lives by ideas and the communication of ideas. It is itself the result of ideas and discussion of ideas, and must depend for its continued sustenance and growth on the circulation of facts, opinions about facts, beliefs developed from these opinions, and decisions reached on the basis of considered judgments. There is today no scarcity of the raw material on which social decisions must be reached and social action taken.

There is a great glut of communication. The individual and the social group are assailed, and sometimes almost overwhelmed, by facts and fiction, by fantasies labeled fantasy, and by other fantasies labeled fact. Truths, partial truths, distortions, mistaken convictions, and deliberate falsehoods confront us everywhere in print and in broadcast speech. The fulsome mouthings of omniscient radio and television commentators, the eternal knowingness of political columnists, freshly agog every day over new and horrendous revelations that they have just divulged and delirious over new alarms that they have originated or helped manufacture, are part of our daily diet. The smirkings of gossip columnists, as they ladle out juicy rumors of marital discord among the glamorous great of the entertainment and sporting world, and post advance notices of obstetrical events among the same group, are as familiar as the syndicated advice of tipsters on romantic love, etiquette, health, and "life." Daily a flood of expertly prepared publicity is released on behalf of corporations, government departments, labor organizations, or anyone willing to pay generously for the purchase of public approval and affection.

With all of this, there is the unceasing clamor of pressure groups of every kind, all intent, for purely selfish reasons, on influencing private and public opinion favorably, and the vociferous outcries of injured minorities—all minorities, seemingly, being injured, and all of them shrilly articulate. So many groups are continually engaged in lobbying, jockeying for advantage, strenuously engaged in putting both their best feet forward in print and on the radio, that the reading public must sometimes be inclined to distrust most of what it reads and hears.

The reputable magazines, "class" or "mass," are comparatively free of the worst material of this type. A glance at the contents of a representative group will bear out the truth of this assertion. Though it would be absurd to attribute to all of them ethical impulses which many of them do not share, or claim for them ethical practices which some of them do not perform, magazine standards of editorial responsibility are fairly high. Magazine traditions, professional pride, and the interest in matters of public concern which the magazines have shown since 1741 account in part for this circumstance. There are practical as well as idealistic reasons.

The reputation, hence the acceptance and circulation, of a magazine can be seriously damaged by publication or irresponsible material. One seriously mistaken article, or an article which is merely sensational, can do almost irreparable damage to a magazine's standing. Again, the national magazines, as business enterprises, are directed at people with the money to buy the products they advertise. These people are apt to be those with enough taste and education to discriminate between reputable and disreputable editorial content, as well as between superior and inferior merchandise. The demands of their audiences operate to keep magazine editorial content at a certain level of intelligence and public usefulness.

The magazines are comparatively free of special pleading, if only for the reason that special pleading will inevitably offend groups of readers whom the magazines wish to retain, readers whom they must retain if they are to keep their circulations at the figures guaranteed to advertisers. The weakness here is that, for the same reason, magazines of wide circulation must be circumspect in their treatment of some controversial issues. Some magazines are so circumspect as to omit treatment of some serious social and political issues altogether, a policy which vitiates their force as instruments of social persuasion. Allied to this avoidance are the superficiality, oversimplification, and glibness which weaken the substance of material of social import communicated in some widely circulated magazines.

The distinctness of individual magazines helps to prevent their publishing some of the kinds of material, running from the vicious to the useless, which are printed or aired today. The magazine which is all things to all men has not yet been developed and will not be. A magazine has to establish its identity in order to be recognized and received. The most successful large magazines—and "successful" is used here to mean financially profitable and widely known, read, and respected—have made themselves as nearly as possible synonymous with specific kinds of editorial attempt and performance. The words or phrases "picture," "news," "business," "women's interest," "literature," "geography," "farm," "fashion," "general weekly," will almost automatically bring to mind the names of specific magazines. These terms serve not only to describe particular magazines, but also to indicate lines of direction through what might be otherwise the trackless morass of public communication in the United States in the mid-twentieth century.

The character of a magazine limits its audience, and thus, to some extent, the spread of its influence, its educational force, its persuasion to belief, and possibly to individual or social action. A reader, on the basis of his experience with the periodical, knows that he will find certain writers, at least writers of certain recognizable types, in one magazine; and that the magazine will consistently display attitudes which he approves or disapproves. He may read or avoid a particular magazine for this reason. He can, if he wishes, read one magazine as an antidote to another. The diversity of magazines enables him to strike a balance between facts as stated and opinions as offered in one magazine, and treatment of the same subject in another magazine. Despite its partisanships—and most of the stronger magazines are partisan politically and socially—one periodical will often present authorities and arguments on several sides of controversial issues.

Magazines are in competition with each other and with the other media of public communication. This competition provides another safeguard against magazine publication of ill-considered material. Magazines do not willingly invite the adverse criticism which is sure to follow its publication. That same competition, of course, is one insurance the public has that the magazines will try to cover every subject of public concern and will offer various interpretations of such subjects. As an integral part of the free press of a free society, magazines share this privilege and responsibility.

Except in arithmetic texts and tables of scientific formulas, little unbiased writing has ever been published. Everything is written by someone, someone with beliefs, emotions, prejudices, and ignorance of his own. Usually a writer has the desire, and sometimes the skill, to sway his readers to his views, but acceptance of what any writer says in any magazine, as in any newspaper or any book, must depend finally on the education and critical intelligence of the reader. Honest and careful magazine editing can screen out obvious inaccuracies and distortions, but the last and final editing the reader must do for himself. For a long time the better magazines have been providing him with the information and helping to develop in him the critical equipment which will enable him to do this.

In recent years much has been written—little has actually been discovered—about how, how much, and in what ways the mass media of communications affect their vast audience. Research in what has come to be called the field of communications is being done continually by sociologists, psychologists, and political scientists drawn to the study; but up to this time few reliable conclusions have been drawn. Most published studies begin or end with the reiterated lament that too little is known and that more study should be done. Wilbur Schramm, in acknowledging and assaying work done by investigators to the end of 1949, could say only that "The present trend of thinking about the study of communications effects is to recognize the full complexity of this problem, and also to recognize that it cannot be solved by any simple and direct attack, but only by analyzing the whole situation minutely and painstakingly, bringing to bear on it all potential evidence from the different social sciences, and then whittling away at the unknown area by means of carefully controlled experiments." [4] Carl I. Hovland, after reviewing studies available five years later, could only repeat in 1954 that some writers thought mass communications were all-powerful while others minimized their effects.[5]

One difficulty which plagues researchers into communications effects is that people must form the basis of their study. If the proper study of mankind is man, as Alexander Pope insisted, he is also the most difficult subject of study. Usually he cannot answer questions accurately about his beliefs and behavior, simply because he does not know. His observed actions, even when controlled under laboratory conditions, are apt to be disconcerting and of small help in reaching valid generalizations. The student of communications must give much of his time and energy to the establishing of study techniques, borrowed many times from marketing research or the pollsters; and, as often as not, he gets lost in the process.

Little of the communications research done thus far has been done specifically on magazines. Magazine publishers make studies continually on the size and composition by age, sex, income, and other social factors of their reading audiences, but these are usually for the purpose of proving to advertisers and potential

---

[4] "The Effects of Mass Communications: A Review," *Journalism Quarterly*, XXVI (December, 1949), No. 4.

[5] "Effects of the Mass Media of Communications," in *Handbook of Social Psychology*, Vol. II, *Special Fields and Applications* (Cambridge, Mass.: Addison-Wesley Publishing Co., 1954). The chapter contains a useful bibliography, pp. 1100–3. Containing, as it does, some of the work of Paul F. Lazarsfeld, Walter Lippmann, Bernard Berelson, Hadley Cantril, Douglas Waples, and other investigators, *Mass Communications* edited by Wilbur Schramm (Urbana, Ill.: University of Illinois Press) is a good indication of the present status of the general study.

advertisers that their magazines reach an interested group of customers and prospects. Such studies are not concerned with the effects of a magazine's editorial content upon its readers. Though they were talking of reading of all kinds of printed media, what Waples, Berelson, and Bradshaw pointed out in 1940 can be applied to magazines. They indicated that people read for information to apply to personal problems, to enhance their self-esteem by reading what praises the group to which they belong, to reinforce positions already taken on controversial issues, and for respite or escape. Their aesthetic experience is usually enriched in some way in the process.[6]

These authors contend, and sensibly, that the effects of reading depend on two forces: the content of the publication and the predispositions of the reader, both of them compounded of many elements, few of which are easily isolated. Joseph T. Klapper in *The Effects of Mass Media* makes the further point that people select material to satisfy already established tastes, and that all the mass media tend to re-expose their audiences to the kind of material which their patrons already like best.[7]

One of the generally accepted opinions resulting from communications study is that radio and television tend to reach all ages and income and cultural levels, while reading is correlated with education. It would seem apparent then that radio and television have become by and large the mass media, while magazines tend to reach a selective audience. Radio and television are "mass" while magazines are "class" from the point of view of editorial appeal as well as from the point of view of the advertiser.

In magazine circles there has been discussion in recent years of "impact." Subjectively, the existence of magazine impact is acknowledged. A given periodical does have distinctive characteristics and does awaken particular responses in its readers. Objectively, impact is difficult to prove, difficult even to describe. Some "impact" is measurable; most of it is not.

[6] D. Waples, B. Berelson, and F. R. Bradshaw, *What Reading Does to People* (Chicago: University of Chicago Press, 1940).
[7] Klapper, *op. cit.*

We speak of the impact of a man's personality, meaning the effect of his physical presence, the sound of his voice, the color and texture of his clothes and how he wears them, what we know of his past or his present or his possibilities—and meaning also our own prejudices, how what we knew of him previously or suspect of him measures against whatever standards and beliefs we have amassed from our own total experience.

Impact is pleasant to the one affected and favorable to the object which provides it, if our previous experience with it has been satisfactory from our own viewpoint. This is true whether the object creating the impact is a man, a circumstance, or a magazine. The impact of a given magazine is a possibility made of a thousand related and diverse impressions. The magazine, in the past, has pleased us by its cover pictures and what it has said about cancer, aspects of St. Paul, Minnesota, the habits of polar bears, or the Formosan situation. It has seemed credible and reliable or has jibed with what we wish to believe. The type and layout, the general makeup, were aesthetically pleasing or, at least, did not annoy. The illustrations were romantic or their colors did not jar. It took very little mental effort to understand what was said about cancer, Formosa, polar bears, or the advisability of buying a particular brand of motor oil. We read the magazine after a good dinner. It pleased, and we assume that it will please again. We have been made receptive. Succeeding issues of the magazine will have impact—they will reach us equipped with the possibility of arousing a favorable response.

This can work the other way, and still be "impact." We distrusted and detested what the magazine said about cancer, Formosa, and the motor lubricant. The periodical has established an effect of annoyance and displeasure. We will not believe what it may say of the Aleutians, tuberculosis, or any motor oil of any kind.

The probability, though, is against the second reaction. The magazine has long been a familiar part of the American scene. It has been able to become so because it has impressed millions, even billions, of its total audience favorably for generations. The probability is that the individual reader is enough like those millions that he too will be receptive to the carefully concocted allure of the periodical. The force of every issue which was ever published, of the fact that the magazine has been around all his life, that his father used to read it, perhaps his grandfather, that it has slick pictures of expensive automobiles and that he can remember poring over them in 1923 or 1930 or 1940, all help.

Because of all these things or things like them, a magazine has impact, the capacity to create an effect. The impact of various magazines, because of the reader's experience with them, is different. The sight of one arouses warm, friendly, reassuring feelings; another, the idea of excitement, cleverness; another stirs troubled feelings of unsolved problems and perplexing issues, though there may be a kind of admiration intermingled with the reader's unease. He makes his choice on the basis of his feelings and his mood of the moment.

There may also be an unconscious element of despair in the reader's choice. "The fact is," Nathaniel Hawthorne wrote in his notebook in 1855, when he was American Consul in Liverpool, "the world is accumulating too many materials for knowledge." The confusion which Hawthorne found perplexing more than a hundred years ago has multiplied until modern man finds it and himself many times worse confounded. Experts and specialists in thousands of fields and the boggy corners of these fields have sprung up in increasing numbers because few can cope with, understand, or attempt even to gather the materials for understanding much of the larger social, political, economic, scientific, and what-else world we live in. Most of us cannot form usable judgments on myriads of subjects that touch us because we have not bases on which to form them and cannot hope to accumulate enough of the pertinent facts to provide them. It is part of modern man's dilemma. It is also part of the reason why he seizes avidly on magazine digests and condensations; why he spends so much time seeking escape in entertainment, why he gladly reads a superficial journalistic foray into some subject he knows influences his world and which he would like, if possible, to know a little about.

Questions and Exercises

1. In what respect does this chapter from *Magazines in the United States* supplement F. S. Cohen's discussion of the origin of prejudice? Can you trace any of your own prejudices to the influence of magazines?

2. Wood's analysis of magazines yields two principal classifications: mass and class. Which magazines, with which you are personally familiar, would you place in either of these two categories? How would you analyze magazines on the basis of the function they perform for readers?

3. Write a paper or give a talk in class on the thesis presented by Wood: "Society lives by ideas and the communication of ideas."

4. Wood mentions the probable effect of magazines on the election of 1928. He does not mention the rumors that were rampant about Al Smith at the time. Determine, if you can, to what extent gossip and rumor affected the outcome of this election. How can false rumors and unsound prejudices be combated?

5. Consider the author's statement: "That magazine circulations have climbed to new heights during the period of television's expansion and arrival can be taken as proof enough that the appearance and use of the new and powerful medium has far from supplanted the older ones." This was written before the demise of *The American Magazine, Collier's,* and *Woman's Home Companion.* How have scholars in the field of mass media of communication explained the collapse of these magazines? See, for example, William D. Patterson's "The Engines of Persuasion," *The Saturday Review,* April 20, 1957.

6. Explain and support the author's statement that "Magazine pressure on the American mind is continuous and unrelenting."

7. What, in your opinion, is the responsibility of a magazine in a free society? Which magazines, of the ones you read consistently, seem to be edited in the public interest? Which ones have obvious, strong vested interests?

8. Explain the author's assertion that "except in arithmetic texts and tables of scientific formulas, little unbiassed writing has ever been published." Point out the author's bias in one or two magazine articles of your own choosing.

9. Compare the format, contents, and design of *Harper's Magazine* fifty years ago and today. How can you explain the differences in terms of what Wood calls "impact"?

10. Find and discuss examples of propaganda in current magazines. Evaluate Wood's statement that "The magazines are comparatively free of special pleading."

11. Discuss ways in which some magazine articles and stories deal unfairly with certain minority groups by character selection, direct expression of attitude, and emotionally toned words and expressions.

12. What are some values of magazine advertising to the reader? What must a reader know for intelligent reading of ads?

13. Discuss the effects of centralized control of magazines upon public opinion.

14. What standards of judgment should a reader employ in criticizing the contents of a particular magazine?

15. What are the essential differences between "pulp," "slick," and "quality" magazines? In what respects is this classification of magazines unrealistic?

16. Read and report to the class on Frederick L. Allen's "The Function of a Magazine in America," University of Missouri Bulletin, No. 46, August 10, 1945, p. 23.

17. Select one magazine on which to make a detailed report to the class covering such items as function, format, size, contents, design, special features, advertizements, editorship, circulation, vested interests, etc.

18. Analyze the contents of several issues of one of the following mass circulation magazines in order to determine what *set of values* it presents to readers:
    Reader's Digest
    The Saturday Evening Post
    Good Housekeeping
    Life
    Time
    Look
    Woman's Day

◆ ◆ ◆

Sight, Sound, and the Fury

MARSHALL McLUHAN

ON HIS recent visit to America, Roy Campbell mentioned that when Dylan Thomas had discovered he could read poetry on the radio, this discovery transformed his later poetry for the better. Thomas discovered a new dimension in his language when he established a new relation with the public.

Until Gutenberg, poetic publication meant the reading or singing of one's poems to a small audience. When poetry began to exist primarily on the printed page, in the seventeenth century, there occurred that strange mixture of sight and sound later known as "metaphysical poetry" which has so much in common with modern poetry.

American colonization began when the only culture available to most men was that of the printed book. European culture was then, as now, as much an affair of music, painting, sculpture, and communication as it was of literature. So that to this day North Americans associate culture mainly with books. But, paradoxically, it is in North America that the new media of sight and sound have had the greatest popular sway. Is it precisely because we make the widest separation between culture and our new media that we are unable to see the new media as serious culture? Have four centuries of book-culture hypnotized us into such concentration on the content of books and the new media that we cannot see that the very form of any medium of communication is as important as anything that it conveys?

Ireland is perhaps the only part of the English-speaking world where the oral tradition of culture has strongly persisted in spite of the printed page. And Ireland has given us Wilde, Shaw, Yeats,

Reprinted from *The Commonweal*, April 9, 1954, by permission of Marshall McLuhan. Copyright 1954 by *The Commonweal*.

Synge, and Joyce in recent years—all of them masters of the magic of the spoken word. A Ballynooley farmer who returned to Ireland from America said to his neighbor: "In three years I didn't meet a man who could sing a ballad, let alone compose one on his feet."

The printed page was itself a highly specialized (and spatialized) form of communication. In 1500 A.D. it was revolutionary. And Erasmus was perhaps the first to grasp the fact that the revolution was going to occur above all in the classroom. He devoted himself to the production of textbooks and to the setting up of grammar schools. The printed book soon liquidated two thousand years of manuscript culture. It created the solitary student. It set up the rule of private interpretation against public disputation. It established the divorce between "literature and life." It created a new and highly abstract culture because it was itself a mechanized form of culture. Today, when the textbook has yielded to the classroom project and the classroom as social workshop and discussion group, it is easier for us to notice what was going on in 1500. Today we know that the turn to the visual on one hand, that is, to photography, and to the auditory media of radio and public address systems on the other hand, has created a totally new environment for the educational process.

André Malraux has recently popularized the notion of the art revolution of our time in his *Museum without Walls*. His theme is that the picture book today can embrace a greater range of art than any museum. By bringing such a range of art within portable compass, however, it has changed even the painter's approach to painting. Again, it is not just a question of message, image, or content. The picture-book as a museum without walls has for the artist a new technical meaning, just as for the spectator, pictorial communication means a large but unconscious shift in his ways of thought and feeling.

We have long been accustomed to the notion that a person's beliefs shape and color his existence. They provide the windows which frame, and through which he views, all events. We are less accustomed to the notion that the shapes of a technological environment are also idea-windows. Every shape (gimmick or metropolis), every situation planned and realized by man's factive intelligence, is a window which reveals or distorts reality. Today when power technology has taken over the entire global environment to be manipulated as the material of art, nature has disappeared with nature-poetry. And the effectiveness of the classroom has diminished with the decline of the monopoly of book-culture. If Erasmus saw the classroom as the new stage for the drama of the printing-press, we can see today that the new situation for young and old alike is classrooms without walls. The entire urban environment has become aggressively pedagogic. Everybody and everything has a message to declare, a line to plug.

This is the time of transition from the commercial age, when it was the production and distribution of commodities which occupied the ingenuity of men. Today we have moved from the production of packaged goods to the packaging of information. Formerly we invaded foreign markets with goods. Today we invade whole cultures with packaged information, entertainment, and ideas. In view of the instantaneous global scope of the new media of sight and sound, even the newspaper is slow. But the press ousted the book in the nineteenth century because the book arrived too late. The newspaper page was not a mere enlargement of the book page. It was, like the movie, a new collective art form.

To retrace some of this ground, it will help to recall that in the *Phaedrus*, Plato argued that the new arrival of writing would revolutionize culture for the worse. He suggested that it would substitute reminiscence for thought and mechanical learning for the true dialectic of the living quest for truth by discourse and conversation. It was as if he foresaw the library of Alexandria and the unending exegesis upon previous exegesis of the scholiasts and grammarians.

It would seem that the great virtue of writing is its power to arrest the swift process of thought for steady contemplation and analysis. Writing is the translation of the audible into the visual. In large measure it is the spatialization of thought. Yet writing on papyrus and parchment fostered a very different set of mental habits from those we associate with print and books. In the first place silent reading was unknown until the macadamized, streamlined surfaces of the printed page arrived to permit swift traverse of the eye alone. In the second place, difficulty of access to manuscripts impelled students to memorize so far as possible everything they read. This led to encyclopedism, but also to having on tap in oral discourse one's entire erudition.

The child at school in the Middle Ages had first to make his own copies of texts from dictation. He had next to compile his own grammar and lexicon and commonplace book. The arrival of plenty of cheap, uniform, printed texts changed all this. The mechanization of writing by means of the assembly line of movable type speedily expanded the range of available reading and just as quickly reduced the habit of oral discourse as a way of learning. During the sixteenth century, however, a degree of equilibrium persisted between oral and written learning which we associate with the special excellence of Elizabethan drama, sermon, and poetry.

In the reverse direction, much of the vivid energy of American speech and writing in the twentieth century is the result of the movement away from book-culture towards oral communication. This non-literary direction of speech has been felt to a much smaller degree in England and in Europe during the same period. Radio in particular has encouraged the return to the panel discussion and the round-table. But the spontaneous move towards the seminar and class discussion as learning process has been helped by press and photography too, in so far as these have challenged the monopoly of the book.

Above all, the habits of the business community in demanding conference and discussion as the swift way of establishing insight into method and procedure in various specialized branches of business—these have prompted the new reliance on speech as a means of discovery. It is significant, for example, that the atomic physicists found that only by daily, face-to-face association could they get on with their tasks during the past war.

It has long been a truism that changes in material culture cause shifts in the patterns of the entire culture. The ancient road made possible armies and empires and destroyed the isolated city states of Greece. But the road depended in the first place on writing. Behind the imperial command of great land areas stood the written word in easily transportable form. In the nineteenth century the newspapers, especially after the telegraph, paid for new roads and faster transport by land and sea. The press altered the forms of government, and the telegraph brought secret diplomacy to an end. When events in Egypt or Russia, London, Paris, or New York were known everywhere at once, the time for secret negotiation was reduced to hours and minutes. And the great national populations of the world, alerted and emotionalized by the press, could confront one another immediately for a show-down.

Printing had from the first fostered nationalism because the vernaculars with their large reading publics were more profitable to commercial publishers than Latin. The press has pushed this nationalism to its ultimate point. There it remains. But photography and movies, like music and painting, are international in their power of appeal. The power of pictures to leap over national frontiers and prejudices is well-known, for good and ill.

One aspect of the press deserves special comment in this same respect. The contents of newspapers, their messages and information, have steadily promoted nationalism. But the form of the newspaper page is powerfully inter-cultural and international. The unformulated message of an assembly of news items from every quarter of the globe is that the world today is one city. All war is civil war. All suffering is our own. So that regardless of the political line, or the time or the place, the mere format of the press exerts a single pressure. Basic acceptance of this fact is recorded in the steady weakening of interest in political parties everywhere.

From the point of view of its format, the press as a daily cross-section of the globe is a mirror of the technological instruments of communication. It is the popular daily book, the great collective poem, the universal entertainment of our age. As such it has modified poetic techniques and in turn has already been modified by the newer media of movie, radio, and television. These represent revolutions in communication as radical as printing itself. In fact, they are "magic casements opening on the foam of perilous seas," on which few of us have yet ventured in thought, art or living. If Erasmus was the first to size up and exploit the printing-press as a new force in art and education, James Joyce was the first to seize upon newspaper, radio, movie, and television to set up his "verbivocovisual" drama in *Finnegans Wake*. Pound and Eliot are, in comparison with Joyce, timid devotees of the book as art form. But most of the difficulties which the ordinary person encounters with the poetry of Pound and Eliot disappear if it is viewed as a historical newsreel of persons, myths, ideas, and events with thematic musical score built in. Joyce had a much greater trust of language and reality than Pound or Eliot. By contrast they give their language and reality the Hollywood glamor treatment. Joyce is closer to a De Sica film with its awareness of the intimate riches of the most ordinary scenes and situations.

But the reader who approaches Pound, Eliot, and Joyce alike as exploiters of the cinematic aspects of language will arrive at appreciation more quickly than the one who unconsciously tries to make sense of them by reducing their use of the new media of communication to the abstract linear forms of the book page.

The basic fact to keep in mind about the movie camera and projector is their resemblance to the process of human cognition. That is the real source of their magical, transforming power. The camera rolls up the external world on a spool. It does this by rapid still shots. The projector unwinds this spool as a kind of magic carpet which conveys the enchanted spectator anywhere in the world in an instant. The camera records and analyzes the daylight world with more than human intensity because of the forty-five degree angle of the camera eye. The projector reveals this daylight world on a dark screen where it becomes a dream world.

The wonderful resemblance in all this to human cognition extends at least this far: in cognition we have to interiorize the exterior world. We have to recreate in the medium of our senses and inner faculties the drama of existence. This is the work of the *logos poietikos*, the agent intellect. In speech we utter that drama which we have analogously recreated within us. In speech we make or *poet* the world even as we may say that the movie parrots the world. Languages themselves are thus the greatest of all works of art. They are the collective hymns to existence. For in cognition itself is the whole of the poetic process. But the artist differs from most men in his power to arrest and then reverse the stages of human apprehension. He learns how to embody the stages of cognition (Aristotle's "plot") in an exterior work which can be held up for contemplation.

Even in this respect the movie resembles the cognitive process since the daylight world which the camera rolls up on the spool is reversed and projected to become the magical dream world of the audience. But all media of communication share something of this cognitive character which only a Thomist vision of existence and cognition dare do justice to.

Television, for example, differs from the movie in the immediacy with which it picks up and renders back the visible. The TV camera is like the microphone in relation to the voice. The movie has no such immediacy of pick-up and feedback. As we begin to look into the inevitably cognitive character of the various media we soon get over the jitters that come from exclusive concern with any one form of communication.

In his *Theory of the Film*, Bela Balazs notes how "the discovery of printing gradually rendered illegible the faces of men. So much could be read from paper that the method of conveying meaning by facial expression fell into desuetude. Victor Hugo wrote once that the printed book took over the part played by the cathedral in the Middle Ages and became the carrier of the spirit of the people. But the thousands of books tore the one spirit . . . into thousands of opinions . . . tore the church into a thousand books. The visible spirit was thus turned into a legible spirit and visual culture into a culture of concepts."

Before printing, a reader was one who discerned and probed riddles. After printing, it meant one who scanned, who skipped along the macadamized surfaces of print. Today at the end of that process we have come to equate reading skill with speed and distraction rather than wisdom. But print, the mechanization of writing, was succeeded in the nineteenth century by photography and then by the mechanization of human gesture in the movie. This was followed by the mechanization of speech in telephone, phonograph and radio. In the talkies, and finally with TV, came the mechanization of the totality of human expression, of voice, gesture, and human figure in action.

Each of these steps in the mechanization of human expression was comparable in its scope to the revolution brought about by the mechanization of writing itself. The changes in the ways of human association, social and political, were telescoped in time and so hidden from casual observers.

If there is a truism in the history of human communication it is that any innovation in the external means of communication brings in its train shock on shock of social change. One effect of writing was to make possible cities, roads, armies, and empires. The letters of the alphabet were indeed the dragon's teeth. The printed book not only fostered nationalism but made it possible to bring the world of the past into every study. The newspaper is a daily book which brings a slice of all the cultures of the world under our eyes every day. To this extent it reverses the tendency of the printing press to accentuate merely national culture. Pictorial journalism and reportage tend strongly in the same international direction. But is this true of radio? Radio has strengthened the oral habit of communication and extended it, via the panel and round-table, to serious learning. Yet radio seems to be a form which also strengthens the national culture. Merely oral societies, for example, are the ultimate in national exclusiveness.

A group of us recently performed an experiment with a large group of students. We divided them into four sections and assigned each section to a separate communication channel. Each section got the identical lecture simultaneously, but one read it, one heard it as a regular lecture in a studio, one heard it on radio and one heard and saw it as a TV broadcast. Immediately afterwards we administered a quiz to determine apprehension and understanding of this new and difficult material. The TV section came out on top, then the radio section, then the studio, and reading sections at the bottom. This was a totally unexpected result and it is too soon to generalize; but it is quite certain that the so-called mass media are not necessarily ordained to be channels of popular entertainment only.

It is "desirable" in thinking about the new media that we should recall that buildings are mass communications and that the first mechanical medium was print from movable type. In fact, the discovery of movable type was the ancestor of all assembly lines, and it would be foolish to overlook the impact of the technological form involved in print on the psychological life of readers. To overlook this would be as unrealistic as to ignore rhythm and tempo in music. Likewise it is only common sense to recognize that the general situation created by a communicative channel and its audience is a large part of that in which and by which the individuals commune. The encoded message cannot be regarded as a mere capsule or pellet produced at one point and consumed at another. Communication is communication all along the line.

One might illustrate from sports. The best brand of football played before fifty people would lack something of the power to communicate. The large enthusiastic crowd is necessary to represent the community at large, just as the players enact a drama which externalizes certain motivations and tensions in the communal life which would not otherwise be visible or available for audience participation. In India huge crowds assemble to experience "*darshan*," which they consider to occur when they are massed in the presence of a visible manifestation of their collective life.

The new media do something similar for us in the West. Movies, radio, and TV establish certain personalities on a new plane of existence. They exist not so much in themselves but as types of collective life felt and perceived through a mass medium. L'il Abner, Bob Hope, Donald Duck, and Marilyn Monroe become points of collective awareness and communication for an entire society. And as technology increasingly undertakes to submit the entire planet as well as the contents of consciousness to the purposes of man's factive intelligence, it behooves us to consider the whole process of magical transformation involved in the media acutely and extensively.

From this point of view it should be obvious, for example, that the framers of the Hollywood morality code were operating with a very inadequate set of perceptions and concepts about the nature of the movie medium. Modern discussions of censorship, in the same way, are helplessly tied to conceptions borrowed from book culture alone. And the defenders of book culture have seldom given any thought to any of the media as art forms, the book least of all. The result is that their "defense" might as well be staged on an abandoned movie lot for all the effect it has on the actual situation.

When I wrote *The Mechanical Bride* some years ago I did not realize that I was attempting a defense of book culture against the new media. I can now see that I was trying to bring some of the critical awareness fostered by literary training to bear on the new media of sight and sound. My strategy was wrong, because my obsession with literary values blinded me to much that was actually happening for good and ill. What we have to defend today is not the values developed in any particular culture or by any one mode of communication. Modern technology presumes to attempt a total transformation of man and his environment. This calls in turn for an inspection and defense of all human values. And so far as merely human aid goes, the citadel of this defense must be located in analytical awareness of the nature of the creative process involved in human cognition. For it is in this citadel that science and technology have already established themselves in their manipulation of the new media.

Questions and Exercises

1. Explain the author's statement that the press has been modified by movies, radio, and television. What is the precise nature of the modification?

2. What does the word "verbivocovisual" demonstrate with regard to linguistic or semantic alterations of the language?
3. In what respects did the earlier "oral tradition" the author speaks of differ from the current "oral tradition"?
4. Comment on the statement "Languages themselves are the greatest of all works of art." What is the meaning of *art* in this context?
5. Discuss the popular theory that television brings the best of culture into the homes of all people.
6. What does McLuhan visualize with regard to the educational possibilities of television and the audio-visual media? How does this support the contention of Kouwenhoven regarding the unfixity of American patterns and customs?
7. How are the new media related to the current emphasis on One World and a holistic view of civilization? (Stuart Chase says "A world state can only be effectively operated by men with a world point of view.")
8. What would you need to know before accepting the author's findings from the experiment of the effectiveness of the various media on the receiver (reader-listener-viewer)?
9. Explain McLuhan's attitude toward censorship. What is the basis of his argument?
10. Explain how recent developments in the techniques of communication help us to understand the workings of the human mind.
11. How does group discussion challenge the authority of single books? To what extent has modern education altered the allegiance once paid to book authorities?
12. What fallacy in reasoning did McLuhan make when he set about to defend book culture against the new media in *The Mechanical Bride?*
13. How does the last paragraph in this essay relate to the "we" words and the "they" words discussed by Cohen in "The Reconstruction of Hidden Value Judgments"?
14. Evaluate the author's statement that the new media of communication became "points of collective awareness and communication for an entire society." What effects will the new media have on regionalism, nationalism, parochialism, and linguistic differences generally?
15. Explain and evaluate the statement that "any innovation in the external means of communication brings in its train shock on shock of social change." Give specific examples to demonstrate the point.

16. In the movie or television version of such literary works as *Moby Dick, The King and I, War and Peace,* why must specific incidents and devices of plot be altered?

17. Many critics of television have deplored the "decline of attention" which it allegedly fosters. What is McLuhan's belief regarding this matter?

18. Detroit police censorship (January, 1957) placed a ban on John O'Hara's prize-winning novel *Ten North Frederick.* The reason was that it allegedly contains "obscene passages." Bennett Cerf declared "This kind of censorship is disgraceful." Read H. S. Canby's "Death of the Iron Virgin" in *The Saturday Review,* April 12, 1947, and present his argument in a brief report to the class.

19. Read the following opinion of the merits of the mass media and suggest specific ways of supporting this view with facts.

    "There is a great deal that is mediocre, repetitious, and patronizing in television, the movies, or any of our popular arts. Yet, if we close our eyes to the significant contributions of the mass media, do we not encourage the very banality we purport to despise?

    "I see substantial amelioration in the uses of our mass media. There has been such a rehearsal of all that is ugly and bathetic in our popular arts by critics whose sincerity cannot be questioned that it is time that the other side of the coin be examined."—David Manning White, "What's Happening to Mass Culture?"

    The Saturday Review, November 3, 1956.

20. Read "The Scandal in TV Licensing" by Louis L. Jaffe in *Harper's Magazine,* September, 1957, and determine to what extent McLuhan's appraisal of TV is too generous.

◆ ◆ ◆

Publicity and Advertising

WILLIAM ALBIG

AT THE close of the nineteenth century and during the first decade of the twenties, there was an age of the muckrakers. Writers for magazines, cartoonists and some newspapermen and many politicians were engaged in various attacks on business organizations. Many corporations needed to assuage public hostility. And so, as Edward L. Bernays notes in the chapter headings of his *Public Relations*, the public-be-damned period (1865 to 1900) was followed by the public-be-informed (1900–1919). The rise of a new profession, the public-relations counsel (1919–1929), developed as public relations came of age (1929–1941).[18]

The press agent of the earlier periods was often crude, blatant and direct in ballyhooing the qualities of his clients, as well as their wares. The public-relations counsel, a functionary distinct from the advertising man with his specific objectives, engaged in securing or avoiding publicity for his clients, usually by indirect means. "Public relations has three meanings: (1) information given to the public, (2) persuasion directed at the public to modify attitudes and actions, and (3) efforts to integrate attitudes and actions of an institution with its publics and of publics with that institution."[19] Publicity as a technique for directing the interest or good will of the public toward some individual or organization is, therefore, but one of the activities of the public-relations man. In his persuasive role, the public-relations counsel is fundamen-

By permission from *Modern Public Opinion* by William Albig. Copyright 1956 McGraw-Hill Book Company, Inc.

[18] E. L. Bernays, *Public Relations*, University of Oklahoma Press, Norman, Okla., 1952. Mr. Bernays is considered by many as the preëminent public-relations counsel of the United States.

[19] *Ibid.*, p. 3.

tally engaged in "the engineering of consent," a phrase frequently encountered in this profession. He is engaged in "opinion engineering in the big time."

Although the overwhelming bulk of advertising in the United States is designed to promote the sale of products and services, there is a substantial and growing publicity for ideas, causes and ideologies. The activity devoted to these campaigns was estimated in 1949 to cost 100 million dollars a year,[20] and by 1950 a single area of this activity, the great free-enterprise campaign, was accounting for 100 million dollars of industry's annual advertising expenditure. Most of such publicity campaigns are initiated by or stimulated by The Advertising Council. The Council is a private, nonprofit organization formed by the agencies to carry on certain public-service campaigns. It is supported by advertisers, agencies and various media groups. The War Advertising Council, formed in 1941, led to the later development of the Council to conduct peacetime campaigns. Illustrative of publicity campaigns to influence ideas have been the United States Bond Sales, the campaigns for the Community Chest, the Go-to-Church movement, the Register-and-Vote campaigns, the Public School Movement, the Blood Bank, CARE, Natural Resources Conservation (Smoky the Bear, etc.), and above all, the free-enterprise campaigns, spread over several years. By many, the free-enterprise campaigns are viewed as the most notable failure in the history of publicity in the United States.[21]

In a crude type of content study in 1949, I developed a simple classification of the dominant appeals in all full-page institutional ads appearing in *Life, Fortune, Time, Newsweek* and *The Saturday Evening Post* for the year 1948. All classification was done by a single classifier, Emily Dunn Scott, so no question of differences of interpretation arose. The dominance of certain themes and types of appeal is indicated by the figures in Table 8, which shows the number of instances in which the dominant appeal,

---

[20] "Admen's Giveaway," *Wall Street Jour.*, November 17, 1949.

[21] The argument as to the fact and reasons for that failure is most cogently presented by William H. Whyte, Assistant Editor of *Fortune* magazine, in *Is Anybody Listening?* Simon & Schuster, Inc., New York, 1952.

according to the classifier, was freedom, service, progress, etc. A great many of the full-page institutional ads in that year were already dealing with the free-enterprise theme, although the peak of the campaign came a little later.[22]

TABLE 8. Frequency of Certain Appeals in Institutional Advertising in Selected Magazines in 1948

	Life	Fortune	Time	News-week	Saturday Evening Post	Total
Freedom	16	18	33	49	13	129
Service	17	23	18	58	68	184
Progress	22	56	66	57	49	250
Prosperity	3	21	30	28	14	96
Equality			6		1	7
Protection	14	7	14	25	33	93
Local Pride	21	28	10	34	30	123
Tolerance	20	3	15	32	29	99
Efficiency	16	4	15	32	45	112
Inefficiency	4	4	5	2	3	18
Superiority	8	18	27	28	25	106
Inferiority		2	2			4
Patriotism	21	6	22	18	22	89

Advertising may be distinguished from propaganda in that the sources of the advertisement are stated and the motives of the advertiser may be readily assumed (when the sources are concealed, as in the case of a food-products company publicizing its claims over the name of a supposed scientific research organization, we have commercial propaganda). There is a perennial debate over the effectiveness of advertising as a creator of markets, but it is quite obvious that advertising has been enormously influential in causing people to buy particular products. At many points commercial advertising has been far more successful in swaying opinions than has propaganda for causes. Aldous Huxley

[22] A good classification of the types of appeal in radio commercials appears in L. I. Pearlin and M. Rosenberg, "Propaganda Techniques in Institutional Advertising," *Pub. Opin. Quar.*, 16:5–26, Spring, 1952.

has reasonably maintained that the commercial advertisers have modified opinions more extensively than the political or ethical propagandists, not because their techniques are superior but because advertising is concerned with matters of no importance. When the political propagandist begins a campaign, he does so because there exist some real differences of opinion among the members of a general public. He deals with issues. But when an advertiser urges one to buy one soap or another of equal merit or worthlessness, or one kind of cigarette among a number of cheap cigarettes, and the like, there is no real issue for the consumer.[23]

As a means of spreading of information, rather than as high-pressure persuasion, advertising has existed from earliest times. Modern persuasive advertising is a product of modern methods of communication, of the historically recent orientation of industry toward the production of masses of consumers' goods and of the development of the advertising business itself which further stimulates its own activity. Advertising of the high-pressure, persuasive type has developed in the period since 1890. American publicity men have been the most effective high priests of commerical publicity.

Advertising itself is a business of very considerable size. The national expenditure on all kinds of advertising has been estimated for 1850 as 50 million dollars, for 1900 as 542 million, 1909 as 1,142 million, 1920 as 2,935 million, 1929 as 3,426 million, 1930 as 2,647 million, 1935 as 1,690 million, and 1940 as 2,087 million. Increasing from that year onward, and in the postwar period increasing rapidly, the volume of advertising in 1953 was 7,809 million dol' rs. Of course, these dollars must be translated into their proportion of the grand total of national income. Speaking thus broadly, we may say that since 1920 the advertising figure is from 2 to 3 per cent of the national income each year.[24] Of the total advertising expenditure in 1953 (a total of 7,809.2 millions), 2,644.8 was expended on newspaper advertising; 667.4 on maga-

---

[23] A. Huxley, "Notes on Propaganda," *Harper's*, 174:32.

[24] These figures are taken from a master table published in the Advertisers' Annual 1955 number of *Printers' Ink*, October 29, 1954, p. 59.

zines; 610.5 on TV; 649.5 on radio; 30.8 on farm publications; 1,099.1 on direct mail; 395.0 on business papers; 176.3 on outdoor advertising; 1,535.8 miscellaneous.

It is quite obvious that advertising has been very effective in swaying popular opinion as to the qualities of consumers' goods and in influencing the choice of those goods. It was primarily the advertising man who lifted the product of the cigarette manufacturers from its status of lowly "coffin nail" to that of a national necessity. Folkways with regard to gum chewing were created by publicity. The citizen's preoccupation with the cleanliness of his teeth and skin surfaces was developed largely from the information provided in the advertisements he read. The hunt for germs in the various orifices and on the surfaces of the body was stimulated by the manufacturers of germicides. Information and misinformation about food values have led to fashions in foods. Cereals used for the American breakfast have been pounded, exploded, inflated, sieved and woven as the "scientific" facts propounded by the advertising man have convinced consumers that their foods should be so treated. And so on. Opinions and behavior have been rapidly changed as the advertiser has presented his phantasmagoria of changing information.

The forces affecting the demand for different consumers' goods are evidently quite various. Indeed, a complex of factors is usually involved so that market research often does not show a simple cause and effect relationship between advertising and demand. Advertising is but one force among many that are involved in determining consumers' attitudes. Sometimes advertising plays little part in the creating or stimulating of primary demands. The average per capita consumption of sugar in 1830 was about 12 pounds, while by 1930 the average per capita consumption had become 112 pounds. Yet direct advertising of sugar has been very limited. It is true that there has been a great deal of advertising of candies, soft drinks and other products using sugar.[25] On the other hand, the demand for spinach has been created almost

[25] See Neil Borden, *The Economic Effects of Advertising*, Richard D. Irwin, Inc., Homewood, Ill., 1947, chap. X.

entirely by advertising. Advertising of shoes is a very small item in comparison to the total sale price of shoes. And so with many primary items of consumption. "Among marketing and advertising executives of companies producing domestic sheeting there is general agreement that advertising probably had little if any effect on the total consumption of sheets and pillow cases."[26] In contrast, dentifrices are so dependent on advertising that the advertising expenditures are from 10 to 15 million dollars to develop retail sales of from 40 to 55 million dollars. And there are scores of products which would be unknown and unused had it not been for intensive advertising. The advertising man works within the context of consumers' attitudes, only a part of which are developed or stimulated by advertising appeals. However, he labors mightily and expensively for the stimulation of selective demand.

It is only since the 1920's that the advertising process has been extensively discussed and attacked. In the 1930's, a number of intellectuals, evidencing that they felt the appeals and wiles of the advertising man to be a personal insult, indicated their revulsion in no uncertain terms.[27] The principal types of discussion have been as follows.

First, the expenditures on advertising have been attacked as economically wasteful. Since 1910 advertising in the United States has cost from 1 billion to almost 8 billion dollars annually. The opponents of modern advertising maintain that the effort and materials utilized in advertising might have been expended on the creation of more goods. The defenders of the process declare that, inasmuch as advertising informs potential consumers of the existence of goods and stimulates purchase, advertising has been responsible for a part of the consumption of goods. They declare that national income, as measured in dol-

[26] *Ibid.*, p. 315.
[27] S. Chase, *The Tragedy of Waste*, The Macmillan Company, New York, 1925, chap. 7; and J. Rorty, *Our Master's Voice*, the John Day Company, Inc., New York, 1934. On a less grim note, see E. S. Turner, *The Shocking History of Advertising*, E. P. Dutton & Company, Inc., New York, 1953; and T. Whiteside, *The Relaxed Sell*, Oxford University Press, New York, 1954.

lars, is, therefore, increased by much more than the billions of dollars spent on advertising. No reputable economist has essayed the difficult, if not impossible, task of calculating just what the advertising expenditure should be to achieve the maximum distribution of goods without waste in the advertising process itself. And, of course, the critics would not desist even if they were convinced that in terms of counters (dollars) the total national income had been increased. They would turn at once to the problem of the relative quality of goods, as—

Second, the critics of advertising say that the appeals of the advertising man have led to the consumption of inferior and ill-selected types of consumers' goods. Instances of adulteration, misrepresentation and quackery are stressed. The advertising man declares, "This, then, is the gist of the matter; somebody must determine what goods are to be produced. The decision must rest either with the government or with consumers. As society is now organized, consumers decide. The only way they can make their decisions effective is through exercising their freedom of choice in the ordinary course of marketing. This freedom of choice constitutes the chief risk of business and gives rise inevitably to profits and losses."[28] "Little by little it seems to be recognized that this demand factor is not a spineless effect but a restless and irresistible cause."[29] But the advertising man does not stress that the psychologically bound consumer—harried, frightened, cajoled, and misinformed—is not free. And it is to the methods of appeal that the critic most violently objects, stating that—

Third, only a small proportion of advertising is based on logical appeals or argumentative procedures (long-circuit appeals); the bulk of advertising is based upon appeals to the emotions, upon unworthy motives or upon direct suggestion (short-circuit appeals). Indeed, a large proportion of the textbooks and articles on the "psychology of advertising" are devoted to the analysis

---

[28] P. T. Cherinton, *The Consumer Looks at Advertising*, Harper & Brothers, New York, 1928, p. 63.
[29] *Ibid.*, p. 38.

of the relative strength of various appeals in relation to particular types of products. D. Starch noted the basic desires as those for food, comfort, mating, power and approbation.[30] A. T. Poffenberger inventoried the fundamental desires as those for drink, food, sex experience, ease, escape from danger, dominance, conformity, parenthood, play, cleanliness, beauty and economy.[31] It is assumed, not that these desires are innate, but simply that they are dominant in our culture. There are scores of such classifications in psychological literature dealing with advertising. Certainly the advertising man knows that however limited the capacity of the common man for sustained logical analysis, his responsiveness to appeals to fundamental desires is almost limitless. The consumer responds to suggested short cuts ("learn French in ten lessons"); to the titillation of sex interests; to the prestige of individuals; to fear (the whole gamut of scare copy of the advertising of germicides, insurance and scores of products); to pseudo science; to numerous other widely distributed appeals. Certainly the advertiser has investigated desires in greater detail than has any other type of special pleader. And he persistently exploits the limited capacity of most of us for logical thinking. To his critics, the defender of persuasive advertising simply replies that he is not responsible for popular dispositions, nor is he the creator of psychological values. He is simply utilizing those which he discovers extant in the general public so that he may distribute the maximum quantity of goods. And many of these goods—though, he sometimes admits, not all of them— add to the general standard of living. Moreover, the advertiser sometimes defiantly asks his critics to answer his contention that the advertising of many products creates values other than those of the immediate utility of the product. A girl buying a beauty product may not be made beautiful thereby, but the advertiser

[30] D. Starch, *Controlling Human Behavior*, The Macmillan Company, New York, 1936, p. 32.

[31] A. T. Poffenberger, *Psychology in Advertising*, McGraw-Hill Book Company, Inc. (Shaw), New York, 1925, chap. 3. For a criticism of the earlier desire inventories, see H. C. Link, *New Psychology of Selling and Advertising*, The Macmillan Company, New York, 1932.

helps to kindle hope. The general issue is fairly clear. The advertising man is not responsible for societal values. But he does at times accentuate values that the moralist deplores. However, it is a waste of time to attack the advertisers personally. Certain of their more extreme activities, especially direct falsehoods, may be regulated in the public interest. Exaggeration, misleading implications, unfounded scientific claims, the use of questionable testimonials and the like may be somewhat more carefully regulated. That is all. Either that, or a dictatorship of consumption. But any interested minority may attempt to educate the general public in values in consumption.[32]

Fourth, the critic also accuses the advertising man of vulgarity, defacing the landscape, a low level of aesthetic appeals and a number of other misdemeanors of which some advertising is obviously guilty. But so are all the media of communication in a culture that stresses a low common denominator of popular appeal. The advertising man is likewise accused of furthering standardization of goods and abetting the creation of a dull uniformity of material things. This uniformity is peculiarly grueling to the aesthetically sensitive. But it is obviously an inevitable concomitant of mass production and distribution.

Those who have attacked advertising have generally left the impression of advertisers as low, unethical fellows involved in chicanery and deceit and having nefarious designs on the welfare of the general public. Obviously, this is sometimes an accurate description. There is much untrue, insincere and misinformative advertising. There is much more of advertising that diseminates false impressions indirectly. Advertising is special pleading, and a highly competitive special pleading at that, so that in many an advertising campaign each side stimulates the other to more and more extreme statements. If advertising is really effective, it leads consumers to make purchases they would not have made without having seen the advertisement. In the quest

[32] In the ten years after 1945, the *Consumers Reports* of Consumers Union astonishingly increased their circulation from a few thousands to about a million per issue.

for these purchasers the advertising man has used every type of appeal that he found to be effective. He is limited only by the attitudes of the general public, by very fragmentary legal restrictions and by the rudimentary ethics of his profession. By experience and by knowledge of the general culture values he learns what will be believed. The attempt to place greater legal restrictions upon his claims has not yet been successful.[33] To some extent, business has regulated the content of advertising. Many of the more blatant untruths have been eliminated from some types of advertising, owing to the activities of business groups with a "Truth in Advertising" slogan. But, of course, distortions of the truth in the special pleading of contemporary advertising are a part of the very fabric of our modern competitive economy. As long as goods compete for markets, the art of "puffing" will play an important part. And granted the wide variety of economic goods for modern consumers, informative advertising would exist under any economy or any political system.

The critic of advertising stresses the more obvious and dramatically antisocial activities of the advertising man. Many of the large advertisers make and sell products of dubious or little value. But, of course, the bulk of advertising consists of special pleading for articles that have raised the standard of living of modern populations. If there is great waste in the competitive clamor about wares, it is also true that this clamor has been in part responsible for the swift acceleration of the production of consumers' goods. It has forced the national economy into the present mold. The selection of which goods shall be produced is in part determined by existing popular wants and, in part, by wants that are to some extent created by the advertiser. But in any case, either when the advertiser verbalizes existing wants or when he tells a public what it should want, the new importance of popular opinion is indicated by the assiduous

---

[33] The question of federal regulation versus voluntary controls is discussed in M. A. Geller, *Advertising at the Crossroads*, The Ronald Press Company, New York, 1952.

cultivation of large publics since the closing decades of the nineteenth century.

Indeed, in the United States, advertising has become a major institution, exercising diverse controls. It is a concomitant of opulence, of the plethora of consumers' goods. As we have seen, publicity and advertising are an inevitable development in our economy. The depth of the advertiser's penetration of American culture is seldom discussed and has never been incisively described, in spite of the hundreds of books devoted to the techniques of advertising. "One might read fairly widely in the literature which treats of public opinion, popular culture, and the mass media in the United States without ever learning that advertising now compares with such long-standing institutions as the school and the church in the magnitude of its social influence. It dominates the media, it has vast power in the shaping of popular standards, and it is really one of the very limited group of institutions which exercise social control."[34]

Questions and Exercises

1. What specific kinds of promotion campaigns can you describe which may be nominated as examples of what Albig calls "opinion engineering in the big time"?
2. What are some of the best examples of "muckraking" in literature? Read chapter 12 of James P. Wood's *Magazines in the United States* (1956), and then cite examples of "muckraking" in current prose or fiction.
3. Discuss the commercial value of such reverse propaganda as censorship or ridicule. Account for the success of "panning the commercials" by such television personalities as George Gobel and Alfred Hitchcock. In this connection, read "Ogilvy the Ineffable Ad Man," *Harper's Magazine*, May, 1955.
4. What specific "gimmicks" are used by modern promotion agents in place of earlier, more direct "ballyhoo"? Read Keith Monroe's "They Made the Cigar Respectable," *Harper's Magazine*, February, 1955.

[34] D. M. Potter, *People of Plenty*, University of Chicago Press, Chicago, 1954, p. 167.

5. Find several advertisements for United States Savings Bonds and analyze the appeals made to the American people. Read John Fischer's discussion of the "World's Finest Investments?" in "The Editor's Easy Chair," *Harper's Magazine*, January, 1957.

6. Using Albig's chart as a guide, find advertisements that exemplify each appeal listed. What appeal do you find most frequently employed?

7. Consider the four major attacks made on advertising by Albig, and find specific advertisements in magazines that deserve each type of criticism.

8. What criticism of advertising techniques can you suggest that Albig has not mentioned?

9. What organizations in America have assumed the responsibility of protecting consumers against pernicious advertising? Study the accomplishments of one such organization and make a detailed oral report of your findings to the class.

10. Refer to *Consumer Reports* regarding a specific commodity advertised and manufactured for public distribution. Compare the findings of the researchers with the claims of the advertiser. What verbal devices do you detect in the advertisement that are designed to deceive or mislead?

11. Find several examples in magazine ads of both "long-circuit" and "short-circuit" appeals.

12. Find advertisements which make an appeal to any of the following motives:
    The need for affection and approval.
    The need for power.
    The need for social recognition or prestige.
    The need for personal admiration.
    The need for personal achievement.
    The need for self-sufficiency and independence.

13. Point out the fallacy in the popular saying, "You get what you pay for."

14. What are some of the specific social results of advertising that Albig refers to in his essay?

15. Make a detailed study of one promotion campaign, such as the March of Dimes, and determine precisely what methods are used to gain favor with the public. Make a list of the specific appeals used, and list them in the order in which they influence your own thoughts, feelings, or emotions.

16. In *The Saturday Review*, January 19, 1957, p. 18, the following announcement was made of awards offered for advertising in the public interest:

"Institutional, public service, public relations or other advertising designed to inform or persuade public opinion is eligible for consideration by the Committee of Judges, a cross-section of editors, educators, advertising executives, public opinion specialists, business leaders, and other communications experts."

The awards for the competition were announced in *The Saturday Review,* April 20, 1957.

Find examples of advertising which you would enter in such a contest. Select a group of five of your classmates to act as judges, and let them present a panel discussion in which they defend the three best entries submitted by the class.

17. Point out the logical fallacies in each of the following:
    a. A typewriter company advertises 20 percent better grades for students who own a particular brand of typewriter.
    b. An ad for a well-known silver plate says: "The happiest brides have Community."
    c. An ad for men's furnishings says: "The well-dressed B.M.O.C. will wear Manhattans."
    d. A manufacturer of toilet soap advertises a magic ingredient which is said to guard against unpleasant body odors.
    e. You, as a preferred customer, are sent a catalog of merchandise offered at greatly reduced prices, not available to the public.
    f. A cigarette manufacturer says that scientific tests prove more people prefer this brand to any other on the market.

18. Find examples of commercial ads which offend the following rules for advertising laid down by the National Better Business Bureau:
    a. Advertising as a whole must not create a misleading impression even though every statement separately considered is literally truthful.
    b. Advertising must be written for the probable effect it produces on ordinary and trusting minds, as well as for those intellectually capable of penetrating analysis.
    c. Advertising must not obscure or conceal material facts.
    d. Advertising must not be artfully contrived to distract and divert readers' attention from the true nature of the terms and conditions of an offer.
    e. Advertising must be free of fraudulent traps and stratagems which induce action which would not result from a forthright disclosure of the true nature of an offer.

19. Read "Is the Bloom off Madison Avenue?" by John McCarthy
     in *Harper's Magazine*, September, 1957, and determine to what
     extent the public is protected against pernicious advertisers.

How to Tell Good Guys from Bad Guys

JOHN STEINBECK

TELEVISION HAS crept upon us so gradually in America that we
have not yet become aware of the extent of its impact for
good or bad. I myself do not look at it very often except for
its coverage of sporting events, news, and politics. Indeed, I get
most of my impressions of the medium from my young sons.

Whether for good or bad, television has taken the place of
the sugartit, soothing syrups, and the mild narcotics parents in
other days used to reduce their children to semiconsciousness
and consequently to seminoisiness. In the past, a harassed parent
would say, "Go sit in a chair!" or "Go outside and play!" or
"If you don't stop that noise, I'm going to beat your dear little
brains out!" The present-day parent suggests, "Why don't you
go look at television?" From that moment the screams, shouts,
revolver shots, and crashes of motor accidents come from the
loudspeaker, not from the child. For some reason, this is presumed to be more relaxing to the parent. The effect on the
child has yet to be determined.

I have observed the physical symptoms of television-looking on children as well as on adults. The mouth grows slack and the lips hang open; the eyes take on a hypnotized or doped look; the nose runs rather more than usual; the backbone turns to water and the fingers slowly and methodically pick the designs out of brocade furniture. Such is the appearance of semiconsciousness that one wonders how much of the "message" of television is getting through to the brain. This wonder is further strengthened by the fact that a television-looker will look at anything at all and for hours. Recently I came into a room to find my eight-year-old son Catbird sprawled in a chair, idiot slackness on his face, with the doped eyes of an opium smoker. On the television screen stood a young woman of mammary distinction with ice-cream hair listening to a man in thick glasses and a doctor's smock.

"What's happening?" I asked.

Catbird answered in the monotone of the sleeptalker which is known as television voice, "She is asking if she should dye her hair."

"What is the doctor's reaction?"

"If she uses Trutone it's all right," said Catbird. "But if she uses ordinary or adulterated products, her hair will split and lose its golden natural sheen. The big economy size is two dollars and ninety-eight cents if you act now," said Catbird.

You see, something was getting through to him. He looked punch-drunk, but he was absorbing. I did not feel it fair to interject a fact I have observed—that natural golden sheen does not exist in nature. But I did think of my friend Elia Kazan's cry of despair, and although it is a digression I shall put it down.

We were having dinner in a lovely little restaurant in California. At the table next to us were six beautiful, young, well-dressed American girls of the age and appearance of magazine advertisements. There was only one difficulty with their perfection. You couldn't tell them apart. Kazan, who is a primitive of a species once known as men, regarded the little beauties with distaste, and finally in more sorrow than anger cried, "It's years since I've seen or smelled a dame! It's all products, Golden Glint, l'Eau d'Eau, Butisan, Elyn's puff-adder cream—I remember I used to like how women smelled. Nowadays it's all products!"

End of digression.

Just when the parent becomes convinced that his child's brain is rotting away from television, he is jerked up in another direction. Catbird has corrected me in the Museum of Natural History when I directed his attention to the mounted skeleton of a tyrannosaur. He said it was a brontosaurus but observed kindly that many people made the same error. He argued with his ten-year-old brother about the relative cleanness of the line in Praxiteles and Phidias. He knows the weight a llama will bear before lying down in protest, and his knowledge of entomology is embarrassing to a parent who likes to impart information to his children. And these things he also got from television. I knew that he was picking up masses of unrelated and probably worthless information from television, incidentally the kind of information I also like best, but I did not know that television was preparing him in criticism and politics, and that is what this piece is really about.

I will have to go back a bit in preparation. When television in America first began to be a threat to the motion-picture industry, that industry fought back by refusing to allow its films to be shown on the home screens. One never saw new pictures, but there were whole blocks of the films called Westerns which were owned by independents, and these were released to the television stations. The result is that at nearly any time of the day or night you can find a Western being shown on some television station. It is not only the children who see them. All of America sees them. They are a typically American conception, the cowboy picture. The story never varies and the conventions are savagely adhered to. The hero never kisses a girl. He loves his horse and he stands for right and justice. Any change in the story or the conventions would be taken as an outrage. Out of these films folk heroes have grown up—

Hopalong Cassidy, the Lone Ranger, Roy Rogers, and Gene Autry. These are more than great men. They are symbols of courage, purity, simplicity, honesty, and right. You must under- stand that nearly every American is drenched in the tradition of the Western, which is, of course, the celebration of a whole pattern of American life that never existed. It is also as set in its form as the *commedia dell' arte.*

End of preparation.

One afternoon, hearing gunfire from the room where our tele- vision set is installed, I went in with that losing intention of fraternizing with my son for a little while. There sat Catbird with the cretinous expression I have learned to recognize. A Western was in progress.

"What's going on?" I asked.

He looked at me in wonder. "What do you mean, what's going on? Don't you know?"

"Well, no. Tell me!"

He was kind to me. Explained as though I were the child.

"Well, the Bad Guy is trying to steal Her father's ranch. But the Good Guy won't let him. Bullet figured out the plot."

"Who is Bullet?"

"Why, the Good Guy's horse." He didn't add "You dope," but his tone implied it.

"Now wait," I said, "which one is the Good Guy?"

"The one with the white hat."

"Then the one with the black hat is the Bad Guy?"

"Anybody knows that," said Catbird.

For a time I watched the picture, and I realized that I had been ignoring a part of our life that everybody knows. I was interested in the characterizations. The girl, known as Her or She, was a blonde, very pretty but completely unvoluptuous because these are Family Pictures. Sometimes she wore a simple gingham dress and sometimes a leather skirt and boots, but always she had a bit of a bow in her hair and her face was untroubled with emotion or, one might almost say, intelligence.

This also is part of the convention. She is a symbol, and any acting would get her thrown out of the picture by popular acclaim.

The Good Guy not only wore a white hat but light-colored clothes, shining boots, tight riding pants, and a shirt embroidered with scrolls and flowers. In my young days I used to work with cattle, and our costume was blue jeans, a leather jacket, and boots with run-over heels. The cleaning bill alone of this gorgeous screen cowboy would have been four times what our pay was in a year.

The Good Guy had very little change of facial expression. He went through his fantastic set of adventures with no show of emotion. This is another convention and proves that he is very brave and very pure. He is also scrubbed and has an immaculate shave.

I turned my attention to the Bad Guy. He wore a black hat and dark clothing, but his clothing was definitely not only unclean but unpressed. He had a stubble of beard but the greatest contrast was in his face. His was not an immobile face. He leered, he sneered, he had a nasty laugh. He bullied and shouted. He looked evil. While he did not swear, because this is a Family Picture, he said things like "Wall dog it" and "You rat" and "I'll cut off your ears and eat 'em," which would indicate that his language was not only coarse but might, off screen, be vulgar. He was, in a word, a Bad Guy. I found a certain interest in the Bad Guy which was lacking in the Good Guy.

"Which one do you like best?" I asked.

Catbird removed his anaesthetized eyes from the screen. "What do you mean?"

"Do you like the Good Guy or the Bad Guy?"

He sighed at my ignorance and looked back at the screen. "Are you kidding?" he asked. "The Good Guy, of course."

Now a new character began to emerge. He puzzled me because he wore a gray hat. I felt a little embarrassed about asking my son, the expert, but I gathered my courage. "Catbird," I asked shyly, "what kind of a guy is that, the one in the gray hat?"

He was sweet to me then. I think until that moment he

had not understood the abysmal extent of my ignorance. "He's the In-Between Guy," Catbird explained kindly. "If he starts bad he ends good and if he starts good he ends bad."

"What's this one going to do?"

"See how he's sneering and needs a shave?" my son asked. "Yes."

"Well, the picture's just started, so that guy is going to end good and help the Good Guy get Her father's ranch back."

"How can you be sure?" I asked.

Catbird gave me a cold look. "He's got a gray hat, hasn't he? Now don't talk. It's about time for the chase."

There it was, not only a tight, true criticism of a whole art form but to a certain extent of life itself. I was deeply impressed because this simple explanation seemed to mean something to me more profound than television or Westerns.

Several nights later I told the Catbird criticism to a friend who is a producer. He has produced many successful musical comedies. My friend has an uncanny perception for the public mind and also for its likes and dislikes. You have to have it you produce musical shows. He listened and nodded and didn't think it was a cute child story. He said, "It's not kid stuff at all. There's a whole generation in this country that makes its judgments pretty much on that basis."

"Give me an example," I asked.

"I'll have to think about it," he said.

Well, that was in March. Soon afterward my wife and I went to Spain and then to Paris and rented a little house. As soon as school was out in New York, my boys flew over to join us in Paris.

In July, my producer friend dropped in to see us. He was going to take an English show to New York, and he had been in London making arrangements.

He told us all of the happenings at home, the gossip and the new jokes and the new songs. Finally I asked him about the McCarthy hearings. "Was it as great a show as we heard?" I asked.

"I couldn't let it alone," he said. "I never saw anything like it. I wonder whether those people knew how they were putting themselves on the screen."

"Well, what do you think will happen?"

"In my opinion, McCarthy is finished," he said, and then he grinned. "I base my opinion on your story about Catbird and the Westerns."

"I don't follow you."

"Have you ever seen McCarthy on television?"

"Sure."

"Just remember," said my friend. "He sneers. He bullies, he has a nasty laugh and he always looks as though he needs a shave. The only thing he lacks is a black hat. McCarthy is the Bad Guy. Everybody who saw him has got it pegged. He's the Bad Guy and people don't like the Bad Guy. I may be wrong but that's what I think. He's finished."

The next morning at breakfast I watched Catbird put butter and two kinds of jam and a little honey on a croissant, then eat the treacherous thing, then lick the jam from the inside of his elbow to his fingers. He took a peach from the basket in the center of the table.

"Catbird," I asked, "did you see any of the McCarthy stuff on television?"

"Sure," he said.

"Was he a Good Guy or a Bad Guy?" I asked.

"Bad Guy," said Catbird, and he bit into the peach.

And do you know, I suspect it is just that simple.

Questions and Exercises

1. Steinbeck suggests that the effects of television on children have yet to be determined. Locate as many studies of this problem as you can, and determine to what extent his statement is still true.

2. What point does Steinbeck make in his announced digression in paragraph 9?

3. What does Steinbeck think of television as an instrument for educating youth? Compare his conviction with the idea suggested by Joseph Wood Krutch in "If You Don't Mind My Saying So . . . ," *The American Scholar*, Summer, 1955. Compare it also with any published statistical study of the results of teaching by television contrasted with the standard classroom method of instruction.

4. Sociologists refer to "mass illusions" as stereotypes. Besides the "good guys" and "bad guys" discussed in this essay, what vocational, professional, national, racial, or religious stereotypes may be defined in America? Read, for example, A. Den Doolard's "A Study in Misunderstanding," *Saturday Review of Literature*, September 24, 1949; or Agnes Rogers Allen's "Is It Anyone We Know?" *Harper's Magazine*, June, 1946.

5. Identify as many stereotyped characters, expressions, situations, plots, customs, etc., as you can of the westerner, as exhibited in western movies and television shows.

6. What is the point Steinbeck makes about the McCarthy hearings? What episodes in American history are similar or parallel?

7. Read a discussion of stereotyping in S. I. Hayakawa's *Language in Thought and Action*, Wendell Johnson's *Your Most Enchanted Listener*, or Anatol Rapoport's *Science and the Goals of Man*, and make a list of suggestions for counteracting the effects of stereotyped thinking.

8. Which of the characters in William Saroyan's "The Circus" is clearly a stereotype?

9. How is the thesis of James Thurber's "Oliver and the Other Ostriches" related to the theme of this essay?

10. What uses do newspapers make of stereotypes? Read S. Stansfeld Sargent, "Stereotypes and the Newspapers" from *Readings in Social Psychology* by Newcomb and Hartley, 1947.

11. How is prejudice related to stereotyping? Consider the stock labels for foreigners discussed by Cohen in "The Reconstruction of Hidden Value Judgments."

12. Show how the following news story demonstrates the dangers of stereotyped thinking. (From *The State Journal*, Lansing, Michigan, January 18, 1957)

> "At 11 a.m. yesterday two airmen stationed at Selfridge Field, Roland G. Edwards, 18, and Dennis Rable, 19, got out of a car and entered the First National Bank. Because

parking space was not available, their companion, Airman Edward Malen, 18, drove around the block while waiting for his pals. Edwards drew $210 from a savings account and was leaving the bank with Rable when the bank's burglar alarm suddenly cut loose. At that instant the two airmen saw Malen passing the bank again and sprinted to the car. Walking a half block away Macomb County Sheriff's Detective Conrad Koltys heard the alarm and saw the running youth. With pistol in hand he raced into the street and stopped their car. Seconds later, Mt. Clemens Police Lt. Russell Girard puffed up after a two-block run. Right behind Girard came three cars carrying 12 patrolmen and deputies. Surrounded by 14 armed officers, the servicemen decided on unconditional surrender. They were handcuffed and taken to headquarters. "We were congratulating ourselves for nabbing three holdup men cold," said Girard, "until we found out the bank hadn't been robbed."

INDEX OF AUTHORS AND TITLES